VAMPI
TALES

VAMPIRE TALES

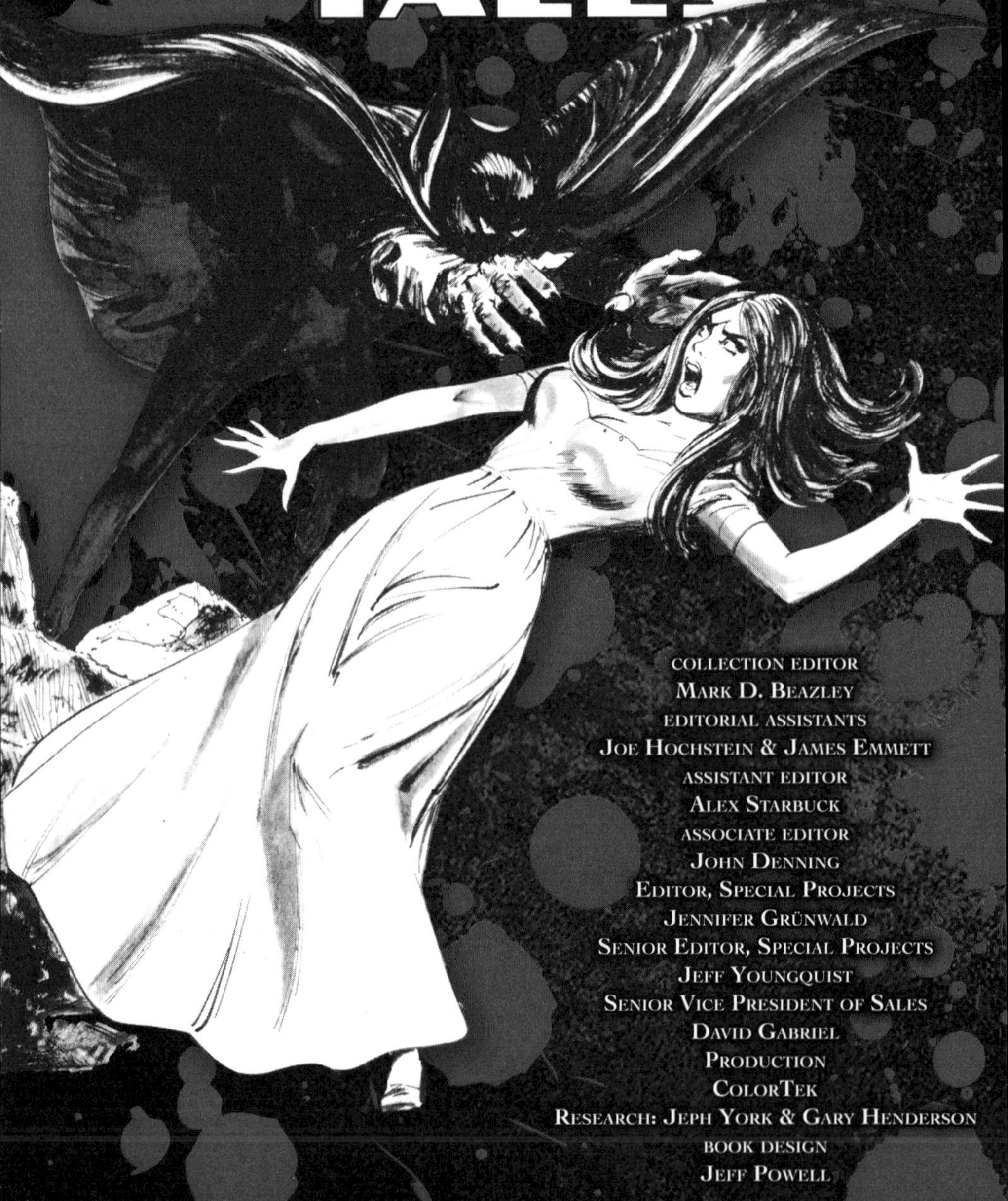

COLLECTION EDITOR
MARK D. BEAZLEY
EDITORIAL ASSISTANTS
JOE HOCHSTEIN & JAMES EMMETT
ASSISTANT EDITOR
ALEX STARBUCK
ASSOCIATE EDITOR
JOHN DENNING
EDITOR, SPECIAL PROJECTS
JENNIFER GRÜNWALD
SENIOR EDITOR, SPECIAL PROJECTS
JEFF YOUNGQUIST
SENIOR VICE PRESIDENT OF SALES
DAVID GABRIEL
PRODUCTION
COLORTEK
RESEARCH: JEPH YORK & GARY HENDERSON
BOOK DESIGN
JEFF POWELL

EDITOR IN CHIEF: JOE QUESADA
PUBLISHER: DAN BUCKLEY
EXECUTIVE PRODUCER: ALAN FINE

VAMPIRE TALES #1

"MORBIUS"
WRITER
STEVE GERBER
ARTIST
PABLO MARCOS

"TO KILL A WEREWOLF"
ARTIST
BILL EVERETT

"THE VAMPYRE!"
PLOT
RON GOULART
SCRIPT
ROY THOMAS
ARTIST
WINSLOW MORTIMER

"SATAN CAN WAIT!"
ARTIST
PAUL REINMAN

"REVENGE OF THE UNLIVING"
WRITER
GARDNER FOX
ARTIST
BERNET

VAMPIRE TALES #2

"THE BLOOD SACRIFICE OF AMANDA SAINT"
WRITER
DON MCGREGOR
PENCILER
RICH BUCKLER
INKER
PABLO MARCOS

"WITCH HUNT"
ARTIST
MANNIE BANKS

"FIVE CLAWS TO TRYPHON"
WRITER
GARDNER FOX
PENCILER
JESUS BLASCO
INKER
JOHN ROMITA

"SATANA"
WRITER
Roy Thomas
ARTIST
JOHN ROMITA

"AT THE STROKE OF MIDNIGHT"
WRITER & ARTIST
JIM STERANKO

"THE PRAYING MANTIS PRINCIPLE"
WRITER
DON MCGREGOR
PENCILER
RICH BUCKLER
INKERS
CARLOS GARZON &
KLAUS JANSON

VAMPIRE TALES #3

"THE KISS OF DEATH"
WRITER
GERRY CONWAY
ARTIST
ESTEBAN MAROTO

"THE COLLECTION"
WRITERS
RUSS JONES &
BHOB STEWART
ARTIST
PAUL REINMAN

"DON'T TRY TO OUTSMART THE DEVIL!"
WRITER
STAN LEE
ARTIST
CARMINE INFANTINO

"BAT'S BELFRY"
WRITER
DON MCGREGOR
ARTIST
VICENTE IBANEZ

"VAMPIRES IN TIME AND SPACE"
WRITER
TONY ISABELLA
ARTIST
PABLO MARCOS

"DEMON FIRE!"
WRITER
DON MCGREGOR
PENCILER
RICH BUCKLER
INKER
KLAUS JANSON

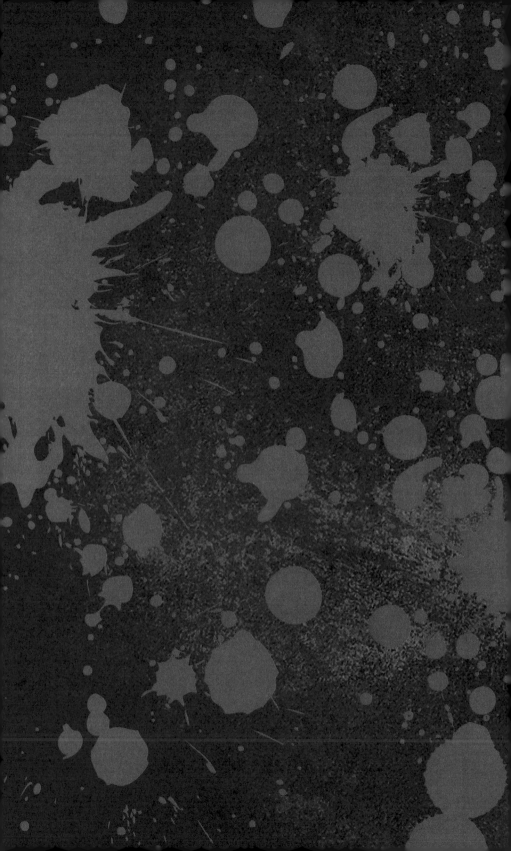

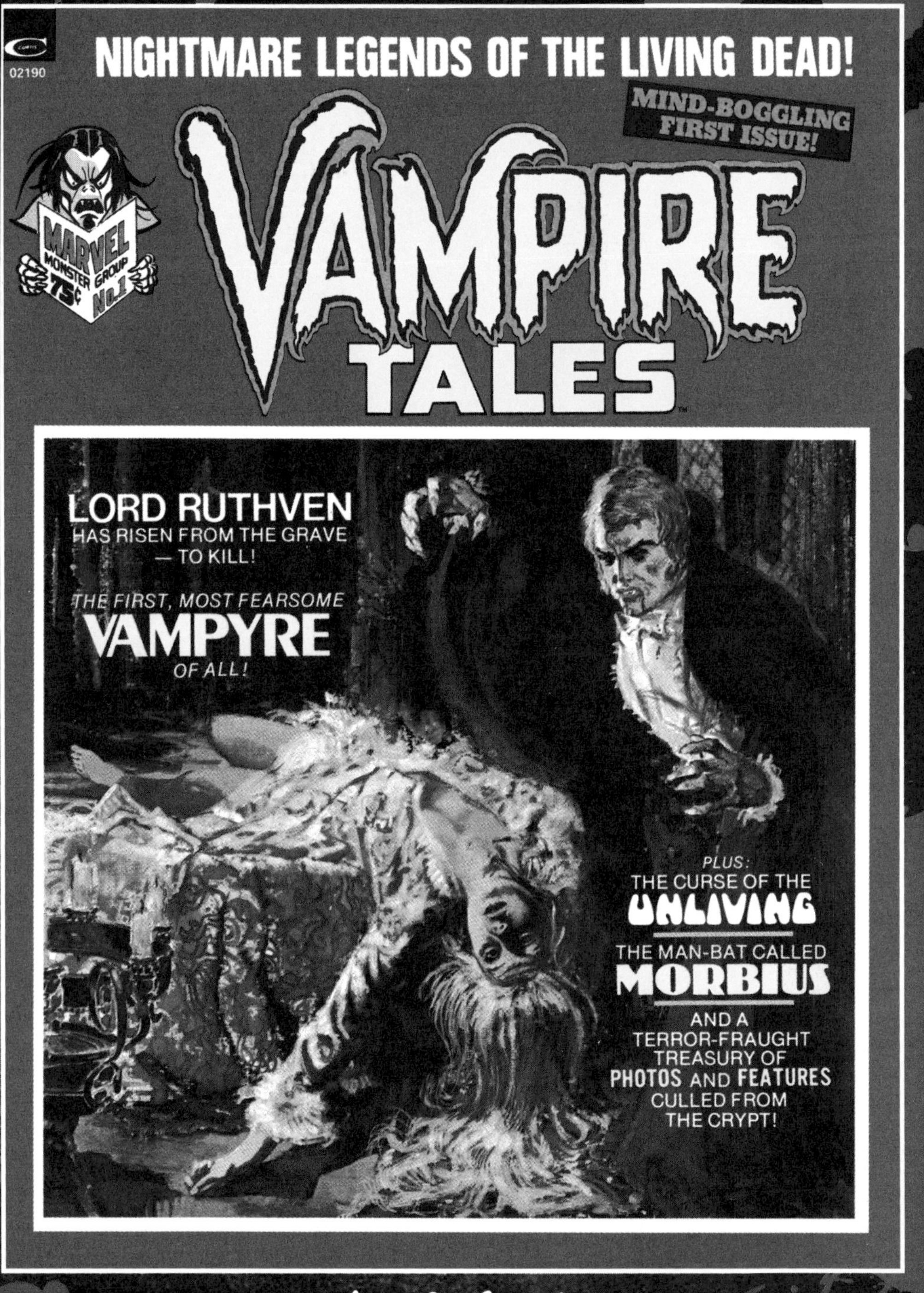
02190
NIGHTMARE LEGENDS OF THE LIVING DEAD!
MIND-BOGGLING FIRST ISSUE!
MARVEL MONSTER GROUP 75¢ No.1
VAMPIRE TALES
LORD RUTHVEN HAS RISEN FROM THE GRAVE — TO KILL!
THE FIRST, MOST FEARSOME VAMPYRE OF ALL!
PLUS:
THE CURSE OF THE UNLIVING
THE MAN-BAT CALLED MORBIUS
AND A TERROR-FRAUGHT TREASURY OF PHOTOS AND FEATURES CULLED FROM THE CRYPT!

ONE

Editor:
ROY THOMAS

Production:
SOL BRODSKY

Staff:
**MARV WOLFMAN
GERRY CONWAY
DON McGREGOR
TONY ISABELLA
MURRAY FRIEDMAN**

Writers This Issue:
**CHRIS CLAREMONT
MARK EVANIER
GARDNER FOX
STEVE GERBER
RON GOULART
ROY THOMAS**

Artists This Issue:
**BERNET
BILL EVERETT
PABLO MARCOS
WINSLOW MORTIMER
PAUL REINMAN**

Cover:
ESTEBAN MAROTO

Spiritual Consultant:
The Late Rev.
MONTAGUE SUMMERS
(Appointment
By Seance Only)

STAN LEE
Presents

Table Of Contents

VAMPIRE TALES is published by MARVEL COMICS GROUP. OFFICE OF PUBLICATION: 575 Madison Avenue, New York, N.Y. 10022. Published Bi-Monthly. Copyright © 1973 by Marvel Comics Group, a Division of Cadence Industries Corporation. All rights reserved 575 Madison Avenue, New York, N.Y. 10022. Vol. 1 No. 1, 1973 issue. Price 75¢ per copy in the U.S. and Canada. No similarity between any of the names, characters, persons and/or institutions in this magazine with those of any living or dead person or institution is intended, and any such similarity which may exist is purely coincidental. Printed in the U.S.A.

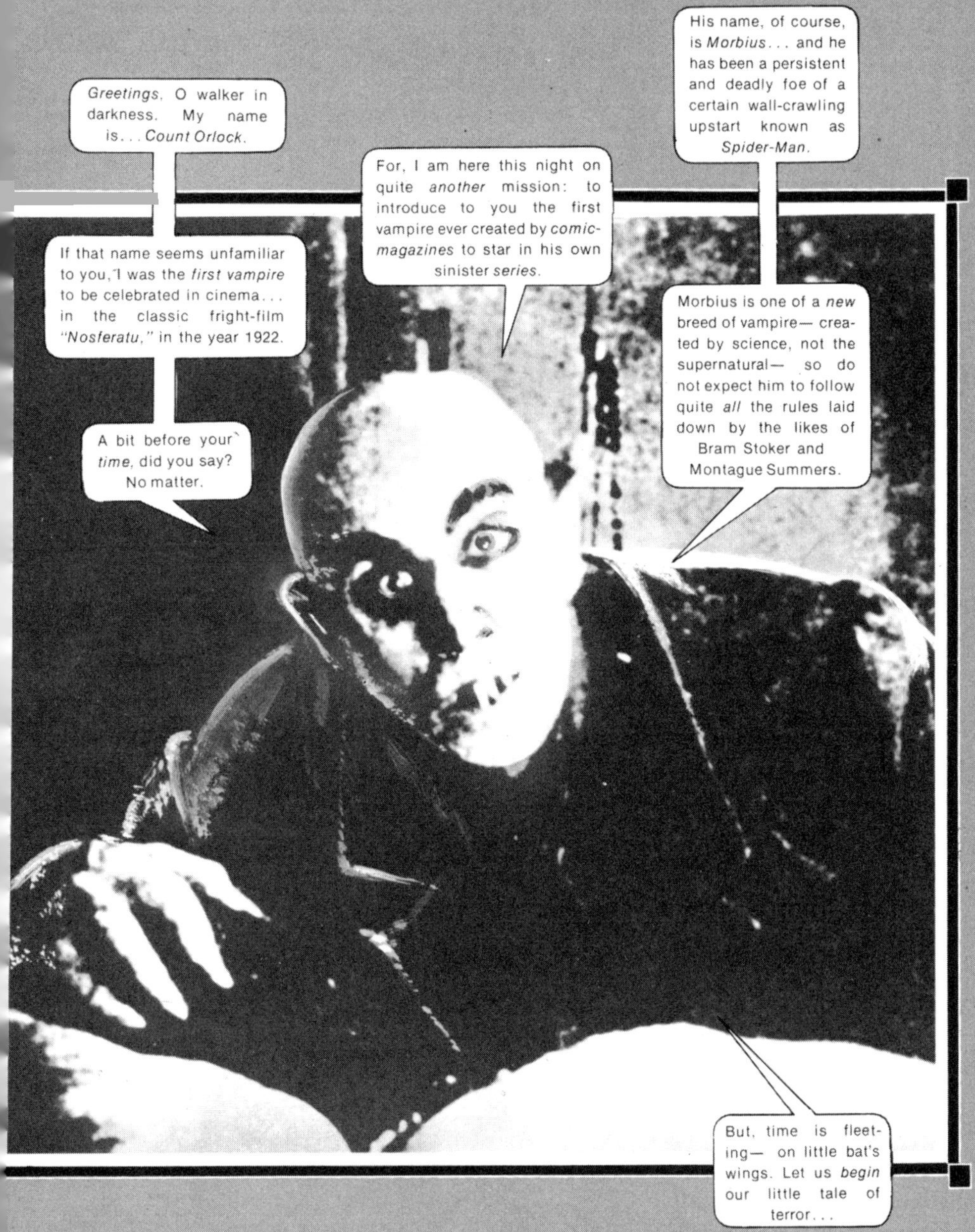
Greetings, O walker in darkness. My name is. . . Count Orlock.
If that name seems unfamiliar to you, I was the first vampire to be celebrated in cinema. . . in the classic fright-film "Nosferatu," in the year 1922.
A bit before your time, did you say? No matter.
For, I am here this night on quite another mission: to introduce to you the first vampire ever created by comic-magazines to star in his own sinister series.
His name, of course, is Morbius. . . and he has been a persistent and deadly foe of a certain wall-crawling upstart known as Spider-Man.
Morbius is one of a new breed of vampire— created by science, not the supernatural— so do not expect him to follow quite all the rules laid down by the likes of Bram Stoker and Montague Summers.
But, time is fleeting— on little bat's wings. Let us begin our little tale of terror. . .

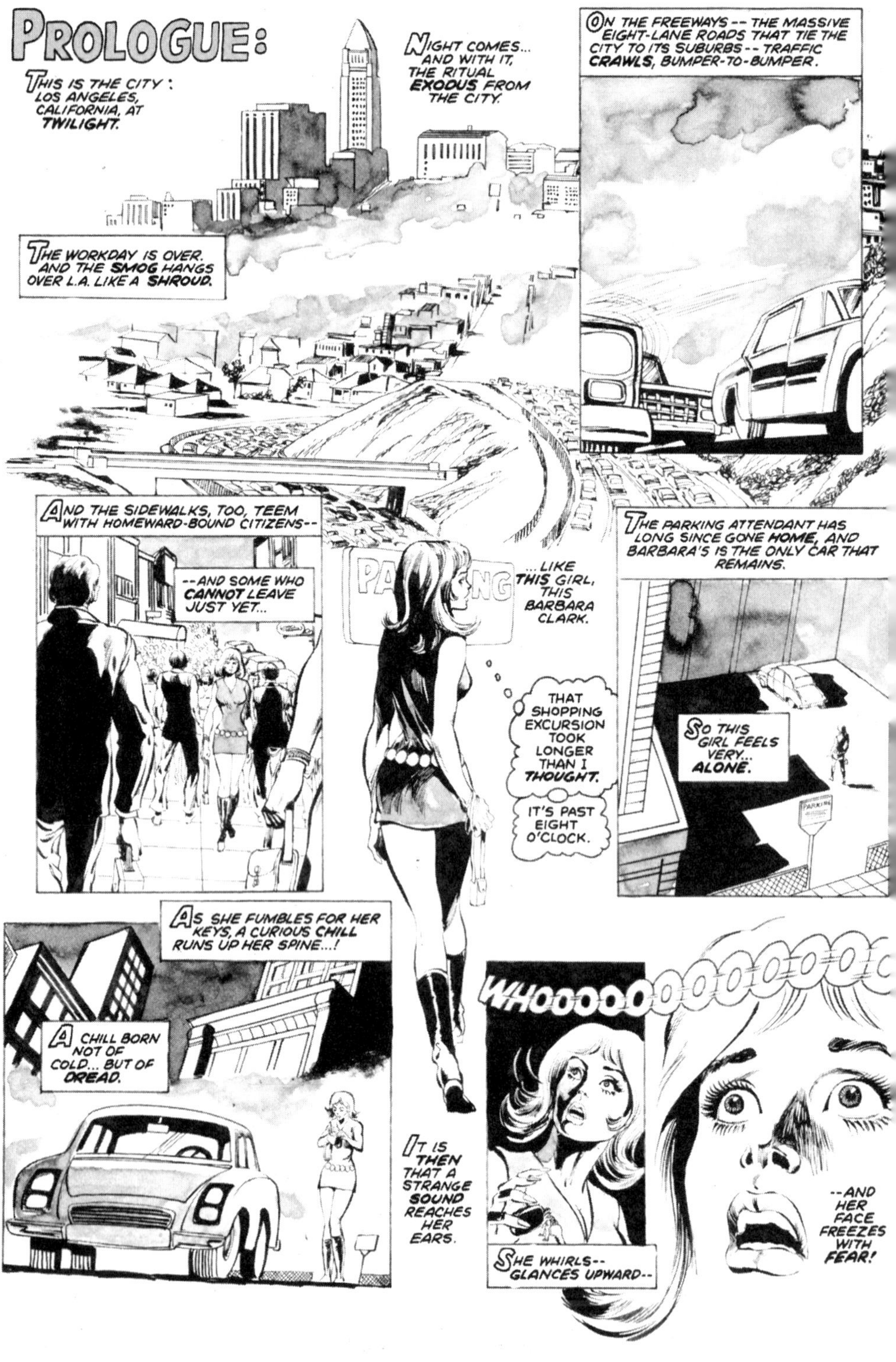
PROLOGUE:
THIS IS THE CITY: LOS ANGELES, CALIFORNIA, AT TWILIGHT.
NIGHT COMES... AND WITH IT, THE RITUAL EXODUS FROM THE CITY.
ON THE FREEWAYS -- THE MASSIVE EIGHT-LANE ROADS THAT TIE THE CITY TO ITS SUBURBS -- TRAFFIC CRAWLS, BUMPER-TO-BUMPER.
THE WORKDAY IS OVER. AND THE SMOG HANGS OVER L.A. LIKE A SHROUD.
AND THE SIDEWALKS, TOO, TEEM WITH HOMEWARD-BOUND CITIZENS--
--AND SOME WHO CANNOT LEAVE JUST YET...
...LIKE THIS GIRL, THIS BARBARA CLARK.
THAT SHOPPING EXCURSION TOOK LONGER THAN I THOUGHT.
IT'S PAST EIGHT O'CLOCK.
THE PARKING ATTENDANT HAS LONG SINCE GONE HOME, AND BARBARA'S IS THE ONLY CAR THAT REMAINS.
SO THIS GIRL FEELS VERY... ALONE.
AS SHE FUMBLES FOR HER KEYS, A CURIOUS CHILL RUNS UP HER SPINE...!
A CHILL BORN NOT OF COLD... BUT OF DREAD.
IT IS THEN THAT A STRANGE SOUND REACHES HER EARS.
WHOOOOOOOOOOOOOOOO
SHE WHIRLS-- GLANCES UPWARD--
--AND HER FACE FREEZES WITH FEAR!

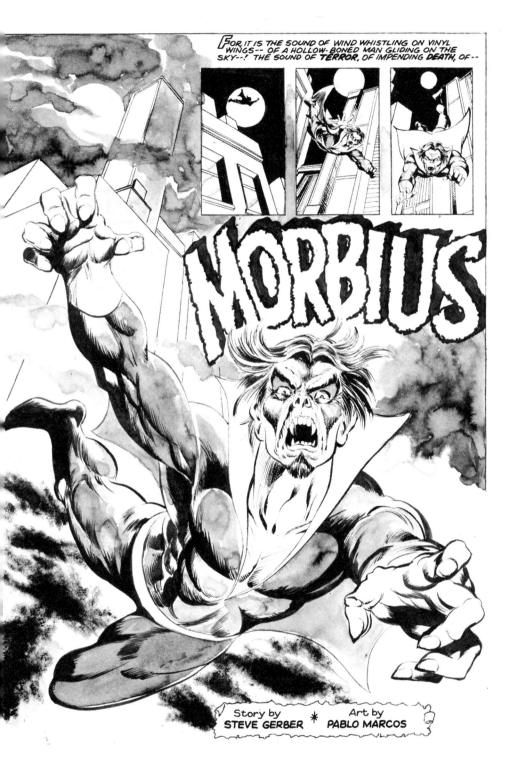

FOR IT IS THE SOUND OF WIND WHISTLING ON VINYL WINGS-- OF A HOLLOW-BONED MAN GLIDING ON THE SKY--! THE SOUND OF **TERROR**, OF IMPENDING **DEATH**, OF--

MORBIUS

Story by
STEVE GERBER
*
Art by
PABLO MARCOS

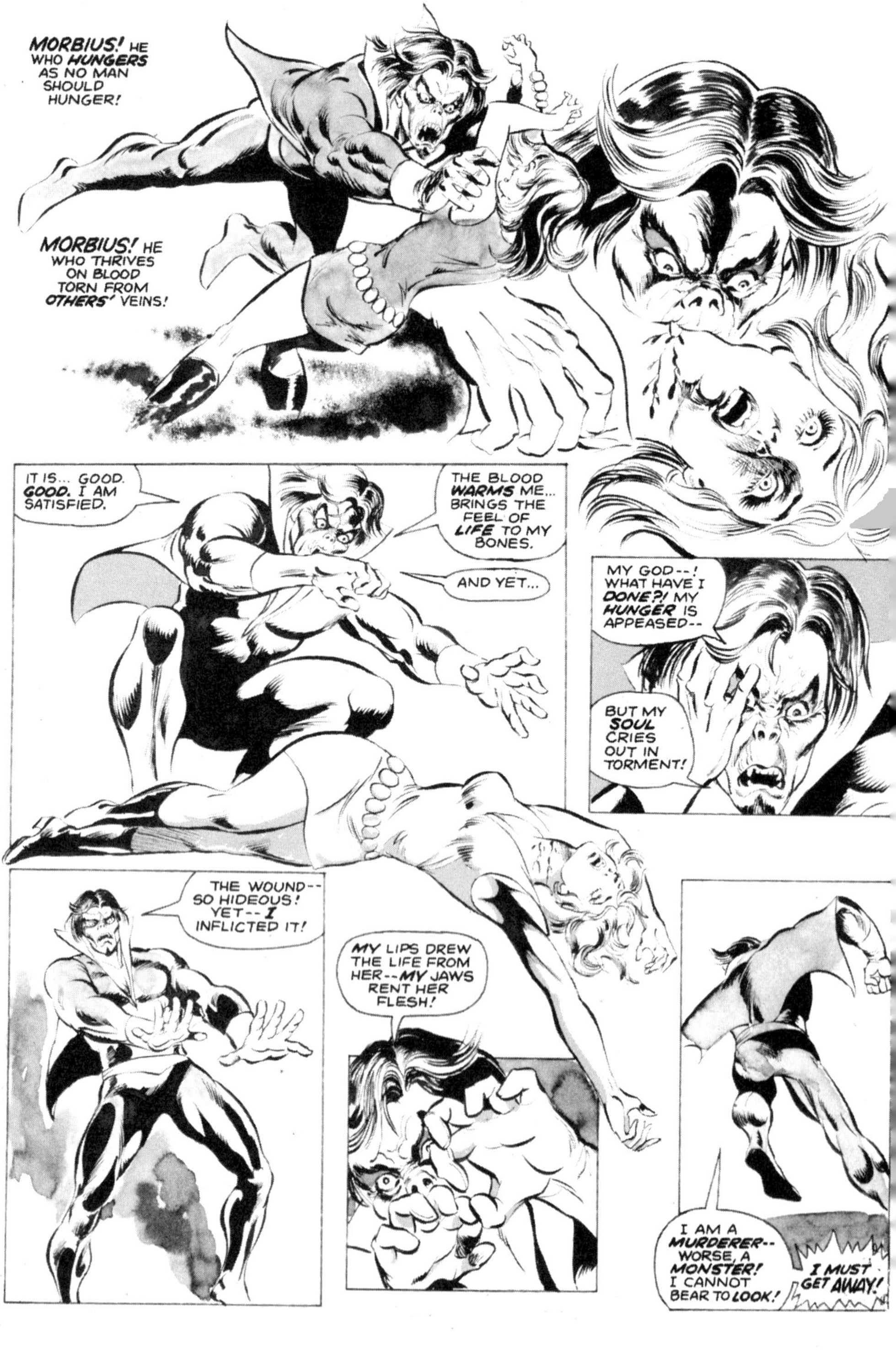
MORBIUS! HE WHO HUNGERS AS NO MAN SHOULD HUNGER!
MORBIUS! HE WHO THRIVES ON BLOOD TORN FROM OTHERS' VEINS!
IT IS... GOOD. GOOD. I AM SATISFIED.
THE BLOOD WARMS ME... BRINGS THE FEEL OF LIFE TO MY BONES.
AND YET...
MY GOD--! WHAT HAVE I DONE?! MY HUNGER IS APPEASED--
BUT MY SOUL CRIES OUT IN TORMENT!
THE WOUND-- SO HIDEOUS! YET--I INFLICTED IT!
MY LIPS DREW THE LIFE FROM HER--MY JAWS RENT HER FLESH!
I AM A MURDERER-- WORSE, A MONSTER! I CANNOT BEAR TO LOOK!
I MUST GET AWAY!

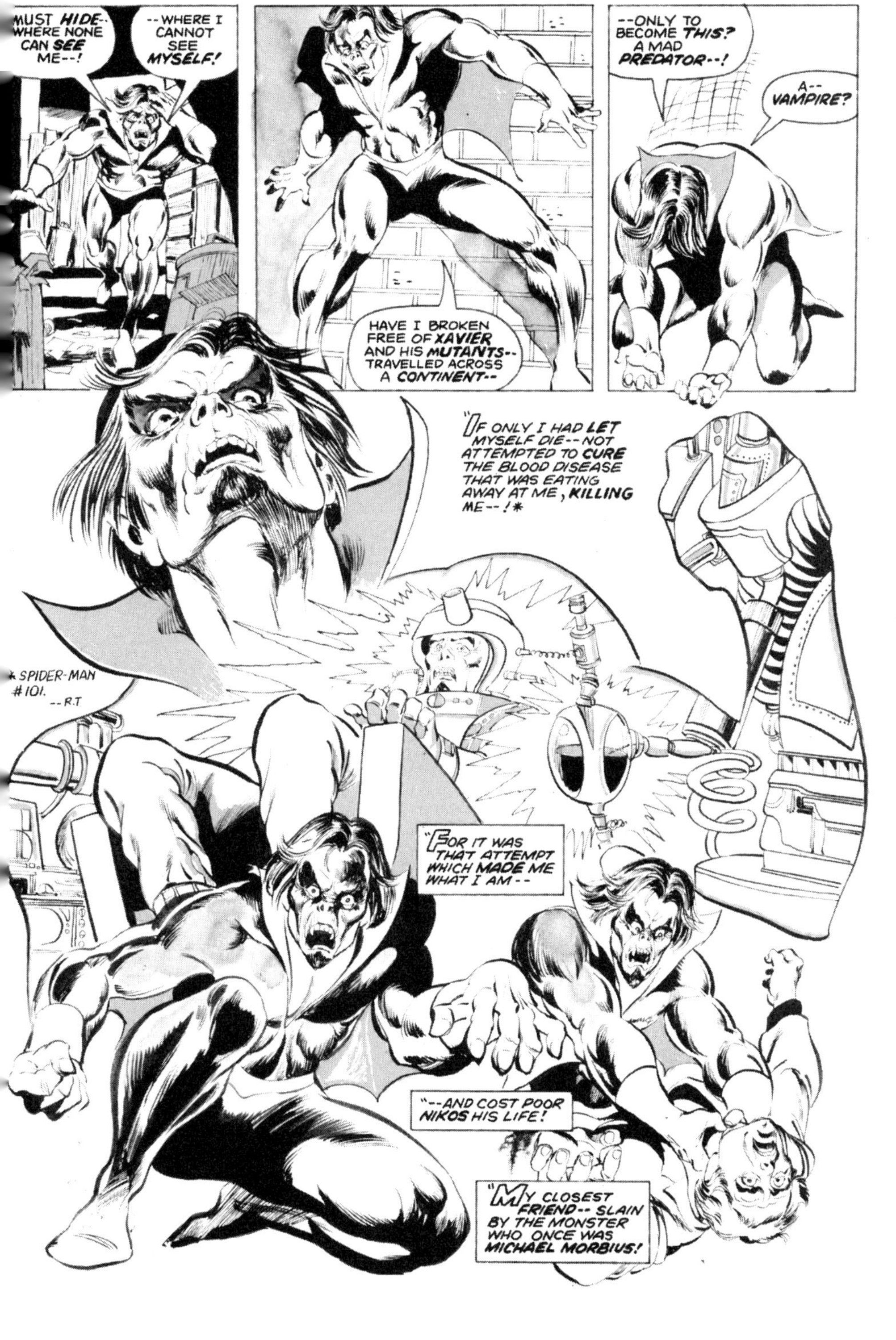
MUST HIDE-- WHERE NONE CAN SEE ME--!
--WHERE I CANNOT SEE MYSELF!
HAVE I BROKEN FREE OF XAVIER AND HIS MUTANTS-- TRAVELLED ACROSS A CONTINENT--
--ONLY TO BECOME THIS? A MAD PREDATOR--!
A-- VAMPIRE?
"IF ONLY I HAD LET MYSELF DIE-- NOT ATTEMPTED TO CURE THE BLOOD DISEASE THAT WAS EATING AWAY AT ME, KILLING ME--!*
*SPIDER-MAN #101. --R.T.
"FOR IT WAS THAT ATTEMPT WHICH MADE ME WHAT I AM--
"--AND COST POOR NIKOS HIS LIFE!
"MY CLOSEST FRIEND-- SLAIN BY THE MONSTER WHO ONCE WAS MICHAEL MORBIUS!

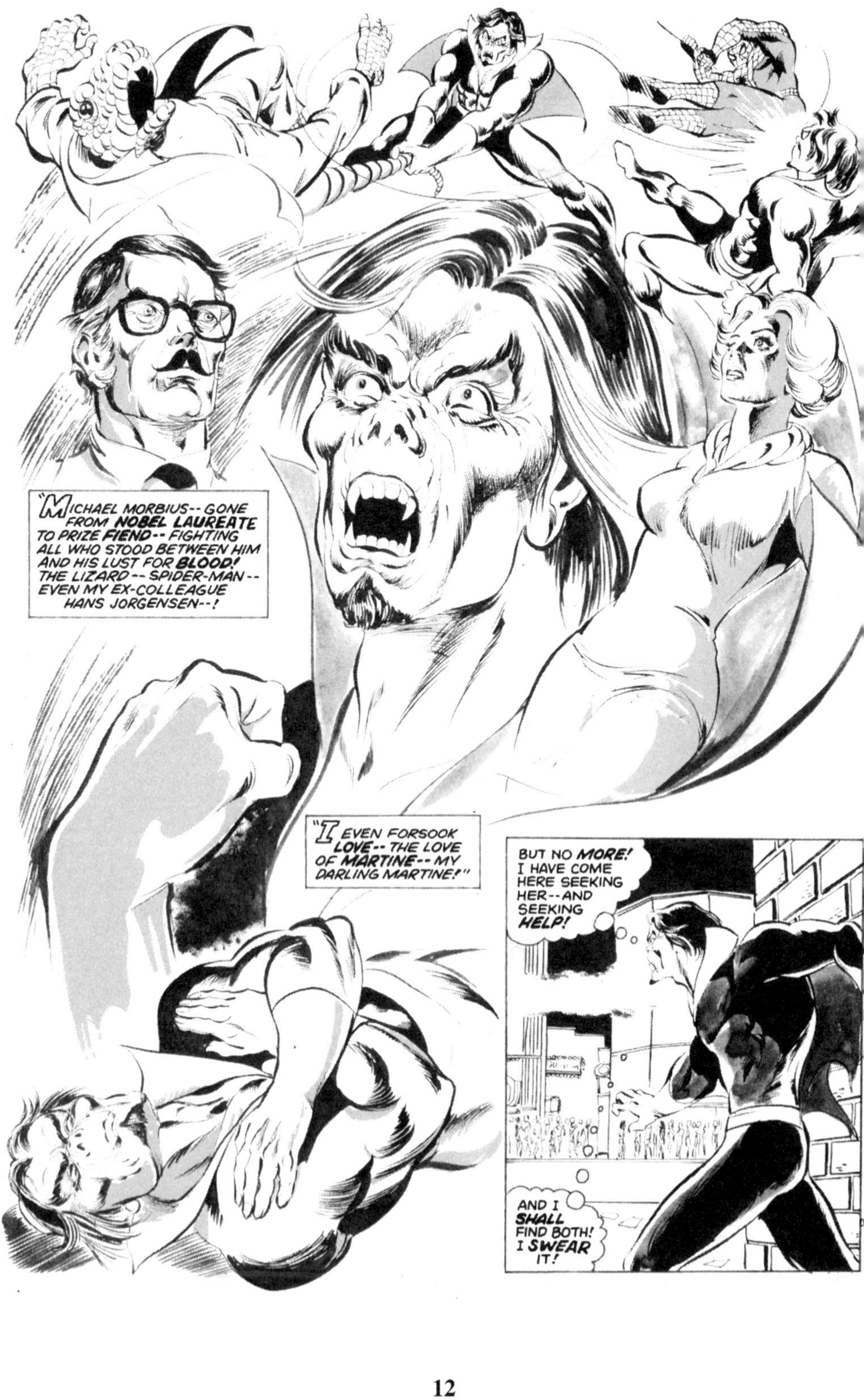
"MICHAEL MORBIUS-- GONE FROM NOBEL LAUREATE TO PRIZE FIEND-- FIGHTING ALL WHO STOOD BETWEEN HIM AND HIS LUST FOR BLOOD! THE LIZARD -- SPIDER-MAN -- EVEN MY EX-COLLEAGUE HANS JORGENSEN--!
"I EVEN FORSOOK LOVE-- THE LOVE OF MARTINE-- MY DARLING MARTINE!"
BUT NO MORE! I HAVE COME HERE SEEKING HER--AND SEEKING HELP!
AND I SHALL FIND BOTH! I SWEAR IT!

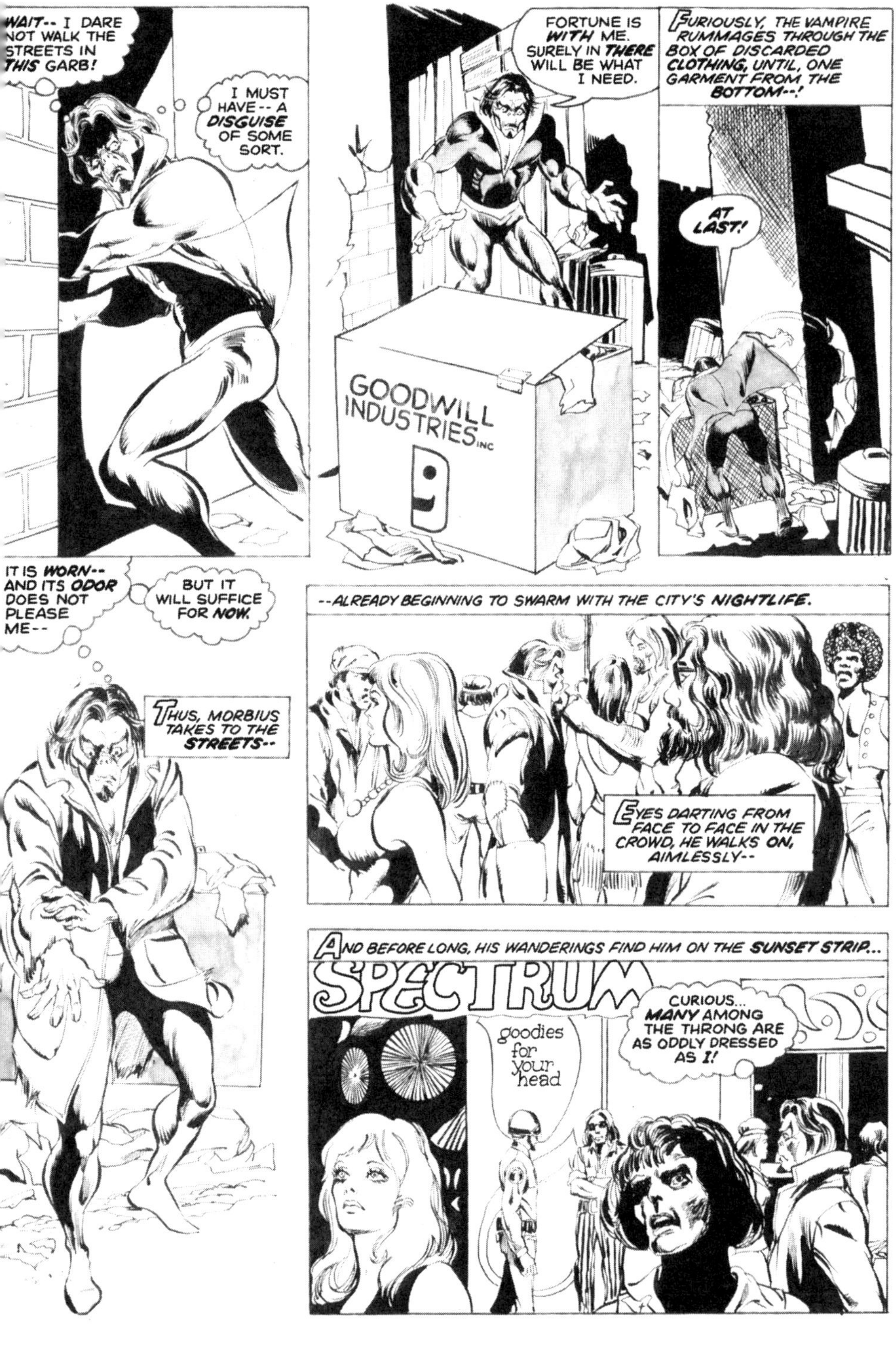

WAIT-- I DARE NOT WALK THE STREETS IN THIS GARB!
I MUST HAVE-- A DISGUISE OF SOME SORT.
FORTUNE IS WITH ME. SURELY IN THERE WILL BE WHAT I NEED.
GOODWILL INDUSTRIES INC
FURIOUSLY, THE VAMPIRE RUMMAGES THROUGH THE BOX OF DISCARDED CLOTHING, UNTIL, ONE GARMENT FROM THE BOTTOM--!
AT LAST!
IT IS WORN-- AND ITS ODOR DOES NOT PLEASE ME--
BUT IT WILL SUFFICE FOR NOW.
THUS, MORBIUS TAKES TO THE STREETS--
--ALREADY BEGINNING TO SWARM WITH THE CITY'S NIGHTLIFE.
EYES DARTING FROM FACE TO FACE IN THE CROWD, HE WALKS ON, AIMLESSLY--
AND BEFORE LONG, HIS WANDERINGS FIND HIM ON THE SUNSET STRIP...
SPECTRUM
goodies for your head
CURIOUS... MANY AMONG THE THRONG ARE AS ODDLY DRESSED AS I!

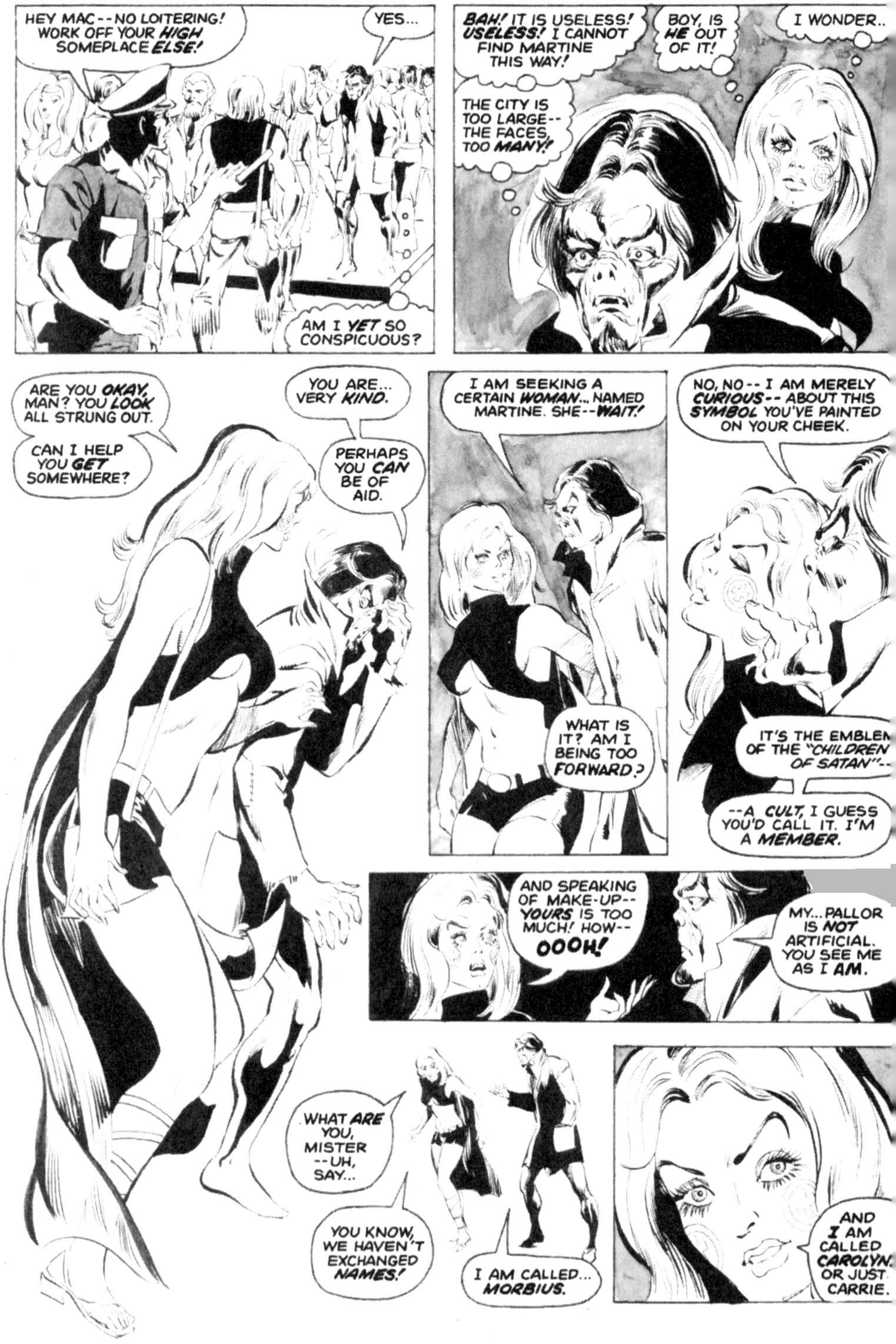
HEY MAC--NO LOITERING! WORK OFF YOUR HIGH SOMEPLACE ELSE!
YES...
AM I YET SO CONSPICUOUS?
BAH! IT IS USELESS! USELESS! I CANNOT FIND MARTINE THIS WAY!
THE CITY IS TOO LARGE-- THE FACES, TOO MANY!
BOY, IS HE OUT OF IT!
I WONDER..
ARE YOU OKAY, MAN? YOU LOOK ALL STRUNG OUT.
CAN I HELP YOU GET SOMEWHERE?
YOU ARE... VERY KIND.
PERHAPS YOU CAN BE OF AID.
I AM SEEKING A CERTAIN WOMAN... NAMED MARTINE. SHE--WAIT!
WHAT IS IT? AM I BEING TOO FORWARD?
NO, NO-- I AM MERELY CURIOUS-- ABOUT THIS SYMBOL YOU'VE PAINTED ON YOUR CHEEK.
IT'S THE EMBLEM OF THE "CHILDREN OF SATAN"--
--A CULT, I GUESS YOU'D CALL IT. I'M A MEMBER.
AND SPEAKING OF MAKE-UP-- YOURS IS TOO MUCH! HOW-- OOOH!
MY... PALLOR IS NOT ARTIFICIAL. YOU SEE ME AS I AM.
WHAT ARE YOU, MISTER --UH, SAY...
YOU KNOW, WE HAVEN'T EXCHANGED NAMES!
I AM CALLED... MORBIUS.
AND I AM CALLED CAROLYN. OR JUST CARRIE.

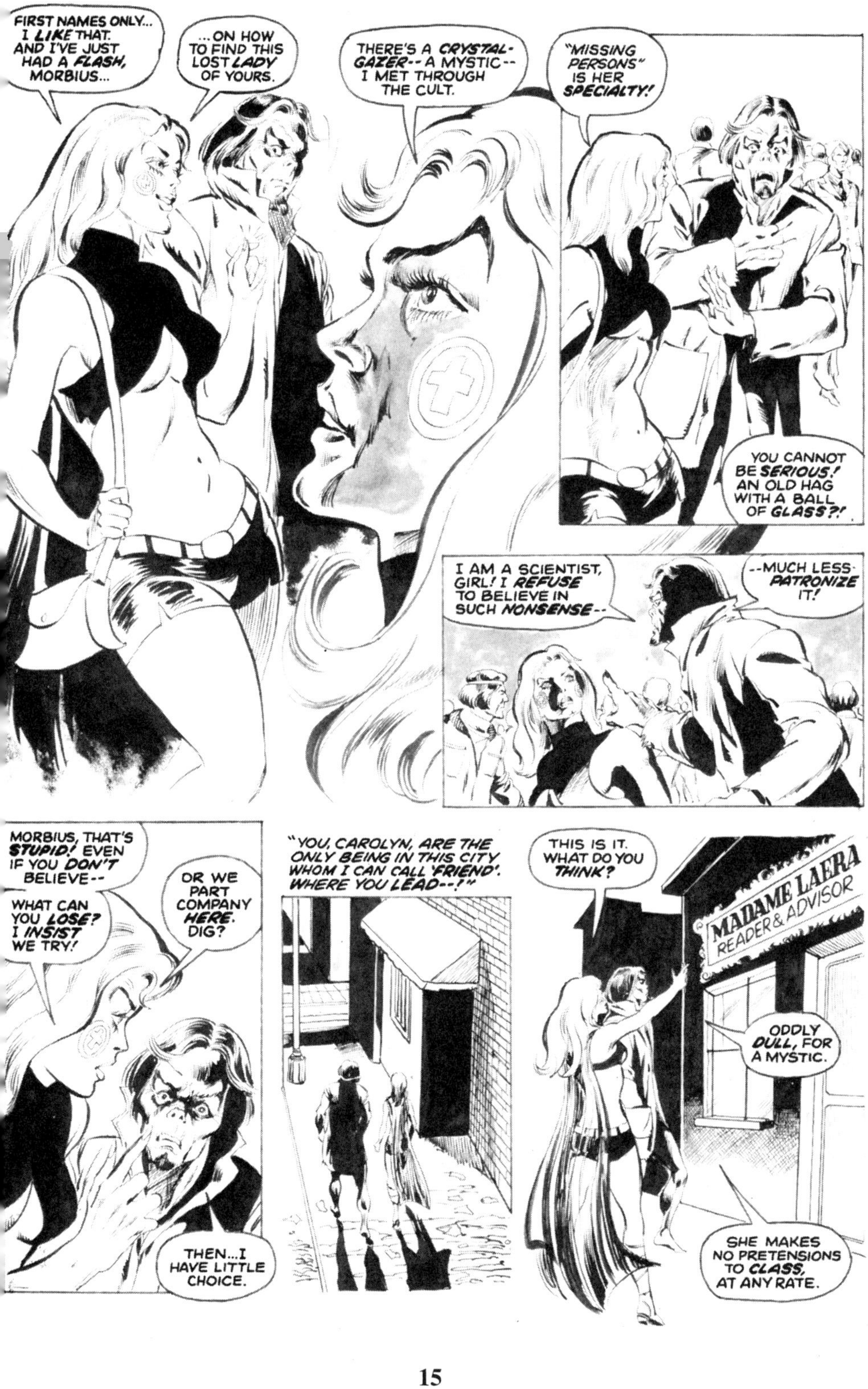
FIRST NAMES ONLY... I LIKE THAT. AND I'VE JUST HAD A FLASH, MORBIUS...
...ON HOW TO FIND THIS LOST LADY OF YOURS.
THERE'S A CRYSTAL-GAZER-- A MYSTIC-- I MET THROUGH THE CULT.
"MISSING PERSONS" IS HER SPECIALTY!
YOU CANNOT BE SERIOUS! AN OLD HAG WITH A BALL OF GLASS?!
I AM A SCIENTIST, GIRL! I REFUSE TO BELIEVE IN SUCH NONSENSE--
--MUCH LESS PATRONIZE IT!
MORBIUS, THAT'S STUPID! EVEN IF YOU DON'T BELIEVE--
WHAT CAN YOU LOSE? I INSIST WE TRY!
OR WE PART COMPANY HERE. DIG?
THEN...I HAVE LITTLE CHOICE.
"YOU, CAROLYN, ARE THE ONLY BEING IN THIS CITY WHOM I CAN CALL 'FRIEND'. WHERE YOU LEAD--!"
THIS IS IT. WHAT DO YOU THINK?
MADAME LAERA
READER & ADVISOR
ODDLY DULL, FOR A MYSTIC.
SHE MAKES NO PRETENSIONS TO CLASS, AT ANY RATE.

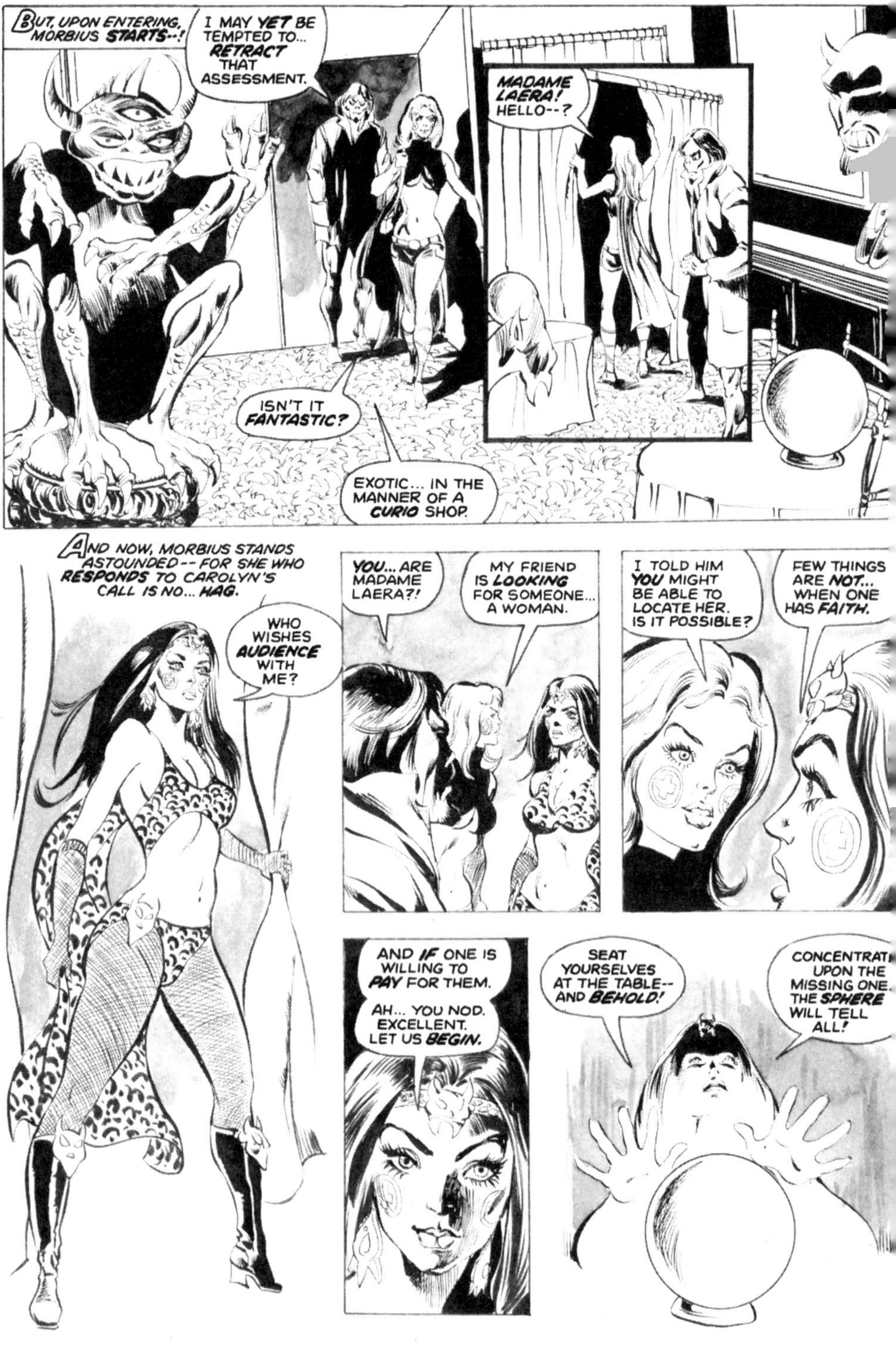
BUT, UPON ENTERING, MORBIUS STARTS--!
I MAY YET BE TEMPTED TO... RETRACT THAT ASSESSMENT.
ISN'T IT FANTASTIC?
EXOTIC... IN THE MANNER OF A CURIO SHOP.
MADAME LAERA! HELLO--?
AND NOW, MORBIUS STANDS ASTOUNDED-- FOR SHE WHO RESPONDS TO CAROLYN'S CALL IS NO... HAG.
WHO WISHES AUDIENCE WITH ME?
YOU... ARE MADAME LAERA?!
MY FRIEND IS LOOKING FOR SOMEONE... A WOMAN.
I TOLD HIM YOU MIGHT BE ABLE TO LOCATE HER. IS IT POSSIBLE?
FEW THINGS ARE NOT... WHEN ONE HAS FAITH.
AND IF ONE IS WILLING TO PAY FOR THEM.
AH... YOU NOD. EXCELLENT. LET US BEGIN.
SEAT YOURSELVES AT THE TABLE-- AND BEHOLD!
CONCENTRAT UPON THE MISSING ONE. THE SPHERE WILL TELL ALL!

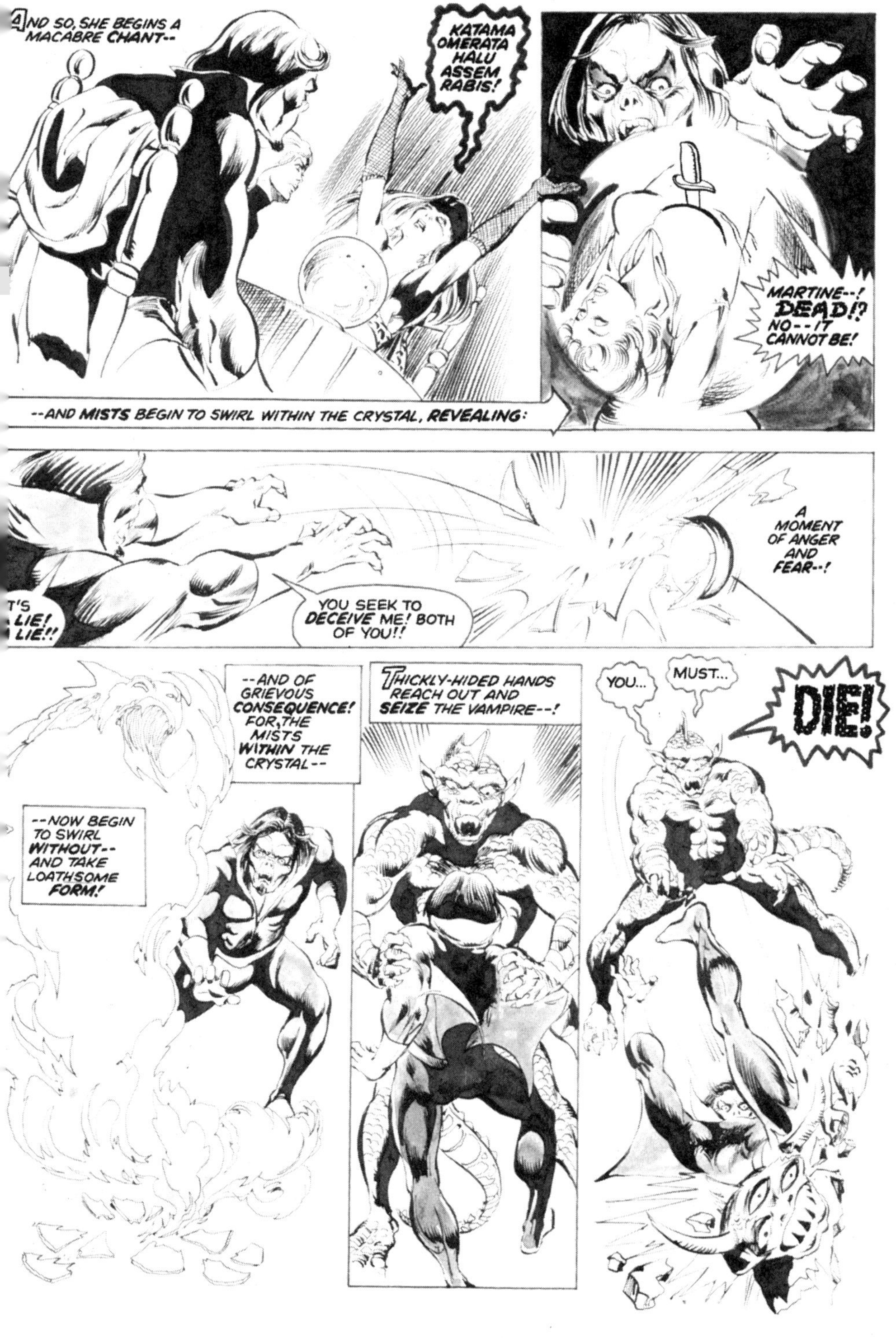
AND SO, SHE BEGINS A MACABRE CHANT--
KATAMA OMERATA HALU ASSEM RABIS!
MARTINE--! DEAD!? NO--IT CANNOT BE!
--AND MISTS BEGIN TO SWIRL WITHIN THE CRYSTAL, REVEALING:
A MOMENT OF ANGER AND FEAR--!
T'S LIE! LIE!!
YOU SEEK TO DECEIVE ME! BOTH OF YOU!!
--AND OF GRIEVOUS CONSEQUENCE! FOR, THE MISTS WITHIN THE CRYSTAL--
--NOW BEGIN TO SWIRL WITHOUT-- AND TAKE LOATHSOME FORM!
THICKLY-HIDED HANDS REACH OUT AND SEIZE THE VAMPIRE--!
YOU...
MUST...
DIE!

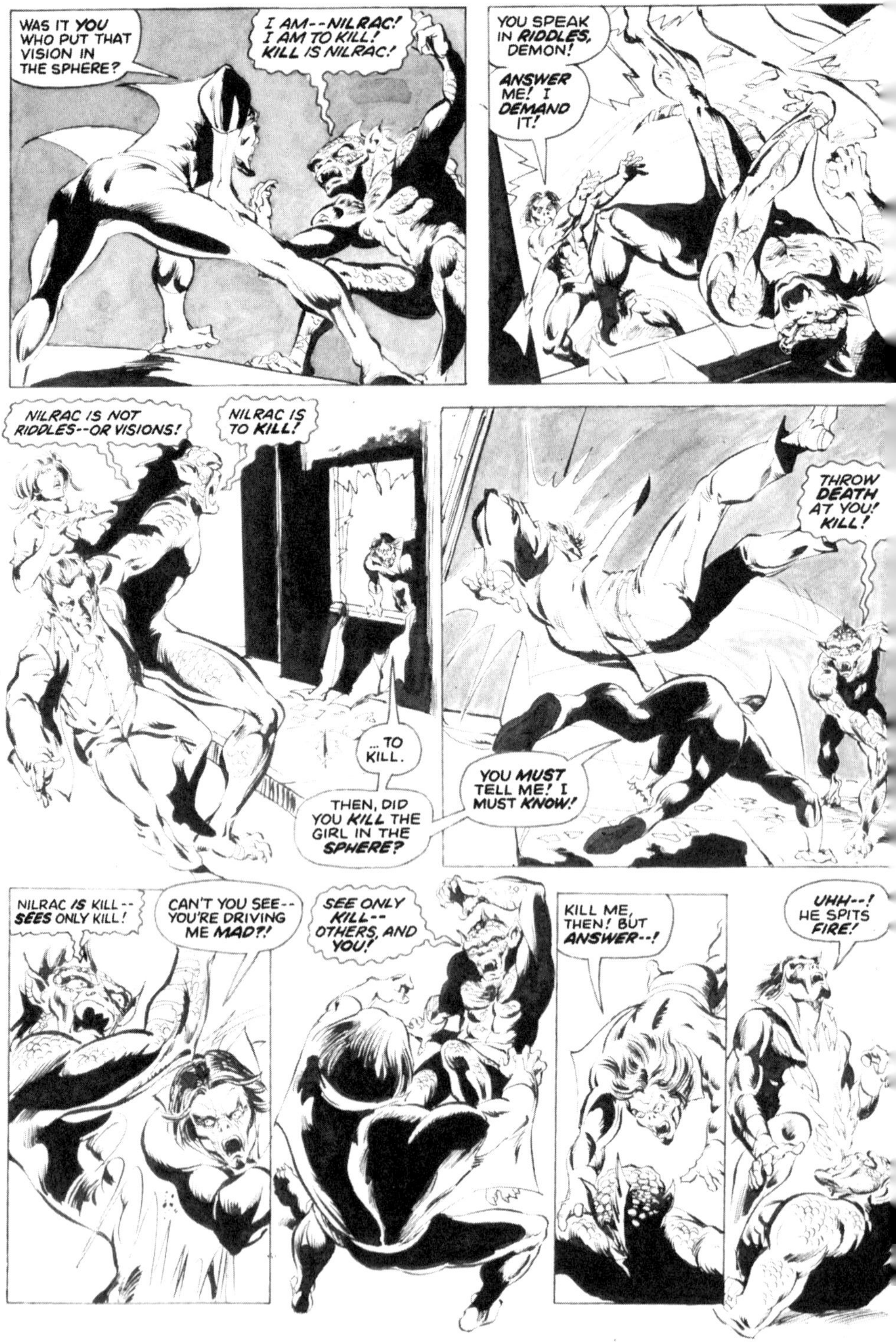

WAS IT YOU WHO PUT THAT VISION IN THE SPHERE?
I AM--NILRAC! I AM TO KILL! KILL IS NILRAC!
YOU SPEAK IN RIDDLES, DEMON!
ANSWER ME! I DEMAND IT!
NILRAC IS NOT RIDDLES--OR VISIONS!
NILRAC IS TO KILL!
... TO KILL.
THEN, DID YOU KILL THE GIRL IN THE SPHERE?
THROW DEATH AT YOU! KILL!
YOU MUST TELL ME! I MUST KNOW!
NILRAC IS KILL-- SEES ONLY KILL!
CAN'T YOU SEE-- YOU'RE DRIVING ME MAD?!
SEE ONLY KILL-- OTHERS, AND YOU!
KILL ME, THEN! BUT ANSWER--!
UHH--! HE SPITS FIRE!

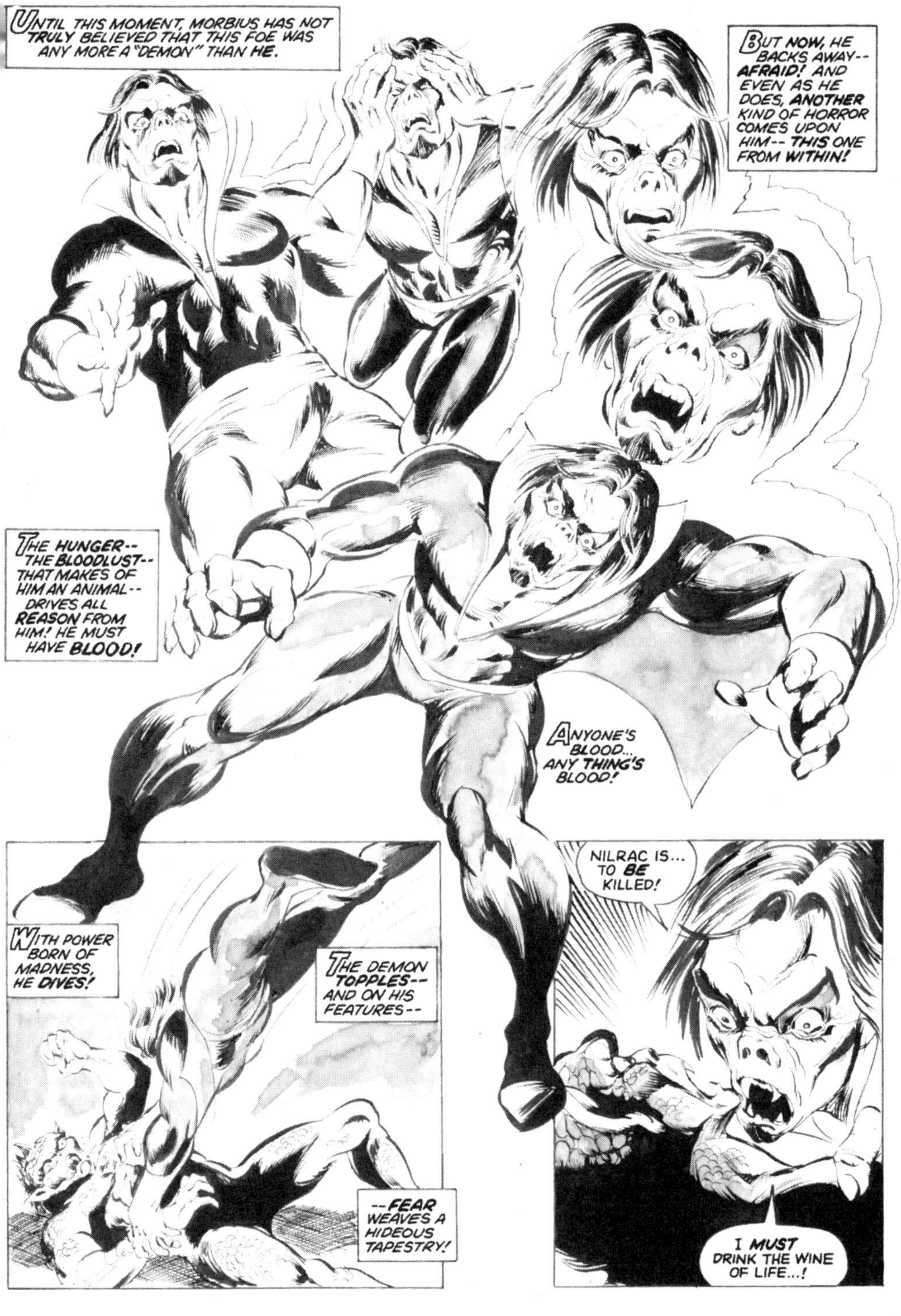
UNTIL THIS MOMENT, MORBIUS HAS NOT TRULY BELIEVED THAT THIS FOE WAS ANY MORE A "DEMON" THAN HE.
BUT NOW, HE BACKS AWAY-- AFRAID! AND EVEN AS HE DOES, ANOTHER KIND OF HORROR COMES UPON HIM-- THIS ONE FROM WITHIN!
THE HUNGER-- THE BLOODLUST-- THAT MAKES OF HIM AN ANIMAL-- DRIVES ALL REASON FROM HIM! HE MUST HAVE BLOOD!
ANYONE'S BLOOD... ANY THING'S BLOOD!
WITH POWER BORN OF MADNESS, HE DIVES!
THE DEMON TOPPLES-- AND ON HIS FEATURES--
--FEAR WEAVES A HIDEOUS TAPESTRY!
NILRAC IS... TO BE KILLED!
I MUST DRINK THE WINE OF LIFE...!

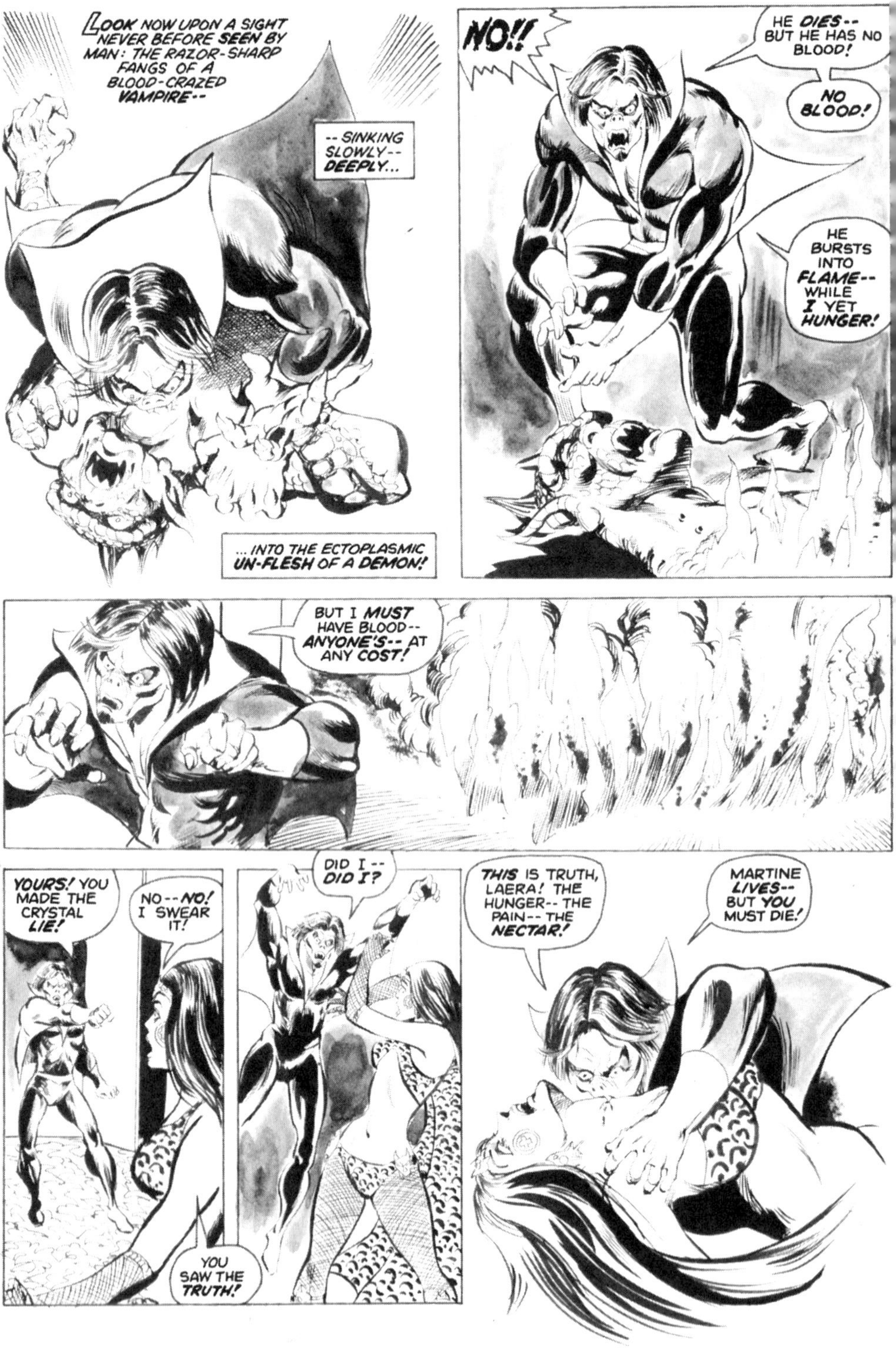
LOOK NOW UPON A SIGHT NEVER BEFORE SEEN BY MAN: THE RAZOR-SHARP FANGS OF A BLOOD-CRAZED VAMPIRE--
-- SINKING SLOWLY-- DEEPLY...
...INTO THE ECTOPLASMIC UN-FLESH OF A DEMON!
NO!!
HE DIES-- BUT HE HAS NO BLOOD!
NO BLOOD!
HE BURSTS INTO FLAME-- WHILE I YET HUNGER!
BUT I MUST HAVE BLOOD-- ANYONE'S-- AT ANY COST!
YOURS! YOU MADE THE CRYSTAL LIE!
NO-- NO! I SWEAR IT!
YOU SAW THE TRUTH!
DID I -- DID I?
THIS IS TRUTH, LAERA! THE HUNGER-- THE PAIN-- THE NECTAR!
MARTINE LIVES-- BUT YOU MUST DIE!

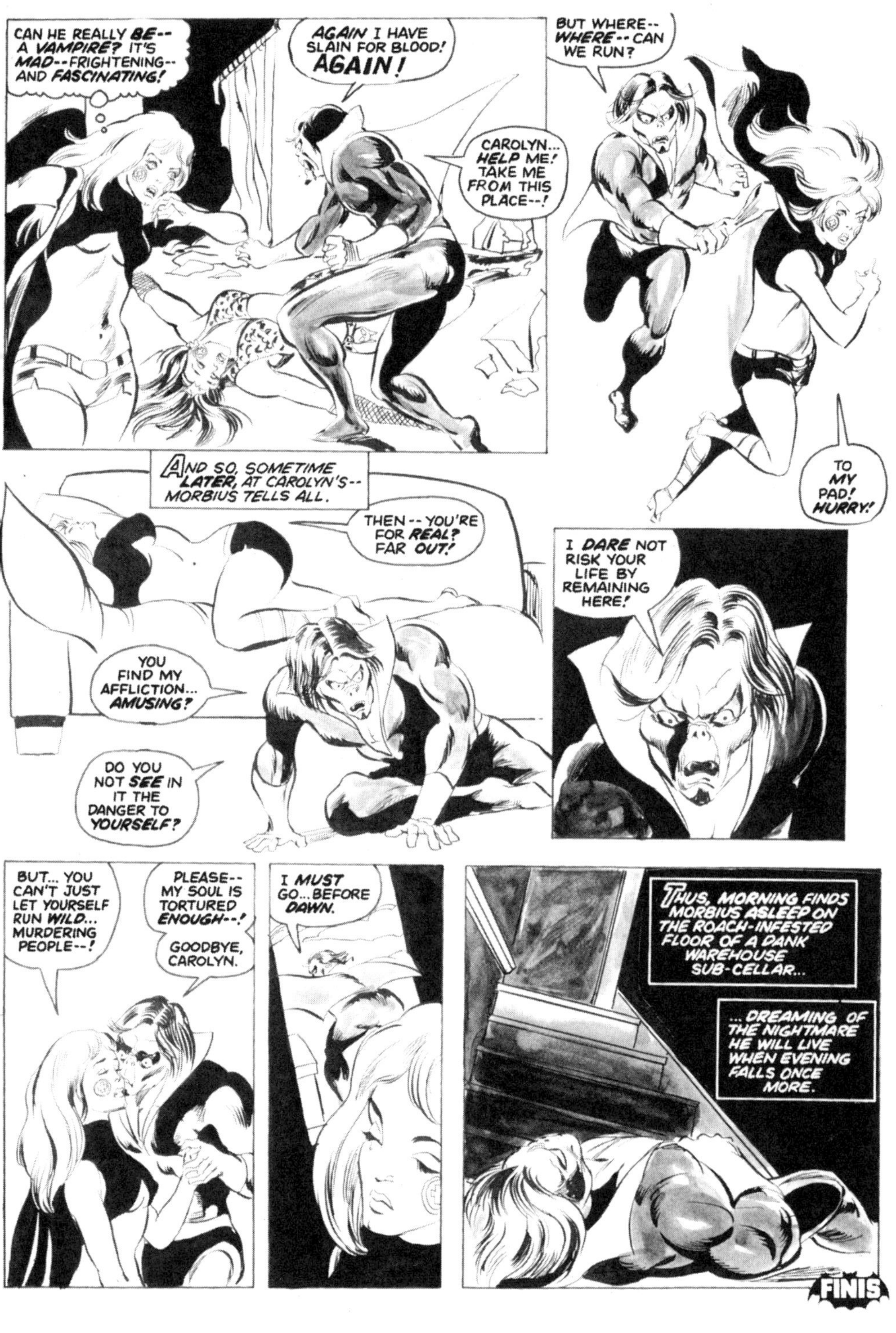
CAN HE REALLY BE-- A VAMPIRE? IT'S MAD--FRIGHTENING-- AND FASCINATING!
AGAIN I HAVE SLAIN FOR BLOOD! AGAIN!
CAROLYN... HELP ME! TAKE ME FROM THIS PLACE--!
BUT WHERE-- WHERE--CAN WE RUN?
TO MY PAD! HURRY!
AND SO, SOMETIME LATER, AT CAROLYN'S-- MORBIUS TELLS ALL.
THEN--YOU'RE FOR REAL? FAR OUT!
YOU FIND MY AFFLICTION... AMUSING?
DO YOU NOT SEE IN IT THE DANGER TO YOURSELF?
I DARE NOT RISK YOUR LIFE BY REMAINING HERE!
BUT... YOU CAN'T JUST LET YOURSELF RUN WILD... MURDERING PEOPLE--!
PLEASE-- MY SOUL IS TORTURED ENOUGH--!
GOODBYE, CAROLYN.
I MUST GO... BEFORE DAWN.
THUS, MORNING FINDS MORBIUS ASLEEP ON THE ROACH-INFESTED FLOOR OF A DANK WAREHOUSE SUB-CELLAR...
...DREAMING OF THE NIGHTMARE HE WILL LIVE WHEN EVENING FALLS ONCE MORE.
FINIS

"Blood is Thicker..."

So you thought Bram Stoker knew all there was to know about vampires, did you?

Or that, at the very least, the knowledge market was cornered between that irascible Irishman and the films by Universal and Hammer?

Well... you were wrong.

By now, it's not exactly the best-kept secret in the waking world that Marvel has a hit on its busy little hands with a giant-size magazine titled DRACULA LIVES!— in addition to its regular color comic-book called THE TOMB OF DRACULA. (Now on sale at your corner cemetery, folks— collect 'em all!)

Still, from the very beginning, Stan and Roy and the rest of the bat-happy Bullpen have set their collective sights rather higher than merely investigating the further adventures of the most famous of all the Living Dead. For, if Dracula is the *king* of vampires, there are likewise princes, barons, nobles— and a coffin-carrying commoner or two. Plus a wealth of untapped information that Bram Stoker never even dreamed of while he was combing Henry Irving's stage wigs.

This first issue of VAMPIRE TALES sets the pace, which we hope all future issues will embellish— with embalming fluid, if necessary.

For, before there was Dracula— more than *half a century* before, to be precise— there was his literary kinsman, Lord Ruthven. This earliest of all Living Deadmen, whose story is told in the tale called "The Vampyre" (sic) a few short pages from now, was the creation of one John Polidori, who was secretary, personal physician, and general travelling companion of the famed English poet, Lord Byron. In fact, in many ways Lord Ruthven *was* Lord Byron— down to Polidori's loving description of his anti-hero's otherworldly ennui and irresistible, nigh-fatal attraction for members of the fair sex. Each lord had his own personal handicap, of course. Byron succeeded in monkey business despite the drawback of a clubfoot, while Ruthven's flaw ran far deeper— was in his *blood*, you might say.

An even more interesting point, for those history-mongers among you: "The Vampyre" was conceived on the same immortal evening as that other far-famed creature, the Frankenstein monster! For, also present that night was a free-wheeling young miss named Mary Godwin (later Mary Shelley, when poet Percy got around to making a more-or-less honest woman of her)— and the two terror-tales birthed at that famous gathering have changed the time and tide. If *Frankenstein* is far better known than Lord Ruthven, it is nonetheless true that the latter in turn was at least the indirect inspiration for a novel called *Dracula*— and thus the obscure Dr. Polidori, too, deserves a place in the Crypt of Fame alongside Mary Wollstonecraft (who seems to have had no less than three names while her eight-foot monster had none— a lamentable instance of favoritism, we're sure you'll agree).

In between Lord Ruthven and Count Dracula, of course, there was a penny-dreadful creation called *Varney the Vampire*, published piecemeal in an early London version of pop culture, circa 1850. Varney, who died more often than Bela Lugosi and Christopher Lee put together, achieved considerable notoreity in his day. Mayhap we'll chronicle the venerable Varney's nighttime exploits sometime— but they run to well over 850 pages (and that name *is* a wee bit too alliterative even for mischievous Marvel, don't you see), so perhaps we'll just settle for a belated review one of these first issues and let it go at that.

Meanwhile, though, we've not wanted to ignore other, more *modern* aspects of the awesome Undead. For instance, few issues of a certain superhero comic-book called THE AMAZING SPIDER-MAN have ever been more warmly received or more greedily collected and hoarded than those which introduced a tortured soul named Morbius. (*Michael* Morbius, to use his full name.) Each time this 20th-century vampire has appeared in print, so great has been the outcry to give him his own magazine that finally nothing was to be done but to grant him a place of honor in this premiere issue of VAMPIRE TALES. And here, hopefully, he'll remain— a more science-fiction-oriented monster in some ways than any before him— in many ways Count Dracula's spiritual descendant, yet because of his nagging conscience in other ways his *opposite*. There are more kinds of vampire in

22

ven and earth than are dreamt of in your philosophy, atio.

nd *one* kind of Living Dead we dare not ignore in these s in which more bras than witches are burned, is the iale of the Species! "Revenge of the Unliving" this ound offers for your edification and enlightenment the y of a liberated young lady (a mere hundred years old, r all) who proves to be every bit as deadly as the male. east, those aren't exactly your every-day *hickeys* on her friend's neck . . . .

loving right along now:

Dracula is the most famous fiction work ever written ut a vampire, by far the most noted *non*-fiction book he subject is a tome called *The Vampire: His Kith and* , by a gent named Montague Summers. In fact, there's nuch legend and lore packed into this several-hundred-e volume that we'll be taking a few issues of VT just to ew it; but by the time we're done, you'll know Every-g You Always Wanted To Know About Vampires But re Afraid To Ask! (Maybe *more!*)

till, it is doubtless Hollywood (with a helping hand n Shepperton Studios in London) that has made Drac his infamous ilk the household word they are today. l so, we felt that no maiden issue of VAMPIRE TALES ld be quite complete without a feature piece on the n-bat in the movies. Just for kicks, though, we decided tart out at the bottom of the barrel and work our way And believe us, after you see this month's article on personal nominees for the worst vampire flicks ever ed, you're going to agree that *up* is the only direction n to us!

And, last and maybe least, we felt that we should make a nod or twain in the direction of other emissaries of evil, just to round out the issue. Hence, we've tossed in a bonus *werewolf* tale (and werewolves are, after all, kissing cousins of the vampire) plus a saga starring the vampire's adoptive father, old Satan himself.

Other, even weirder wonders await you in future issues. There'll be more of the most fabulous, most fearful vampire stories ever written— both by your Bullpen Stalwarts and by past masters like Robert Bloch, August Derleth, *et al.* There'll be vampires in contemporary settings— the rat-infested alleys of Harlem, the polluted pleasure-palaces of Las Vegas, and all points in between.

Just the same, in the long run, this is *your* magazine more than ours. Let us know what *you* want to see, and what you prefer to remain at rest in its spider-webbed coffin. Do you want more movie features? More macabre adventures of Morbius? *Longer* stories? *Shorter* stories? Perchance a double-page spread of the fingerprints of Barnabas Collins?

As we've previously said in DRACULA LIVES, MONSTERS UNLEASHED, and TALES OF THE ZOMBIE— let us know!

Send those carrier pigeons and carrion bats to:

VAMPIRE TALES
c/o Marvel Monster Group
575 Madison Ave., 9th Floor
New York, N.Y. 10022

Oh yes, and by the bye— try leaving your window open next week between the hours of sunset and dawn.

Maybe you'll even get a *personal* reply . . . !

FINIS

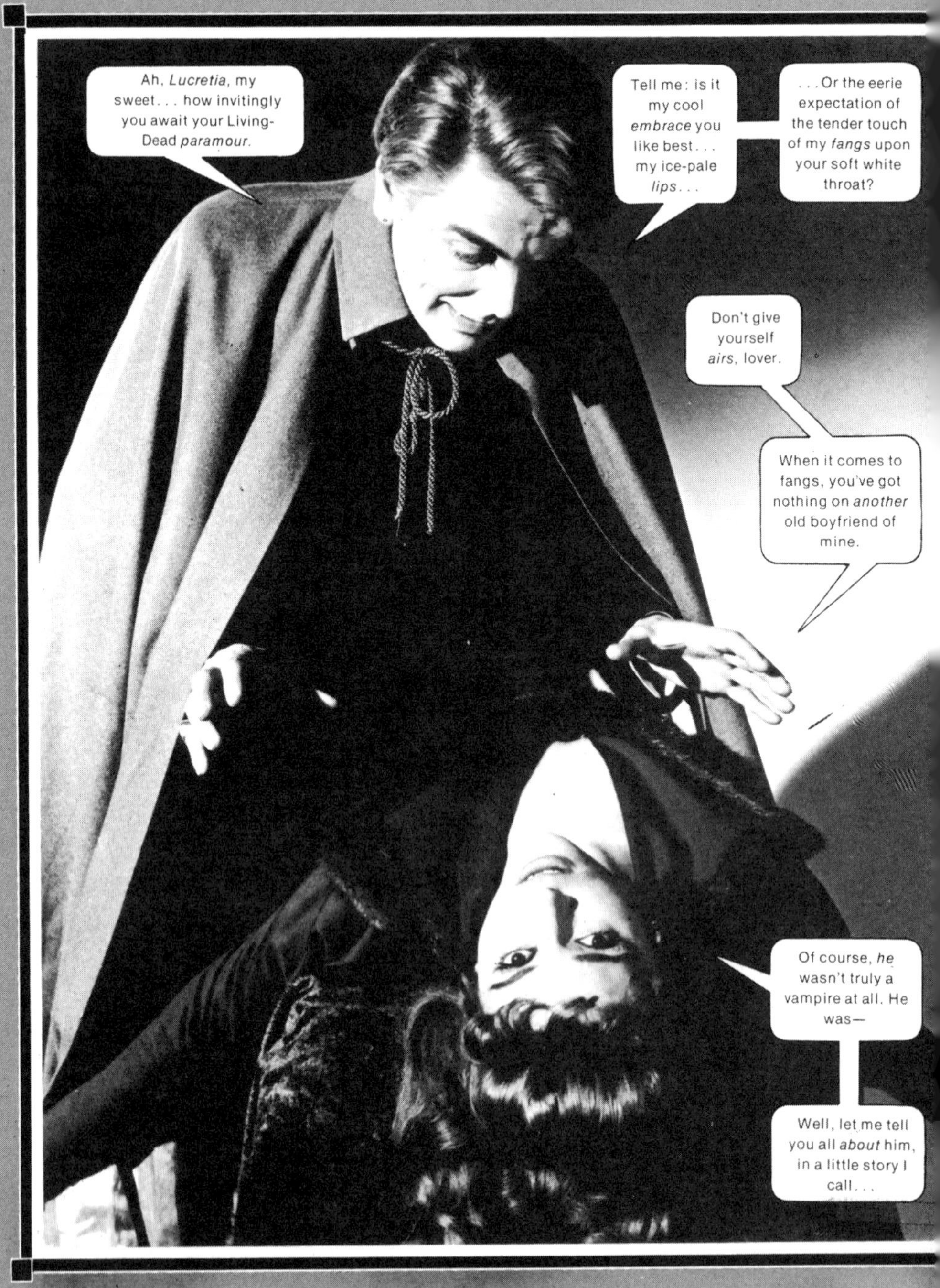
Ah, *Lucretia*, my sweet. . . how invitingly you await your Living-Dead *paramour.*
Tell me: is it my cool *embrace* you like best. . . my ice-pale *lips*. . .
. . . Or the eerie expectation of the tender touch of my *fangs* upon your soft white throat?
Don't give yourself *airs*, lover.
When it comes to fangs, you've got nothing on *another* old boyfriend of mine.
Of course, *he* wasn't truly a vampire at all. He was—
Well, let me tell you all *about* him, in a little story I call. . .

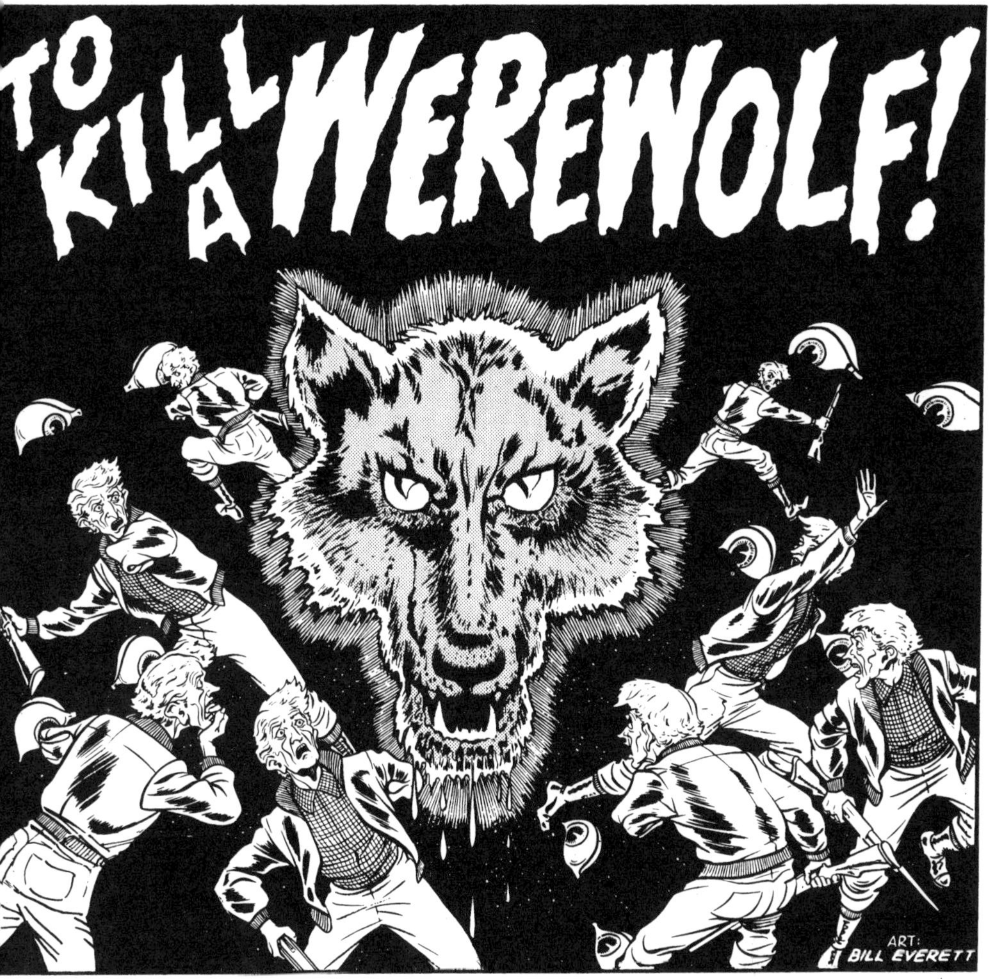
TO KILL A WEREWOLF!
ART: BILL EVERETT

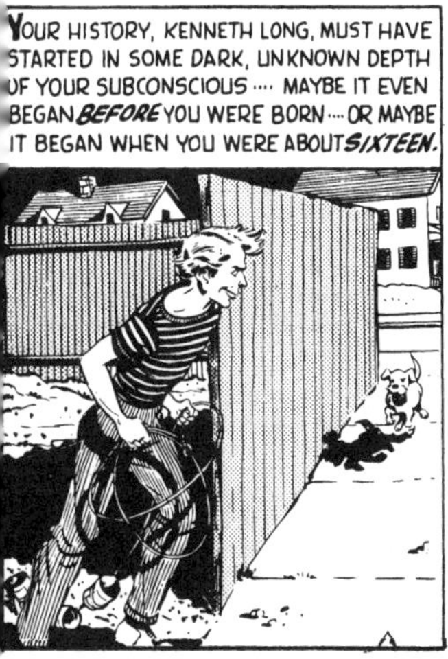
YOUR HISTORY, KENNETH LONG, MUST HAVE STARTED IN SOME DARK, UNKNOWN DEPTH OF YOUR SUBCONSCIOUS .... MAYBE IT EVEN BEGAN *BEFORE* YOU WERE BORN .... OR MAYBE IT BEGAN WHEN YOU WERE ABOUT *SIXTEEN*.

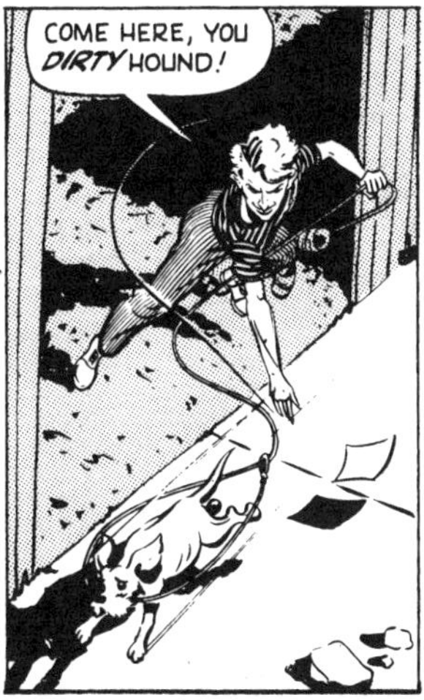
COME HERE, YOU *DIRTY* HOUND!

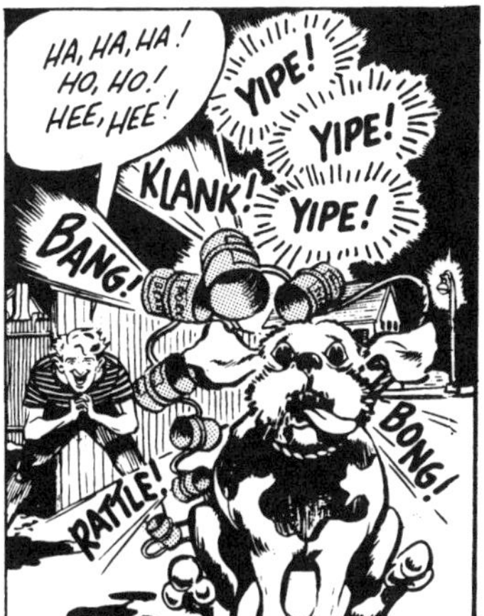
HA, HA, HA! HO, HO! HEE, HEE!
YIPE!
YIPE!
YIPE!
KLANK!
BANG!
BONG!
RATTLE!

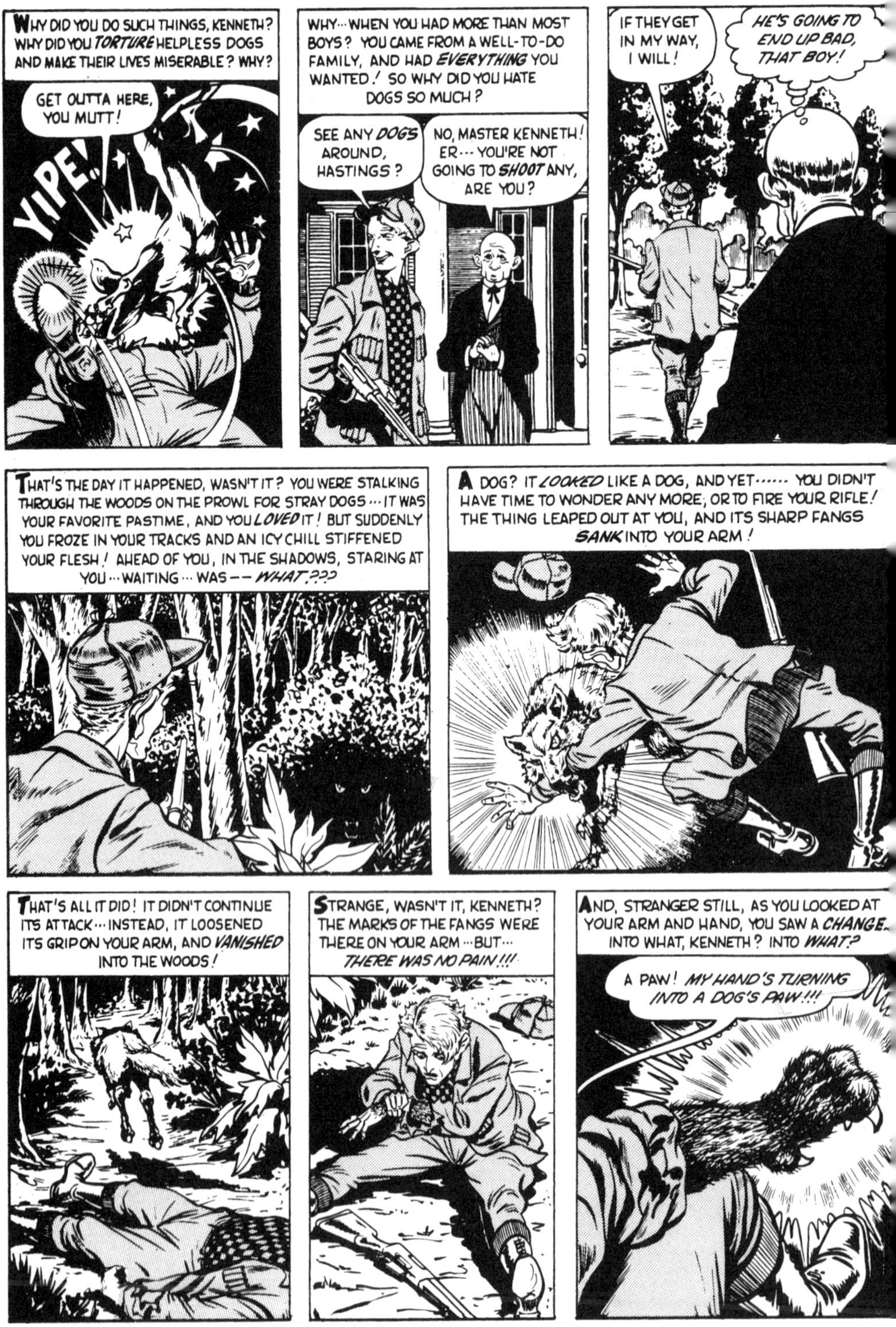
WHY DID YOU DO SUCH THINGS, KENNETH? WHY DID YOU TORTURE HELPLESS DOGS AND MAKE THEIR LIVES MISERABLE? WHY?
GET OUTTA HERE, YOU MUTT!
YIPE!
WHY... WHEN YOU HAD MORE THAN MOST BOYS? YOU CAME FROM A WELL-TO-DO FAMILY, AND HAD EVERYTHING YOU WANTED! SO WHY DID YOU HATE DOGS SO MUCH?
SEE ANY DOGS AROUND, HASTINGS?
NO, MASTER KENNETH! ER... YOU'RE NOT GOING TO SHOOT ANY, ARE YOU?
IF THEY GET IN MY WAY, I WILL!
HE'S GOING TO END UP BAD, THAT BOY!
THAT'S THE DAY IT HAPPENED, WASN'T IT? YOU WERE STALKING THROUGH THE WOODS ON THE PROWL FOR STRAY DOGS... IT WAS YOUR FAVORITE PASTIME, AND YOU LOVED IT! BUT SUDDENLY YOU FROZE IN YOUR TRACKS AND AN ICY CHILL STIFFENED YOUR FLESH! AHEAD OF YOU, IN THE SHADOWS, STARING AT YOU... WAITING... WAS -- WHAT???
A DOG? IT LOOKED LIKE A DOG, AND YET...... YOU DIDN'T HAVE TIME TO WONDER ANY MORE; OR TO FIRE YOUR RIFLE! THE THING LEAPED OUT AT YOU, AND ITS SHARP FANGS SANK INTO YOUR ARM!
THAT'S ALL IT DID! IT DIDN'T CONTINUE ITS ATTACK... INSTEAD, IT LOOSENED ITS GRIP ON YOUR ARM, AND VANISHED INTO THE WOODS!
STRANGE, WASN'T IT, KENNETH? THE MARKS OF THE FANGS WERE THERE ON YOUR ARM... BUT... THERE WAS NO PAIN!!!
AND, STRANGER STILL, AS YOU LOOKED AT YOUR ARM AND HAND, YOU SAW A CHANGE. INTO WHAT, KENNETH? INTO WHAT?
A PAW! MY HAND'S TURNING INTO A DOG'S PAW!!!

OU ALMOST WENT MAD WITH HORROR! YOUR FAMILY CALLED IN HE BEST DOCTORS! YOUR WEIRD MALADY BAFFLED THEM, AND THEY HAD ONLY *ONE* SOLUTION···

HATEVER IT IS, IT'S PREADING! SOON I'LL REACH HIS HOULDER···THEN···

WE'LL HAVE TO *AMPUTATE!*

ANYTHING! DO *ANYTHING*, BUT STOP IT FROM SPREADING!!

YEARS PASSED, KENNETH···YOUR PARENTS DIED, LEAVING YOU A FORTUNE OF MILLIONS! AND YOUR HATRED FOR DOGS GREW EVEN *GREATER!* THAT'S WHY YOU BUILT A HOUSE OUT IN THE LONELY MARSHLANDS···SO YOU COULD HUNT AND KILL WILD DOGS···EVEN WITH ONLY ONE ARM!!

AEEE-YIPE!!

BANG!

AHA! ONE LESS *CUR* ON EARTH!

ND THAT'S WHY YOU HIRED LLOYD WAYNE, A SHARPSHOOTER, AS A GUARD FOR YOUR NEW PROPERTY···

LL I WANT YOU TO DO IS TO SHOOT *EVERY* DOG YOU SEE.! UNDERSTAND?

FOR THE DOUGH YOU PAY ME, I CAN UNDERSTAND *ANYTHING!*

EVERY DOG, UNDERSTAND? EVERY DOG YOU SEE! SHOOT 'IM ON SIGHT!

YES, *SIR!!*

AND THEN YOU WERE PERFECTLY HAPPY, WEREN'T YOU, KENNETH? YOU HAD *EVERY-THING* YOU WANTED···EXPENSIVE TRAPS, THE FINEST RIFLES, POISON, A MAN TO HELP YOU KILL YOUR CANINE ENEMIES, AND ALL THE TIME AND MONEY YOU COULD USE! WHAT *MORE* COULD ANYONE ASK?

HAT MORE, KENNETH? YOU KNOW, DON'T YOU? THERE'S JUST *ONE* MORE THING YOU WANT, BUT YOU KNOW YOU'LL NEVER HAVE IT! THAT'S *FREEDOM FROM FEAR*···THE FEAR THAT IS ALWAYS WITH YOU! THEY CUT OFF YOUR ARM, BUT THEY COULDN'T CUT OFF THE FEAR THAT CREPT THROUGH THE REST OF YOUR BODY, COULD THEY, KENNETH?

DID IT DO ANY GOOD TO AMPUTATE MY ARM? WAS IT ALREADY TOO LATE ???

LOOK, KENNETH! *LOOK CLOSELY!* WHAT DO YOU SEE? YOUR FACE, YES ···BUT WHAT IS IT BEGINNING TO LOOK LIKE, KENNETH?

A *DOG!* MY FACE···IT'S CHANGING···INTO A *DOG'S* FACE !!!

27

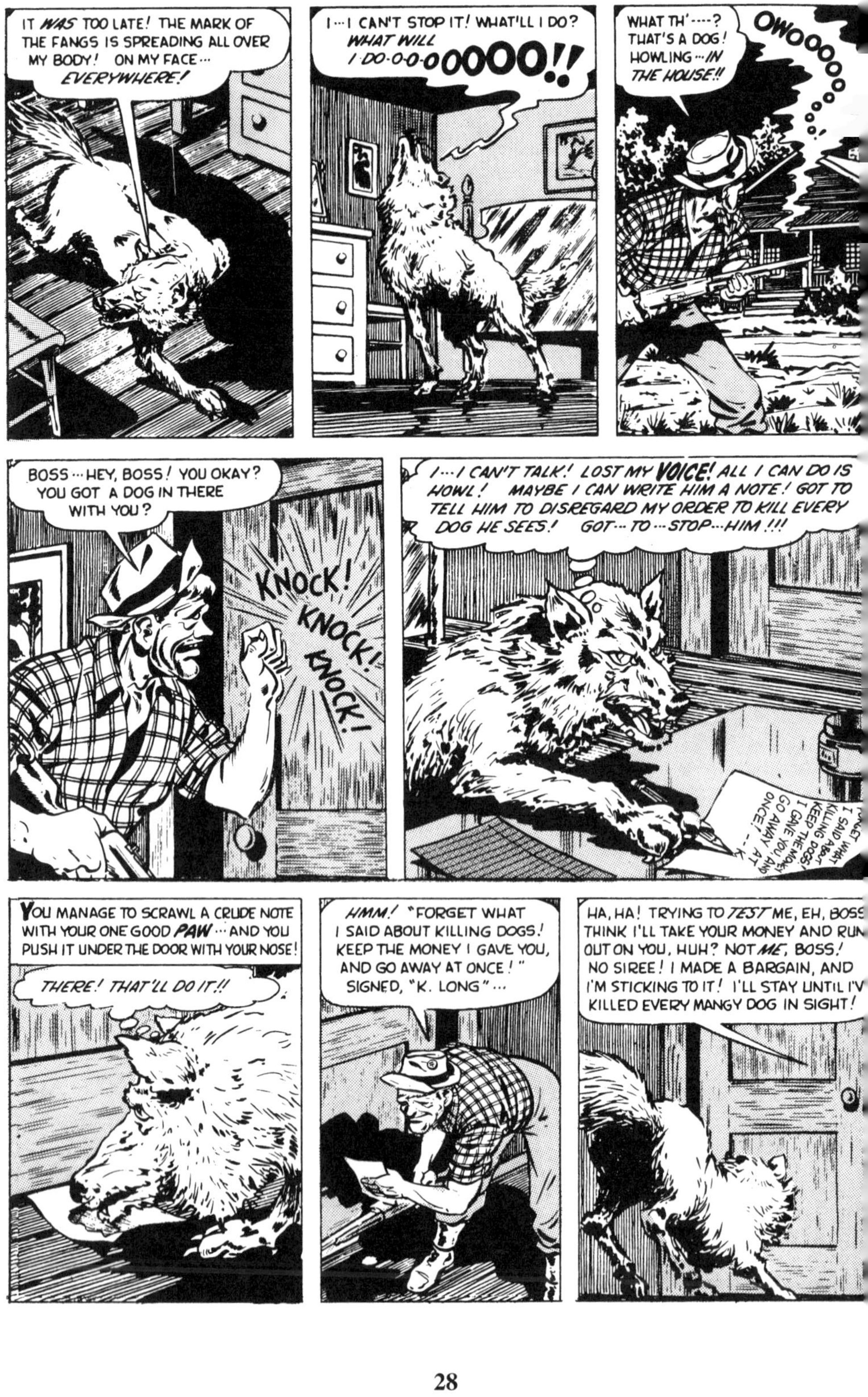

IT WAS TOO LATE! THE MARK OF THE FANGS IS SPREADING ALL OVER MY BODY! ON MY FACE... EVERYWHERE!
I... I CAN'T STOP IT! WHAT'LL I DO? WHAT WILL I DO-O-O-OOOOO!!
WHAT TH'----? THAT'S A DOG! HOWLING... IN THE HOUSE!!
OWOOOOOOOOO!
BOSS... HEY, BOSS! YOU OKAY? YOU GOT A DOG IN THERE WITH YOU?
KNOCK! KNOCK! KNOCK!
I... I CAN'T TALK! LOST MY VOICE! ALL I CAN DO IS HOWL! MAYBE I CAN WRITE HIM A NOTE! GOT TO TELL HIM TO DISREGARD MY ORDER TO KILL EVERY DOG HE SEES! GOT... TO... STOP... HIM!!!
I SAID ABOUT KILLING DOGS! KEEP THE MONEY I GAVE YOU AND GO AWAY AT ONCE! --K
YOU MANAGE TO SCRAWL A CRUDE NOTE WITH YOUR ONE GOOD PAW... AND YOU PUSH IT UNDER THE DOOR WITH YOUR NOSE!
THERE! THAT'LL DO IT!!
HMM! "FORGET WHAT I SAID ABOUT KILLING DOGS! KEEP THE MONEY I GAVE YOU, AND GO AWAY AT ONCE!" SIGNED, "K. LONG"...
HA, HA! TRYING TO TEST ME, EH, BOSS THINK I'LL TAKE YOUR MONEY AND RUN OUT ON YOU, HUH? NOT ME, BOSS! NO SIREE! I MADE A BARGAIN, AND I'M STICKING TO IT! I'LL STAY UNTIL I'V KILLED EVERY MANGY DOG IN SIGHT!

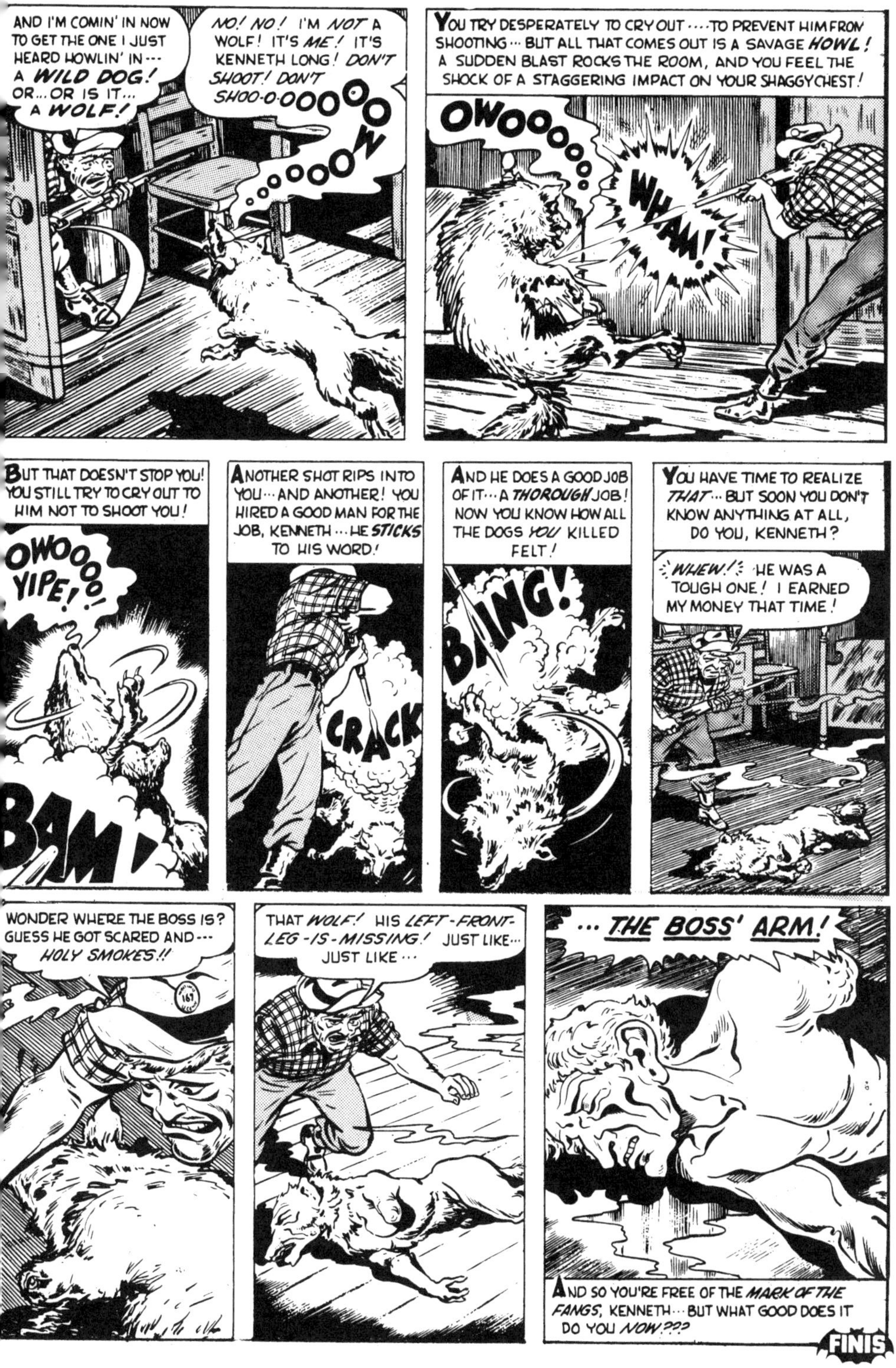
AND I'M COMIN' IN NOW TO GET THE ONE I JUST HEARD HOWLIN' IN --- A WILD DOG! OR... OR IS IT... A WOLF!
NO! NO! I'M NOT A WOLF! IT'S ME! IT'S KENNETH LONG! DON'T SHOOT! DON'T SHOO-O-OOOOOOOOW
...OOOOOOW
YOU TRY DESPERATELY TO CRY OUT ····TO PREVENT HIM FROM SHOOTING··· BUT ALL THAT COMES OUT IS A SAVAGE HOWL! A SUDDEN BLAST ROCKS THE ROOM, AND YOU FEEL THE SHOCK OF A STAGGERING IMPACT ON YOUR SHAGGY CHEST!
OWOOOOOOO
WHAM!
BUT THAT DOESN'T STOP YOU! YOU STILL TRY TO CRY OUT TO HIM NOT TO SHOOT YOU!
OWOOOOO! YIPE!
BAM!
ANOTHER SHOT RIPS INTO YOU··· AND ANOTHER! YOU HIRED A GOOD MAN FOR THE JOB, KENNETH ··· HE STICKS TO HIS WORD!
CRACK
AND HE DOES A GOOD JOB OF IT··· A THOROUGH JOB! NOW YOU KNOW HOW ALL THE DOGS YOU KILLED FELT!
BANG!
YOU HAVE TIME TO REALIZE THAT··· BUT SOON YOU DON'T KNOW ANYTHING AT ALL, DO YOU, KENNETH?
WHEW! HE WAS A TOUGH ONE! I EARNED MY MONEY THAT TIME!
WONDER WHERE THE BOSS IS? GUESS HE GOT SCARED AND --- HOLY SMOKES!!
THAT WOLF! HIS LEFT-FRONT-LEG-IS-MISSING! JUST LIKE··· JUST LIKE···
... THE BOSS' ARM!
AND SO YOU'RE FREE OF THE MARK OF THE FANGS, KENNETH··· BUT WHAT GOOD DOES IT DO YOU NOW???
FINIS

THE VAMPIRE

Article by Chris Claremont

HIS KITH AND KIN

An Analysis in Five Parts of the Book by Montague Summers

Part I: The Origin of The Vampire

Vampire.

From the Magyar, *vampir*, and the Russian *upyr*: loosely defined as a kind of blood-drunkenness.

What does the word mean to you? A Gene Colan-drawn spectacular? William Marshall totaling the LAPD? Or for the classicists among you, does it birth images of Chris Lee snarling at Peter Cushing just before he's zapped for the last (?) time. And then there is the patriarch of the cinematic cult, Lugosi himself; who can forget his chilling "Good e-ven-ing, Mr. Ren-field "?

A joke, right; a fiction, not to be taken seriously.

Yet there is a saying, that every legend had, at some time and in some way, its birth in fact. Ever wonder about that part of it, pilgrim? About those who did and those who were done unto? As near as two centuries ago, vampires were a reality and Mankind walked without the comforting protection of the silver screen to whisper in their ears, "Don't worry; this is only make-believe." Accused vampires, like accused witches, were executed on the flimsiest evidence—if any at all—and the manner of their executions was not pleasant. And few raised objections; where vampires were concerned, the moral choice was simple—us or them; no quarter asked or given.

So which is it? Man or demon? A fantasy we can laugh at or a reality we should respect and, perhaps, fear?

All of which brings us to a man, one Montague Summers, an ecclesiastical scholar of the early twentieth century whose specialites lay in the oddly juxtaposed fields of the occult and daemonic phenomena, and Elizabethan and Restoration theatre—he was extremely well-known in the '20's for his work editing the plays of Jonson, Wycherley, and Congreve, much more so than for his book *The Vampire: His Kith and Kin*.

Summers was born in 1880, in England. Upon graduation from Trinity College, Oxford, he—as he wrote himself—". . . gave concentrated study to theology, and after ordination (as a Roman Catholic priest) I worked for some time in the slums of London, and also on more than one country mission. For health's sake, I resided abroad during considerable periods, mainly in Italy and Southern France." Eventually, he returned to Oxford to study and to teach—and to write *Vampire*.

On the surface, a nice enough chap—though a trifle unforgiving to those who opposed his views—yet if one probes behind the facade, darker strains begin intruding

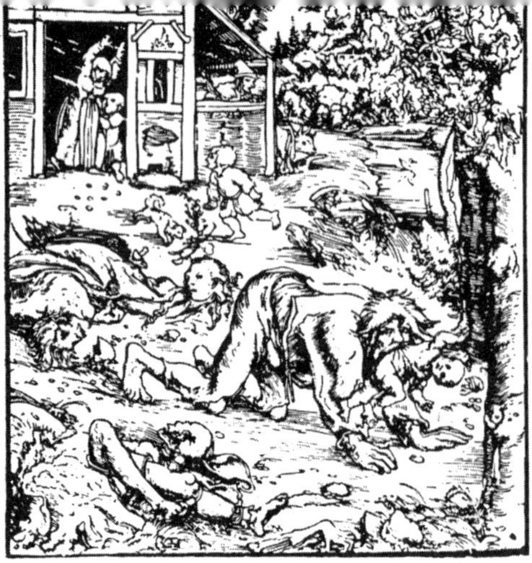

"Vampires beset men, women, and children alike. . ."

on the picture. He was born into the Church of England, not the Catholic faith, and while there is evidence of his conversion while travelling in Europe, there is no record of his ever having been ordained a priest. And there were rumors concerning those trips around the Continent, rumors that his writings on the occult were based on first-hand experience, that Summers had been an Initiate, perhaps even an Adept, in the Left-Hand Path.

As with the vampire, there are many stories about Summers; and little, if any, proof to back them u

The legend of the vampire is old, as old as Man, and knows no geographic boundaries. It is mentioned by t Assyrians—indeed, their tombs bear carvings of fange blood-sucking demons (but more on Assyria later)—ar the Chinese. The Mexican peoples knew of the vampi before Cortes; and the Arabs have their own tales ghouls who haunt ill-omened tombs and lonely roads attack and devour hapless travellers. And, of course, t Slavic races of Eastern Europe know it well. Very we indeed.

So, what is this vampire?

According to Summers he is neither demon nor ghos but he is Satanically-inspired and he possesses elemen of both natures. He has a corporeal body and he ca move, and he must feed to maintain a healthy—if t word really applies—existence; yet he is dead. As Joh Zopfius said in his *Dissertatio de Vampiris Seruiensib* (Halle, 1733): "Vampires issue forth from their graves the night, attack people sleeping quietly in their bed suck out all their blood from their bodies and destr them. They beset men, women, and children alik sparing neither age nor sex. Those who are under t fatal malignity of their influence complain of suffocati and a total deficiency of spirits, after which they soo expire. Some who, when at the point of death, have bee asked if they can tell what is causing their decease, rep that such and such persons, lately dead, have arisen fro the tomb to torment and torture them."

Another learned treatise, written about the same tin by a learned French theologian, Dom Augustin Calme describes the vampire in similar terms, but continues c

"The vampire must feed to maintain a healthy existence. . ."

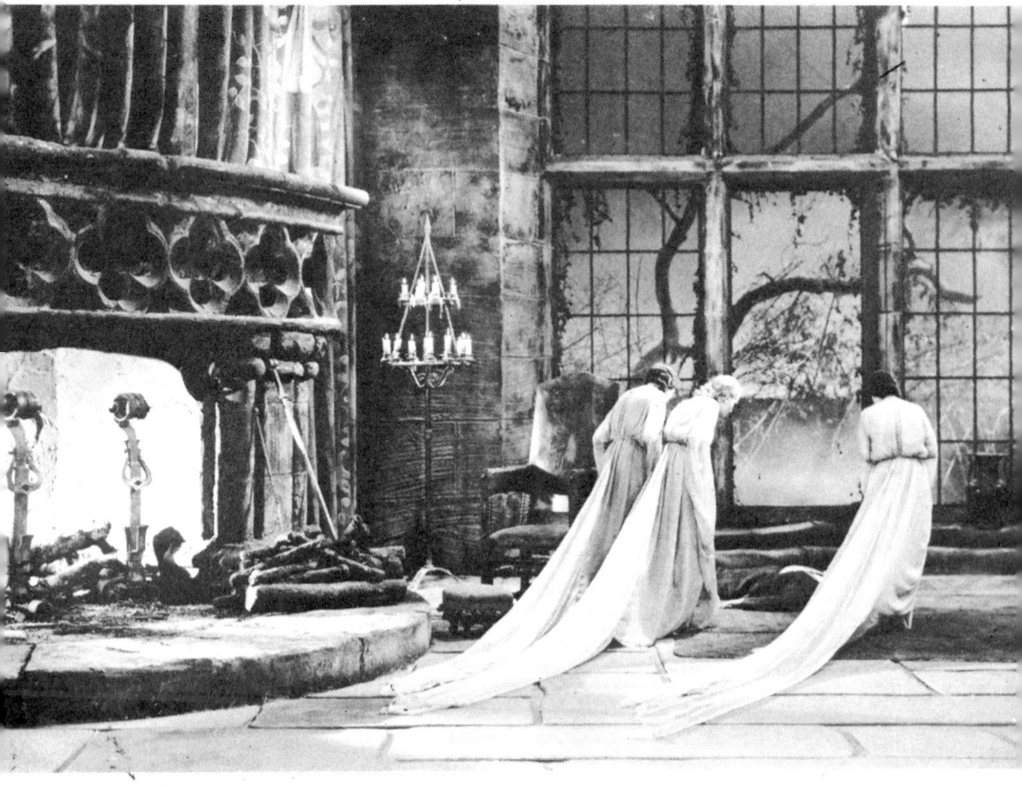

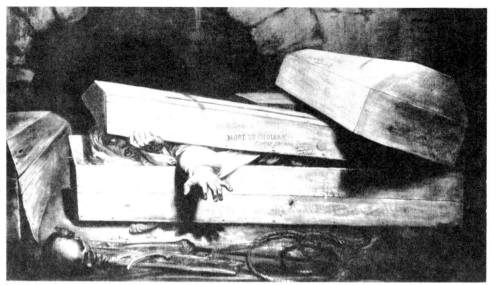

"Vampires issue forth from their graves in the night . . ."

to detail how one deals with them. The Undead corpses must be dug up from their graves and a stake driven through their hearts; then, the head must be cut off and the heart ripped from the body. An alternative is just to burn the suspect corpse to ashes.

From these and other examples (many, *many* others; Summers is nothing if not prolific in his citation of sources—if he heard about it, he put it on paper)—unfortunately, he presupposes his reader has a classical education and leaves a good third of his quotations in their original Greek, Latin, French or German, *sans* translation), we have an idea of what the vampire is. The question is, how did it all get started?

Summers theorizes that early man, as he evolved the concepts of religion and life-after-death, concluded that "heaven" was probably not too far away from earth, that a man going there would still remember the events of his life and could even return if the need was great enough. From this, it was an easy step to the idea that if a corpse were not "sent off" with the proper respect due it from its family and friends, it might come back to deal with those who slighted it. Many of these beliefs are tied in to the sanctity of the body after death and, most especially, with the necessity of not spilling any blood around it during the burial. The Bible, for example, is full of specific injunctions against cannibalism, whatever the reason; and Homer's *Odyssey* describes a scene in which Odysseus summons his dead crew by filling a pit with the blood of sacrificed animals, which the spirits come forth and drink.

Now, consider the plight of the cataleptic. A person whose physiological processes have slowed to such a degree that he seems dead. So, his family/friends stick the supposed corpse in the ground—invariably fatal—or in a tomb, in which case the "corpse" rises when the attack wears off and "returns from the dead." A short step, indeed, from here to the concept of the Undead, the dead who walk and seem to live.

And, in a slightly branching vein, there is the necrophiliac, a person whose psychological foul-ups prompt him to prey on newly interred corpses, abusing them—often sexually—and occasionally progressing to attacks on the living, killing and maiming travellers for both food and thrills. The brutality and bloodlust of the vampire could easily be ascribed to warped sadists such as these, a classic example being the Countess Elisabeth Bathory of Hungary, who bathed in the blood of some two hundred virgins in the hope that it would give her eternal youth; another being Vlad Tepes—Vlad the Impaler, believed by many to be the model for Stoker's Dracula (and ironically, a hero to many Hungarians; the Turks he impaled felt otherwise)—who impaled some 100,000 people on stakes, among other things.

So, what do we have? Many beliefs, all tied in to the idea of life after death and the ability of the soul—perhaps the body—to return to this earth, usually for some malignant purpose. And we have physical and psychological aberrations, barely understood today, infinitely more frightening in pre-Renaissance days, which could so easily be misconstrued as the handiwork of Satan. Does this mean the vampire, the ultimate horror, is only an accident of ignorance? Perhaps. But too many questions remain to be totally sure—and the legends have persisted too long for one to safely scoff at them. In the next few articles, we'll try to deal with these questions: the generation of the vampire; traits and practices of vampirism; the vampire in ancient civilizations; and, finally, the vampire in literature (and though the book only goes up to Stoker's epic, we'll throw in a sentence about the Lancer "masterpieces" just to bring it up to date for you *gothic* freaks).

When we're through with you, you should know a bit more than you do now. You may not sleep any easier, but at least you'll know why.

Stick around, pilgrim; as they say on the midnight boob-tube, there's more to come.

NEXT: THE GENERATION OF THE VAMPIRE

33

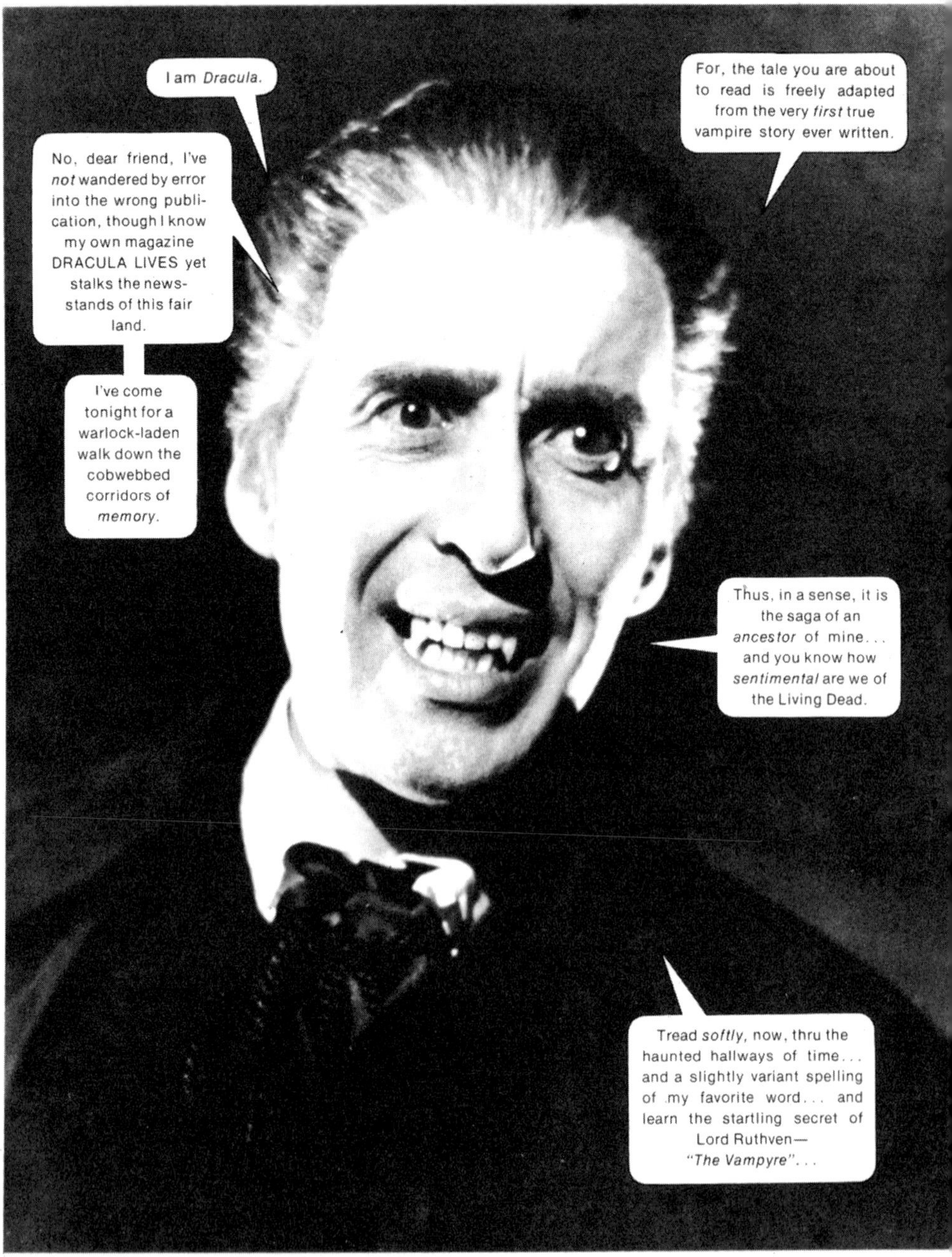
I am *Dracula*.
No, dear friend, I've *not* wandered by error into the wrong publication, though I know my own magazine DRACULA LIVES yet stalks the newsstands of this fair land.
I've come tonight for a warlock-laden walk down the cobwebbed corridors of *memory*.
For, the tale you are about to read is freely adapted from the very *first* true vampire story ever written.
Thus, in a sense, it is the saga of an *ancestor* of mine... and you know how *sentimental* are we of the Living Dead.
Tread *softly*, now, thru the haunted hallways of time... and a slightly variant spelling of my favorite word... and learn the startling secret of Lord Ruthven— *"The Vampyre"*...

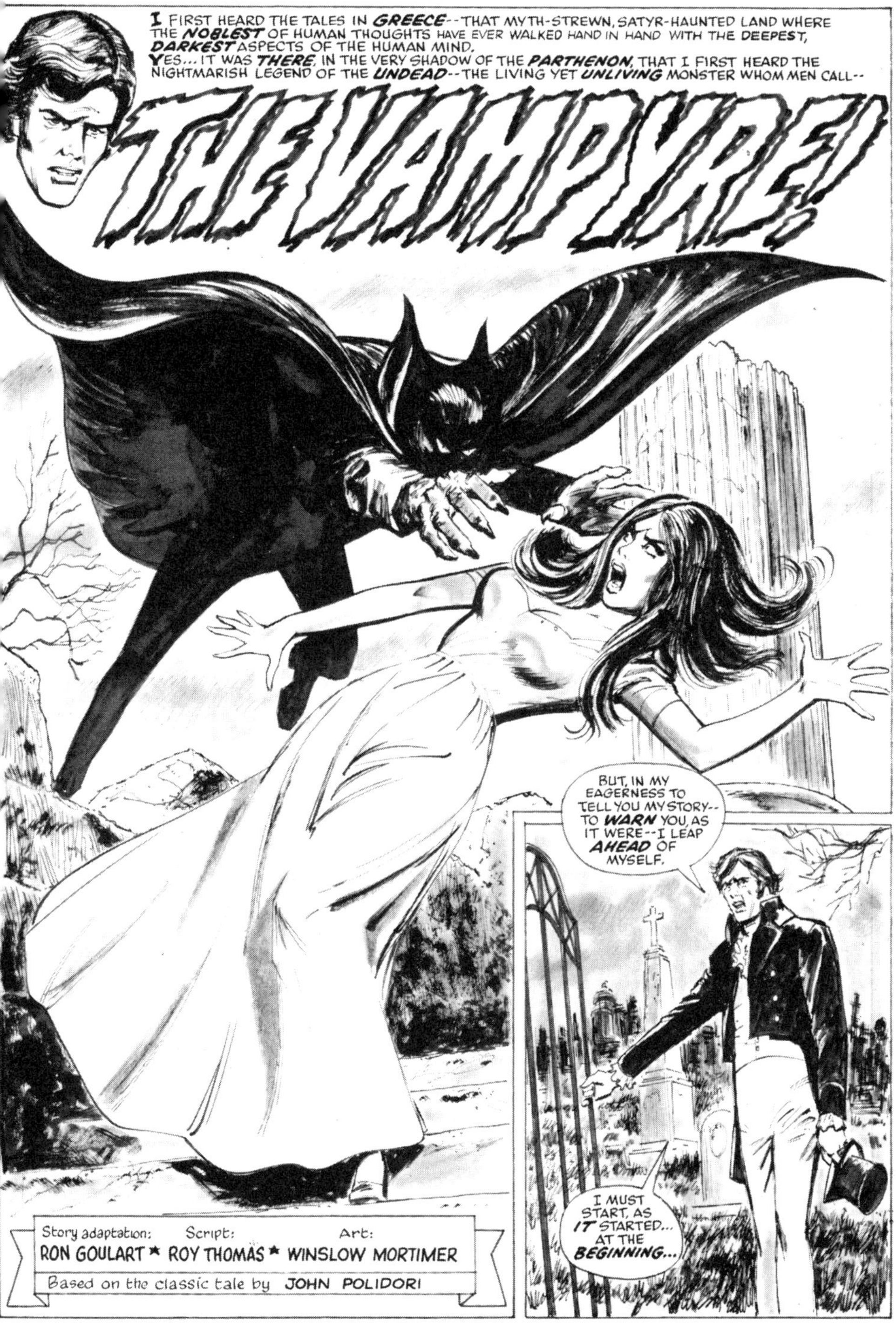
I FIRST HEARD THE TALES IN GREECE--THAT MYTH-STREWN, SATYR-HAUNTED LAND WHERE THE NOBLEST OF HUMAN THOUGHTS HAVE EVER WALKED HAND IN HAND WITH THE DEEPEST, DARKEST ASPECTS OF THE HUMAN MIND.
YES... IT WAS THERE, IN THE VERY SHADOW OF THE PARTHENON, THAT I FIRST HEARD THE NIGHTMARISH LEGEND OF THE UNDEAD--THE LIVING YET UNLIVING MONSTER WHOM MEN CALL--
THE VAMPYRE!
BUT, IN MY EAGERNESS TO TELL YOU MY STORY--TO WARN YOU, AS IT WERE--I LEAP AHEAD OF MYSELF.
I MUST START, AS IT STARTED... AT THE BEGINNING...
Story adaptation: RON GOULART ★ Script: ROY THOMAS ★ Art: WINSLOW MORTIMER
Based on the classic tale by JOHN POLIDORI

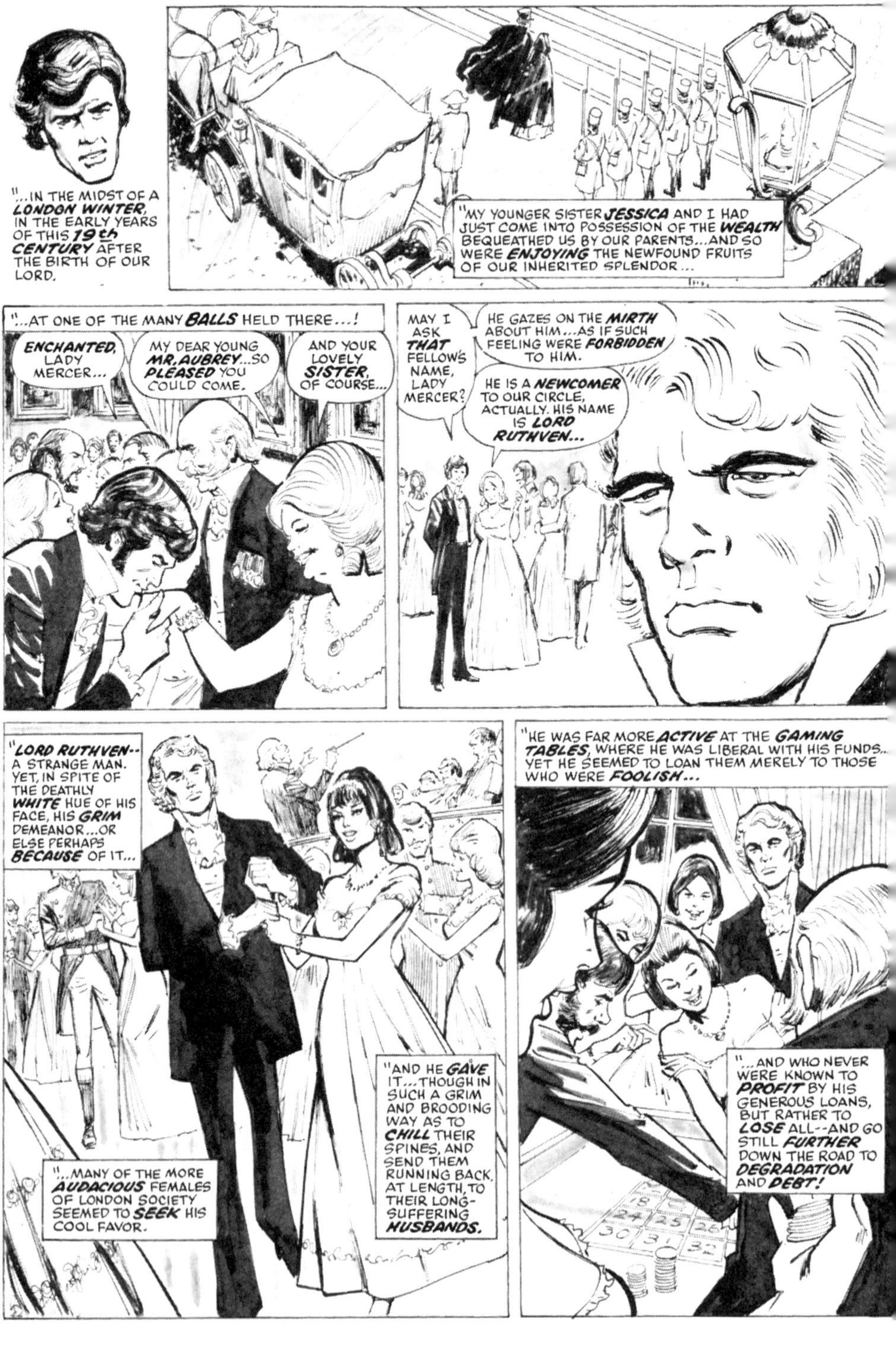
"...IN THE MIDST OF A LONDON WINTER, IN THE EARLY YEARS OF THIS 19th CENTURY AFTER THE BIRTH OF OUR LORD.
"MY YOUNGER SISTER JESSICA AND I HAD JUST COME INTO POSSESSION OF THE WEALTH BEQUEATHED US BY OUR PARENTS...AND SO WERE ENJOYING THE NEWFOUND FRUITS OF OUR INHERITED SPLENDOR...
"...AT ONE OF THE MANY BALLS HELD THERE...!
ENCHANTED, LADY MERCER...
MY DEAR YOUNG MR. AUBREY...SO PLEASED YOU COULD COME.
AND YOUR LOVELY SISTER, OF COURSE...
MAY I ASK THAT FELLOW'S NAME, LADY MERCER?
HE GAZES ON THE MIRTH ABOUT HIM...AS IF SUCH FEELING WERE FORBIDDEN TO HIM.
HE IS A NEWCOMER TO OUR CIRCLE, ACTUALLY. HIS NAME IS LORD RUTHVEN...
"LORD RUTHVEN-- A STRANGE MAN. YET, IN SPITE OF THE DEATHLY WHITE HUE OF HIS FACE, HIS GRIM DEMEANOR...OR ELSE PERHAPS BECAUSE OF IT...
"...MANY OF THE MORE AUDACIOUS FEMALES OF LONDON SOCIETY SEEMED TO SEEK HIS COOL FAVOR.
"AND HE GAVE IT...THOUGH IN SUCH A GRIM AND BROODING WAY AS TO CHILL THEIR SPINES, AND SEND THEM RUNNING BACK, AT LENGTH, TO THEIR LONG-SUFFERING HUSBANDS.
"HE WAS FAR MORE ACTIVE AT THE GAMING TABLES, WHERE HE WAS LIBERAL WITH HIS FUNDS.. YET HE SEEMED TO LOAN THEM MERELY TO THOSE WHO WERE FOOLISH...
"...AND WHO NEVER WERE KNOWN TO PROFIT BY HIS GENEROUS LOANS, BUT RATHER TO LOSE ALL--AND GO STILL FURTHER DOWN THE ROAD TO DEGRADATION AND DEBT!

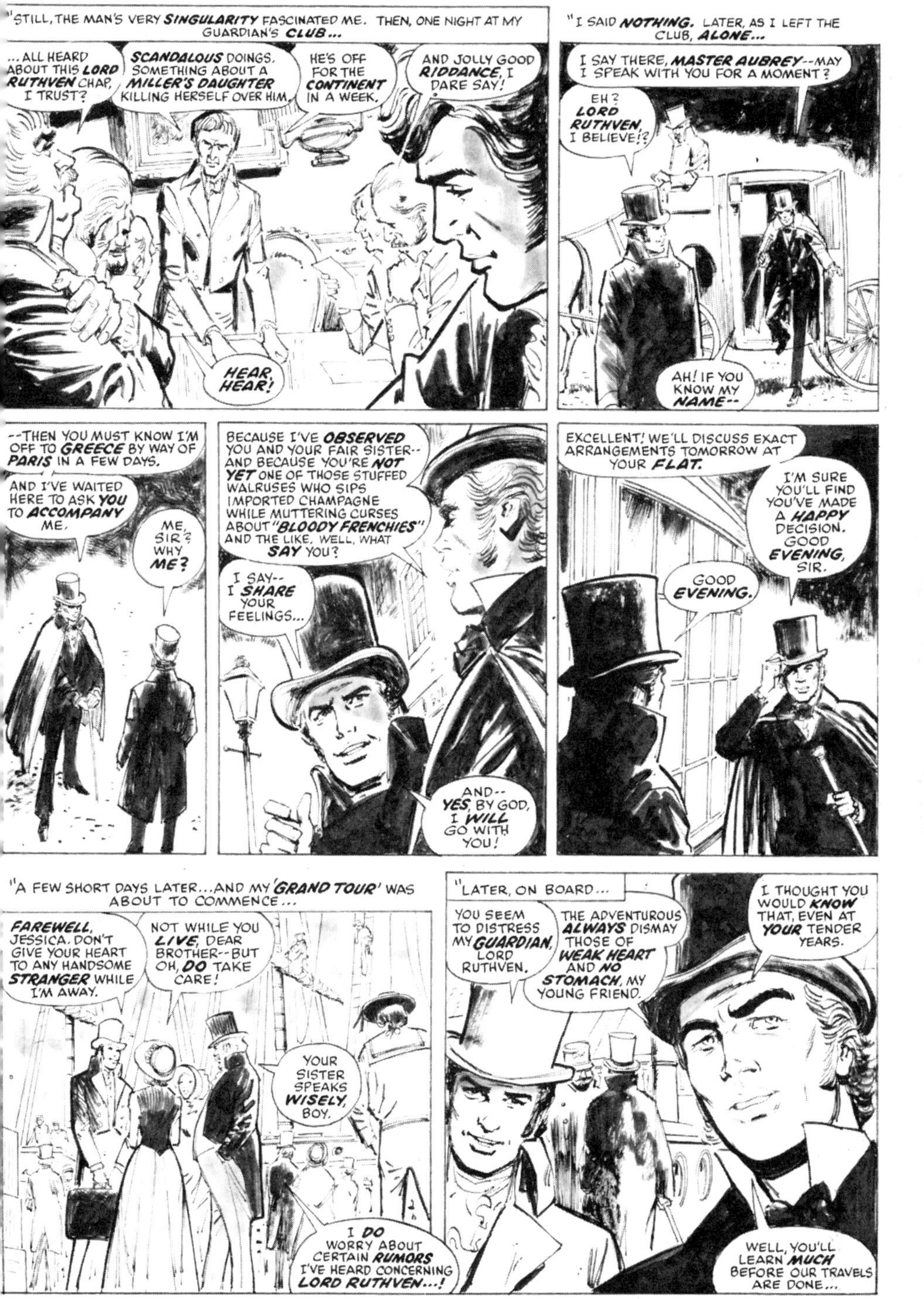
"STILL, THE MAN'S VERY SINGULARITY FASCINATED ME. THEN, ONE NIGHT AT MY GUARDIAN'S CLUB...
...ALL HEARD ABOUT THIS LORD RUTHVEN CHAP, I TRUST?
SCANDALOUS DOINGS. SOMETHING ABOUT A MILLER'S DAUGHTER KILLING HERSELF OVER HIM.
HE'S OFF FOR THE CONTINENT IN A WEEK.
AND JOLLY GOOD RIDDANCE, I DARE SAY!
HEAR, HEAR!
"I SAID NOTHING. LATER, AS I LEFT THE CLUB, ALONE...
I SAY THERE, MASTER AUBREY--MAY I SPEAK WITH YOU FOR A MOMENT?
EH? LORD RUTHVEN, I BELIEVE!?
AH! IF YOU KNOW MY NAME--
--THEN YOU MUST KNOW I'M OFF TO GREECE BY WAY OF PARIS IN A FEW DAYS.
AND I'VE WAITED HERE TO ASK YOU TO ACCOMPANY ME.
ME, SIR? WHY ME?
BECAUSE I'VE OBSERVED YOU AND YOUR FAIR SISTER--AND BECAUSE YOU'RE NOT YET ONE OF THOSE STUFFED WALRUSES WHO SIPS IMPORTED CHAMPAGNE WHILE MUTTERING CURSES ABOUT "BLOODY FRENCHIES" AND THE LIKE. WELL, WHAT SAY YOU?
I SAY--I SHARE YOUR FEELINGS...
AND--YES, BY GOD, I WILL GO WITH YOU!
EXCELLENT! WE'LL DISCUSS EXACT ARRANGEMENTS TOMORROW AT YOUR FLAT.
I'M SURE YOU'LL FIND YOU'VE MADE A HAPPY DECISION. GOOD EVENING, SIR.
GOOD EVENING.
"A FEW SHORT DAYS LATER...AND MY 'GRAND TOUR' WAS ABOUT TO COMMENCE...
FAREWELL, JESSICA. DON'T GIVE YOUR HEART TO ANY HANDSOME STRANGER WHILE I'M AWAY.
NOT WHILE YOU LIVE, DEAR BROTHER--BUT OH, DO TAKE CARE!
YOUR SISTER SPEAKS WISELY, BOY.
I DO WORRY ABOUT CERTAIN RUMORS I'VE HEARD CONCERNING LORD RUTHVEN...!
"LATER, ON BOARD...
YOU SEEM TO DISTRESS MY GUARDIAN, LORD RUTHVEN.
THE ADVENTUROUS ALWAYS DISMAY THOSE OF WEAK HEART AND NO STOMACH, MY YOUNG FRIEND.
I THOUGHT YOU WOULD KNOW THAT, EVEN AT YOUR TENDER YEARS.
WELL, YOU'LL LEARN MUCH BEFORE OUR TRAVELS ARE DONE...

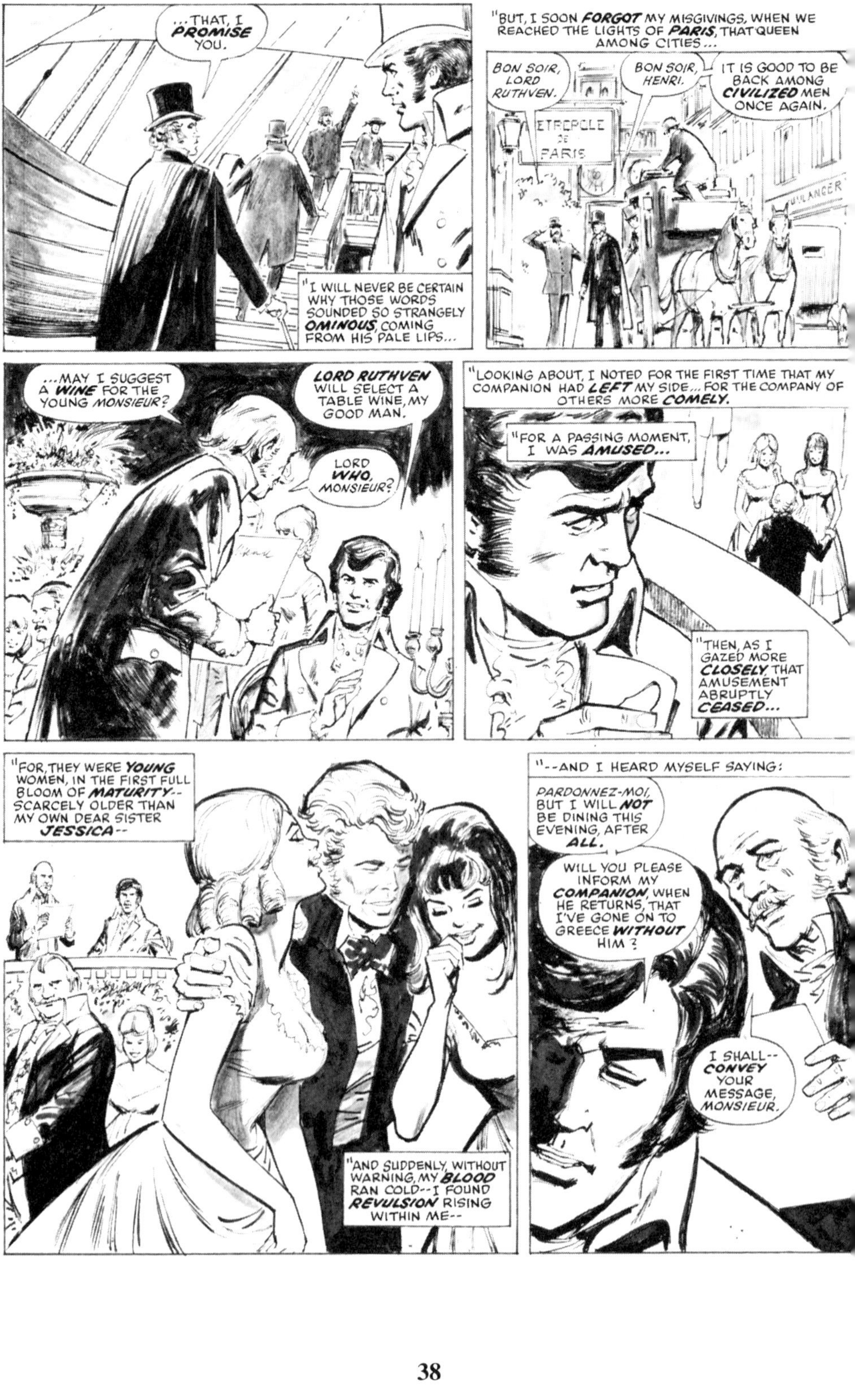
...THAT, I PROMISE YOU.
"I WILL NEVER BE CERTAIN WHY THOSE WORDS SOUNDED SO STRANGELY OMINOUS, COMING FROM HIS PALE LIPS...
"BUT, I SOON FORGOT MY MISGIVINGS, WHEN WE REACHED THE LIGHTS OF PARIS, THAT QUEEN AMONG CITIES...
BON SOIR, LORD RUTHVEN.
BON SOIR, HENRI.
IT IS GOOD TO BE BACK AMONG CIVILIZED MEN ONCE AGAIN.
...MAY I SUGGEST A WINE FOR THE YOUNG MONSIEUR?
LORD RUTHVEN WILL SELECT A TABLE WINE, MY GOOD MAN.
LORD WHO, MONSIEUR?
"LOOKING ABOUT, I NOTED FOR THE FIRST TIME THAT MY COMPANION HAD LEFT MY SIDE... FOR THE COMPANY OF OTHERS MORE COMELY.
"FOR A PASSING MOMENT, I WAS AMUSED...
"THEN, AS I GAZED MORE CLOSELY, THAT AMUSEMENT ABRUPTLY CEASED...
"FOR, THEY WERE YOUNG WOMEN, IN THE FIRST FULL BLOOM OF MATURITY-- SCARCELY OLDER THAN MY OWN DEAR SISTER JESSICA--
"AND SUDDENLY, WITHOUT WARNING, MY BLOOD RAN COLD--I FOUND REVULSION RISING WITHIN ME--
"--AND I HEARD MYSELF SAYING:
PARDONNEZ-MOI, BUT I WILL NOT BE DINING THIS EVENING, AFTER ALL.
WILL YOU PLEASE INFORM MY COMPANION, WHEN HE RETURNS, THAT I'VE GONE ON TO GREECE WITHOUT HIM?
I SHALL-- CONVEY YOUR MESSAGE, MONSIEUR.

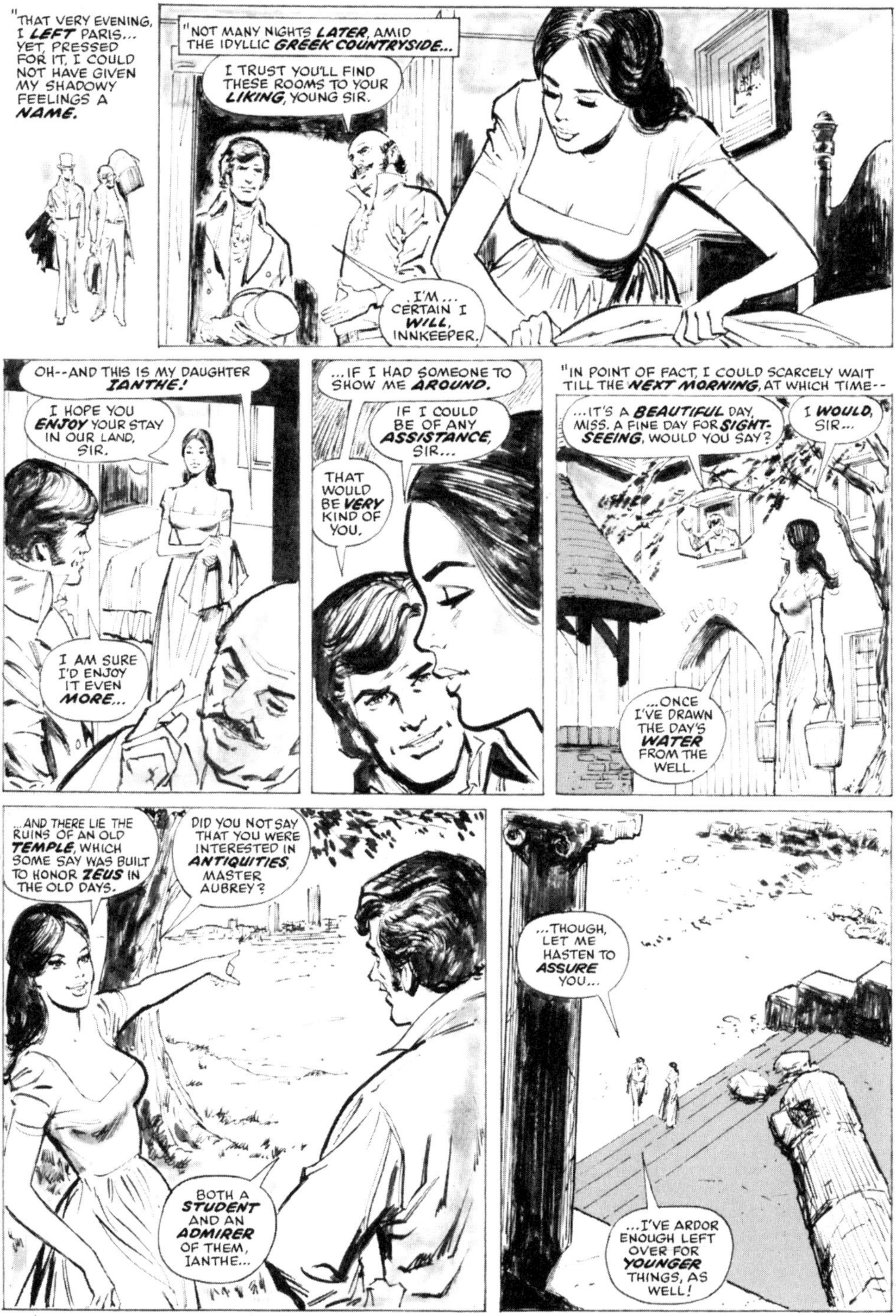
"THAT VERY EVENING, I LEFT PARIS... YET, PRESSED FOR IT, I COULD NOT HAVE GIVEN MY SHADOWY FEELINGS A NAME.
"NOT MANY NIGHTS LATER, AMID THE IDYLLIC GREEK COUNTRYSIDE...
I TRUST YOU'LL FIND THESE ROOMS TO YOUR LIKING, YOUNG SIR.
I'M... CERTAIN I WILL, INNKEEPER.
OH--AND THIS IS MY DAUGHTER IANTHE!
I HOPE YOU ENJOY YOUR STAY IN OUR LAND, SIR.
I AM SURE I'D ENJOY IT EVEN MORE...
...IF I HAD SOMEONE TO SHOW ME AROUND.
IF I COULD BE OF ANY ASSISTANCE, SIR...
THAT WOULD BE VERY KIND OF YOU.
"IN POINT OF FACT, I COULD SCARCELY WAIT TILL THE NEXT MORNING, AT WHICH TIME--
...IT'S A BEAUTIFUL DAY, MISS. A FINE DAY FOR SIGHT-SEEING, WOULD YOU SAY?
I WOULD, SIR...
...ONCE I'VE DRAWN THE DAY'S WATER FROM THE WELL.
...AND THERE LIE THE RUINS OF AN OLD TEMPLE, WHICH SOME SAY WAS BUILT TO HONOR ZEUS IN THE OLD DAYS.
DID YOU NOT SAY THAT YOU WERE INTERESTED IN ANTIQUITIES, MASTER AUBREY?
BOTH A STUDENT AND AN ADMIRER OF THEM, IANTHE...
...THOUGH, LET ME HASTEN TO ASSURE YOU...
...I'VE ARDOR ENOUGH LEFT OVER FOR YOUNGER THINGS, AS WELL!

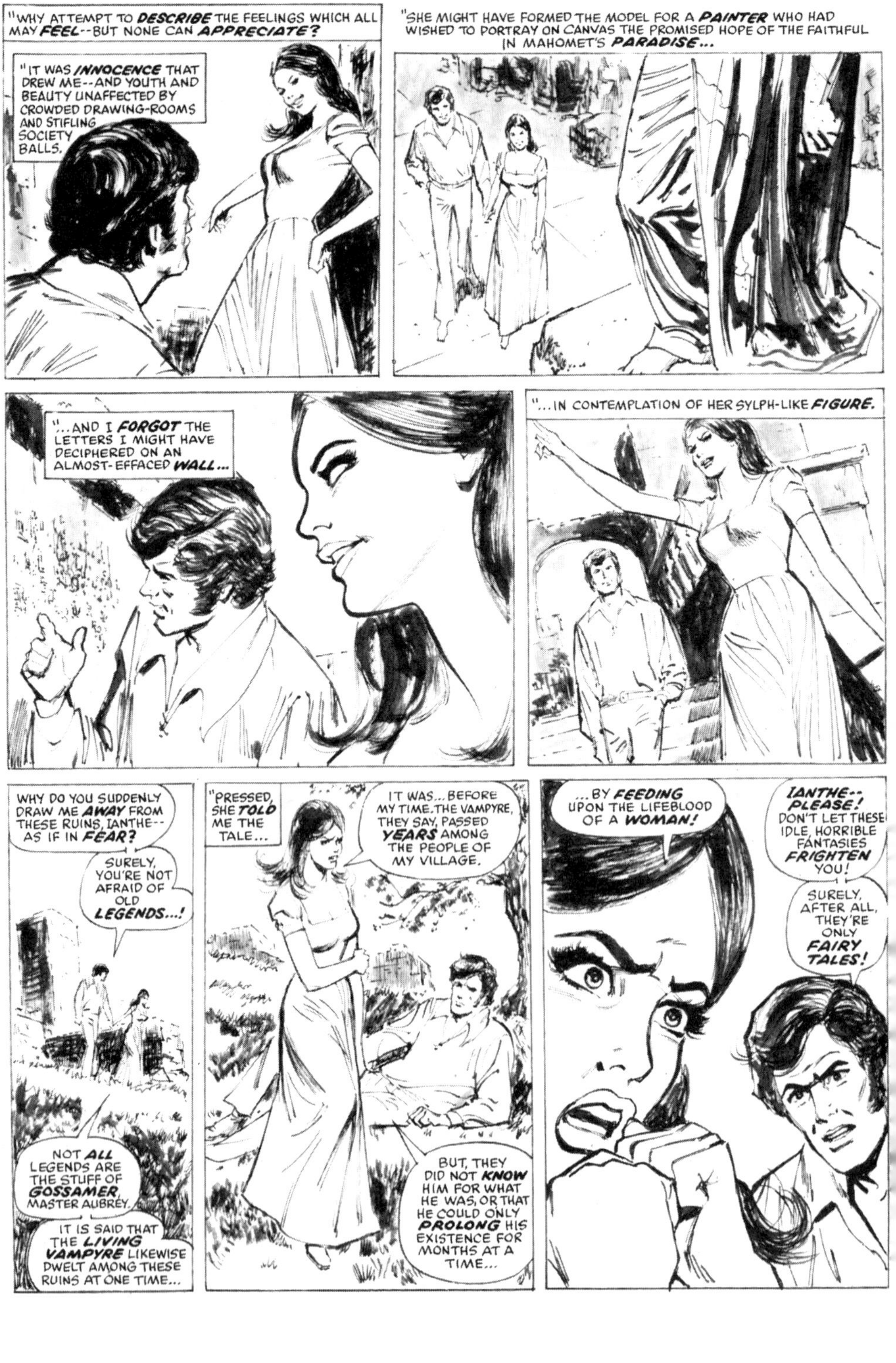
"WHY ATTEMPT TO DESCRIBE THE FEELINGS WHICH ALL MAY FEEL--BUT NONE CAN APPRECIATE?
"IT WAS INNOCENCE THAT DREW ME--AND YOUTH AND BEAUTY UNAFFECTED BY CROWDED DRAWING-ROOMS AND STIFLING SOCIETY BALLS.
"SHE MIGHT HAVE FORMED THE MODEL FOR A PAINTER WHO HAD WISHED TO PORTRAY ON CANVAS THE PROMISED HOPE OF THE FAITHFUL IN MAHOMET'S PARADISE...
"...AND I FORGOT THE LETTERS I MIGHT HAVE DECIPHERED ON AN ALMOST-EFFACED WALL...
"...IN CONTEMPLATION OF HER SYLPH-LIKE FIGURE.
WHY DO YOU SUDDENLY DRAW ME AWAY FROM THESE RUINS, IANTHE--AS IF IN FEAR?
SURELY, YOU'RE NOT AFRAID OF OLD LEGENDS...!
NOT ALL LEGENDS ARE THE STUFF OF GOSSAMER, MASTER AUBREY.
IT IS SAID THAT THE LIVING VAMPYRE LIKEWISE DWELT AMONG THESE RUINS AT ONE TIME...
"PRESSED, SHE TOLD ME THE TALE...
IT WAS... BEFORE MY TIME. THE VAMPYRE, THEY SAY, PASSED YEARS AMONG THE PEOPLE OF MY VILLAGE.
BUT, THEY DID NOT KNOW HIM FOR WHAT HE WAS, OR THAT HE COULD ONLY PROLONG HIS EXISTENCE FOR MONTHS AT A TIME...
...BY FEEDING UPON THE LIFEBLOOD OF A WOMAN!
IANTHE--PLEASE! DON'T LET THESE IDLE, HORRIBLE FANTASIES FRIGHTEN YOU!
SURELY, AFTER ALL, THEY'RE ONLY FAIRY TALES!

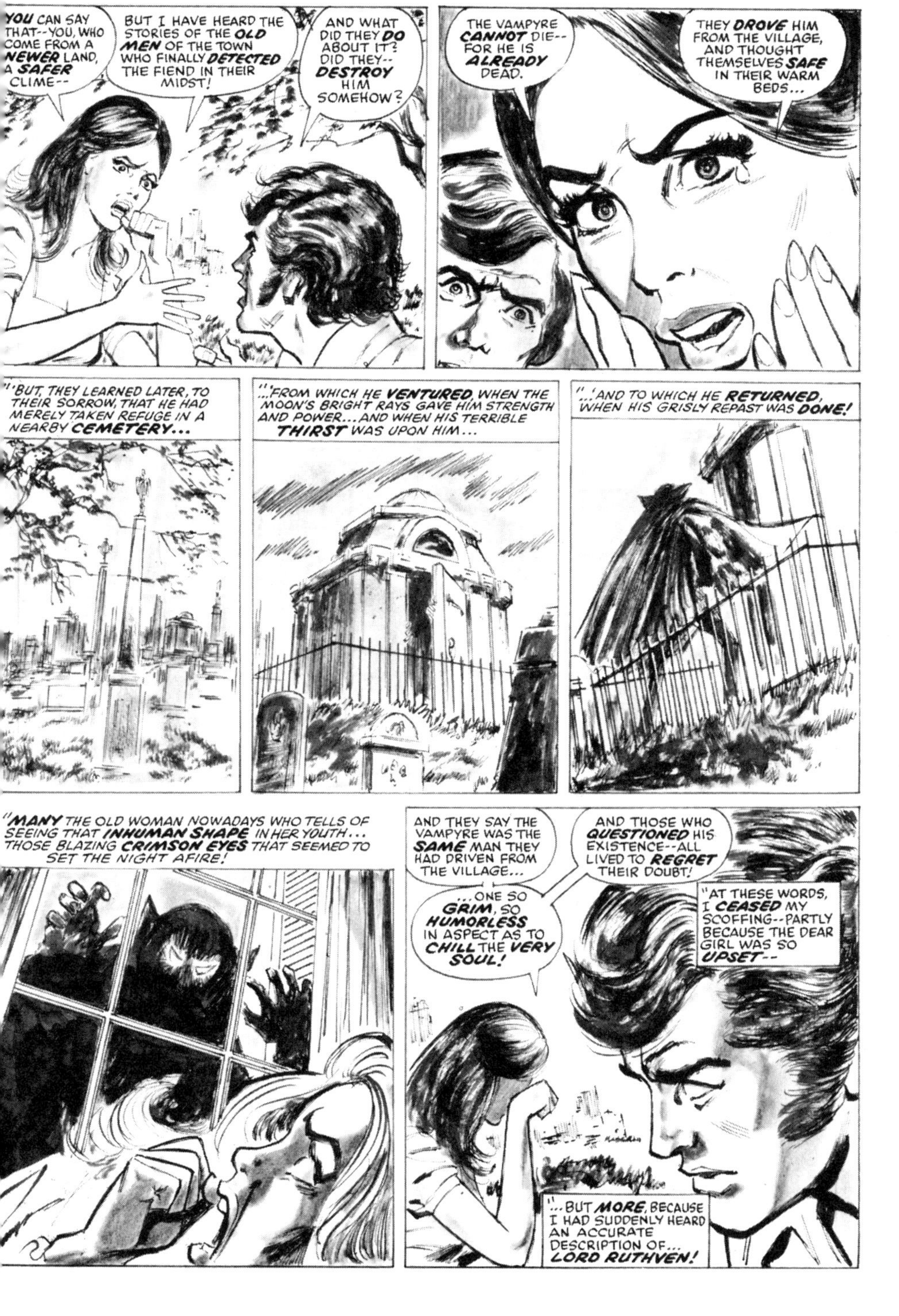
YOU CAN SAY THAT--YOU, WHO COME FROM A NEWER LAND, A SAFER CLIME--
BUT I HAVE HEARD THE STORIES OF THE OLD MEN OF THE TOWN WHO FINALLY DETECTED THE FIEND IN THEIR MIDST!
AND WHAT DID THEY DO ABOUT IT? DID THEY--DESTROY HIM SOMEHOW?
THE VAMPYRE CANNOT DIE--FOR HE IS ALREADY DEAD.
THEY DROVE HIM FROM THE VILLAGE, AND THOUGHT THEMSELVES SAFE IN THEIR WARM BEDS...
"BUT, THEY LEARNED LATER, TO THEIR SORROW, THAT HE HAD MERELY TAKEN REFUGE IN A NEARBY CEMETERY...
"...FROM WHICH HE VENTURED, WHEN THE MOON'S BRIGHT RAYS GAVE HIM STRENGTH AND POWER... AND WHEN HIS TERRIBLE THIRST WAS UPON HIM...
"...AND TO WHICH HE RETURNED, WHEN HIS GRISLY REPAST WAS DONE!
"MANY THE OLD WOMAN NOWADAYS WHO TELLS OF SEEING THAT INHUMAN SHAPE IN HER YOUTH... THOSE BLAZING CRIMSON EYES THAT SEEMED TO SET THE NIGHT AFIRE!
AND THEY SAY THE VAMPYRE WAS THE SAME MAN THEY HAD DRIVEN FROM THE VILLAGE...
...ONE SO GRIM, SO HUMORLESS IN ASPECT AS TO CHILL THE VERY SOUL!
AND THOSE WHO QUESTIONED HIS EXISTENCE--ALL LIVED TO REGRET THEIR DOUBT!
"AT THESE WORDS, I CEASED MY SCOFFING--PARTLY BECAUSE THE DEAR GIRL WAS SO UPSET--
"...BUT MORE, BECAUSE I HAD SUDDENLY HEARD AN ACCURATE DESCRIPTION OF... LORD RUTHVEN!

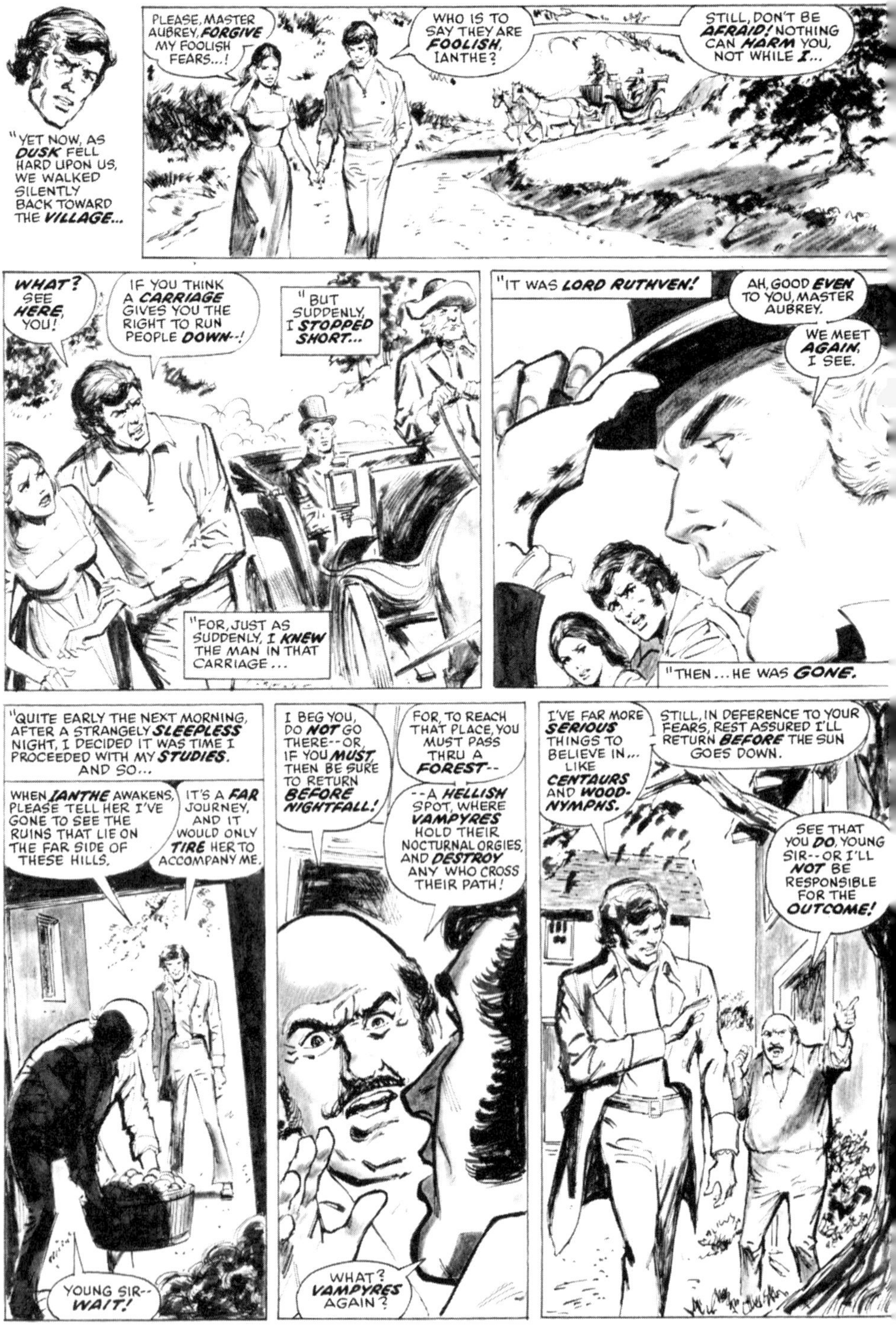

"YET NOW, AS DUSK FELL HARD UPON US, WE WALKED SILENTLY BACK TOWARD THE VILLAGE...
PLEASE, MASTER AUBREY, FORGIVE MY FOOLISH FEARS...!
WHO IS TO SAY THEY ARE FOOLISH, IANTHE?
STILL, DON'T BE AFRAID! NOTHING CAN HARM YOU, NOT WHILE I...
WHAT? SEE HERE, YOU!
IF YOU THINK A CARRIAGE GIVES YOU THE RIGHT TO RUN PEOPLE DOWN--!
"BUT SUDDENLY, I STOPPED SHORT...
"FOR, JUST AS SUDDENLY, I KNEW THE MAN IN THAT CARRIAGE...
"IT WAS LORD RUTHVEN!
AH, GOOD EVEN TO YOU, MASTER AUBREY.
WE MEET AGAIN, I SEE.
"THEN... HE WAS GONE.
"QUITE EARLY THE NEXT MORNING, AFTER A STRANGELY SLEEPLESS NIGHT, I DECIDED IT WAS TIME I PROCEEDED WITH MY STUDIES. AND SO...
WHEN IANTHE AWAKENS, PLEASE TELL HER I'VE GONE TO SEE THE RUINS THAT LIE ON THE FAR SIDE OF THESE HILLS.
IT'S A FAR JOURNEY, AND IT WOULD ONLY TIRE HER TO ACCOMPANY ME.
YOUNG SIR-- WAIT!
I BEG YOU, DO NOT GO THERE--OR, IF YOU MUST, THEN BE SURE TO RETURN BEFORE NIGHTFALL!
FOR, TO REACH THAT PLACE, YOU MUST PASS THRU A FOREST--
--A HELLISH SPOT, WHERE VAMPYRES HOLD THEIR NOCTURNAL ORGIES, AND DESTROY ANY WHO CROSS THEIR PATH!
WHAT? VAMPYRES AGAIN?
I'VE FAR MORE SERIOUS THINGS TO BELIEVE IN... LIKE CENTAURS AND WOOD-NYMPHS.
STILL, IN DEFERENCE TO YOUR FEARS, REST ASSURED I'LL RETURN BEFORE THE SUN GOES DOWN.
SEE THAT YOU DO, YOUNG SIR--OR I'LL NOT BE RESPONSIBLE FOR THE OUTCOME!

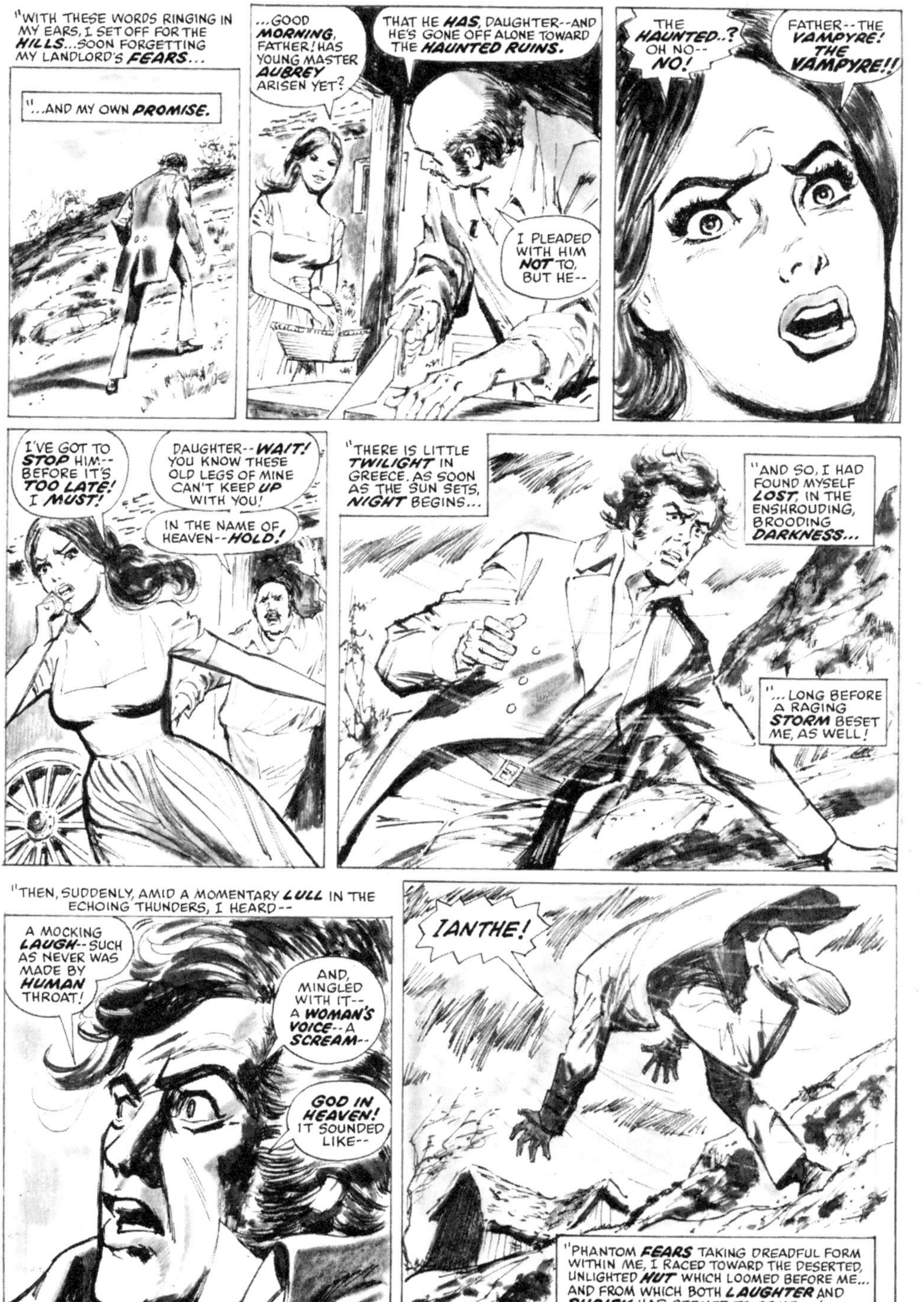
"WITH THESE WORDS RINGING IN MY EARS, I SET OFF FOR THE HILLS...SOON FORGETTING MY LANDLORD'S FEARS...
"...AND MY OWN PROMISE.
...GOOD MORNING, FATHER! HAS YOUNG MASTER AUBREY ARISEN YET?
THAT HE HAS, DAUGHTER--AND HE'S GONE OFF ALONE TOWARD THE HAUNTED RUINS.
I PLEADED WITH HIM NOT TO, BUT HE--
THE HAUNTED..? OH NO--NO!
FATHER--THE VAMPYRE! THE VAMPYRE!!
I'VE GOT TO STOP HIM--BEFORE IT'S TOO LATE! I MUST!
DAUGHTER--WAIT! YOU KNOW THESE OLD LEGS OF MINE CAN'T KEEP UP WITH YOU!
IN THE NAME OF HEAVEN--HOLD!
"THERE IS LITTLE TWILIGHT IN GREECE. AS SOON AS THE SUN SETS, NIGHT BEGINS...
"AND SO, I HAD FOUND MYSELF LOST, IN THE ENSHROUDING, BROODING DARKNESS...
"...LONG BEFORE A RAGING STORM BESET ME, AS WELL!
"THEN, SUDDENLY, AMID A MOMENTARY LULL IN THE ECHOING THUNDERS, I HEARD--
A MOCKING LAUGH--SUCH AS NEVER WAS MADE BY HUMAN THROAT!
AND, MINGLED WITH IT--A WOMAN'S VOICE--A SCREAM--
GOD IN HEAVEN! IT SOUNDED LIKE--
IANTHE!
"PHANTOM FEARS TAKING DREADFUL FORM WITHIN ME, I RACED TOWARD THE DESERTED, UNLIGHTED HUT WHICH LOOMED BEFORE ME... AND FROM WHICH BOTH LAUGHTER AND SHRIEK HAD SEEMED TO COME...!

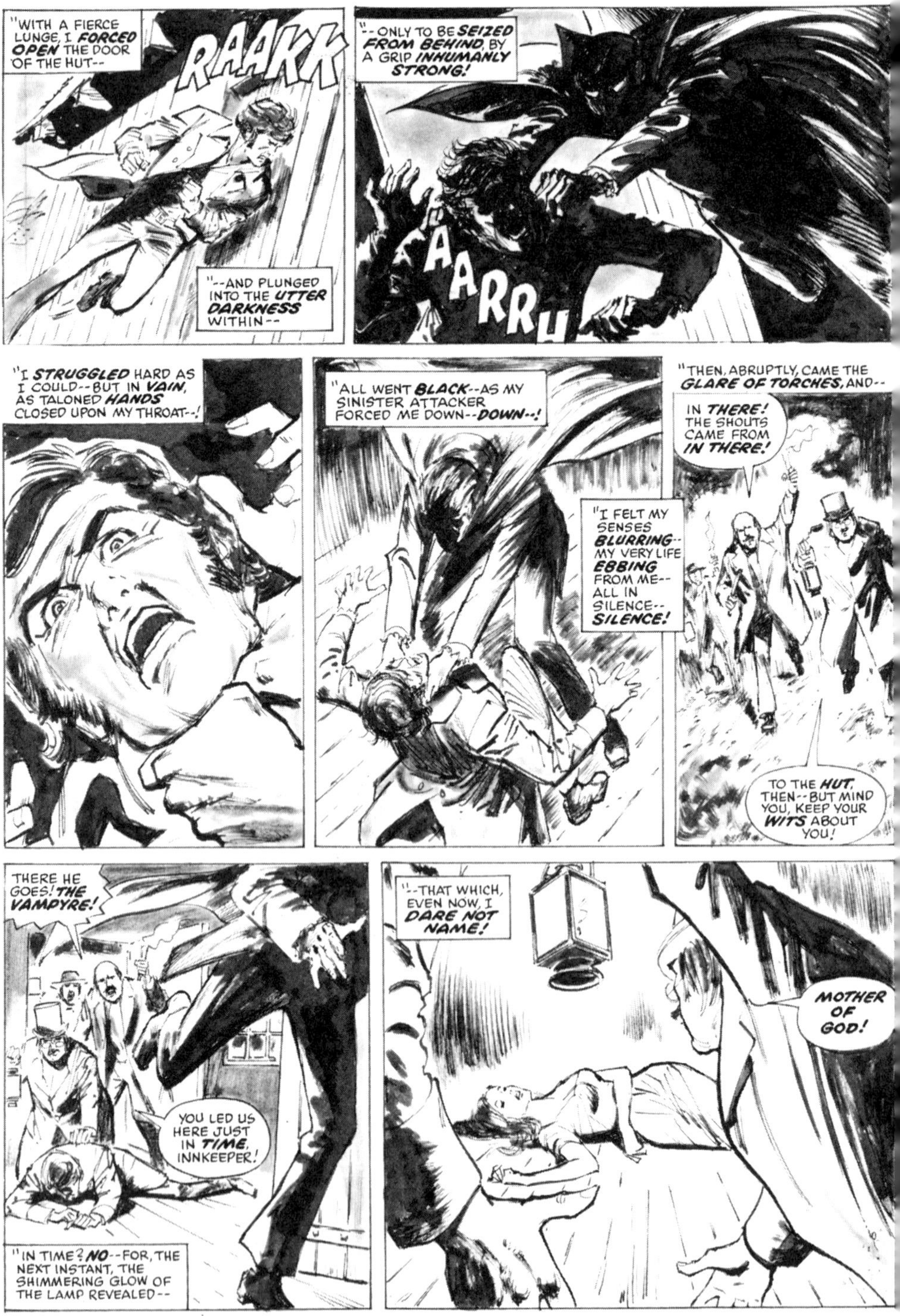
"WITH A FIERCE LUNGE, I FORCED OPEN THE DOOR OF THE HUT--
RAAKK
"--AND PLUNGED INTO THE UTTER DARKNESS WITHIN--
"--ONLY TO BE SEIZED FROM BEHIND, BY A GRIP INHUMANLY STRONG!
AARRH
"I STRUGGLED HARD AS I COULD--BUT IN VAIN, AS TALONED HANDS CLOSED UPON MY THROAT--!
"ALL WENT BLACK--AS MY SINISTER ATTACKER FORCED ME DOWN--DOWN--!
"I FELT MY SENSES BLURRING--MY VERY LIFE EBBING FROM ME--ALL IN SILENCE--SILENCE!
"THEN, ABRUPTLY, CAME THE GLARE OF TORCHES, AND--
IN THERE! THE SHOUTS CAME FROM IN THERE!
TO THE HUT, THEN--BUT MIND YOU, KEEP YOUR WITS ABOUT YOU!
THERE HE GOES! THE VAMPYRE!
YOU LED US HERE JUST IN TIME, INNKEEPER!
"IN TIME? NO--FOR, THE NEXT INSTANT, THE SHIMMERING GLOW OF THE LAMP REVEALED--
"--THAT WHICH, EVEN NOW, I DARE NOT NAME!
MOTHER OF GOD!

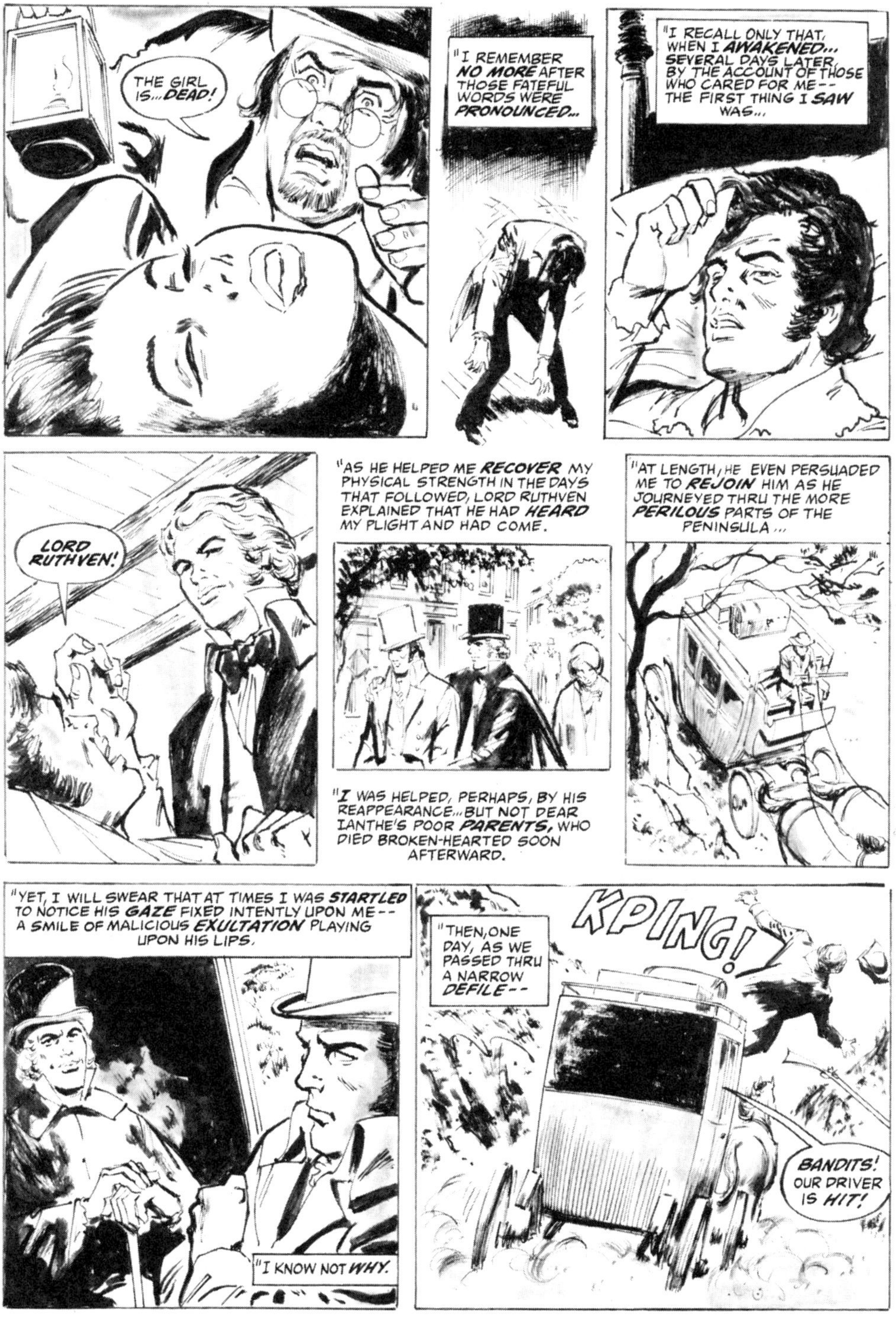
THE GIRL IS...DEAD!
"I REMEMBER NO MORE AFTER THOSE FATEFUL WORDS WERE PRONOUNCED...
"I RECALL ONLY THAT, WHEN I AWAKENED... SEVERAL DAYS LATER, BY THE ACCOUNT OF THOSE WHO CARED FOR ME-- THE FIRST THING I SAW WAS...
LORD RUTHVEN!
"AS HE HELPED ME RECOVER MY PHYSICAL STRENGTH IN THE DAYS THAT FOLLOWED, LORD RUTHVEN EXPLAINED THAT HE HAD HEARD MY PLIGHT AND HAD COME.
"I WAS HELPED, PERHAPS, BY HIS REAPPEARANCE... BUT NOT DEAR IANTHE'S POOR PARENTS, WHO DIED BROKEN-HEARTED SOON AFTERWARD.
"AT LENGTH, HE EVEN PERSUADED ME TO REJOIN HIM AS HE JOURNEYED THRU THE MORE PERILOUS PARTS OF THE PENINSULA...
"YET, I WILL SWEAR THAT AT TIMES I WAS STARTLED TO NOTICE HIS GAZE FIXED INTENTLY UPON ME-- A SMILE OF MALICIOUS EXULTATION PLAYING UPON HIS LIPS.
"I KNOW NOT WHY.
"THEN, ONE DAY, AS WE PASSED THRU A NARROW DEFILE--
KPING!
BANDITS! OUR DRIVER IS HIT!

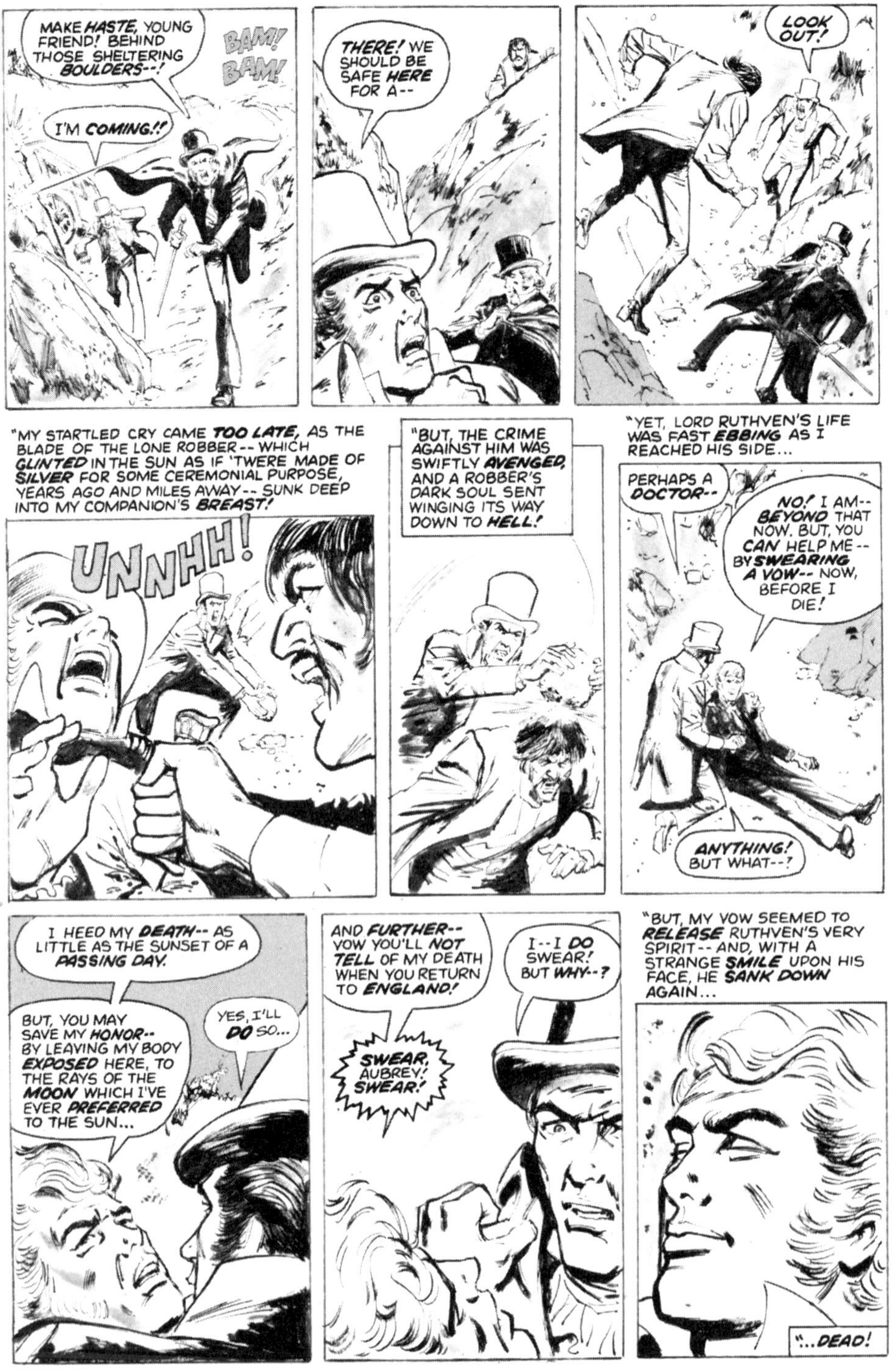
MAKE HASTE, YOUNG FRIEND! BEHIND THOSE SHELTERING BOULDERS--!
BAM! BAM!
I'M COMING!!
THERE! WE SHOULD BE SAFE HERE FOR A--
LOOK OUT!
"MY STARTLED CRY CAME TOO LATE, AS THE BLADE OF THE LONE ROBBER-- WHICH GLINTED IN THE SUN AS IF 'TWERE MADE OF SILVER FOR SOME CEREMONIAL PURPOSE, YEARS AGO AND MILES AWAY-- SUNK DEEP INTO MY COMPANION'S BREAST!
UNNHH!
"BUT, THE CRIME AGAINST HIM WAS SWIFTLY AVENGED, AND A ROBBER'S DARK SOUL SENT WINGING ITS WAY DOWN TO HELL!
"YET, LORD RUTHVEN'S LIFE WAS FAST EBBING AS I REACHED HIS SIDE...
PERHAPS A DOCTOR--
NO! I AM-- BEYOND THAT NOW. BUT, YOU CAN HELP ME-- BY SWEARING A VOW-- NOW, BEFORE I DIE!
ANYTHING! BUT WHAT--?
I HEED MY DEATH-- AS LITTLE AS THE SUNSET OF A PASSING DAY.
BUT, YOU MAY SAVE MY HONOR-- BY LEAVING MY BODY EXPOSED HERE, TO THE RAYS OF THE MOON WHICH I'VE EVER PREFERRED TO THE SUN...
YES, I'LL DO SO...
AND FURTHER-- VOW YOU'LL NOT TELL OF MY DEATH WHEN YOU RETURN TO ENGLAND!
SWEAR, AUBREY! SWEAR!
I--I DO SWEAR! BUT WHY--?
"BUT, MY VOW SEEMED TO RELEASE RUTHVEN'S VERY SPIRIT-- AND, WITH A STRANGE SMILE UPON HIS FACE, HE SANK DOWN AGAIN...
"...DEAD!

"THE **BANDITS**, IT TURNED OUT, SOUGHT MERELY A **RANSOM**, NOT TROUBLE WITH ENGLISHMEN.

"THUS, THEY DEPARTED ON ITS PAYING.

"THE **MOON'S RAYS** WERE JUST STARTING TO LIGHT THE DARKENING SKY AS I FULFILLED THE **FIRST** OF MY VOWS... THEN **LEFT**...

"...AND, INWARDLY PROMISING TO KEEP MY **SECOND** VOW TO HIM AS WELL -- NO MATTER **WHAT** IT MIGHT COST ME--I SET SAIL SOON AFTERWARD FOR **BRITAIN**.

"--TILL I STOOD ONCE MORE IN THE STREETS OF MY BELOVED **LONDON**.

"THERE, I **FORGOT** ALL ELSE FOR A MOMENT, IN MY **JOY** AT THE PROSPECT OF SEEING AGAIN MY DEAR **SISTER**...

JESSICA! I'M HOME! I'M HOME!

"I TRIED TO PUT LORD RUTHVEN'S EERIE REQUESTS FROM MY **MIND**-- BUT FOUND THAT I COULD **NOT**--

JESSICA... DIDN'T YOU **HEAR** ME? YOU DON'T SEEM **SURPRISED** TO...

HOW **COULD** I BE, WHEN WORD OF YOUR IMPENDING ARRIVAL REACHED ME **DAYS** AGO--

--FROM **THIS** GENTLEMAN, WHO HAS DONE ME THE VERY GREAT HONOR OF REQUESTING MY HAND IN **MARRIAGE**.

AND I HAVE **ACCEPTED**, FOR WHO COULD DO **LESS**--

-- TO ONE **WHO SAVED HER DEAR BROTHER'S LIFE?**

YOUR **VOW**, YOUNG FRIEND.

REMEMBER YOUR SACRED **VOW**...

... FOR AS LONG AS YOU MAY **LIVE!**

WELL! IT LOOKS AS IF LORD RUTHVEN WAS ONE OF AN **OLDER** BREED OF VAMPIRE -- A WEE BIT **DIFFERENT** FROM BRAM STOKER'S LATER CLASSIC INTERPRETATION. BUT, THAT DOESN'T SEEM TO HAVE MADE HIM ANY MORE **AMIABLE**. AFTER ALL, BOYS WILL BE **BOYS**, THEY SAY-- AND **VAMPIRES WILL OUT!**

FINIS

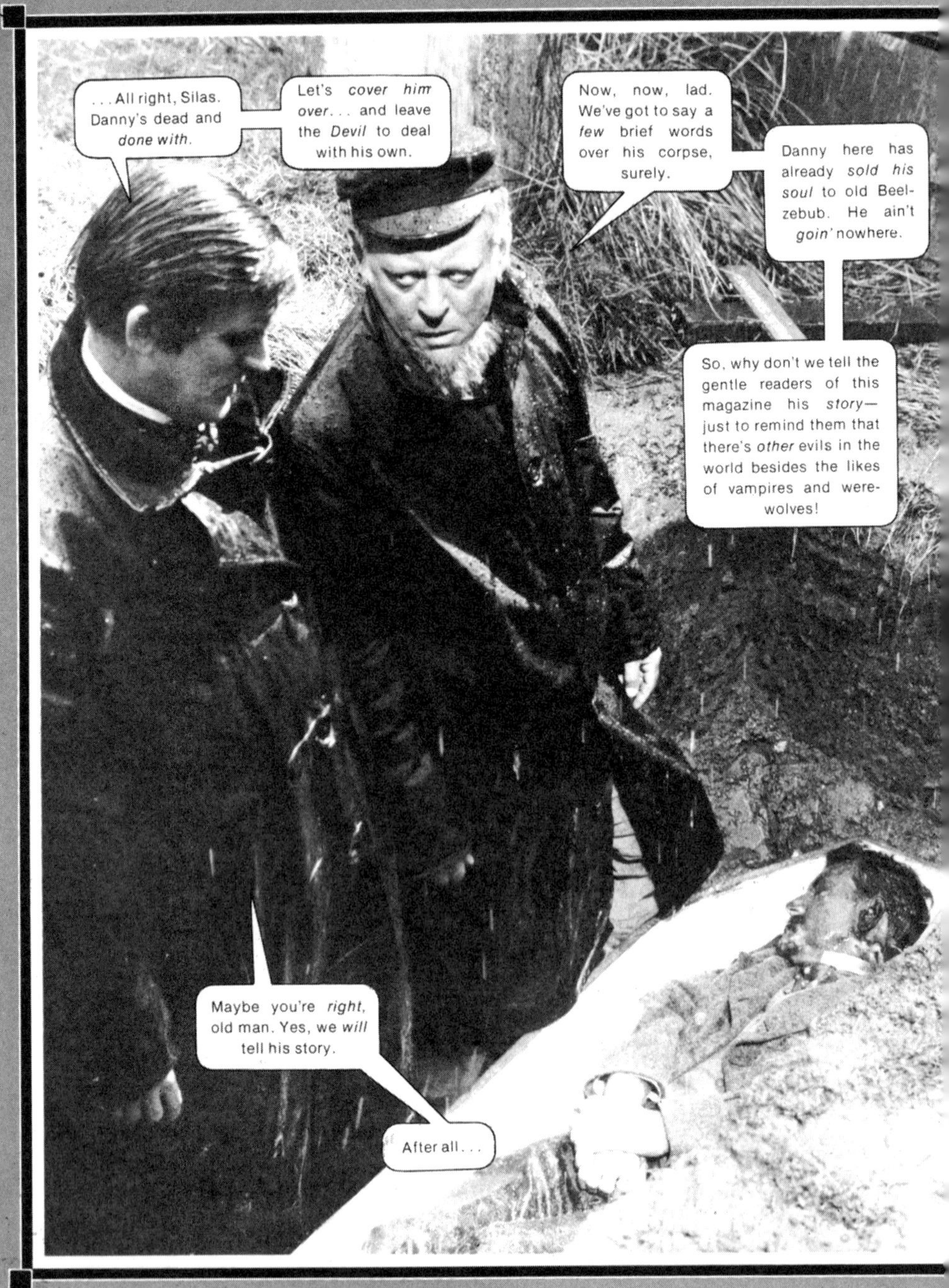

. . . All right, Silas. Danny's dead and *done with*.
Let's *cover him over*. . . and leave the *Devil* to deal with his own.
Now, now, lad. We've got to say a *few* brief words over his corpse, surely.
Danny here has already *sold his soul* to old Beelzebub. He ain't *goin'* nowhere.
So, why don't we tell the gentle readers of this magazine his *story*—just to remind them that there's *other* evils in the world besides the likes of vampires and werewolves!
Maybe you're *right*, old man. Yes, we *will* tell his story.
After all . . .

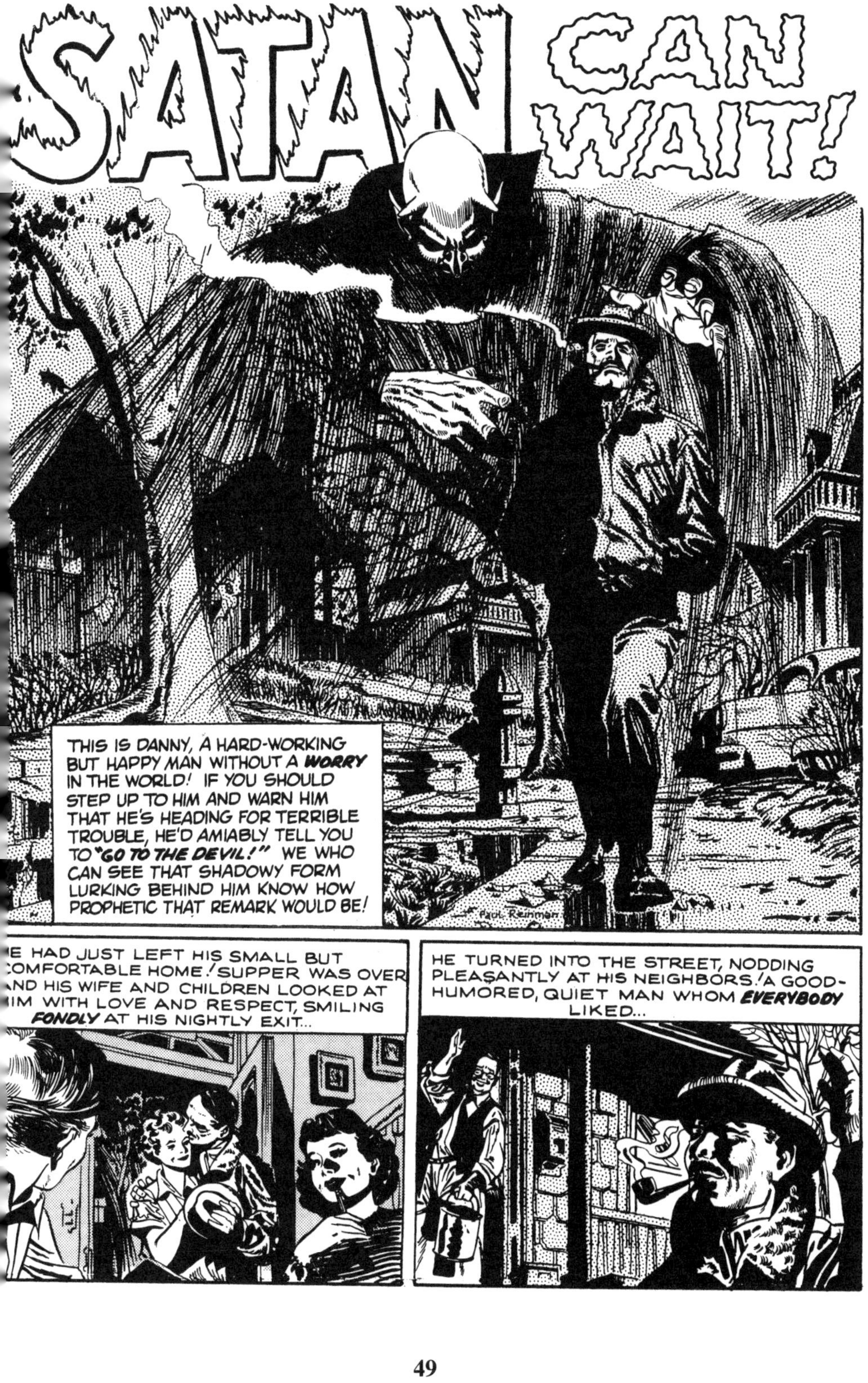

SATAN CAN WAIT!
THIS IS DANNY, A HARD-WORKING BUT HAPPY MAN WITHOUT A **WORRY** IN THE WORLD! IF YOU SHOULD STEP UP TO HIM AND WARN HIM THAT HE'S HEADING FOR TERRIBLE TROUBLE, HE'D AMIABLY TELL YOU TO **"GO TO THE DEVIL!"** WE WHO CAN SEE THAT SHADOWY FORM LURKING BEHIND HIM KNOW HOW PROPHETIC THAT REMARK WOULD BE!
E HAD JUST LEFT HIS SMALL BUT OMFORTABLE HOME! SUPPER WAS OVER ND HIS WIFE AND CHILDREN LOOKED AT IM WITH LOVE AND RESPECT, SMILING **FONDLY** AT HIS NIGHTLY EXIT...
HE TURNED INTO THE STREET, NODDING PLEASANTLY AT HIS NEIGHBORS! A GOOD-HUMORED, QUIET MAN WHOM **EVERYBODY** LIKED...

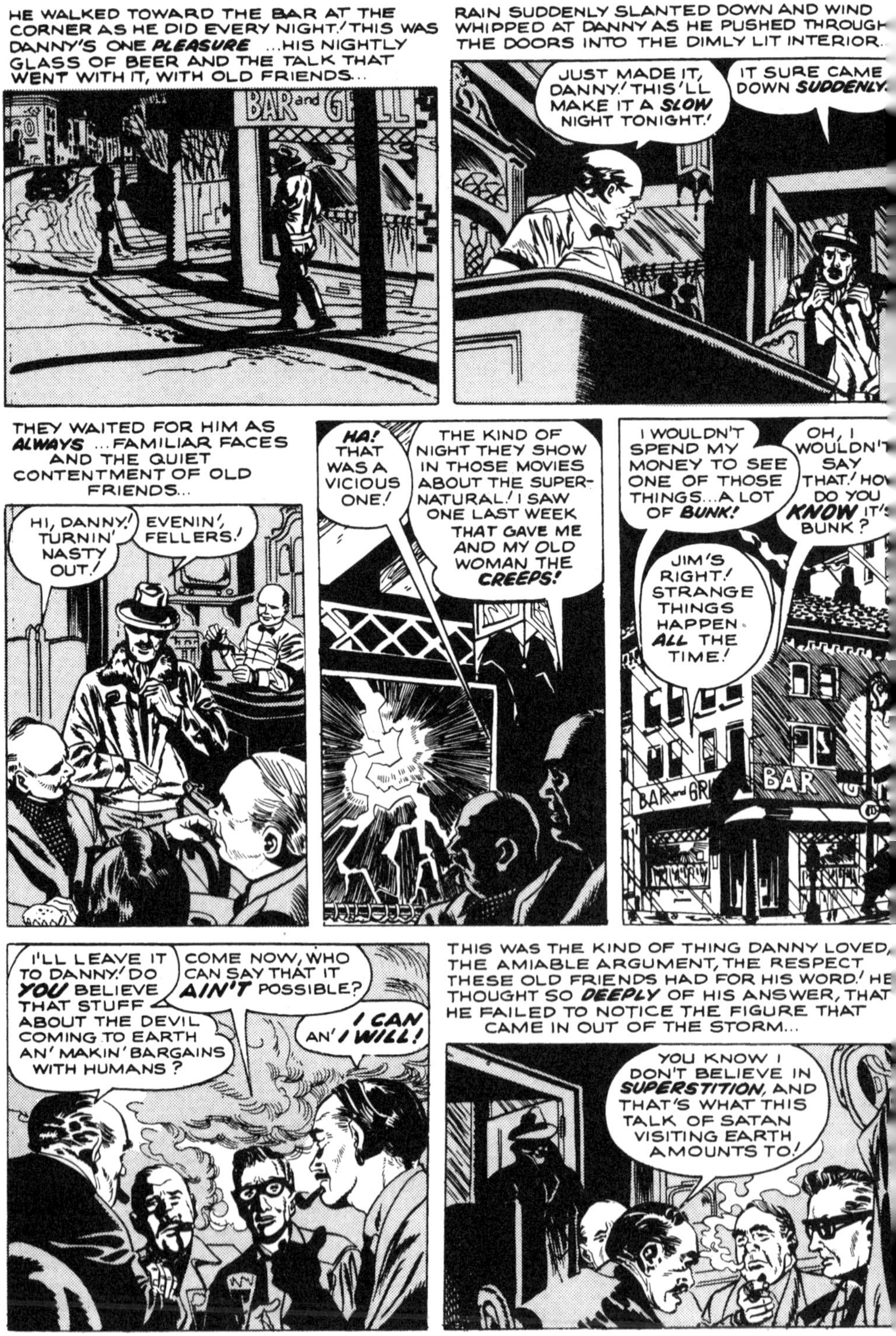

HE WALKED TOWARD THE BAR AT THE CORNER AS HE DID EVERY NIGHT! THIS WAS DANNY'S ONE PLEASURE ...HIS NIGHTLY GLASS OF BEER AND THE TALK THAT WENT WITH IT, WITH OLD FRIENDS...
BAR and GRILL
RAIN SUDDENLY SLANTED DOWN AND WIND WHIPPED AT DANNY AS HE PUSHED THROUGH THE DOORS INTO THE DIMLY LIT INTERIOR...
JUST MADE IT, DANNY! THIS'LL MAKE IT A SLOW NIGHT TONIGHT!
IT SURE CAME DOWN SUDDENLY!
THEY WAITED FOR HIM AS ALWAYS ...FAMILIAR FACES AND THE QUIET CONTENTMENT OF OLD FRIENDS...
HI, DANNY! TURNIN' NASTY OUT!
EVENIN', FELLERS!
HA! THAT WAS A VICIOUS ONE!
THE KIND OF NIGHT THEY SHOW IN THOSE MOVIES ABOUT THE SUPER-NATURAL! I SAW ONE LAST WEEK THAT GAVE ME AND MY OLD WOMAN THE CREEPS!
I WOULDN'T SPEND MY MONEY TO SEE ONE OF THOSE THINGS...A LOT OF BUNK!
OH, I WOULDN'T SAY THAT! HOW DO YOU KNOW IT'S BUNK?
JIM'S RIGHT! STRANGE THINGS HAPPEN ALL THE TIME!
BAR and GRILL
BAR
I'LL LEAVE IT TO DANNY! DO YOU BELIEVE THAT STUFF ABOUT THE DEVIL COMING TO EARTH AN' MAKIN' BARGAINS WITH HUMANS?
COME NOW, WHO CAN SAY THAT IT AIN'T POSSIBLE?
I CAN AN' I WILL!
THIS WAS THE KIND OF THING DANNY LOVED, THE AMIABLE ARGUMENT, THE RESPECT THESE OLD FRIENDS HAD FOR HIS WORD! HE THOUGHT SO DEEPLY OF HIS ANSWER, THAT HE FAILED TO NOTICE THE FIGURE THAT CAME IN OUT OF THE STORM...
YOU KNOW I DON'T BELIEVE IN SUPERSTITION, AND THAT'S WHAT THIS TALK OF SATAN VISITING EARTH AMOUNTS TO!

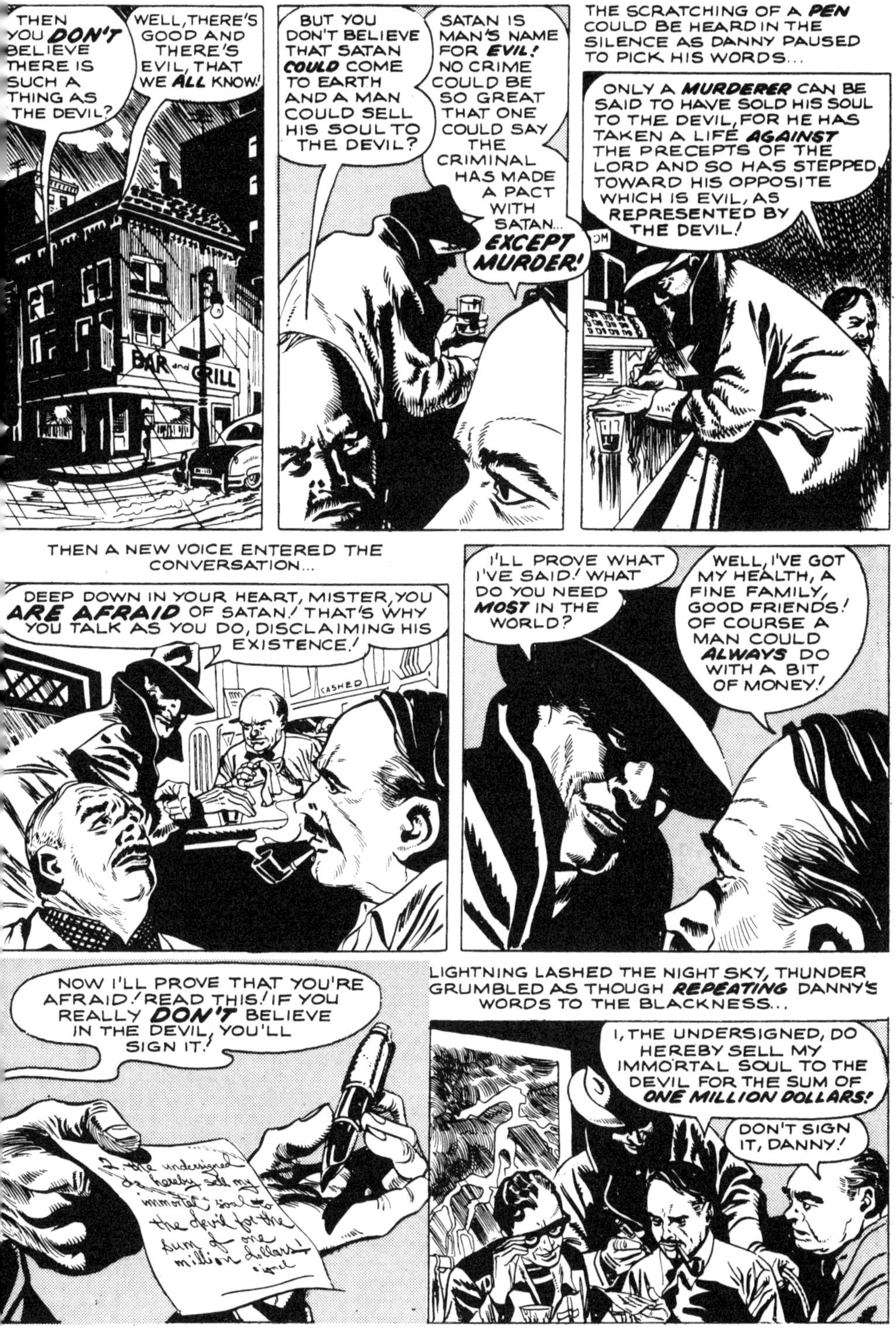
THEN YOU DON'T BELIEVE THERE IS SUCH A THING AS THE DEVIL?
WELL, THERE'S GOOD AND THERE'S EVIL, THAT WE ALL KNOW!
BAR and GRILL
BUT YOU DON'T BELIEVE THAT SATAN COULD COME TO EARTH AND A MAN COULD SELL HIS SOUL TO THE DEVIL?
SATAN IS MAN'S NAME FOR EVIL! NO CRIME COULD BE SO GREAT THAT ONE COULD SAY THE CRIMINAL HAS MADE A PACT WITH SATAN... EXCEPT MURDER!
THE SCRATCHING OF A PEN COULD BE HEARD IN THE SILENCE AS DANNY PAUSED TO PICK HIS WORDS...
ONLY A MURDERER CAN BE SAID TO HAVE SOLD HIS SOUL TO THE DEVIL, FOR HE HAS TAKEN A LIFE AGAINST THE PRECEPTS OF THE LORD AND SO HAS STEPPED TOWARD HIS OPPOSITE WHICH IS EVIL, AS REPRESENTED BY THE DEVIL!
THEN A NEW VOICE ENTERED THE CONVERSATION...
DEEP DOWN IN YOUR HEART, MISTER, YOU ARE AFRAID OF SATAN! THAT'S WHY YOU TALK AS YOU DO, DISCLAIMING HIS EXISTENCE!
CASHED
I'LL PROVE WHAT I'VE SAID! WHAT DO YOU NEED MOST IN THE WORLD?
WELL, I'VE GOT MY HEALTH, A FINE FAMILY, GOOD FRIENDS! OF COURSE A MAN COULD ALWAYS DO WITH A BIT OF MONEY!
NOW I'LL PROVE THAT YOU'RE AFRAID! READ THIS! IF YOU REALLY DON'T BELIEVE IN THE DEVIL, YOU'LL SIGN IT!
I, the undersigned do hereby sell my immortal soul to the devil for the sum of one million dollars! signed
LIGHTNING LASHED THE NIGHT SKY, THUNDER GRUMBLED AS THOUGH REPEATING DANNY'S WORDS TO THE BLACKNESS...
I, THE UNDERSIGNED, DO HEREBY SELL MY IMMORTAL SOUL TO THE DEVIL FOR THE SUM OF ONE MILLION DOLLARS!
DON'T SIGN IT, DANNY!

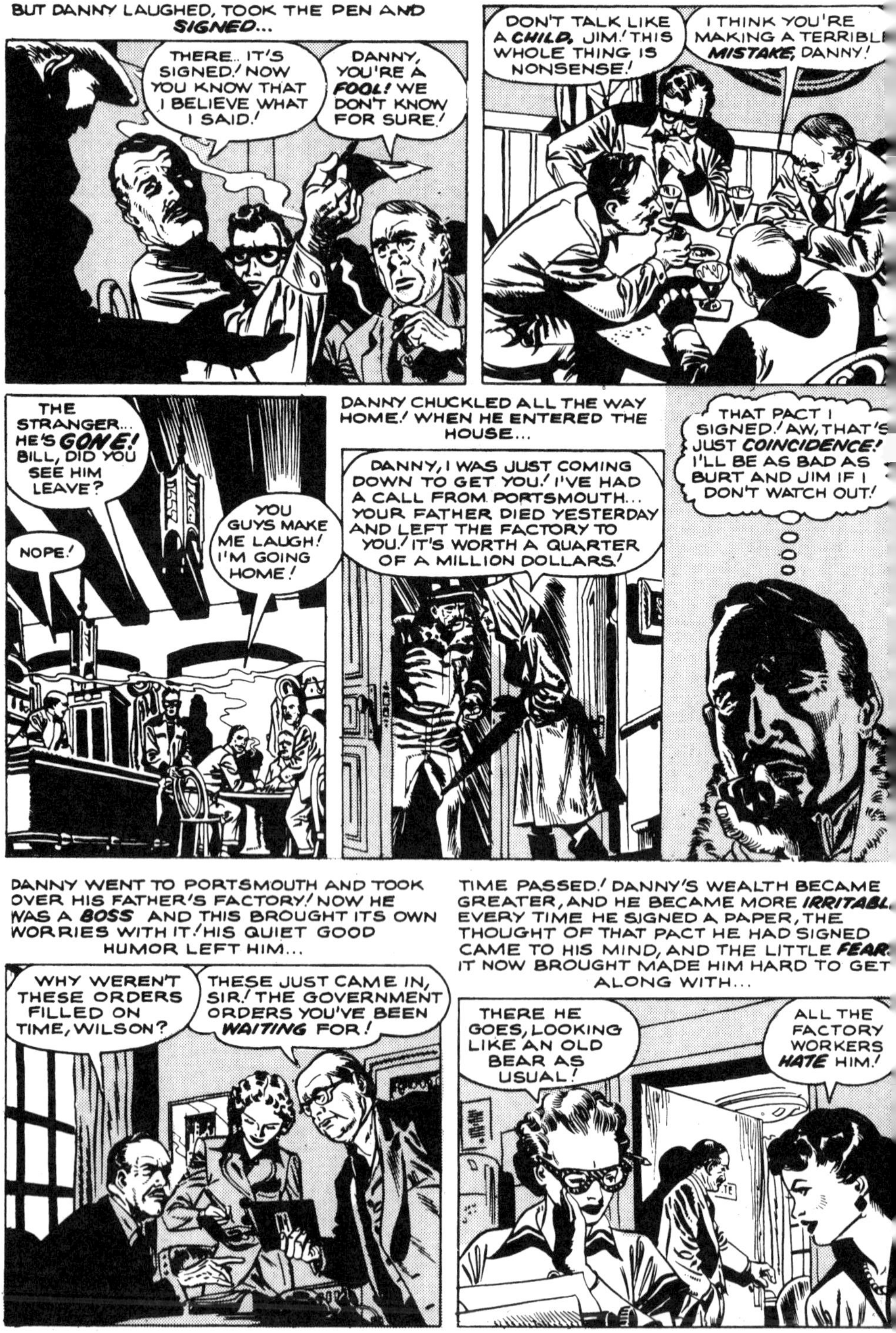
BUT DANNY LAUGHED, TOOK THE PEN AND SIGNED...
THERE.. IT'S SIGNED! NOW YOU KNOW THAT I BELIEVE WHAT I SAID!
DANNY, YOU'RE A FOOL! WE DON'T KNOW FOR SURE!
DON'T TALK LIKE A CHILD, JIM! THIS WHOLE THING IS NONSENSE!
I THINK YOU'RE MAKING A TERRIBL MISTAKE, DANNY!
THE STRANGER... HE'S GONE! BILL, DID YOU SEE HIM LEAVE?
NOPE!
YOU GUYS MAKE ME LAUGH! I'M GOING HOME!
DANNY CHUCKLED ALL THE WAY HOME! WHEN HE ENTERED THE HOUSE...
DANNY, I WAS JUST COMING DOWN TO GET YOU! I'VE HAD A CALL FROM PORTSMOUTH... YOUR FATHER DIED YESTERDAY AND LEFT THE FACTORY TO YOU! IT'S WORTH A QUARTER OF A MILLION DOLLARS!
THAT PACT I SIGNED! AW, THAT'S JUST COINCIDENCE! I'LL BE AS BAD AS BURT AND JIM IF I DON'T WATCH OUT!
DANNY WENT TO PORTSMOUTH AND TOOK OVER HIS FATHER'S FACTORY! NOW HE WAS A BOSS AND THIS BROUGHT ITS OWN WORRIES WITH IT! HIS QUIET GOOD HUMOR LEFT HIM...
WHY WEREN'T THESE ORDERS FILLED ON TIME, WILSON?
THESE JUST CAME IN, SIR! THE GOVERNMENT ORDERS YOU'VE BEEN WAITING FOR!
TIME PASSED! DANNY'S WEALTH BECAME GREATER, AND HE BECAME MORE IRRITABL EVERY TIME HE SIGNED A PAPER, THE THOUGHT OF THAT PACT HE HAD SIGNED CAME TO HIS MIND, AND THE LITTLE FEAR IT NOW BROUGHT MADE HIM HARD TO GET ALONG WITH...
THERE HE GOES, LOOKING LIKE AN OLD BEAR AS USUAL!
ALL THE FACTORY WORKERS HATE HIM!

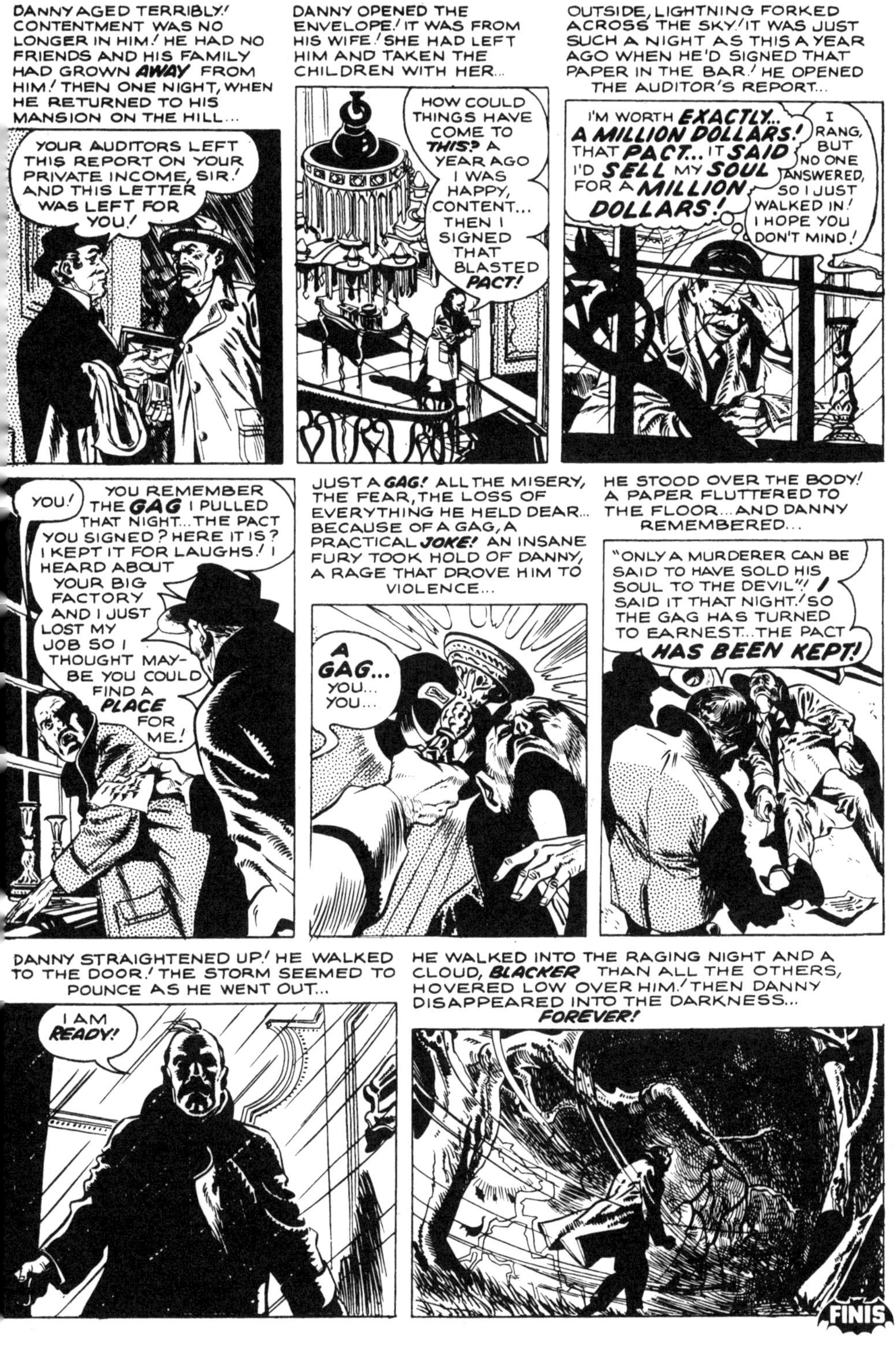
DANNY AGED TERRIBLY! CONTENTMENT WAS NO LONGER IN HIM! HE HAD NO FRIENDS AND HIS FAMILY HAD GROWN AWAY FROM HIM! THEN ONE NIGHT, WHEN HE RETURNED TO HIS MANSION ON THE HILL...
YOUR AUDITORS LEFT THIS REPORT ON YOUR PRIVATE INCOME, SIR! AND THIS LETTER WAS LEFT FOR YOU!
DANNY OPENED THE ENVELOPE! IT WAS FROM HIS WIFE! SHE HAD LEFT HIM AND TAKEN THE CHILDREN WITH HER...
HOW COULD THINGS HAVE COME TO THIS? A YEAR AGO I WAS HAPPY, CONTENT... THEN I SIGNED THAT BLASTED PACT!
OUTSIDE, LIGHTNING FORKED ACROSS THE SKY! IT WAS JUST SUCH A NIGHT AS THIS A YEAR AGO WHEN HE'D SIGNED THAT PAPER IN THE BAR! HE OPENED THE AUDITOR'S REPORT...
I'M WORTH EXACTLY... A MILLION DOLLARS! THAT PACT... IT SAID I'D SELL MY SOUL FOR A MILLION DOLLARS!
I RANG, BUT NO ONE ANSWERED, SO I JUST WALKED IN! I HOPE YOU DON'T MIND!
YOU!
YOU REMEMBER THE GAG I PULLED THAT NIGHT... THE PACT YOU SIGNED? HERE IT IS? I KEPT IT FOR LAUGHS! I HEARD ABOUT YOUR BIG FACTORY AND I JUST LOST MY JOB SO I THOUGHT MAY-BE YOU COULD FIND A PLACE FOR ME!
JUST A GAG! ALL THE MISERY, THE FEAR, THE LOSS OF EVERYTHING HE HELD DEAR... BECAUSE OF A GAG, A PRACTICAL JOKE! AN INSANE FURY TOOK HOLD OF DANNY, A RAGE THAT DROVE HIM TO VIOLENCE...
A GAG... YOU... YOU...
HE STOOD OVER THE BODY! A PAPER FLUTTERED TO THE FLOOR... AND DANNY REMEMBERED...
"ONLY A MURDERER CAN BE SAID TO HAVE SOLD HIS SOUL TO THE DEVIL"! I SAID IT THAT NIGHT! SO THE GAG HAS TURNED TO EARNEST... THE PACT HAS BEEN KEPT!
DANNY STRAIGHTENED UP! HE WALKED TO THE DOOR! THE STORM SEEMED TO POUNCE AS HE WENT OUT...
I AM READY!
HE WALKED INTO THE RAGING NIGHT AND A CLOUD, BLACKER THAN ALL THE OTHERS, HOVERED LOW OVER HIM! THEN DANNY DISAPPEARED INTO THE DARKNESS... FOREVER!
FINIS

THE WORST (No Kiddin'!) VAMPIRE FILMS EVER MADE!

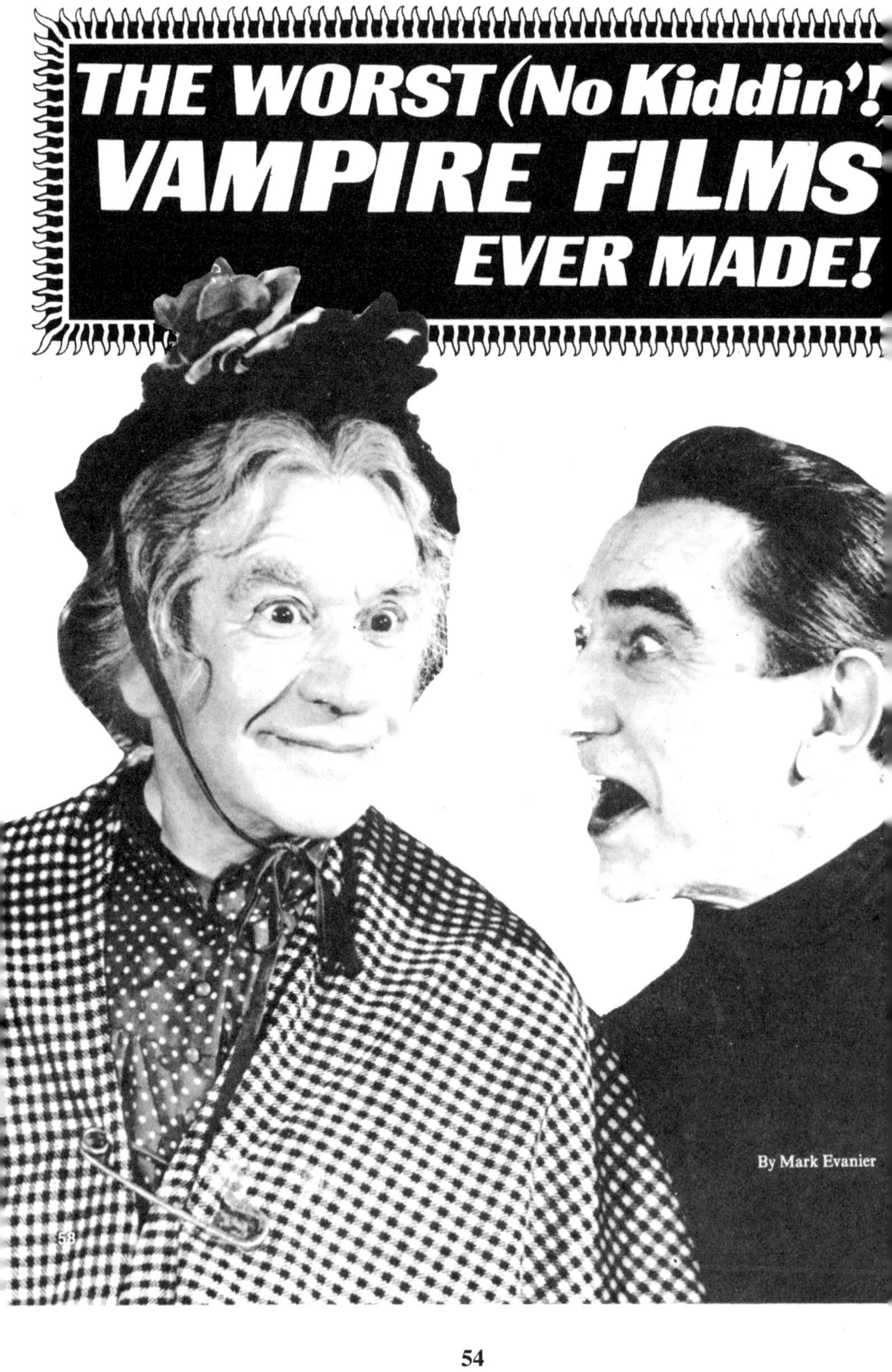

By Mark Evanier

Amidst the grand and glorious heritage of the cinema mpire, there have been some films that were...shall say, *lesser efforts*? Shall we be totally accurate and y, *outright stinkers?* The lot of the vampire movie buff no easy one, what with the excess of blood-curdlers at *look* promising, from a distance—but do unto the dience far greater agony than is inflicted on any reen victim. For a true connoisseur, nothing is quite so crutiating as sitting out some Transylvanian trashie in movie theatre, watching the faith mauled by the nkest of incompetents. The fan may squirm and fidget his well-gummed seat, try to catch some reflection off e screen on his watch dial, or contemplate what other foray to the lobby refreshment center will do to s wallet and waist. But there is no out, really—the cket has been paid for and the film he *really* wanted to e is always second on the double-bill. To the eatre-owners of America, "mercy" is as alien a concept having a candy bar that costs less than fifty cents.

One would think that the television vampire-watcher ould have it much better. And one would be wrong. hough relief is but a channel-switch away, the TV mphile must contend with the shlock-shockers of both st and present. Programming directors are miraculously adept at dredging up the lowest of the low from the m archives. Any given issue of *TV Guide* is usually ammed solid with listings for bad vampire films. Thus, e vampire aficianado often finds himself turning from me dread Dracula emulation to some other program here badly-costumed creatures emit idiotic shrieks and t like mindless idiots. You can imagine his nbarrassment when he discovers that he's now tuned in "Let's Make a Deal!"

LOOD OF DRACULA.
is film inspired a TV series—Stand Up and Jeer!

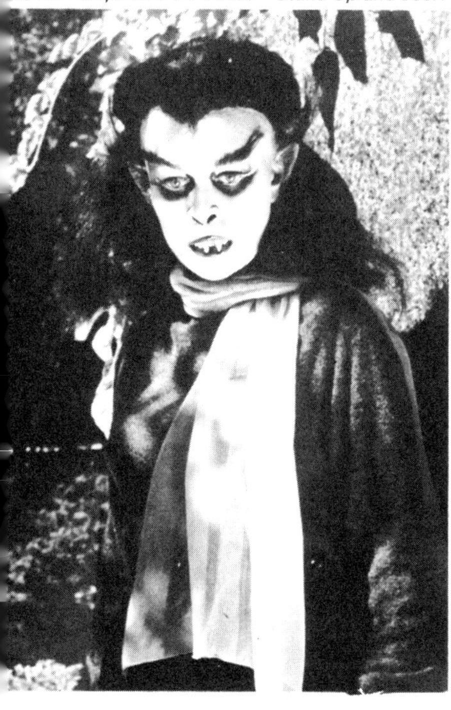

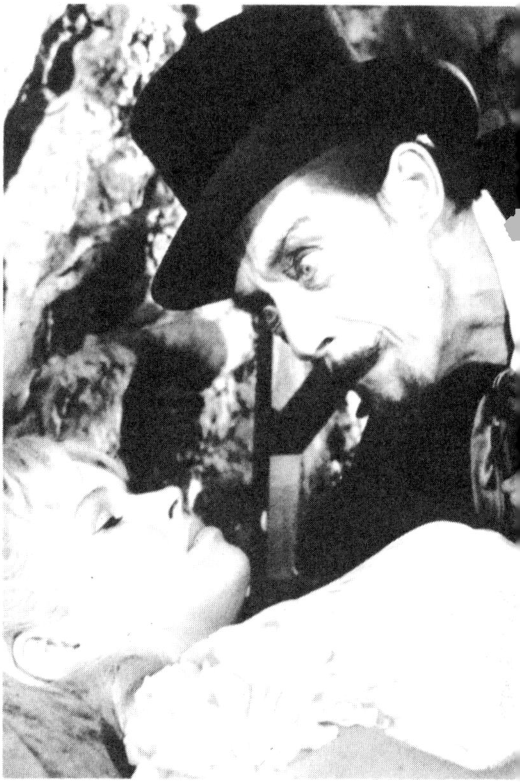

THE VAMPIRE GOES WEST.
The audience went east.

Consider such a celluloid indiscretion as CURSE OF THE UNDEAD, a little gem that turns up on TV as often as Charles Nelson Reilly...and is much funnier. In this fifties' mixture of vampires and the Mild Wild West, Eric Fleming is trying to ward off the jugular designs of Michael Pate. While the glistening globe of Universal Studios usually heralds a product of some quality, CURSE OF THE UNDEAD is the kind of film that big studios usually place their contract players in, to punish them for some misbehavior. Eric Fleming must have incurred an awesome amount of some executive's wrath to warrant this brand of capital punishment. If you *can* tolerate the sight of cowboys galloping off in search of the town vampire, the ending will get you. (And it will ruin absolutely no one's enjoyment of the film to reveal that ending here. Throughout recorded vampire-watching history, only three fans managed to endure this picture to the very end. Two of them, alas, did *not* live to regret it, having perished from terminal mindrot. The third, currently confined to a rubber room, gave us the ending between shock treatments.) The vampire is finally felled by a bullet to which a fragment of Holy Cross has been affixed. And some people wonder why Universal doesn't make vampire films any more...

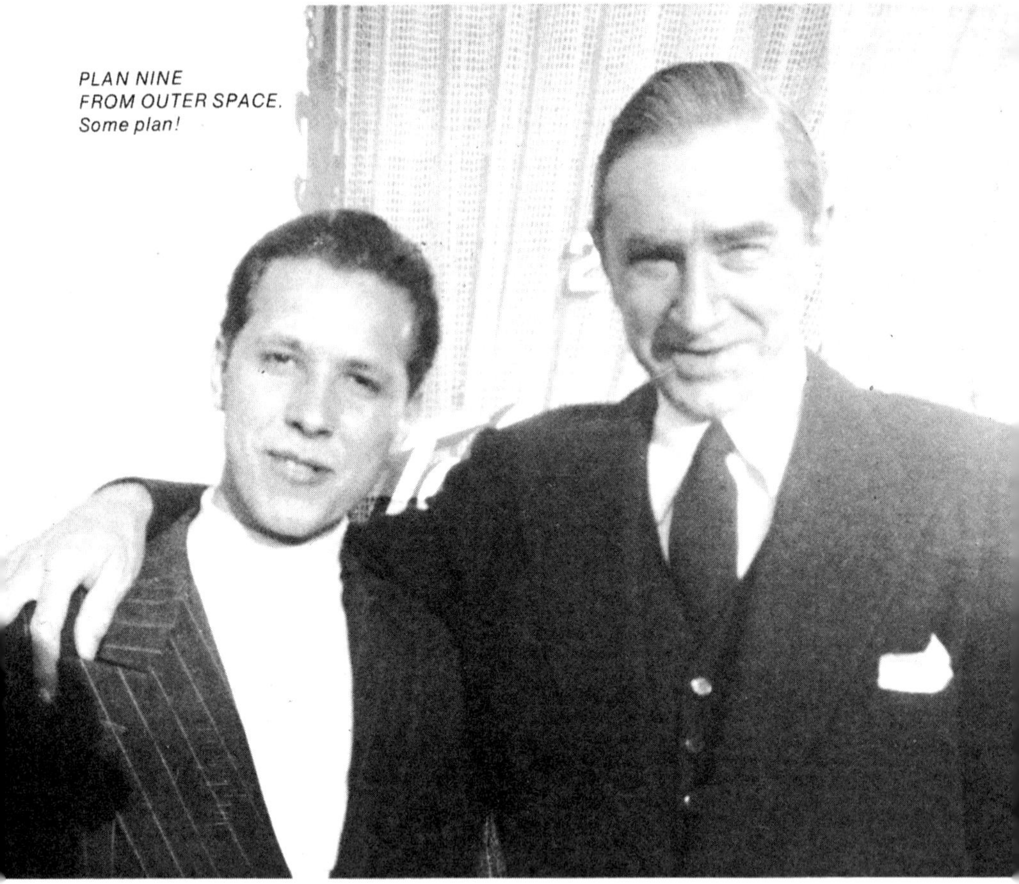

PLAN NINE FROM OUTER SPACE. Some plan!

Even worse, however, if such a thing is possible, is BILLY THE KID VS. DRACULA. When you expect very little, you often get much less. Billy wants to settle down and live the simple, honest life with the girl of his dreams. He finds the girl but his dreams hadn't included her being the daughter of Dracula- - played gamely by John Carradine, a trooper to the very end. But even a horror veteran of Carradine's stature and talent couldn't save this turkey. A few years later, both Carradine *and* Lon Chaney, Jr., failed to elevate DR. TERROR'S GALLERY OF HORRORS above loser stature. (Also known as RETURN FROM THE PAST for obscure reasons and not to be confused with DOCTOR TERROR'S HOUSE OF HORRORS). The presence of a monster superstar does not always indicate quality—in fact, it can often be torturesome watching a good actor struggle with a wretched script.

Bela Lugosi's last film is just such an agony. PLAN NINE FROM OUTER SPACE is also known today as GRAVE ROBBERS FROM OUTER SPACE and, by any name, it still smells. Lugosi died during its production and looks terrible during his few brief scenes. A pastiche of zombies, vampires, and science-fiction, features TV's Vampira and, thus, has *some* sm amount of historical interest. But, then, so did the S Francisco Earthquake.

TRACK OF THE VAMPIRE has no such historic interest, unless you be a student of the Theatre of t Inane. In this must-miss item, the vampire is artistic— paints portraits of his victims before putting the bite them. There may have been worse horror movies made 1966 than this one—but all of them were eight mi meter.

Even the hallowed name of DRACULA is guarantee of quality in a film. Last year, *Variety* report that the general consensus of movie-makers was that t name of *Dracula* in a film title was worth nearly million dollars' additional gross to the film, regardless content. Thus, many wretched pictures have gone o capitalizing on the good name of the Count himse

As far back as BLOOD OF DRACULA (1958) a even before, the name of Dracula was affixed to films no merit — thus luring in unsuspecting Dracu devotees. In BLOOD OF DRACULA, an all-girls' sch is terrorized by a student placed under a vampire's cur y her teacher . . . perhaps not the worst damage that a acher has ever inflicted on her charges, but among the ost ludicrous plots ever inflicted on an audience. Even at, however, pales by comparison to GUESS WHAT APPENED TO COUNT DRACULA! — which has the ubious distinction of being probably the *worst* vampire lm ever made, eight-millimeter or otherwise. The ampire of this turkey is named Count Adrian, *not* racula, making it all the more curious when theatre arquees asked the musical question, GUESS WHAT APPENED TO DRACULA! The producers offered no nswers to choose from, but if they had, they would robably have read something like this: *A*] He was played y an actor in the worst make-up job of any horror film, ast or present. *B*] He fumbled around in a plotless and ept rehash of traditional *ad nauseum* vampire cliches.] His name was exploited to draw unaware Dracula fans to see a bomb of epic proportions. The correct answer , of course: *D*] All of the above.

Needless to say, no survey of the jugular junkheap ould be complete without acknowledgment of the epths to which *foreign producers* have gone to undercut e standards of the afore-mentioned lemons. Though e average British monster fare has usually been ood-to-excellent (DRACULA A.D. '72, notwithstand- g), the producers in Mexico and Italy have done their est to sever diplomatic relations with these United ates, by sending deadly weapons in, right past nsuspecting customs officials. From the former ation—which also gave us chihuahuas, tacos, and Texas - we've had such Mexican mediocrites as INVASION F THE VAMPIRES and THE MONSTER- ESTROYER. From the latter country—along with aghetti, Sophia Loren, and that organization that oesn't *really* exist—have come such Italian idiocies as NCLE WAS A VAMPIRE and the legendary TOM-AGE VAMPIRE. In all fairness, though, it must e noted that the main flaw in such films (aside from the ct that they were made in the first place) is the inept ubbing. In UNCLE WAS A VAMPIRE, for instance, e action suggests that the film might have been mewhat amusing in its original Italian—but the ubbed version is very bland and tedious in its dialogue. ny regular reader of *Monster Madness* could have done far better job of filling in English words to fit the ctures. In fact, the second-best way to enjoy such inane ports is to turn the volume knob down and off—and ake up your own dialogue! The *best* way, naturally is to rn off the picture, as well.

So. . . the plentiful supply of stench vampire films may me as a bane to the vampire buff—but that surplus of uddies merely attests to the eternal popularity of mpires on screen. Vampires are so popular that even e worst-made film about them can attract enough of an idience to clear a profit. Bad film-makers have made any more low-calibre vampictures than are itemized ere. With but a camera, some film, a bottle of Heinz he slowest) ketchup, and a girl who can scream, they go . . . desecrating the good name of vampires and, in articular, Dracula! The worst is yet to come. FINIS

Coming soon at your local third-rate movie house:
FANGS FOR THE MEMORY
and GIDGET GOES VAMPIRIC!
Don't dare miss them!

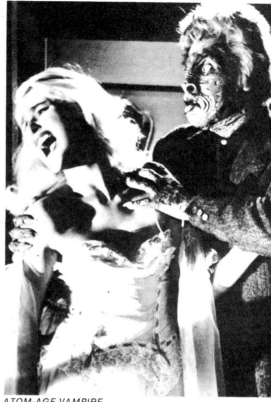

ATOM-AGE VAMPIRE.
The biggest bomb since Hiroshima.

CURSE OF THE UNDEAD.
The audience reaction was phenomenal.

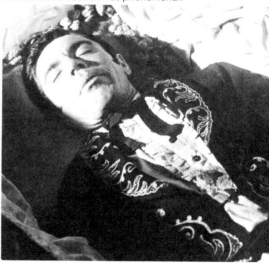

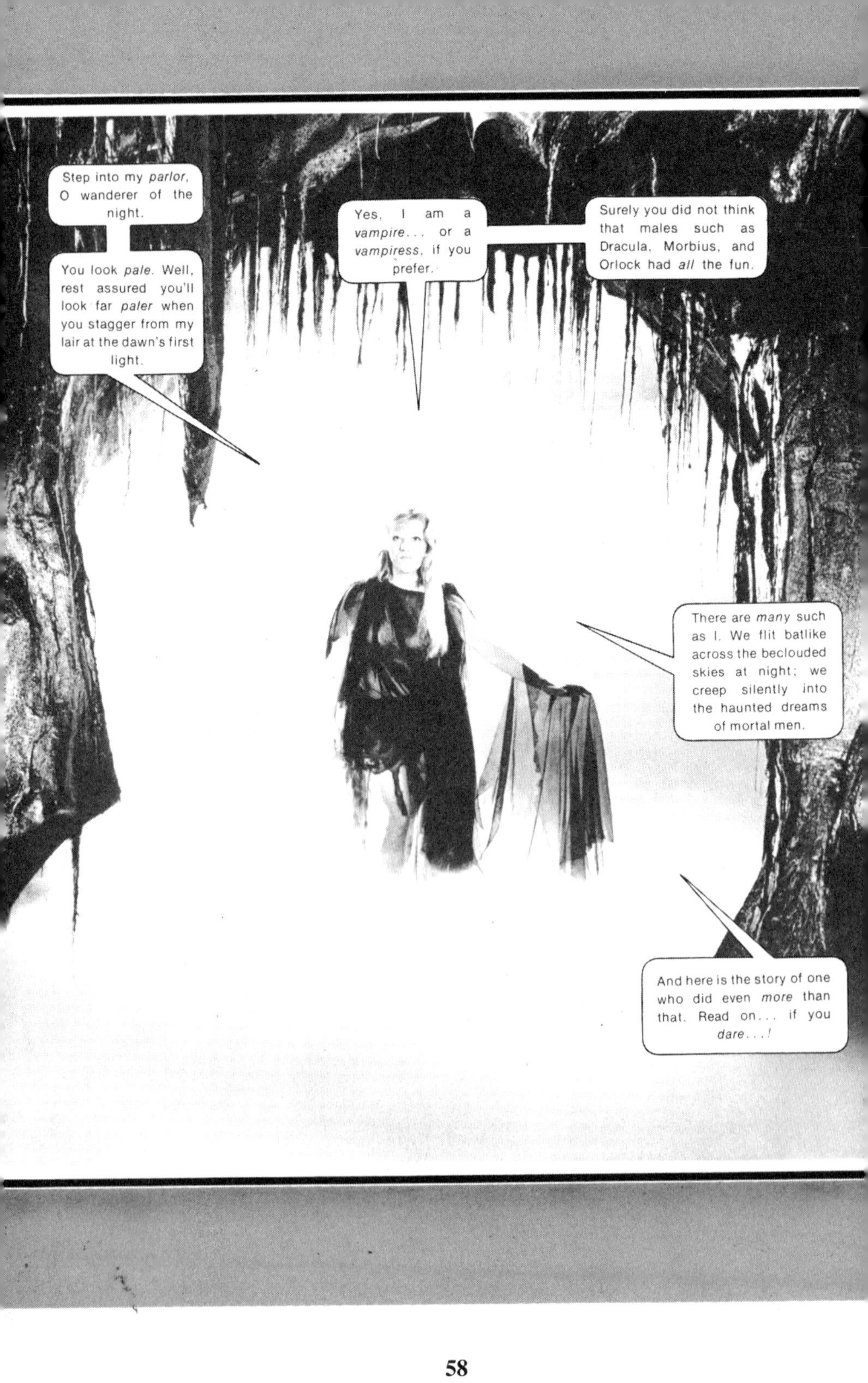

Step into my *parlor*, O wanderer of the night.
You look *pale.* Well, rest assured you'll look far *paler* when you stagger from my lair at the dawn's first light.
Yes, I am a *vampire*... or a *vampiress*, if you prefer.
Surely you did not think that males such as Dracula, Morbius, and Orlock had *all* the fun.
There are *many* such as I. We flit batlike across the beclouded skies at night; we creep silently into the haunted dreams of mortal men.
And here is the story of one who did even *more* than that. Read on... if you *dare*...!

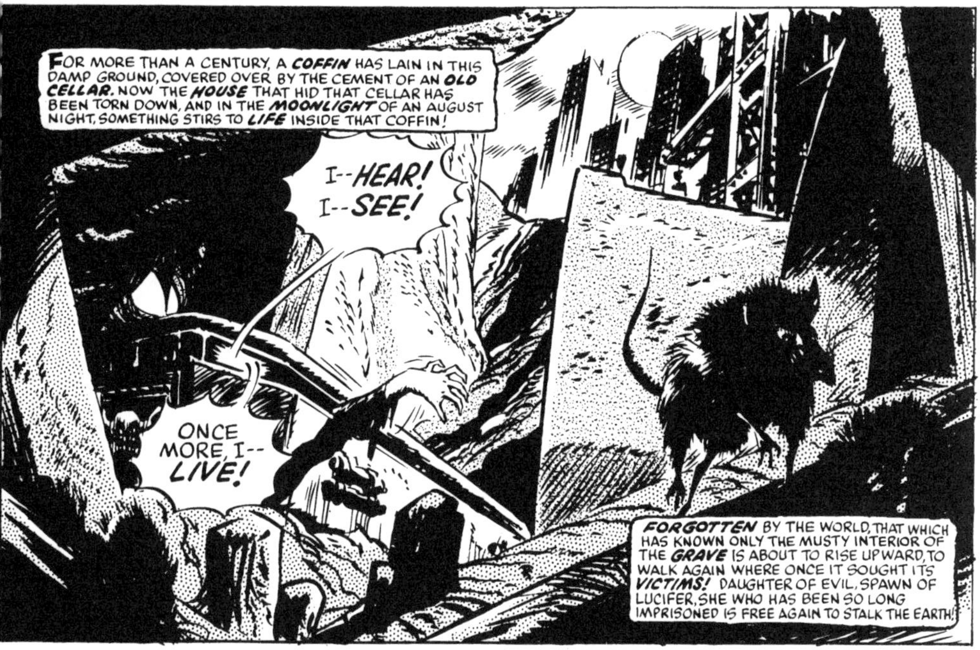
FOR MORE THAN A CENTURY, A COFFIN HAS LAIN IN THIS DAMP GROUND, COVERED OVER BY THE CEMENT OF AN OLD CELLAR. NOW THE HOUSE THAT HID THAT CELLAR HAS BEEN TORN DOWN, AND IN THE MOONLIGHT OF AN AUGUST NIGHT, SOMETHING STIRS TO LIFE INSIDE THAT COFFIN!
I--HEAR! I--SEE!
ONCE MORE, I-- LIVE!
FORGOTTEN BY THE WORLD, THAT WHICH HAS KNOWN ONLY THE MUSTY INTERIOR OF THE GRAVE IS ABOUT TO RISE UPWARD, TO WALK AGAIN WHERE ONCE IT SOUGHT ITS VICTIMS! DAUGHTER OF EVIL, SPAWN OF LUCIFER, SHE WHO HAS BEEN SO LONG IMPRISONED IS FREE AGAIN TO STALK THE EARTH!

REVENGE of the UNLIVING!

SCRIPT: GARDNER FOX

ART: BERNET

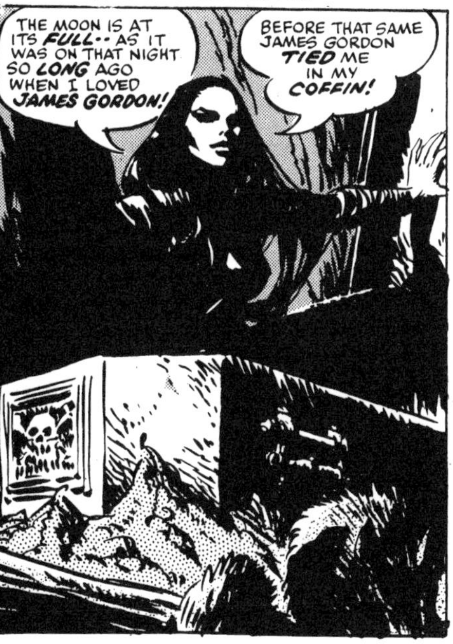
THE MOON IS AT ITS FULL-- AS IT WAS ON THAT NIGHT SO LONG AGO WHEN I LOVED JAMES GORDON!
BEFORE THAT SAME JAMES GORDON TIED ME IN MY COFFIN!

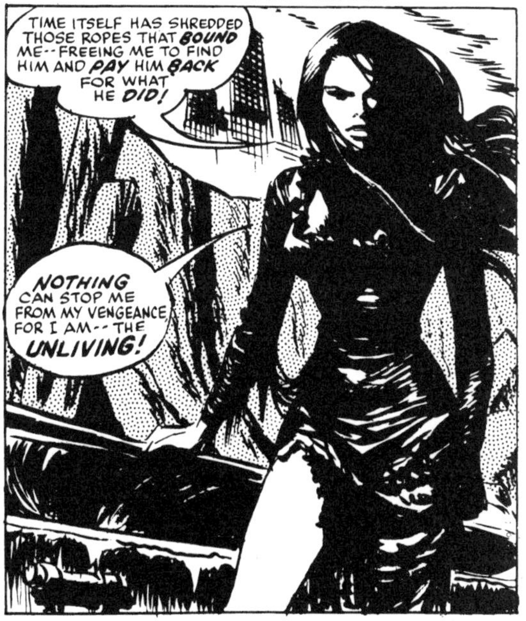
TIME ITSELF HAS SHREDDED THOSE ROPES THAT BOUND ME--FREEING ME TO FIND HIM AND PAY HIM BACK FOR WHAT HE DID!
NOTHING CAN STOP ME FROM MY VENGEANCE, FOR I AM-- THE UNLIVING!

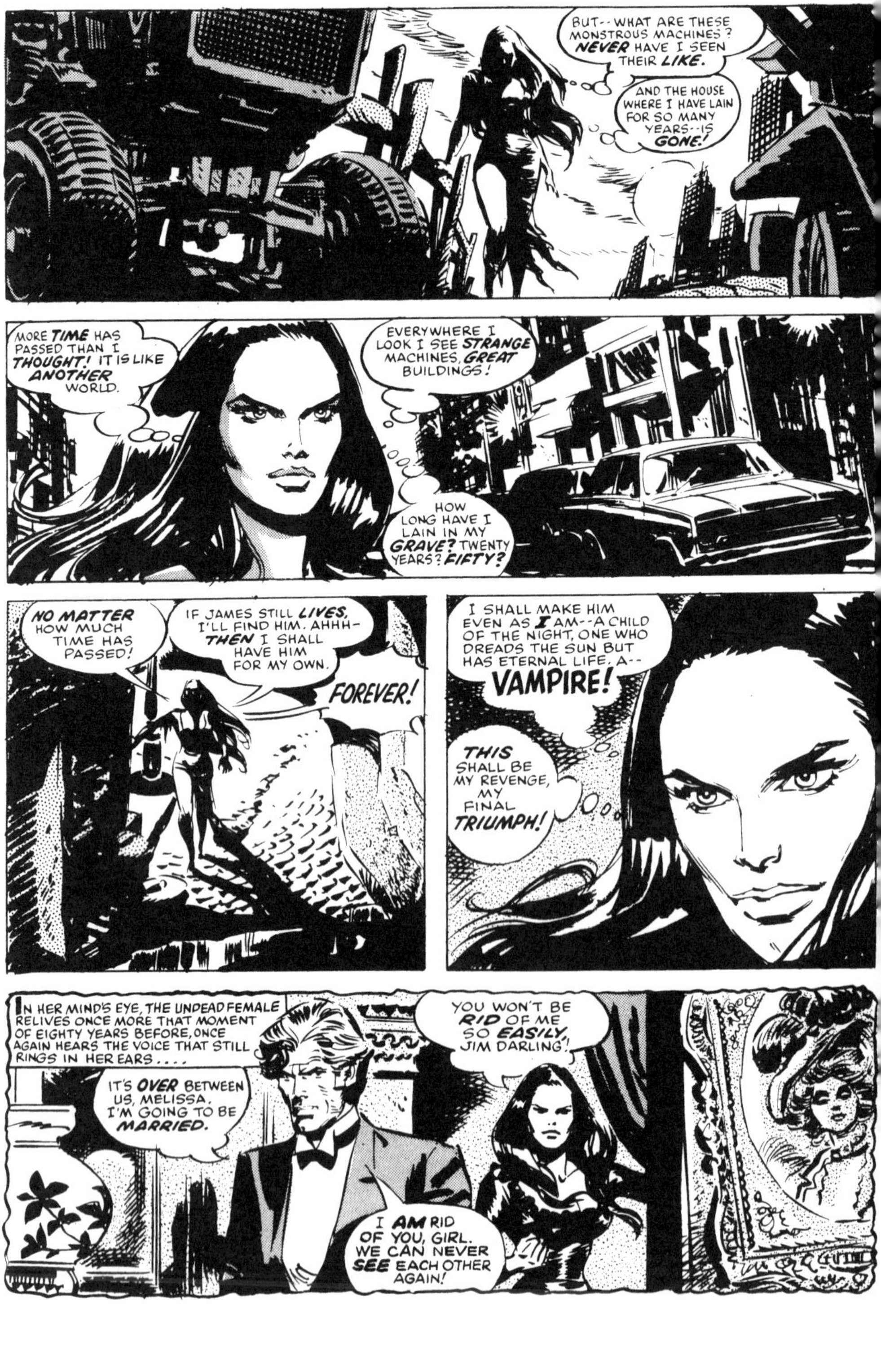
BUT--WHAT ARE THESE MONSTROUS MACHINES? NEVER HAVE I SEEN THEIR LIKE.
AND THE HOUSE WHERE I HAVE LAIN FOR SO MANY YEARS--IS GONE!
MORE TIME HAS PASSED THAN I THOUGHT! IT IS LIKE ANOTHER WORLD.
EVERYWHERE I LOOK I SEE STRANGE MACHINES, GREAT BUILDINGS!
HOW LONG HAVE I LAIN IN MY GRAVE? TWENTY YEARS? FIFTY?
NO MATTER HOW MUCH TIME HAS PASSED!
IF JAMES STILL LIVES, I'LL FIND HIM. AHHH-THEN I SHALL HAVE HIM FOR MY OWN.
FOREVER!
I SHALL MAKE HIM EVEN AS I AM--A CHILD OF THE NIGHT, ONE WHO DREADS THE SUN BUT HAS ETERNAL LIFE. A--
VAMPIRE!
THIS SHALL BE MY REVENGE, MY FINAL TRIUMPH!
IN HER MIND'S EYE, THE UNDEAD FEMALE RELIVES ONCE MORE THAT MOMENT OF EIGHTY YEARS BEFORE, ONCE AGAIN HEARS THE VOICE THAT STILL RINGS IN HER EARS....
IT'S OVER BETWEEN US, MELISSA. I'M GOING TO BE MARRIED.
YOU WON'T BE RID OF ME SO EASILY, JIM DARLING!
I AM RID OF YOU, GIRL. WE CAN NEVER SEE EACH OTHER AGAIN!

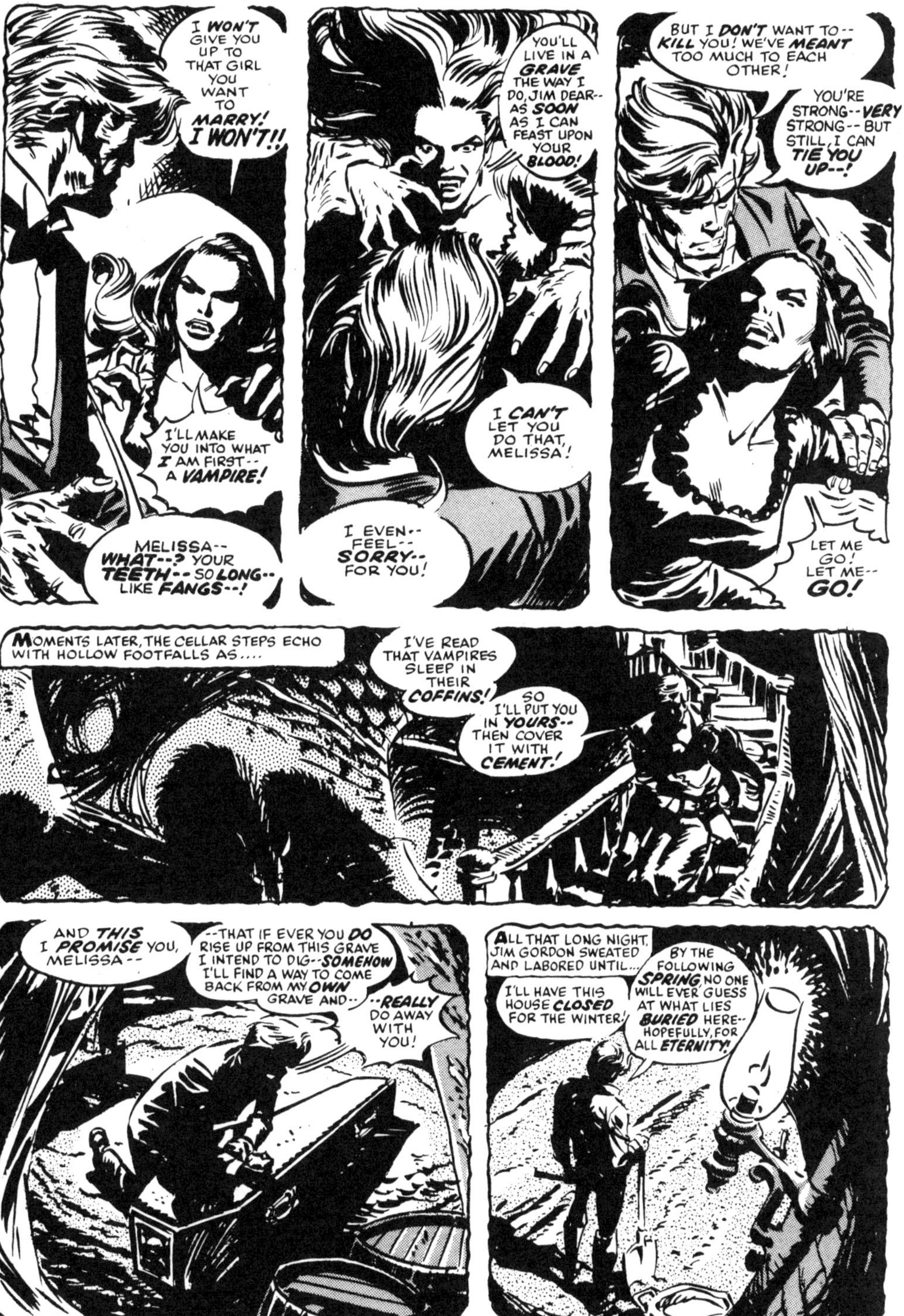

I WON'T GIVE YOU UP TO THAT GIRL YOU WANT TO MARRY! I WON'T!!
I'LL MAKE YOU INTO WHAT I AM FIRST-- A VAMPIRE!
MELISSA-- WHAT--? YOUR TEETH-- SO LONG-- LIKE FANGS--!
YOU'LL LIVE IN A GRAVE THE WAY I DO, JIM DEAR-- AS SOON AS I CAN FEAST UPON YOUR BLOOD!
I CAN'T LET YOU DO THAT, MELISSA!
I EVEN-- FEEL-- SORRY-- FOR YOU!
BUT I DON'T WANT TO-- KILL YOU! WE'VE MEANT TOO MUCH TO EACH OTHER!
YOU'RE STRONG-- VERY STRONG-- BUT STILL, I CAN TIE YOU UP--!
LET ME GO! LET ME-- GO!
MOMENTS LATER, THE CELLAR STEPS ECHO WITH HOLLOW FOOTFALLS AS....
I'VE READ THAT VAMPIRES SLEEP IN THEIR COFFINS!
SO I'LL PUT YOU IN YOURS-- THEN COVER IT WITH CEMENT!
AND THIS I PROMISE YOU, MELISSA--
--THAT IF EVER YOU DO RISE UP FROM THIS GRAVE I INTEND TO DIG-- SOMEHOW I'LL FIND A WAY TO COME BACK FROM MY OWN GRAVE AND--
--REALLY DO AWAY WITH YOU!
ALL THAT LONG NIGHT, JIM GORDON SWEATED AND LABORED UNTIL...
I'LL HAVE THIS HOUSE CLOSED FOR THE WINTER!
BY THE FOLLOWING SPRING, NO ONE WILL EVER GUESS AT WHAT LIES BURIED HERE-- HOPEFULLY, FOR ALL ETERNITY!

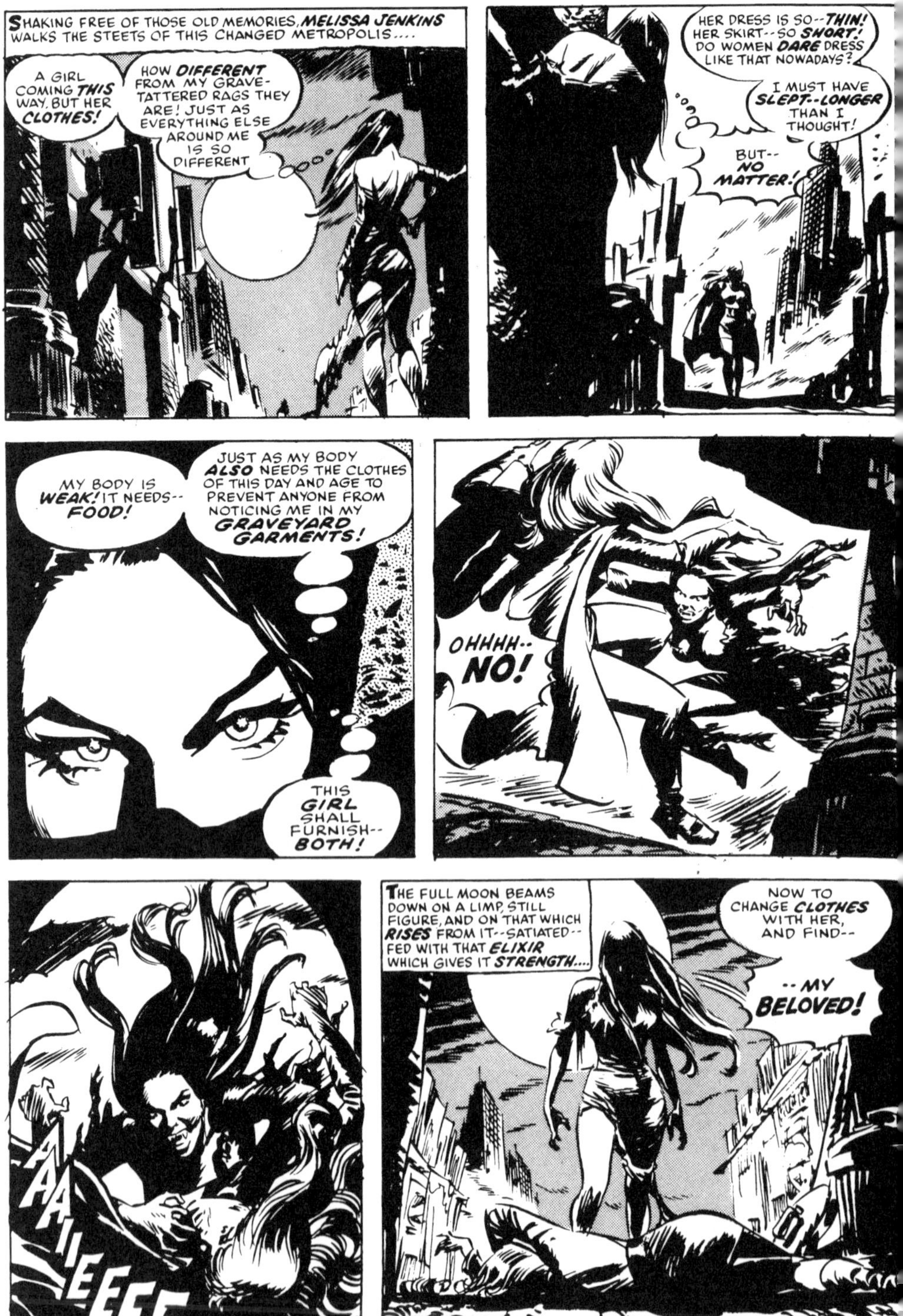

SHAKING FREE OF THOSE OLD MEMORIES, MELISSA JENKINS WALKS THE STEETS OF THIS CHANGED METROPOLIS....
A GIRL COMING THIS WAY. BUT HER CLOTHES!
HOW DIFFERENT FROM MY GRAVE-TATTERED RAGS THEY ARE! JUST AS EVERYTHING ELSE AROUND ME IS SO DIFFERENT
HER DRESS IS SO--THIN! HER SKIRT--SO SHORT! DO WOMEN DARE DRESS LIKE THAT NOWADAYS?
I MUST HAVE SLEPT--LONGER THAN I THOUGHT!
BUT--NO MATTER!
MY BODY IS WEAK! IT NEEDS--FOOD!
JUST AS MY BODY ALSO NEEDS THE CLOTHES OF THIS DAY AND AGE TO PREVENT ANYONE FROM NOTICING ME IN MY GRAVEYARD GARMENTS!
THIS GIRL SHALL FURNISH--BOTH!
OHHHH--NO!
AAIIEEEE
THE FULL MOON BEAMS DOWN ON A LIMP, STILL FIGURE, AND ON THAT WHICH RISES FROM IT--SATIATED--FED WITH THAT ELIXIR WHICH GIVES IT STRENGTH....
NOW TO CHANGE CLOTHES WITH HER, AND FIND--
--MY BELOVED!

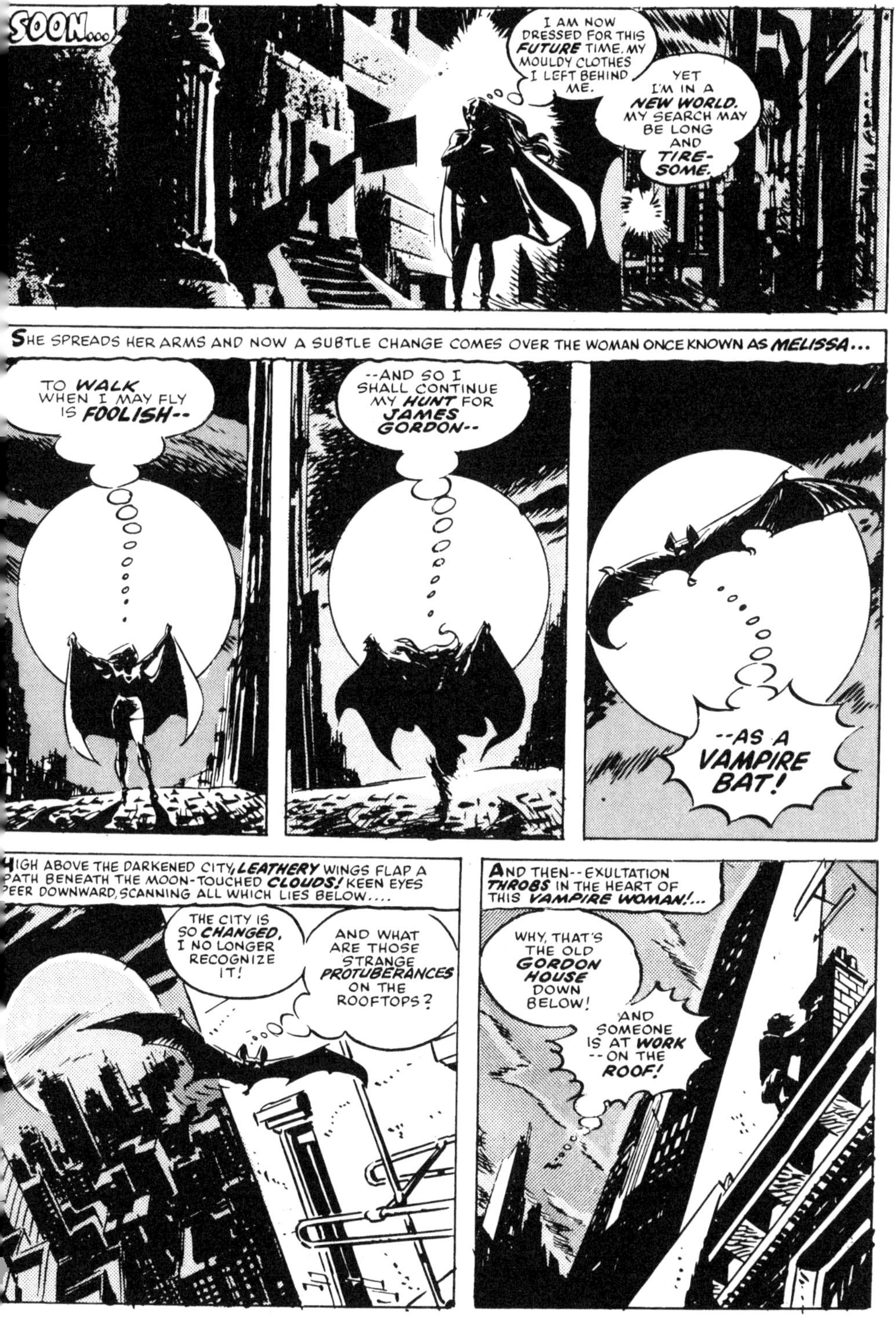
SOON...
I AM NOW DRESSED FOR THIS FUTURE TIME, MY MOULDY CLOTHES I LEFT BEHIND ME.
YET I'M IN A NEW WORLD. MY SEARCH MAY BE LONG AND TIRE-SOME.
SHE SPREADS HER ARMS AND NOW A SUBTLE CHANGE COMES OVER THE WOMAN ONCE KNOWN AS MELISSA...
TO WALK WHEN I MAY FLY IS FOOLISH--
--AND SO I SHALL CONTINUE MY HUNT FOR JAMES GORDON--
--AS A VAMPIRE BAT!
HIGH ABOVE THE DARKENED CITY, LEATHERY WINGS FLAP A PATH BENEATH THE MOON-TOUCHED CLOUDS! KEEN EYES PEER DOWNWARD, SCANNING ALL WHICH LIES BELOW....
THE CITY IS SO CHANGED, I NO LONGER RECOGNIZE IT!
AND WHAT ARE THOSE STRANGE PROTUBERANCES ON THE ROOFTOPS?
AND THEN--EXULTATION THROBS IN THE HEART OF THIS VAMPIRE WOMAN!...
WHY, THAT'S THE OLD GORDON HOUSE DOWN BELOW!
AND SOMEONE IS AT WORK --ON THE ROOF!

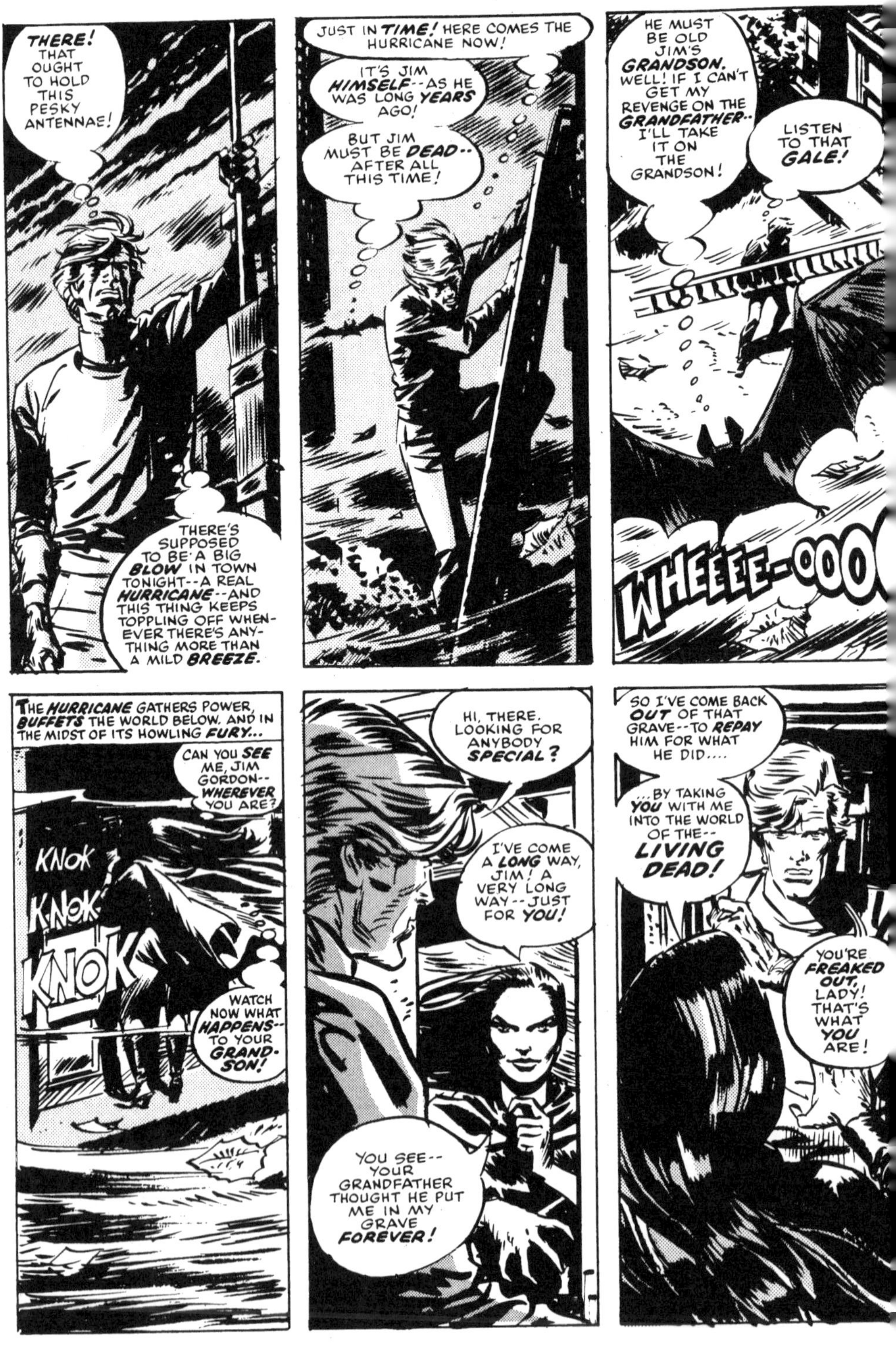
THERE! THAT OUGHT TO HOLD THIS PESKY ANTENNAE!
THERE'S SUPPOSED TO BE A BIG BLOW IN TOWN TONIGHT--A REAL HURRICANE--AND THIS THING KEEPS TOPPLING OFF WHENEVER THERE'S ANYTHING MORE THAN A MILD BREEZE.
JUST IN TIME! HERE COMES THE HURRICANE NOW!
IT'S JIM HIMSELF--AS HE WAS LONG YEARS AGO!
BUT JIM MUST BE DEAD--AFTER ALL THIS TIME!
HE MUST BE OLD JIM'S GRANDSON. WELL! IF I CAN'T GET MY REVENGE ON THE GRANDFATHER--I'LL TAKE IT ON THE GRANDSON!
LISTEN TO THAT GALE!
WHEEEE-OOO
THE HURRICANE GATHERS POWER, BUFFETS THE WORLD BELOW, AND IN THE MIDST OF ITS HOWLING FURY...
CAN YOU SEE ME, JIM GORDON--WHEREVER YOU ARE?
KNOK
KNOK
KNOK
WATCH NOW WHAT HAPPENS--TO YOUR GRANDSON!
HI, THERE. LOOKING FOR ANYBODY SPECIAL?
I'VE COME A LONG WAY, JIM! A VERY LONG WAY--JUST FOR YOU!
YOU SEE--YOUR GRANDFATHER THOUGHT HE PUT ME IN MY GRAVE FOREVER!
SO I'VE COME BACK OUT OF THAT GRAVE--TO REPAY HIM FOR WHAT HE DID....
...BY TAKING YOU WITH ME INTO THE WORLD OF THE--LIVING DEAD!
YOU'RE FREAKED OUT, LADY! THAT'S WHAT YOU ARE!

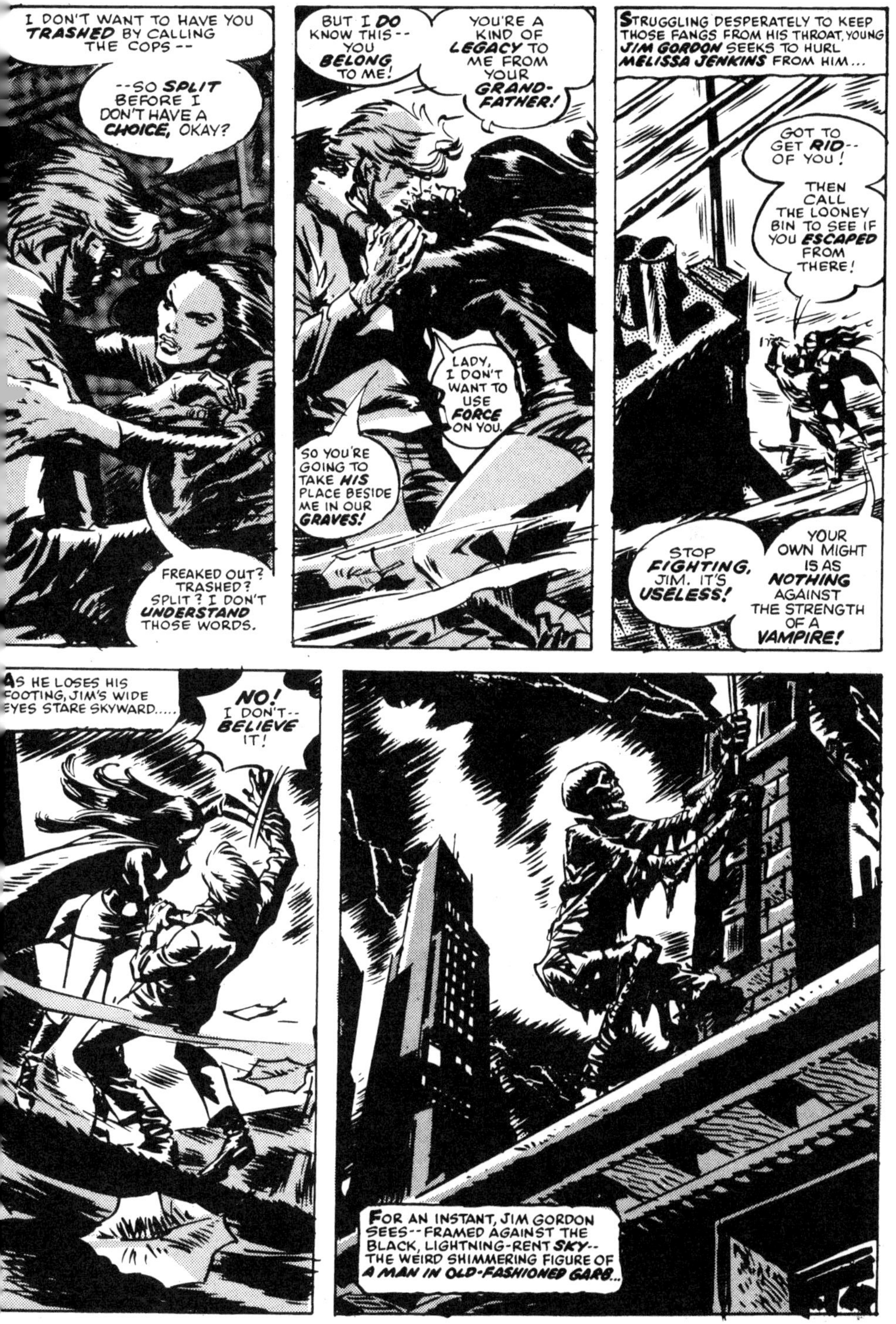
I DON'T WANT TO HAVE YOU TRASHED BY CALLING THE COPS --
--SO SPLIT BEFORE I DON'T HAVE A CHOICE, OKAY?
FREAKED OUT? TRASHED? SPLIT? I DON'T UNDERSTAND THOSE WORDS.
BUT I DO KNOW THIS-- YOU BELONG TO ME!
YOU'RE A KIND OF LEGACY TO ME FROM YOUR GRAND-FATHER!
LADY, I DON'T WANT TO USE FORCE ON YOU.
SO YOU'RE GOING TO TAKE HIS PLACE BESIDE ME IN OUR GRAVES!
STRUGGLING DESPERATELY TO KEEP THOSE FANGS FROM HIS THROAT, YOUNG JIM GORDON SEEKS TO HURL MELISSA JENKINS FROM HIM...
GOT TO GET RID-- OF YOU!
THEN CALL THE LOONEY BIN TO SEE IF YOU ESCAPED FROM THERE!
STOP FIGHTING, JIM. IT'S USELESS!
YOUR OWN MIGHT IS AS NOTHING AGAINST THE STRENGTH OF A VAMPIRE!
AS HE LOSES HIS FOOTING, JIM'S WIDE EYES STARE SKYWARD.....
NO! I DON'T-- BELIEVE IT!
FOR AN INSTANT, JIM GORDON SEES--FRAMED AGAINST THE BLACK, LIGHTNING-RENT SKY-- THE WEIRD SHIMMERING FIGURE OF A MAN IN OLD-FASHIONED GARB...

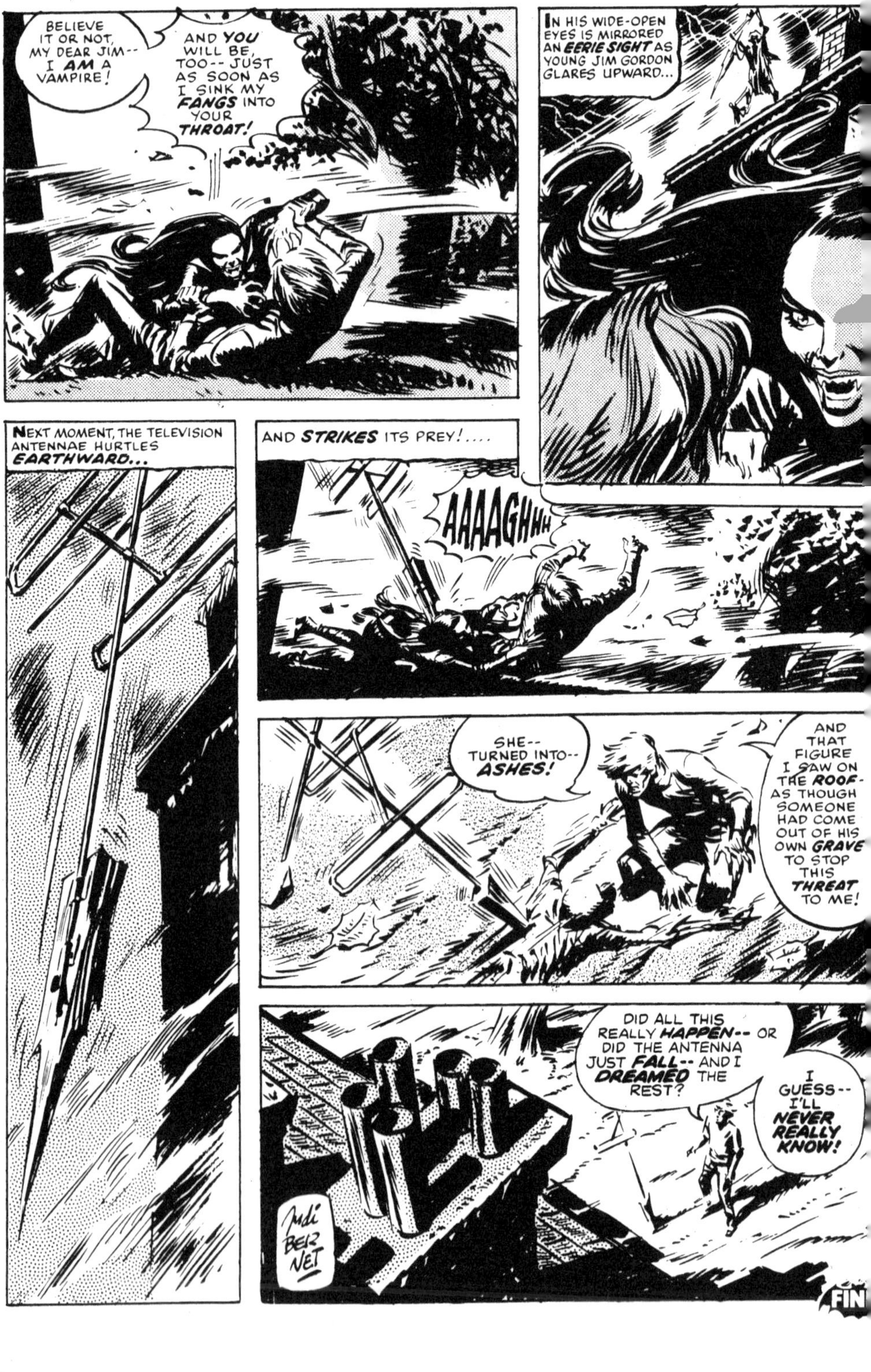
BELIEVE IT OR NOT, MY DEAR JIM-- I AM A VAMPIRE!
AND YOU WILL BE, TOO-- JUST AS SOON AS I SINK MY FANGS INTO YOUR THROAT!
IN HIS WIDE-OPEN EYES IS MIRRORED AN EERIE SIGHT AS YOUNG JIM GORDON GLARES UPWARD...
NEXT MOMENT, THE TELEVISION ANTENNAE HURTLES EARTHWARD...
AND STRIKES ITS PREY!....
AAAAGHHH
SHE-- TURNED INTO-- ASHES!
AND THAT FIGURE I SAW ON THE ROOF-- AS THOUGH SOMEONE HAD COME OUT OF HIS OWN GRAVE TO STOP THIS THREAT TO ME!
DID ALL THIS REALLY HAPPEN-- OR DID THE ANTENNA JUST FALL-- AND I DREAMED THE REST?
I GUESS-- I'LL NEVER REALLY KNOW!
FIN

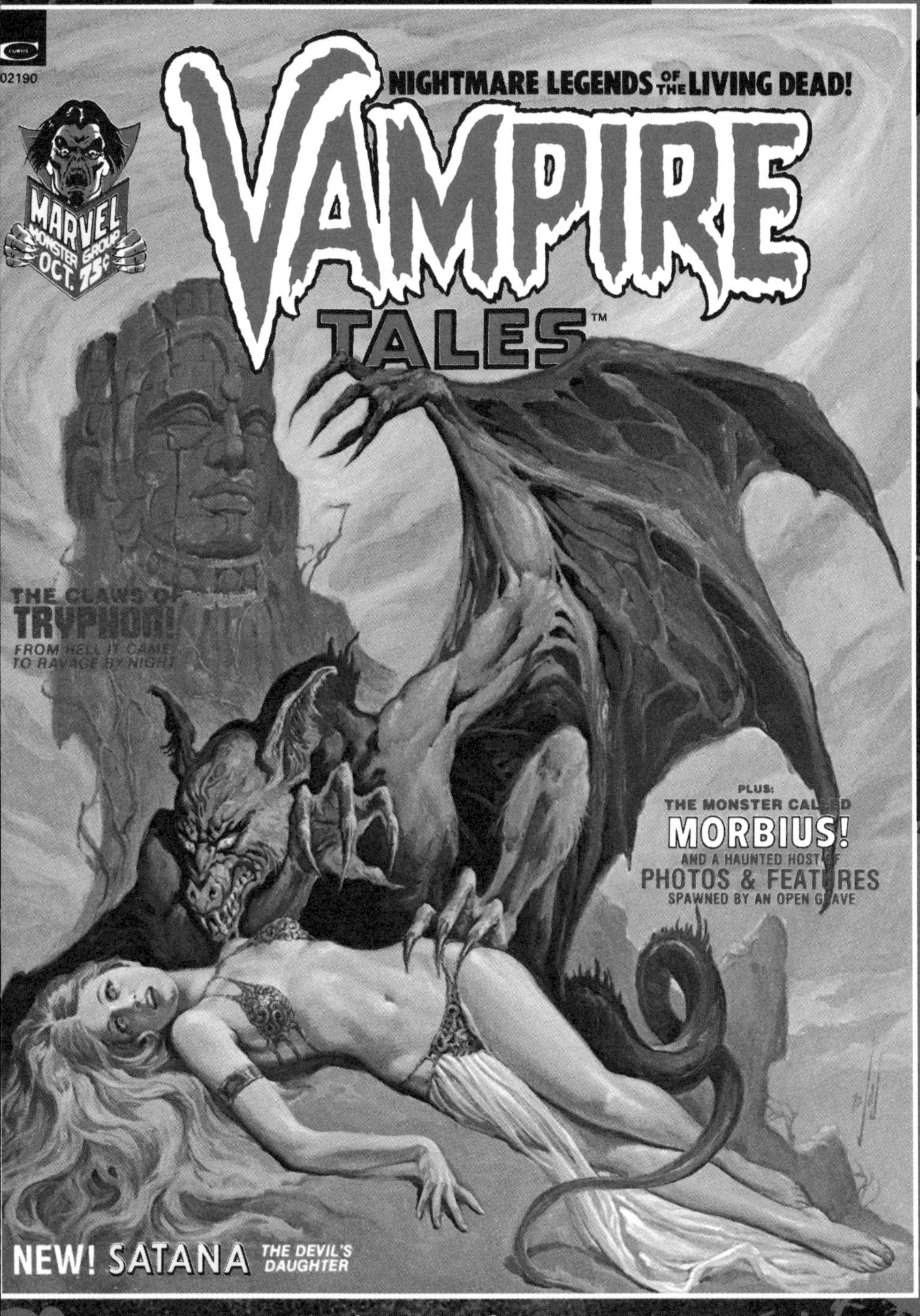
02190
NIGHTMARE LEGENDS OF THE LIVING DEAD!
MARVEL MONSTER GROUP
OCT. 75¢
VAMPIRE
TALES™
THE CLAWS OF
TRYPHON!
FROM HELL IT CAME TO RAVAGE BY NIGHT
PLUS:
THE MONSTER CALLED
MORBIUS!
AND A HAUNTED HOST OF
PHOTOS & FEATURES
SPAWNED BY AN OPEN GRAVE
NEW! SATANA THE DEVIL'S DAUGHTER

TWO

No. 2   OCTOBER, 1973

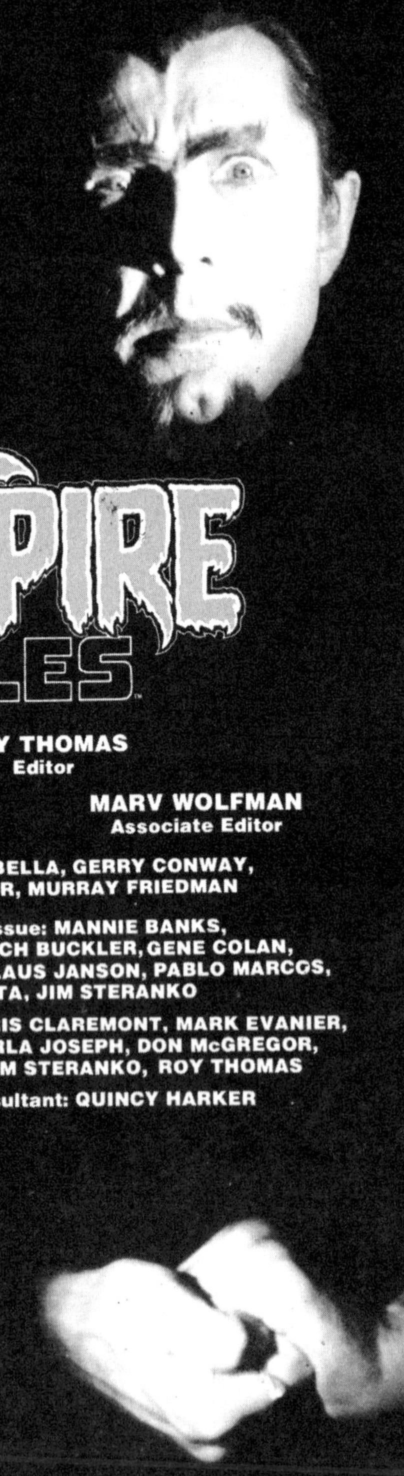

STAN LEE
presents

ROY THOMAS
Editor

SOL BRODSKY   MARV WOLFMAN
Production   Associate Editor

Staff: TONY ISABELLA, GERRY CONWAY,
DON McGREGOR, MURRAY FRIEDMAN

Artists This Issue: MANNIE BANKS,
JESUS BLASCO, RICH BUCKLER, GENE COLAN,
CARLOS GARZON, KLAUS JANSON, PABLO MARCOS,
JOHN ROMITA, JIM STERANKO

Writers This Issue: CHRIS CLAREMONT, MARK EVANIER,
GARDNER FOX, CARLA JOSEPH, DON McGREGOR,
DOUG MOENCH, JIM STERANKO, ROY THOMAS

Research Consultant: QUINCY HARKER

VAMPIRE TALES is published by
MARVEL COMICS GROUP. OFFICE
OF PUBLICATION: 575 Madison Avenue, New York, N.Y. 10022. Published
Bi-Monthly. Copyright © 1973 by Marvel Comics Group, a Division of
Cadence Industries Corporation. All
rights reserved 575 Madison Avenue,
New York, N.Y. 10022. Vol.1 No. 2, Oct.
1973 issue. Price 75 ¢ per copy in the
U.S. and Canada. No similarity between any of the names, characters,
persons and or institutions in this
magazine with those of any living or
dead person or institution is intended, and any such similarity
which may exist is purely coincidental. Printed in the U.S.A.

Cover:

3

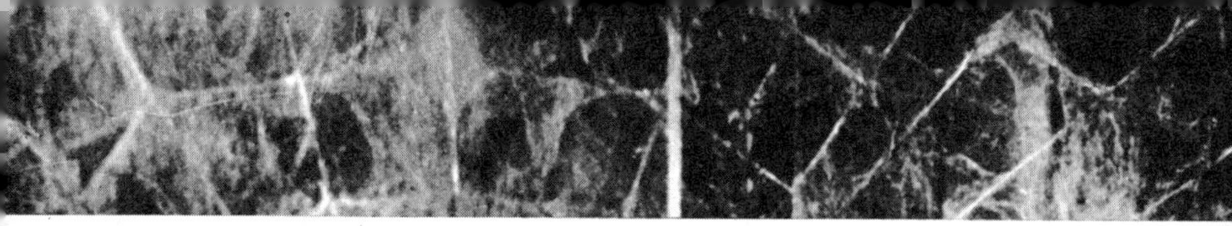

Vampires. From Vlad Tepes to Barnabas Collins. From Lugosi to Lee. These are the damned, the cursed Undead, doomed to spend eternity feasting on the blood of others.

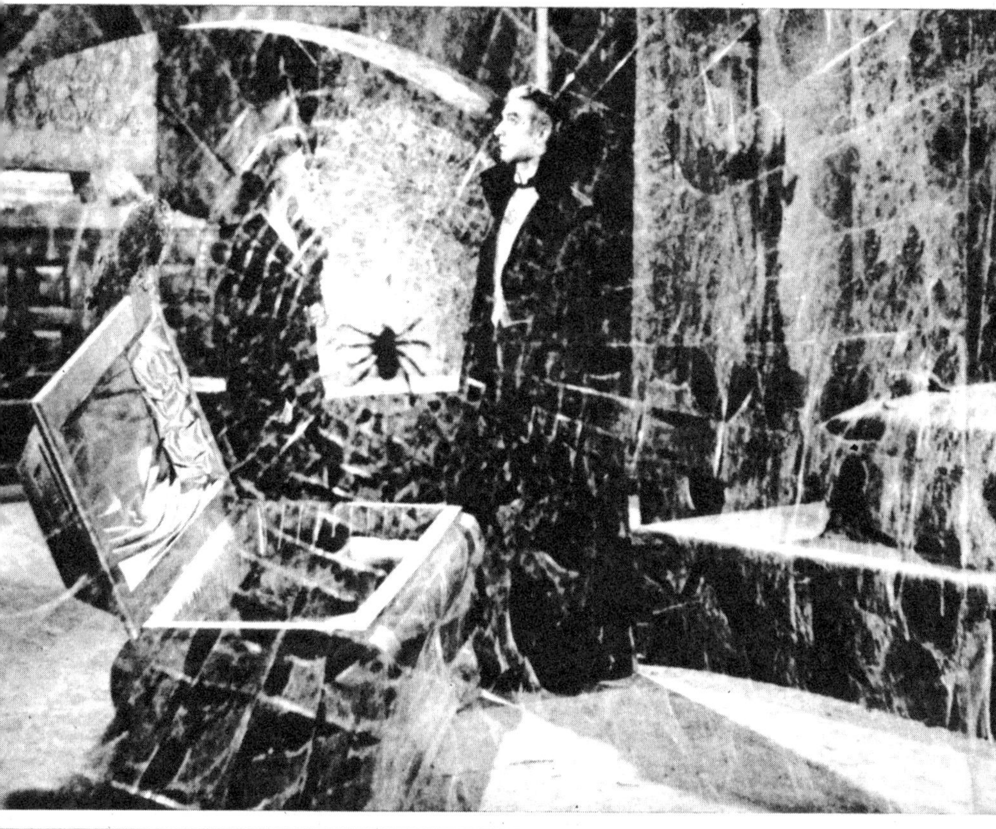

And then there's Michael Morbius. Something *different.* A product of test tubes, not cauldrons—scientific theories, not pacts with Satan—knowledge not superstition. *Morbius.* Something different. And yet—no less cursed for it . . . !

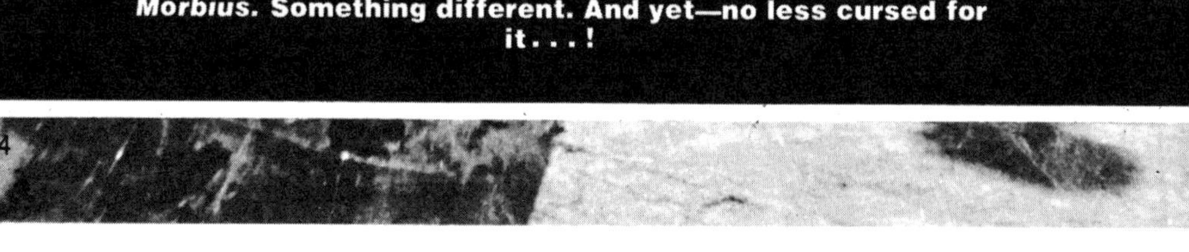

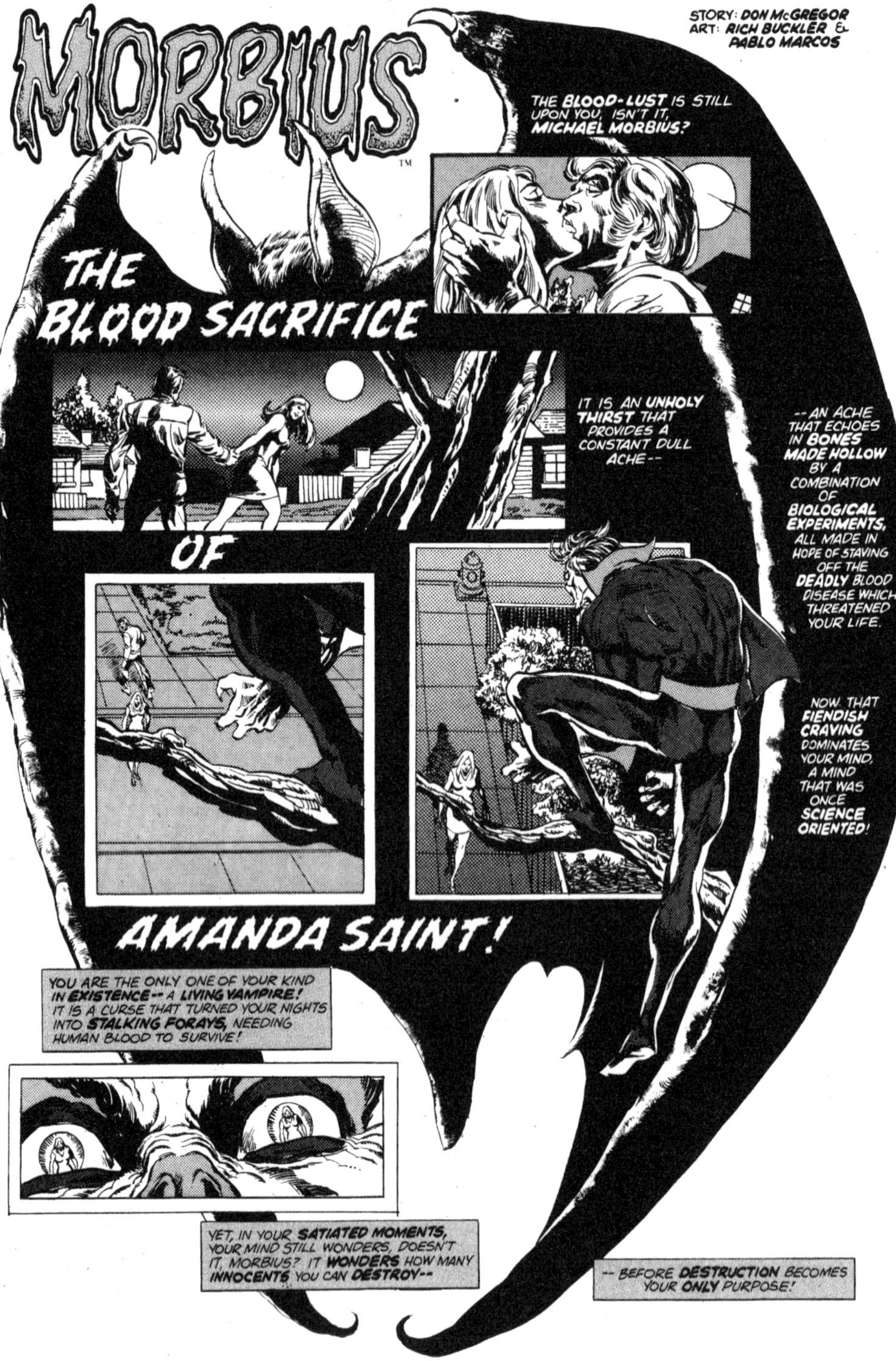
MORBIUS
STORY: DON McGREGOR
ART: RICH BUCKLER & PABLO MARCOS
THE BLOOD-LUST IS STILL UPON YOU, ISN'T IT, MICHAEL MORBIUS?
THE BLOOD SACRIFICE OF AMANDA SAINT!
IT IS AN UNHOLY THIRST THAT PROVIDES A CONSTANT DULL ACHE--
--AN ACHE THAT ECHOES IN BONES MADE HOLLOW BY A COMBINATION OF BIOLOGICAL EXPERIMENTS, ALL MADE IN HOPE OF STAVING OFF THE DEADLY BLOOD DISEASE WHICH THREATENED YOUR LIFE.
NOW THAT FIENDISH CRAVING DOMINATES YOUR MIND, A MIND THAT WAS ONCE SCIENCE ORIENTED!
YOU ARE THE ONLY ONE OF YOUR KIND IN EXISTENCE-- A LIVING VAMPIRE! IT IS A CURSE THAT TURNED YOUR NIGHTS INTO STALKING FORAYS, NEEDING HUMAN BLOOD TO SURVIVE!
YET, IN YOUR SATIATED MOMENTS, YOUR MIND STILL WONDERS, DOESN'T IT, MORBIUS? IT WONDERS HOW MANY INNOCENTS YOU CAN DESTROY--
-- BEFORE DESTRUCTION BECOMES YOUR ONLY PURPOSE!

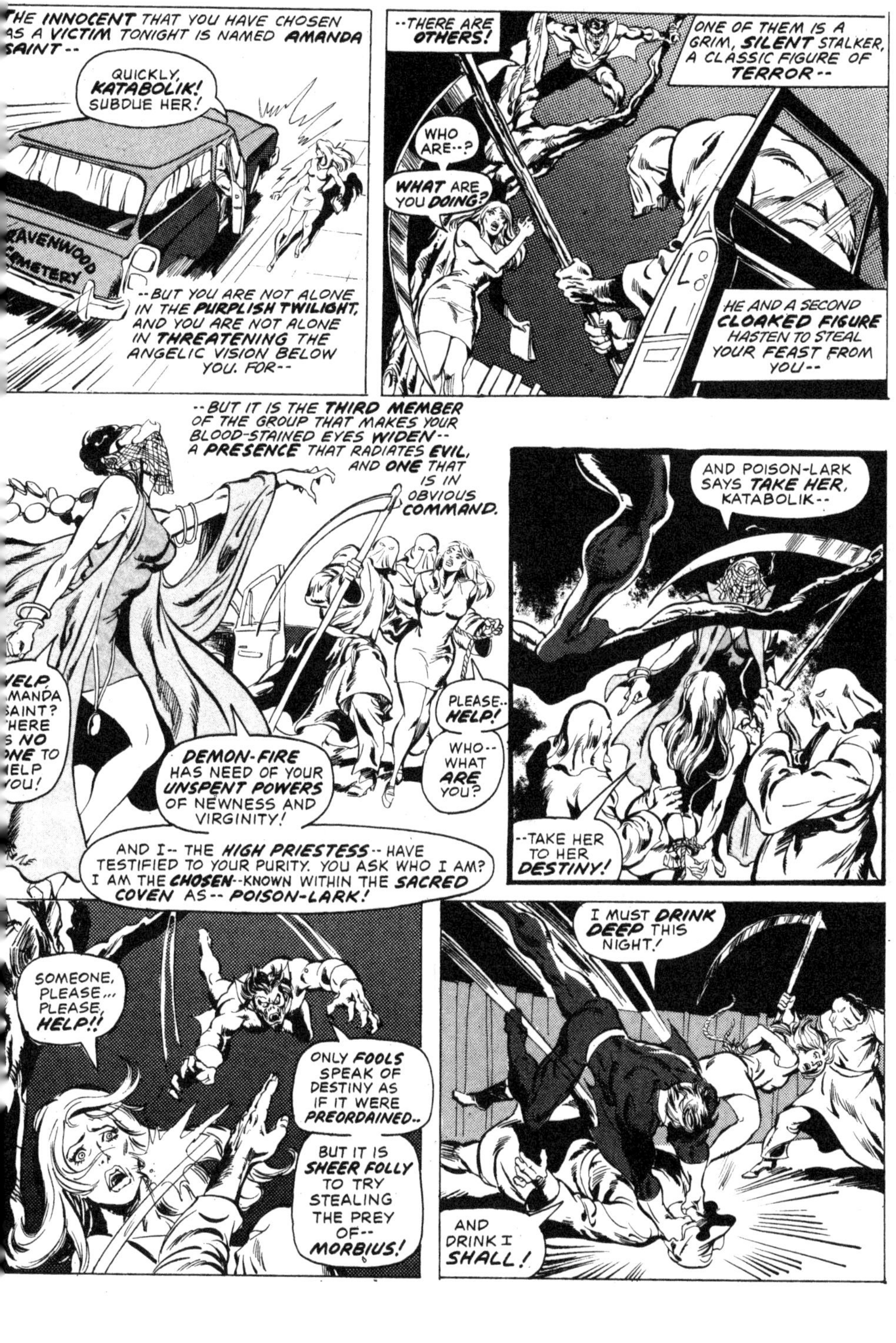
THE INNOCENT THAT YOU HAVE CHOSEN AS A VICTIM TONIGHT IS NAMED AMANDA SAINT--
QUICKLY, KATABOLIK! SUBDUE HER!
RAVENWOOD CEMETERY
--BUT YOU ARE NOT ALONE IN THE PURPLISH TWILIGHT, AND YOU ARE NOT ALONE IN THREATENING THE ANGELIC VISION BELOW YOU. FOR--
--THERE ARE OTHERS!
ONE OF THEM IS A GRIM, SILENT STALKER, A CLASSIC FIGURE OF TERROR--
WHO ARE--?
WHAT ARE YOU DOING?
HE AND A SECOND CLOAKED FIGURE HASTEN TO STEAL YOUR FEAST FROM YOU--
--BUT IT IS THE THIRD MEMBER OF THE GROUP THAT MAKES YOUR BLOOD-STAINED EYES WIDEN-- A PRESENCE THAT RADIATES EVIL, AND ONE THAT IS IN OBVIOUS COMMAND.
HELP, AMANDA SAINT? THERE IS NO ONE TO HELP YOU!
PLEASE.. HELP!
WHO-- WHAT ARE YOU?
DEMON-FIRE HAS NEED OF YOUR UNSPENT POWERS OF NEWNESS AND VIRGINITY!
AND I-- THE HIGH PRIESTESS-- HAVE TESTIFIED TO YOUR PURITY. YOU ASK WHO I AM? I AM THE CHOSEN--KNOWN WITHIN THE SACRED COVEN AS-- POISON-LARK!
AND POISON-LARK SAYS TAKE HER, KATABOLIK--
--TAKE HER TO HER DESTINY!
SOMEONE, PLEASE... PLEASE, HELP!!
ONLY FOOLS SPEAK OF DESTINY AS IF IT WERE PREORDAINED..
BUT IT IS SHEER FOLLY TO TRY STEALING THE PREY OF-- MORBIUS!
I MUST DRINK DEEP THIS NIGHT!
AND DRINK I SHALL!

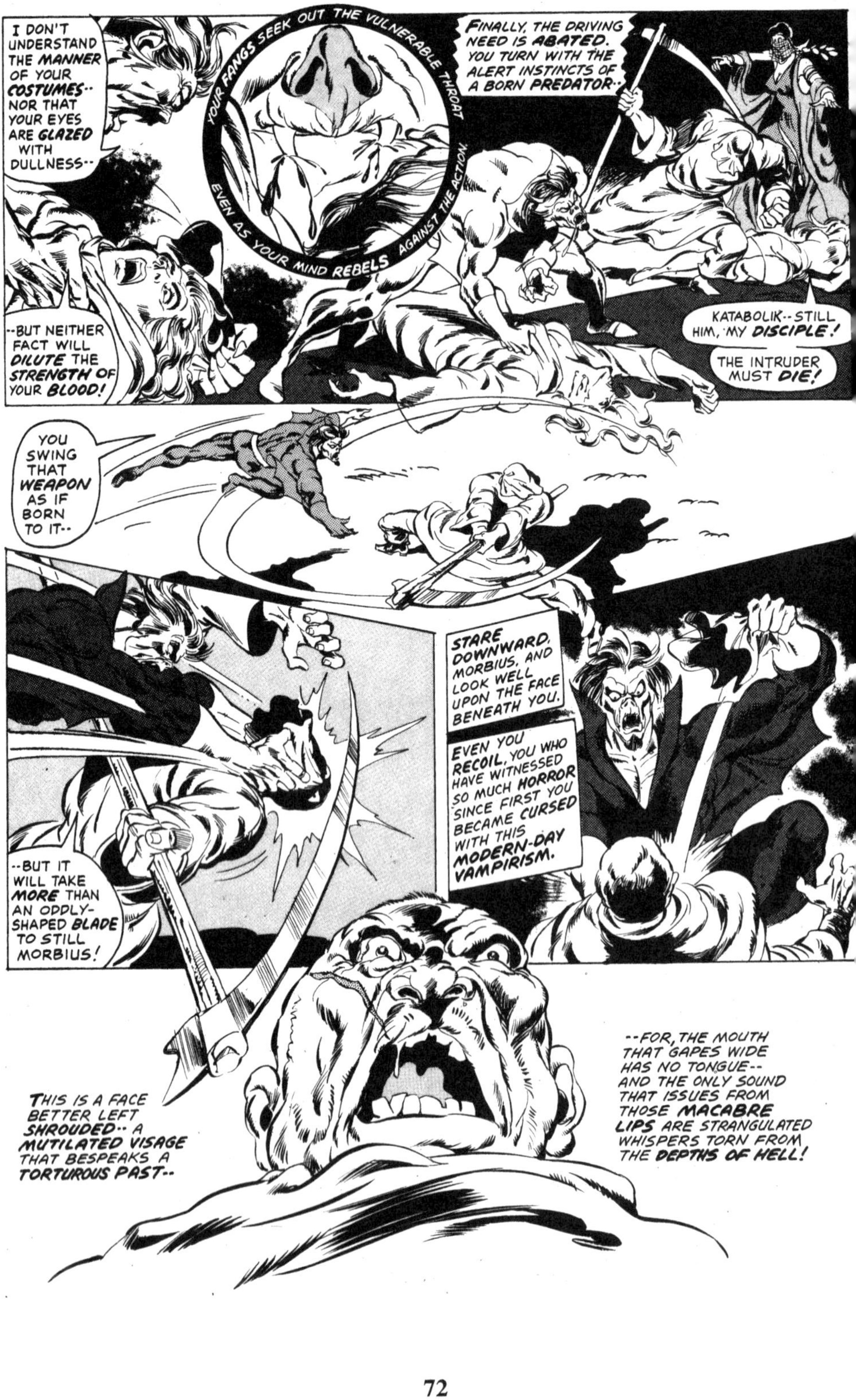
I DON'T UNDERSTAND THE MANNER OF YOUR COSTUMES-- NOR THAT YOUR EYES ARE GLAZED WITH DULLNESS--
--BUT NEITHER FACT WILL DILUTE THE STRENGTH OF YOUR BLOOD!
YOUR FANGS SEEK OUT THE VULNERABLE THROAT EVEN AS YOUR MIND REBELS AGAINST THE ACTION.
FINALLY, THE DRIVING NEED IS ABATED. YOU TURN WITH THE ALERT INSTINCTS OF A BORN PREDATOR--
KATABOLIK-- STILL HIM, MY DISCIPLE!
THE INTRUDER MUST DIE!
YOU SWING THAT WEAPON AS IF BORN TO IT--
--BUT IT WILL TAKE MORE THAN AN ODDLY-SHAPED BLADE TO STILL MORBIUS!
STARE DOWNWARD, MORBIUS, AND LOOK WELL UPON THE FACE BENEATH YOU.
EVEN YOU RECOIL, YOU WHO HAVE WITNESSED SO MUCH HORROR SINCE FIRST YOU BECAME CURSED WITH THIS MODERN-DAY VAMPIRISM.
THIS IS A FACE BETTER LEFT SHROUDED-- A MUTILATED VISAGE THAT BESPEAKS A TORTUROUS PAST--
--FOR, THE MOUTH THAT GAPES WIDE HAS NO TONGUE-- AND THE ONLY SOUND THAT ISSUES FROM THOSE MACABRE LIPS ARE STRANGULATED WHISPERS TORN FROM THE DEPTHS OF HELL!

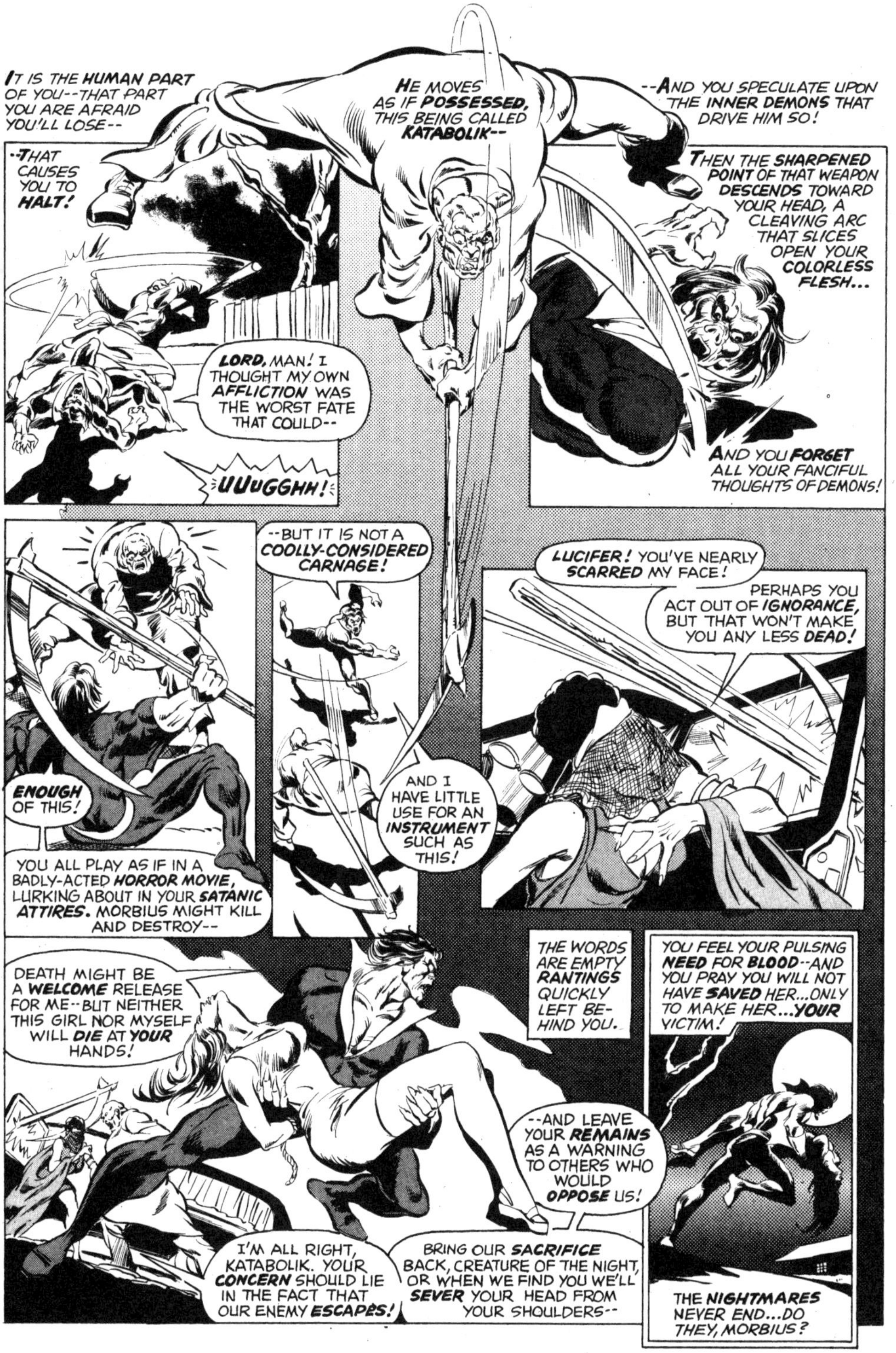
IT IS THE HUMAN PART OF YOU--THAT PART YOU ARE AFRAID YOU'LL LOSE--
--THAT CAUSES YOU TO HALT!
HE MOVES AS IF POSSESSED, THIS BEING CALLED KATABOLIK--
--AND YOU SPECULATE UPON THE INNER DEMONS THAT DRIVE HIM SO!
THEN THE SHARPENED POINT OF THAT WEAPON DESCENDS TOWARD YOUR HEAD, A CLEAVING ARC THAT SLICES OPEN YOUR COLORLESS FLESH...
LORD, MAN! I THOUGHT MY OWN AFFLICTION WAS THE WORST FATE THAT COULD--
UUUGGHH!
AND YOU FORGET ALL YOUR FANCIFUL THOUGHTS OF DEMONS!
ENOUGH OF THIS!
YOU ALL PLAY AS IF IN A BADLY-ACTED HORROR MOVIE, LURKING ABOUT IN YOUR SATANIC ATTIRES. MORBIUS MIGHT KILL AND DESTROY--
--BUT IT IS NOT A COOLLY-CONSIDERED CARNAGE!
AND I HAVE LITTLE USE FOR AN INSTRUMENT SUCH AS THIS!
LUCIFER! YOU'VE NEARLY SCARRED MY FACE!
PERHAPS YOU ACT OUT OF IGNORANCE, BUT THAT WON'T MAKE YOU ANY LESS DEAD!
DEATH MIGHT BE A WELCOME RELEASE FOR ME--BUT NEITHER THIS GIRL NOR MYSELF WILL DIE AT YOUR HANDS!
THE WORDS ARE EMPTY RANTINGS QUICKLY LEFT BEHIND YOU.
--AND LEAVE YOUR REMAINS AS A WARNING TO OTHERS WHO WOULD OPPOSE US!
I'M ALL RIGHT, KATABOLIK. YOUR CONCERN SHOULD LIE IN THE FACT THAT OUR ENEMY ESCAPES!
BRING OUR SACRIFICE BACK, CREATURE OF THE NIGHT, OR WHEN WE FIND YOU WE'LL SEVER YOUR HEAD FROM YOUR SHOULDERS--
YOU FEEL YOUR PULSING NEED FOR BLOOD--AND YOU PRAY YOU WILL NOT HAVE SAVED HER...ONLY TO MAKE HER...YOUR VICTIM!
THE NIGHTMARES NEVER END...DO THEY, MORBIUS?

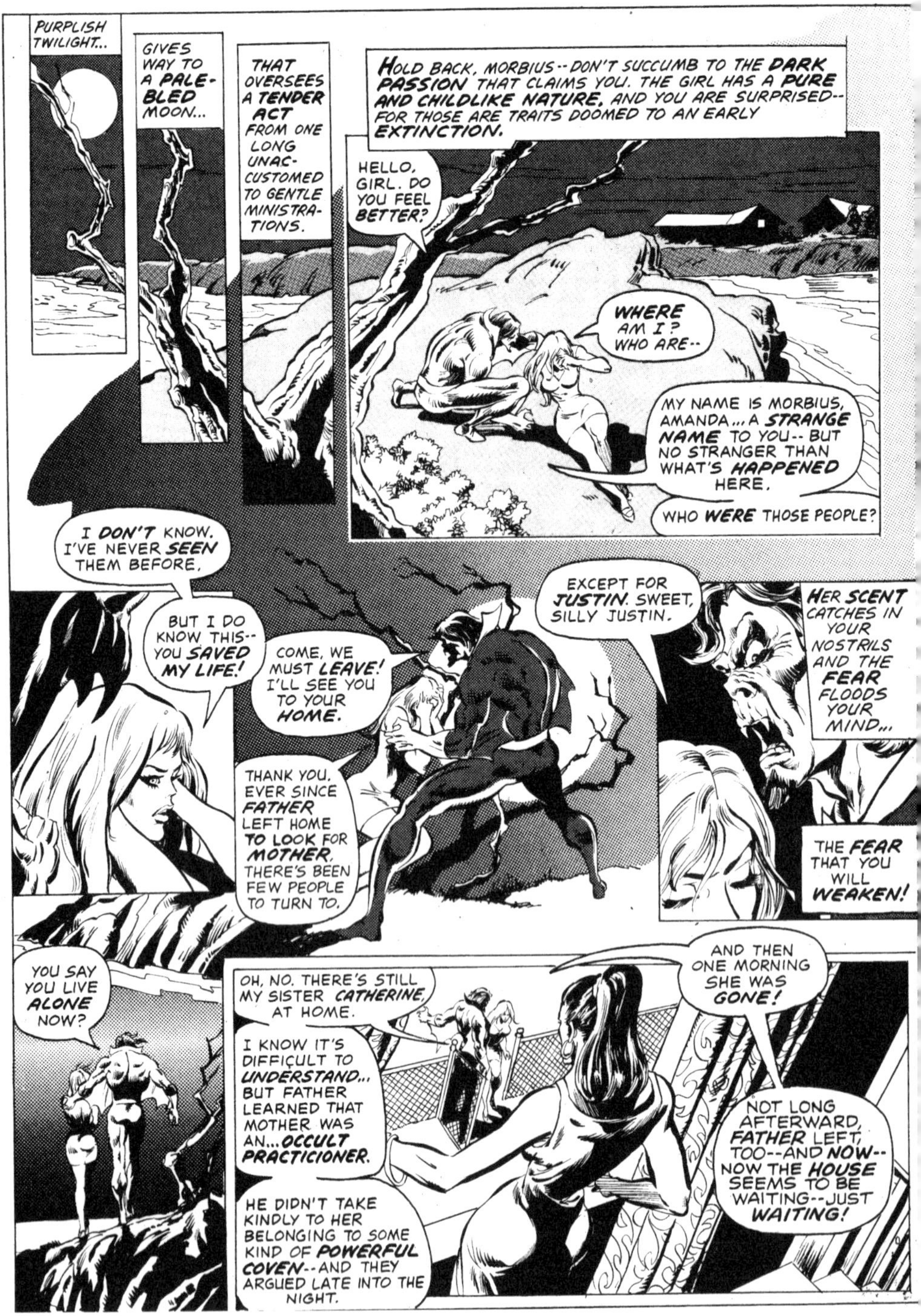

PURPLISH TWILIGHT...
GIVES WAY TO A PALE-BLED MOON...
THAT OVERSEES A TENDER ACT FROM ONE LONG UNACCUSTOMED TO GENTLE MINISTRATIONS.
HOLD BACK, MORBIUS -- DON'T SUCCUMB TO THE DARK PASSION THAT CLAIMS YOU. THE GIRL HAS A PURE AND CHILDLIKE NATURE, AND YOU ARE SURPRISED-- FOR THOSE ARE TRAITS DOOMED TO AN EARLY EXTINCTION.
HELLO, GIRL. DO YOU FEEL BETTER?
WHERE AM I? WHO ARE--
MY NAME IS MORBIUS, AMANDA... A STRANGE NAME TO YOU-- BUT NO STRANGER THAN WHAT'S HAPPENED HERE.
WHO WERE THOSE PEOPLE?
I DON'T KNOW. I'VE NEVER SEEN THEM BEFORE.
BUT I DO KNOW THIS-- YOU SAVED MY LIFE!
COME, WE MUST LEAVE! I'LL SEE YOU TO YOUR HOME.
THANK YOU. EVER SINCE FATHER LEFT HOME TO LOOK FOR MOTHER, THERE'S BEEN FEW PEOPLE TO TURN TO.
EXCEPT FOR JUSTIN. SWEET, SILLY JUSTIN.
HER SCENT CATCHES IN YOUR NOSTRILS AND THE FEAR FLOODS YOUR MIND...
THE FEAR THAT YOU WILL WEAKEN!
YOU SAY YOU LIVE ALONE NOW?
OH, NO. THERE'S STILL MY SISTER CATHERINE, AT HOME.
I KNOW IT'S DIFFICULT TO UNDERSTAND... BUT FATHER LEARNED THAT MOTHER WAS AN... OCCULT PRACTICIONER.
HE DIDN'T TAKE KINDLY TO HER BELONGING TO SOME KIND OF POWERFUL COVEN--AND THEY ARGUED LATE INTO THE NIGHT.
AND THEN ONE MORNING SHE WAS GONE!
NOT LONG AFTERWARD, FATHER LEFT, TOO--AND NOW-- NOW THE HOUSE SEEMS TO BE WAITING--JUST WAITING!

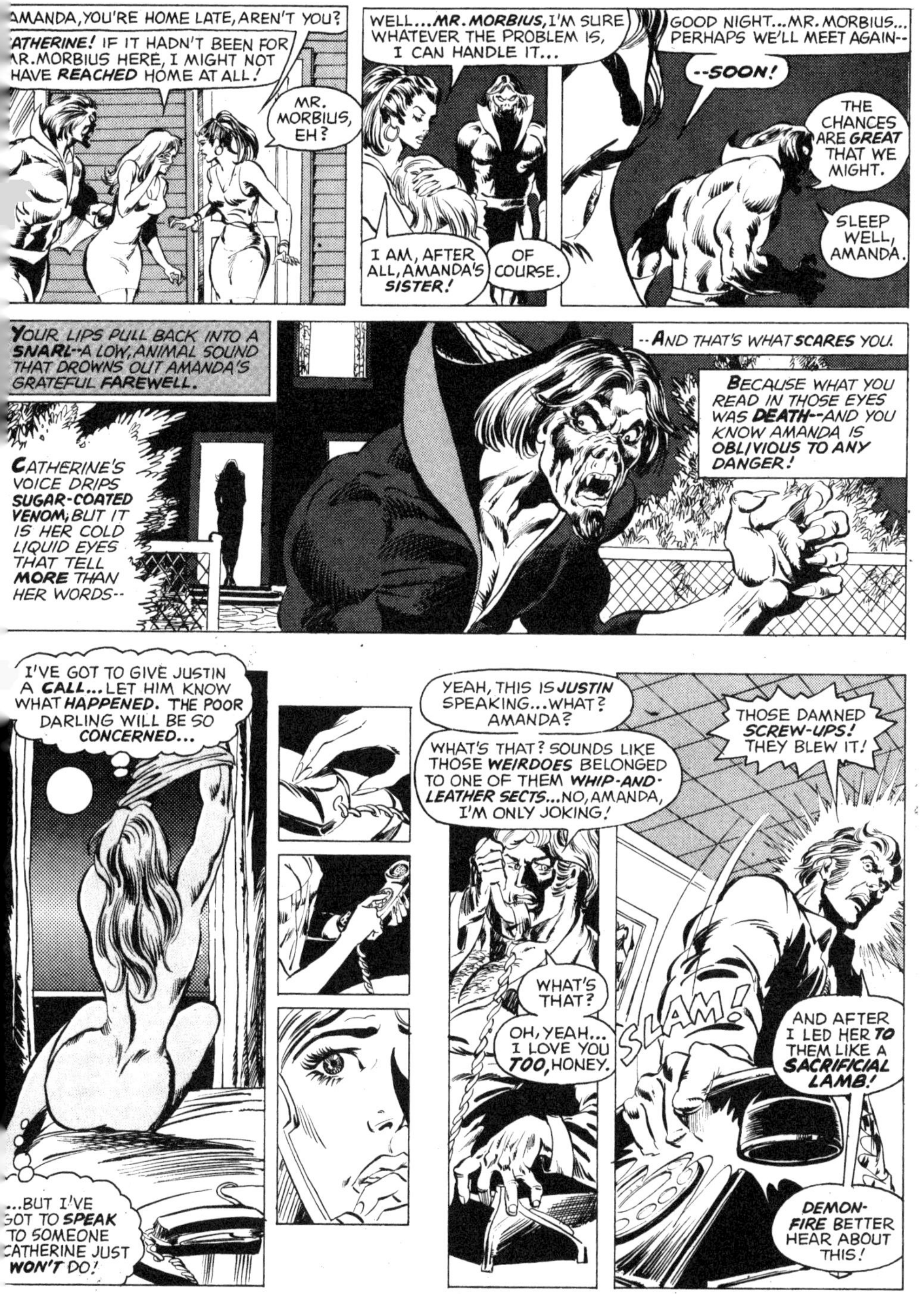

AMANDA, YOU'RE HOME LATE, AREN'T YOU?
ATHERINE! IF IT HADN'T BEEN FOR R.MORBIUS HERE, I MIGHT NOT HAVE REACHED HOME AT ALL!
MR. MORBIUS, EH?
WELL... MR. MORBIUS, I'M SURE WHATEVER THE PROBLEM IS, I CAN HANDLE IT...
I AM, AFTER ALL, AMANDA'S SISTER!
OF COURSE.
GOOD NIGHT... MR. MORBIUS... PERHAPS WE'LL MEET AGAIN--
--SOON!
THE CHANCES ARE GREAT THAT WE MIGHT.
SLEEP WELL, AMANDA.
YOUR LIPS PULL BACK INTO A SNARL--A LOW, ANIMAL SOUND THAT DROWNS OUT AMANDA'S GRATEFUL FAREWELL.
CATHERINE'S VOICE DRIPS SUGAR-COATED VENOM; BUT IT IS HER COLD LIQUID EYES THAT TELL MORE THAN HER WORDS--
--AND THAT'S WHAT SCARES YOU.
BECAUSE WHAT YOU READ IN THOSE EYES WAS DEATH--AND YOU KNOW AMANDA IS OBLIVIOUS TO ANY DANGER!
I'VE GOT TO GIVE JUSTIN A CALL... LET HIM KNOW WHAT HAPPENED. THE POOR DARLING WILL BE SO CONCERNED...
...BUT I'VE GOT TO SPEAK TO SOMEONE CATHERINE JUST WON'T DO!
YEAH, THIS IS JUSTIN SPEAKING... WHAT? AMANDA?
WHAT'S THAT? SOUNDS LIKE THOSE WEIRDOES BELONGED TO ONE OF THEM WHIP-AND-LEATHER SECTS... NO, AMANDA, I'M ONLY JOKING!
WHAT'S THAT?
OH, YEAH... I LOVE YOU TOO, HONEY.
THOSE DAMNED SCREW-UPS! THEY BLEW IT!
SLAM!
AND AFTER I LED HER TO THEM LIKE A SACRIFICIAL LAMB!
DEMON-FIRE BETTER HEAR ABOUT THIS!

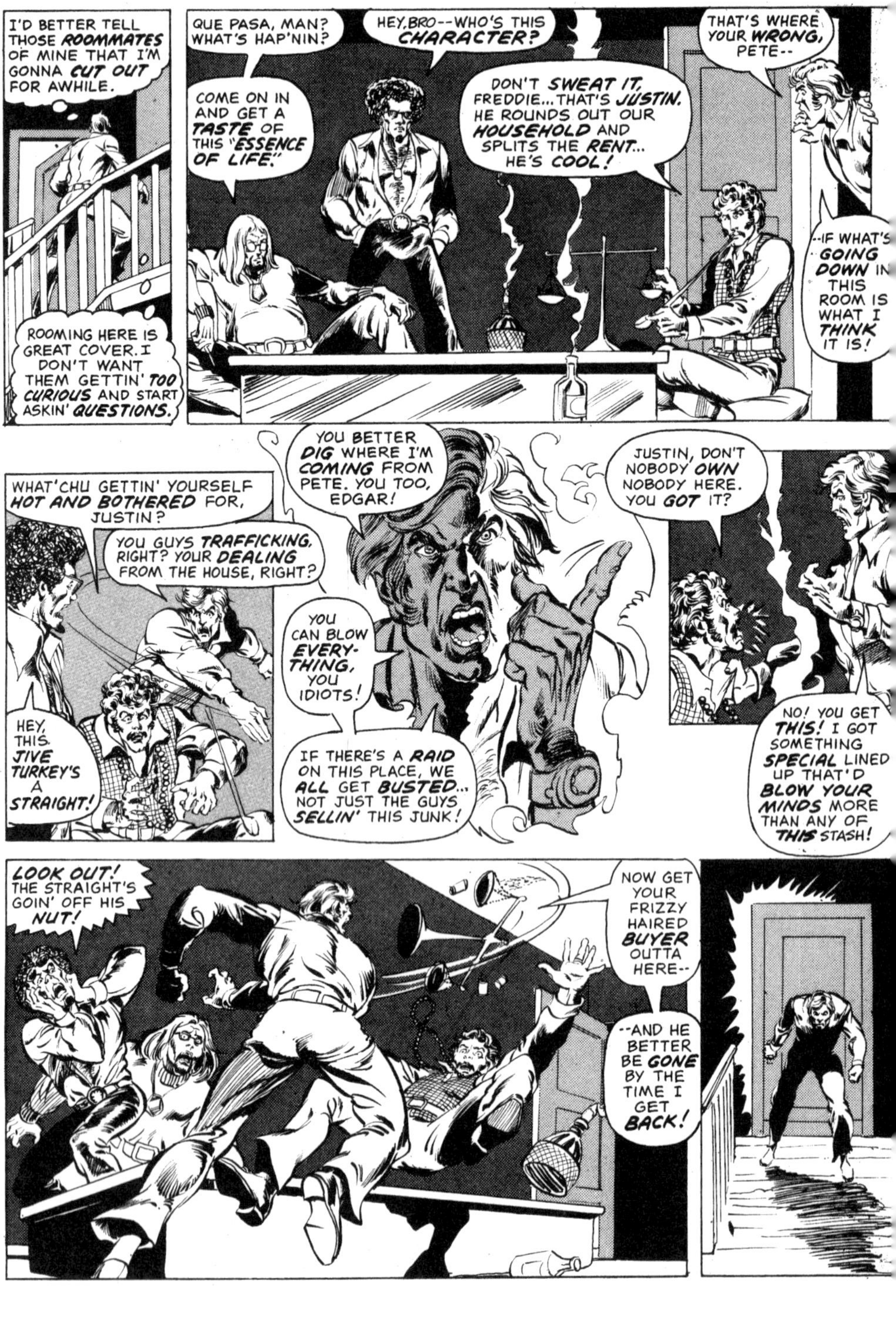

I'D BETTER TELL THOSE ROOMMATES OF MINE THAT I'M GONNA CUT OUT FOR AWHILE.
ROOMING HERE IS GREAT COVER. I DON'T WANT THEM GETTIN' TOO CURIOUS AND START ASKIN' QUESTIONS.
QUE PASA, MAN? WHAT'S HAP'NIN?
COME ON IN AND GET A TASTE OF THIS "ESSENCE OF LIFE."
HEY, BRO--WHO'S THIS CHARACTER?
DON'T SWEAT IT, FREDDIE... THAT'S JUSTIN. HE ROUNDS OUT OUR HOUSEHOLD AND SPLITS THE RENT... HE'S COOL!
THAT'S WHERE YOUR WRONG, PETE--
--IF WHAT'S GOING DOWN IN THIS ROOM IS WHAT I THINK IT IS!
WHAT'CHU GETTIN' YOURSELF HOT AND BOTHERED FOR, JUSTIN?
YOU GUYS TRAFFICKING, RIGHT? YOUR DEALING FROM THE HOUSE, RIGHT?
HEY, THIS JIVE TURKEY'S A STRAIGHT!
YOU BETTER DIG WHERE I'M COMING FROM PETE. YOU TOO, EDGAR!
YOU CAN BLOW EVERY-THING, YOU IDIOTS!
IF THERE'S A RAID ON THIS PLACE, WE ALL GET BUSTED... NOT JUST THE GUYS SELLIN' THIS JUNK!
JUSTIN, DON'T NOBODY OWN NOBODY HERE. YOU GOT IT?
NO! YOU GET THIS! I GOT SOMETHING SPECIAL LINED UP THAT'D BLOW YOUR MINDS MORE THAN ANY OF THIS STASH!
LOOK OUT! THE STRAIGHT'S GOIN' OFF HIS NUT!
NOW GET YOUR FRIZZY HAIRED BUYER OUTTA HERE--
--AND HE BETTER BE GONE BY THE TIME I GET BACK!

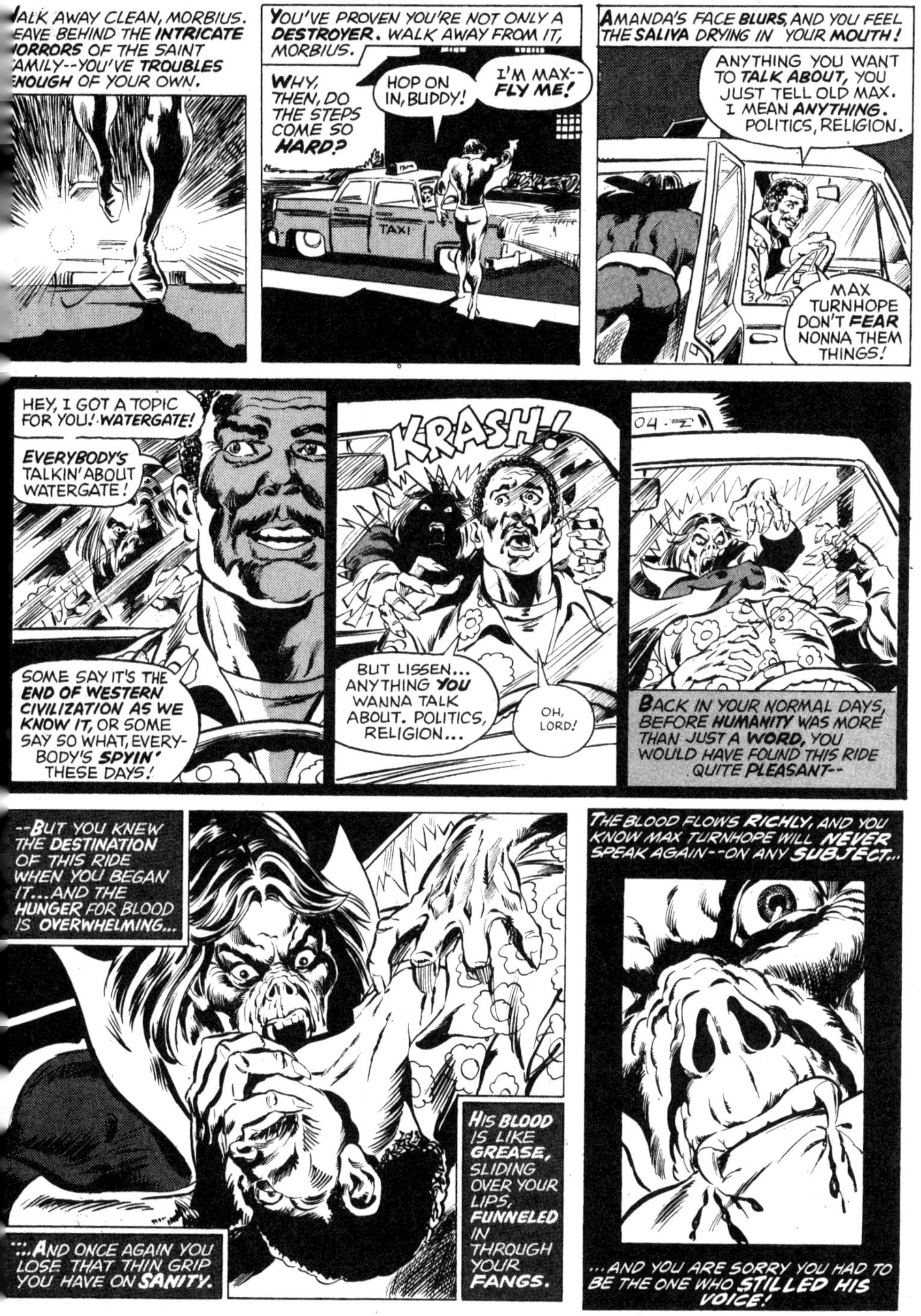

ALK AWAY CLEAN, MORBIUS. EAVE BEHIND THE INTRICATE ORRORS OF THE SAINT AMILY--YOU'VE TROUBLES NOUGH OF YOUR OWN.
YOU'VE PROVEN YOU'RE NOT ONLY A DESTROYER. WALK AWAY FROM IT, MORBIUS.
WHY, THEN, DO THE STEPS COME SO HARD?
HOP ON IN, BUDDY!
I'M MAX--FLY ME!
TAXI
AMANDA'S FACE BLURS, AND YOU FEEL THE SALIVA DRYING IN YOUR MOUTH!
ANYTHING YOU WANT TO TALK ABOUT, YOU JUST TELL OLD MAX. I MEAN ANYTHING. POLITICS, RELIGION.
MAX TURNHOPE DON'T FEAR NONNA THEM THINGS!
HEY, I GOT A TOPIC FOR YOU! WATERGATE!
EVERYBODY'S TALKIN' ABOUT WATERGATE!
SOME SAY IT'S THE END OF WESTERN CIVILIZATION AS WE KNOW IT, OR SOME SAY SO WHAT, EVERY-BODY'S SPYIN' THESE DAYS!
KRASH!
BUT LISSEN... ANYTHING YOU WANNA TALK ABOUT. POLITICS, RELIGION...
OH, LORD!
BACK IN YOUR NORMAL DAYS, BEFORE HUMANITY WAS MORE THAN JUST A WORD, YOU WOULD HAVE FOUND THIS RIDE QUITE PLEASANT--
--BUT YOU KNEW THE DESTINATION OF THIS RIDE WHEN YOU BEGAN IT...AND THE HUNGER FOR BLOOD IS OVERWHELMING...
...AND ONCE AGAIN YOU LOSE THAT THIN GRIP YOU HAVE ON SANITY.
HIS BLOOD IS LIKE GREASE, SLIDING OVER YOUR LIPS, FUNNELED IN THROUGH YOUR FANGS.
THE BLOOD FLOWS RICHLY, AND YOU KNOW MAX TURNHOPE WILL NEVER SPEAK AGAIN--ON ANY SUBJECT...
...AND YOU ARE SORRY YOU HAD TO BE THE ONE WHO STILLED HIS VOICE!

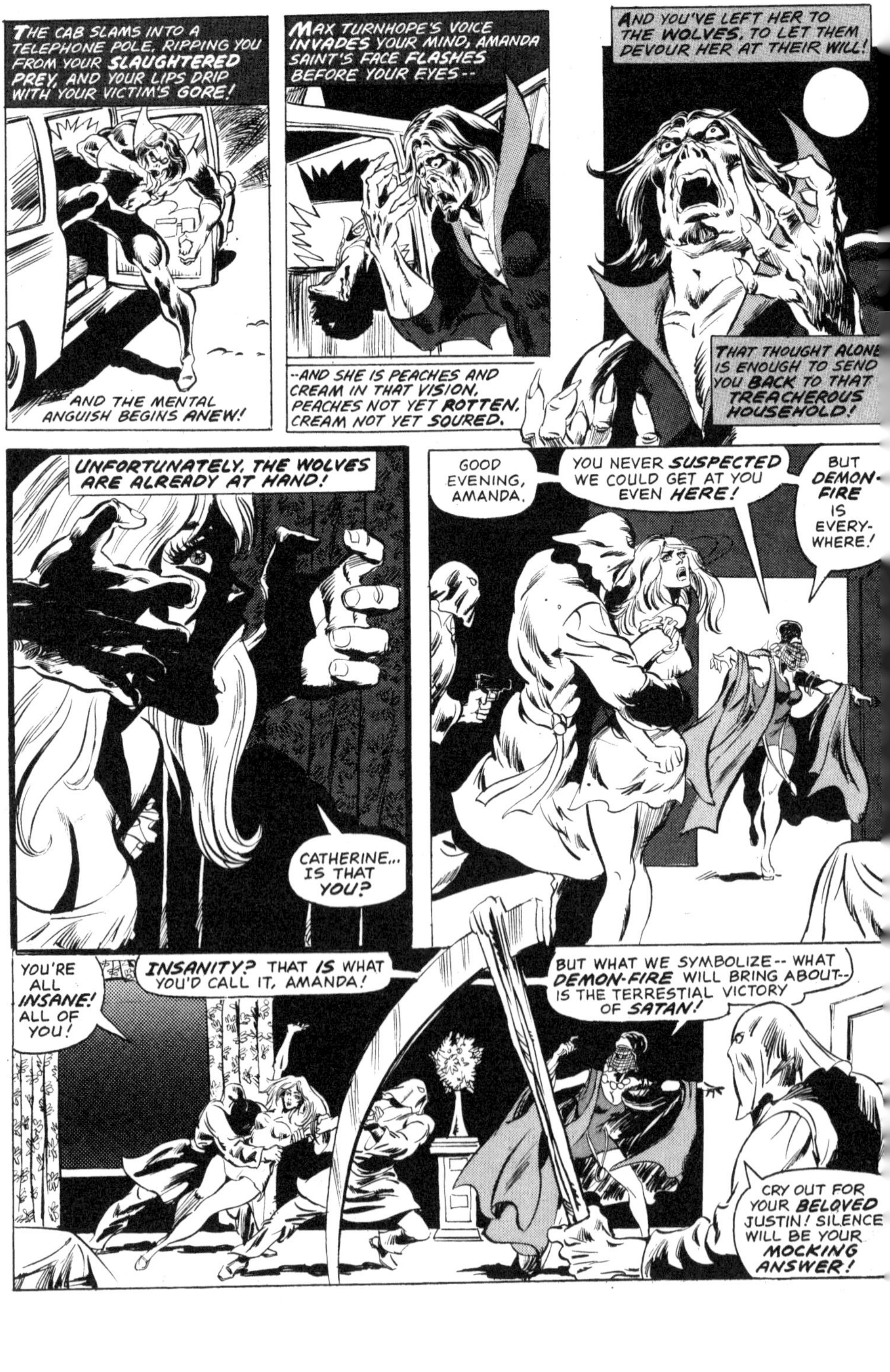
THE CAB SLAMS INTO A TELEPHONE POLE, RIPPING YOU FROM YOUR SLAUGHTERED PREY, AND YOUR LIPS DRIP WITH YOUR VICTIM'S GORE!
AND THE MENTAL ANGUISH BEGINS ANEW!
MAX TURNHOPE'S VOICE INVADES YOUR MIND, AMANDA SAINT'S FACE FLASHES BEFORE YOUR EYES--
--AND SHE IS PEACHES AND CREAM IN THAT VISION, PEACHES NOT YET ROTTEN, CREAM NOT YET SOURED.
AND YOU'VE LEFT HER TO THE WOLVES, TO LET THEM DEVOUR HER AT THEIR WILL!
THAT THOUGHT ALONE IS ENOUGH TO SEND YOU BACK TO THAT TREACHEROUS HOUSEHOLD!
UNFORTUNATELY, THE WOLVES ARE ALREADY AT HAND!
CATHERINE... IS THAT YOU?
GOOD EVENING, AMANDA.
YOU NEVER SUSPECTED WE COULD GET AT YOU EVEN HERE!
BUT DEMON-FIRE IS EVERYWHERE!
YOU'RE ALL INSANE! ALL OF YOU!
INSANITY? THAT IS WHAT YOU'D CALL IT, AMANDA!
BUT WHAT WE SYMBOLIZE-- WHAT DEMON-FIRE WILL BRING ABOUT-- IS THE TERRESTIAL VICTORY OF SATAN!
CRY OUT FOR YOUR BELOVED JUSTIN! SILENCE WILL BE YOUR MOCKING ANSWER!

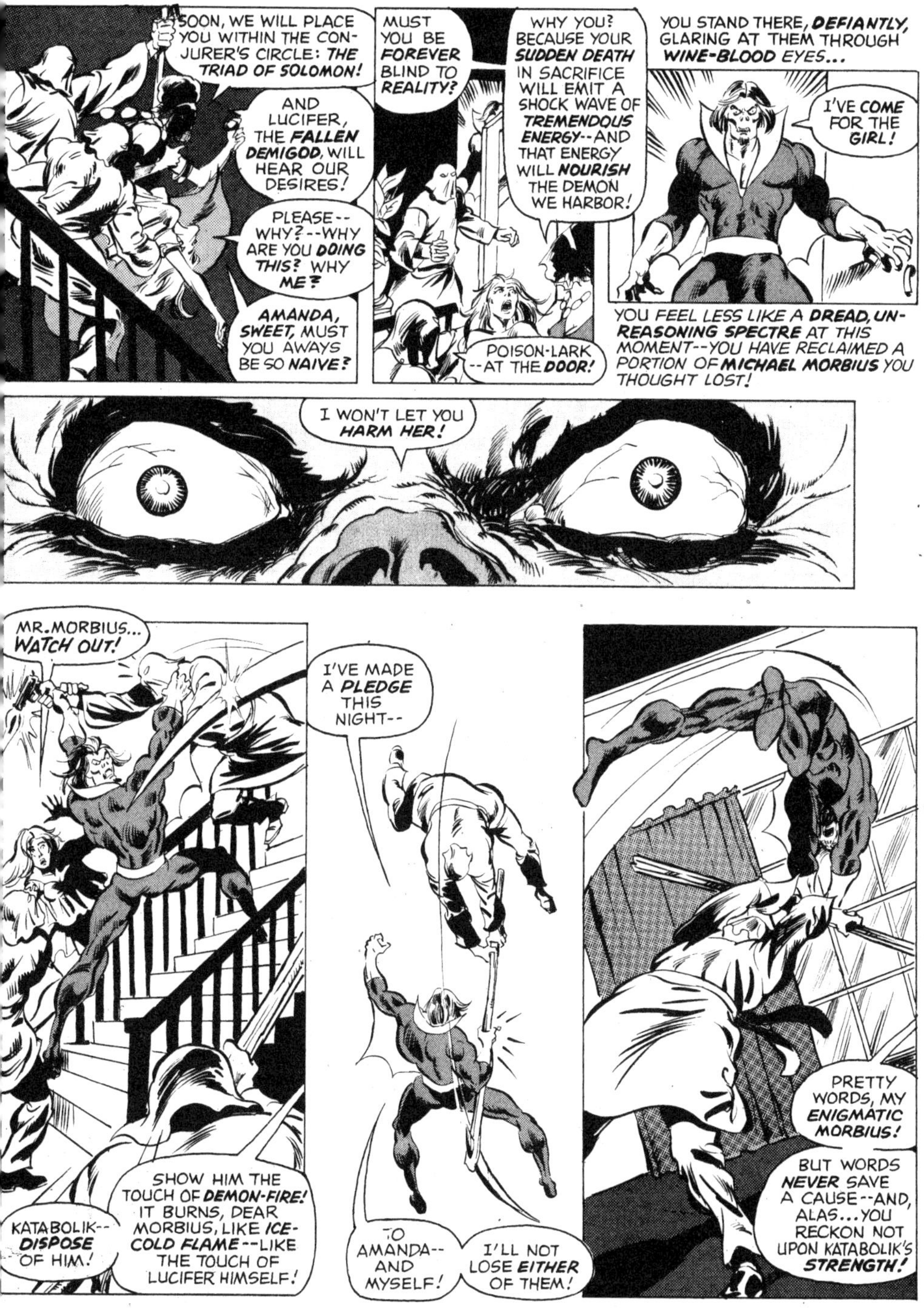
SOON, WE WILL PLACE YOU WITHIN THE CONJURER'S CIRCLE: THE TRIAD OF SOLOMON!
AND LUCIFER, THE FALLEN DEMIGOD, WILL HEAR OUR DESIRES!
PLEASE-- WHY?--WHY ARE YOU DOING THIS? WHY ME?
AMANDA, SWEET, MUST YOU AWAYS BE SO NAIVE?
MUST YOU BE FOREVER BLIND TO REALITY?
WHY YOU? BECAUSE YOUR SUDDEN DEATH IN SACRIFICE WILL EMIT A SHOCK WAVE OF TREMENDOUS ENERGY--AND THAT ENERGY WILL NOURISH THE DEMON WE HARBOR!
POISON-LARK --AT THE DOOR!
YOU STAND THERE, DEFIANTLY, GLARING AT THEM THROUGH WINE-BLOOD EYES...
I'VE COME FOR THE GIRL!
YOU FEEL LESS LIKE A DREAD, UNREASONING SPECTRE AT THIS MOMENT--YOU HAVE RECLAIMED A PORTION OF MICHAEL MORBIUS YOU THOUGHT LOST!
I WON'T LET YOU HARM HER!
MR. MORBIUS... WATCH OUT!
SHOW HIM THE TOUCH OF DEMON-FIRE! IT BURNS, DEAR MORBIUS, LIKE ICE-COLD FLAME--LIKE THE TOUCH OF LUCIFER HIMSELF!
KATABOLIK-- DISPOSE OF HIM!
I'VE MADE A PLEDGE THIS NIGHT--
TO AMANDA-- AND MYSELF!
I'LL NOT LOSE EITHER OF THEM!
PRETTY WORDS, MY ENIGMATIC MORBIUS!
BUT WORDS NEVER SAVE A CAUSE--AND, ALAS...YOU RECKON NOT UPON KATABOLIK'S STRENGTH!

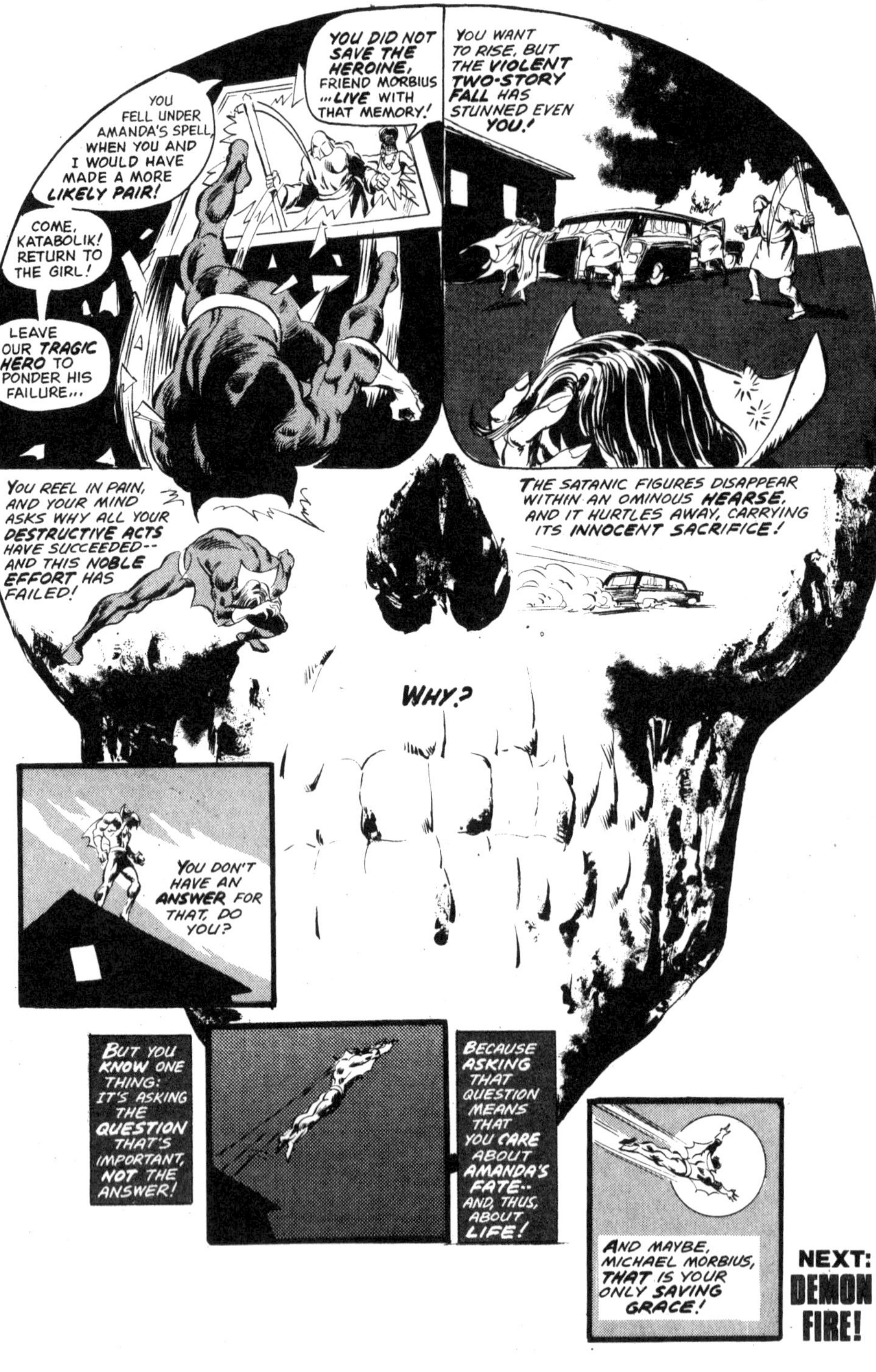
YOU FELL UNDER AMANDA'S SPELL, WHEN YOU AND I WOULD HAVE MADE A MORE LIKELY PAIR!
YOU DID NOT SAVE THE HEROINE, FRIEND MORBIUS ...LIVE WITH THAT MEMORY!
COME, KATABOLIK! RETURN TO THE GIRL!
LEAVE OUR TRAGIC HERO TO PONDER HIS FAILURE...
YOU WANT TO RISE, BUT THE VIOLENT TWO-STORY FALL HAS STUNNED EVEN YOU!
YOU REEL IN PAIN, AND YOUR MIND ASKS WHY ALL YOUR DESTRUCTIVE ACTS HAVE SUCCEEDED-- AND THIS NOBLE EFFORT HAS FAILED!
THE SATANIC FIGURES DISAPPEAR WITHIN AN OMINOUS HEARSE, AND IT HURTLES AWAY, CARRYING ITS INNOCENT SACRIFICE!
WHY?
YOU DON'T HAVE AN ANSWER FOR THAT, DO YOU?
BUT YOU KNOW ONE THING: IT'S ASKING THE QUESTION THAT'S IMPORTANT, NOT THE ANSWER!
BECAUSE ASKING THAT QUESTION MEANS THAT YOU CARE ABOUT AMANDA'S FATE-- AND, THUS, ABOUT LIFE!
AND MAYBE, MICHAEL MORBIUS, THAT IS YOUR ONLY SAVING GRACE!
NEXT: DEMON FIRE!

80

V is for Vampire!

Rumors of the death of the Vampire Legend have been grossly exaggerated.

For some years now, your editor has been reading of how the advances of modern technology have finally sounded the death-knell of such quaint middle-European myth-monsters as the vampire and the werewolf, and of their inevitable replacement by another kind (or rather, by *several* kinds) of horror.

The Arkham-stalking, star-spawned weirdness of an H.P. Lovecraft, for instance.

Or the sheer, un-supernatural terror of Robert Bloch's and Hitchcock's *Psycho*.

All well and good, as far as they go. And, indeed, perhaps such horrors as lurk beyond the blackest voids of space or within the deepest reaches of the human mind *are* the wave of the future's Brave New World.

But the final verdict isn't in yet.

For, all the while that psychological and psuedo-scientific weirdnesses have been staking out their claim on the psyche of man, Count Dracula and his quasi-human ilk have been thriving, as well.

Witness, for instance, the phenomenal popularity of the daytime TV program "Dark Shadows" only a couple of years back—which featured an occasional werewolf—and which starred a very human vampire named Barnabas Collins.

Witness the continued success of the Hammer Dracula films, as well as whole late-movie cults built around the Universal movies of the 30's and 40's.

Witness the spate of books, in just the past twelve-month or so, dealing with vampires and vampirism.

Witness also a May 1973 newspaper account, telling how several unidentified strangers were hacked to death by a mob in Calcutta, India, because someone spread the rumor that they were vampires who possessed blood-sucking devices which would rob sleeping people of their precious bodily fluids.

The vampire may be dead, yes.

But that never stopped him from walking around *before*, did it?

Case in point: This issue's tale of Morbius, the Living Vampire. Not a true scion of Dracula at all—except perhaps in spirit—but a man possessed of an apparently incurable disease which forces him to sustain his own life by drinking the warm blood of others. The idea has been explored before, of course—most notably by Richard Matheson in his celebrated novel *I Am Legend*—but never before has it formed the basis of a continuing character. Beginning this issue, writer Don McGregor and artist Rich Buckler combine their considerable talents to explore perhaps the strangest, most terrifying curse that can befall a man—in this century or any other.

One other series debut—or *semi*-debut, rather—with this issue: "Satana, the Devil's Daughter." She's not *quite* a vampire, for what she takes from her unlucky victims is not blood, but something even more vital. Ye Editor had a ball on this one—for, in his nearly a decade at Marvel, he had never before had the exquisite privilege of working with artist John Romita, and it was beginning to look as if he never would. And, with our next issue, the full-scale feature-length series will be launched by still another team supreme: Steve Engelhart and Esteban Maroto.

On the non-series front, Don McGregor returns (again in tandem with Rich Buckler) with "The Preying Mantis Principle," an offbeat tale of a league of vampires with perhaps the most unique "front" of all time. And there's also our cover feature, scripted by Gardner Fox in the timeless tradition of A. Merritt and H. Rider Haggard and drawn by Jesus Blasco. All this, plus the second installment of Chris Claremont's skilled abridgement of *The Vampire: His Kith and Kin*, plus a feature on that most venerable of movie monsters, Bela Lugosi, who it turns out played many another fanged fiend besides the Tyrant of Transylvania.

The Vampire—a thing of the forgotten, obsolescent past?

Maybe.

Still, as mehitabel the cat said to a cockroach named archy: *"there's a dance in the old girl yet."* **FINIS**

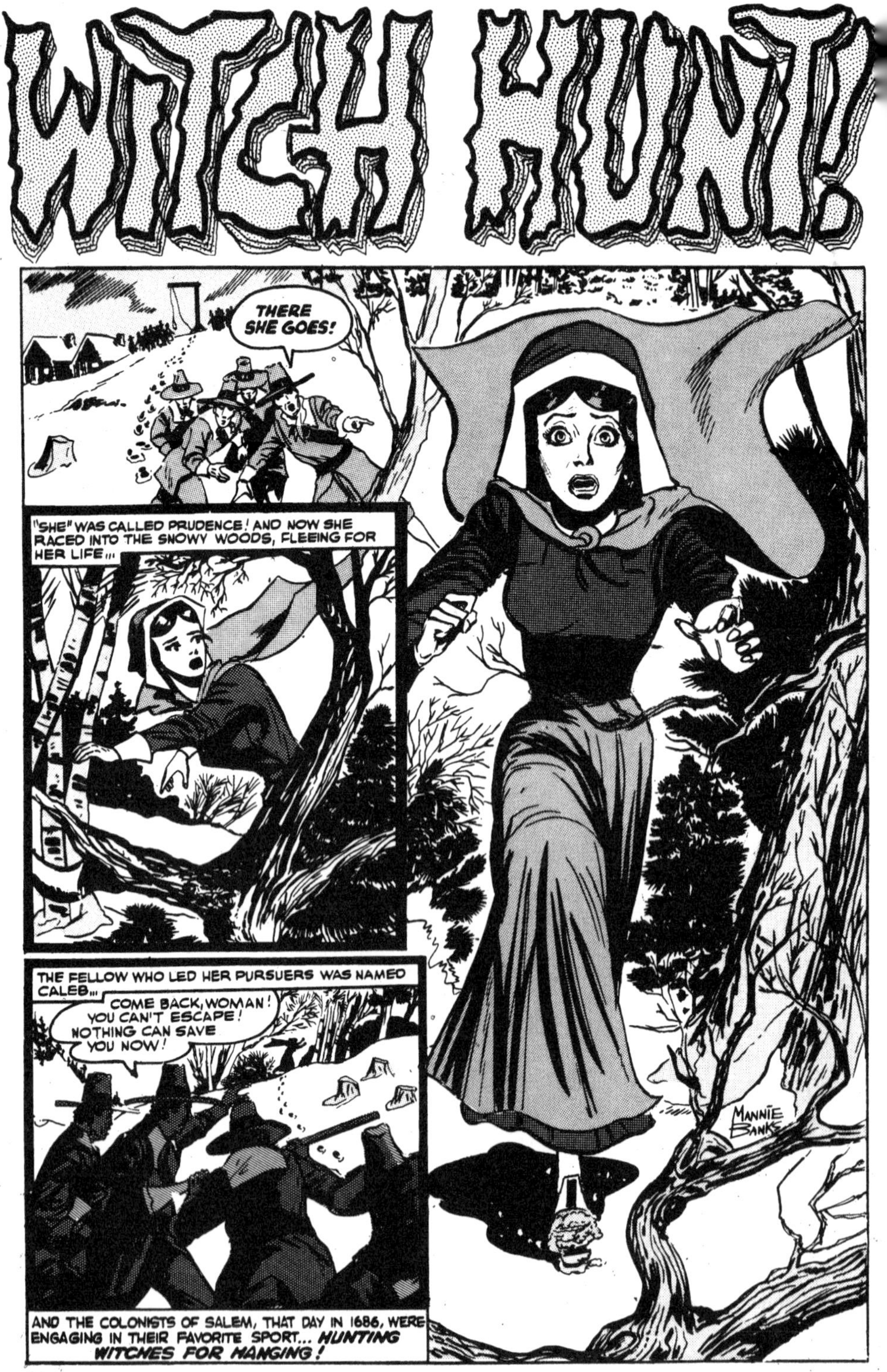
WITCH HUNT!
THERE SHE GOES!
"SHE" WAS CALLED PRUDENCE! AND NOW SHE RACED INTO THE SNOWY WOODS, FLEEING FOR HER LIFE...
THE FELLOW WHO LED HER PURSUERS WAS NAMED CALEB...
COME BACK, WOMAN! YOU CAN'T ESCAPE! NOTHING CAN SAVE YOU NOW!
AND THE COLONISTS OF SALEM, THAT DAY IN 1686, WERE ENGAGING IN THEIR FAVORITE SPORT... HUNTING WITCHES FOR HANGING!
MANNIE BANKS

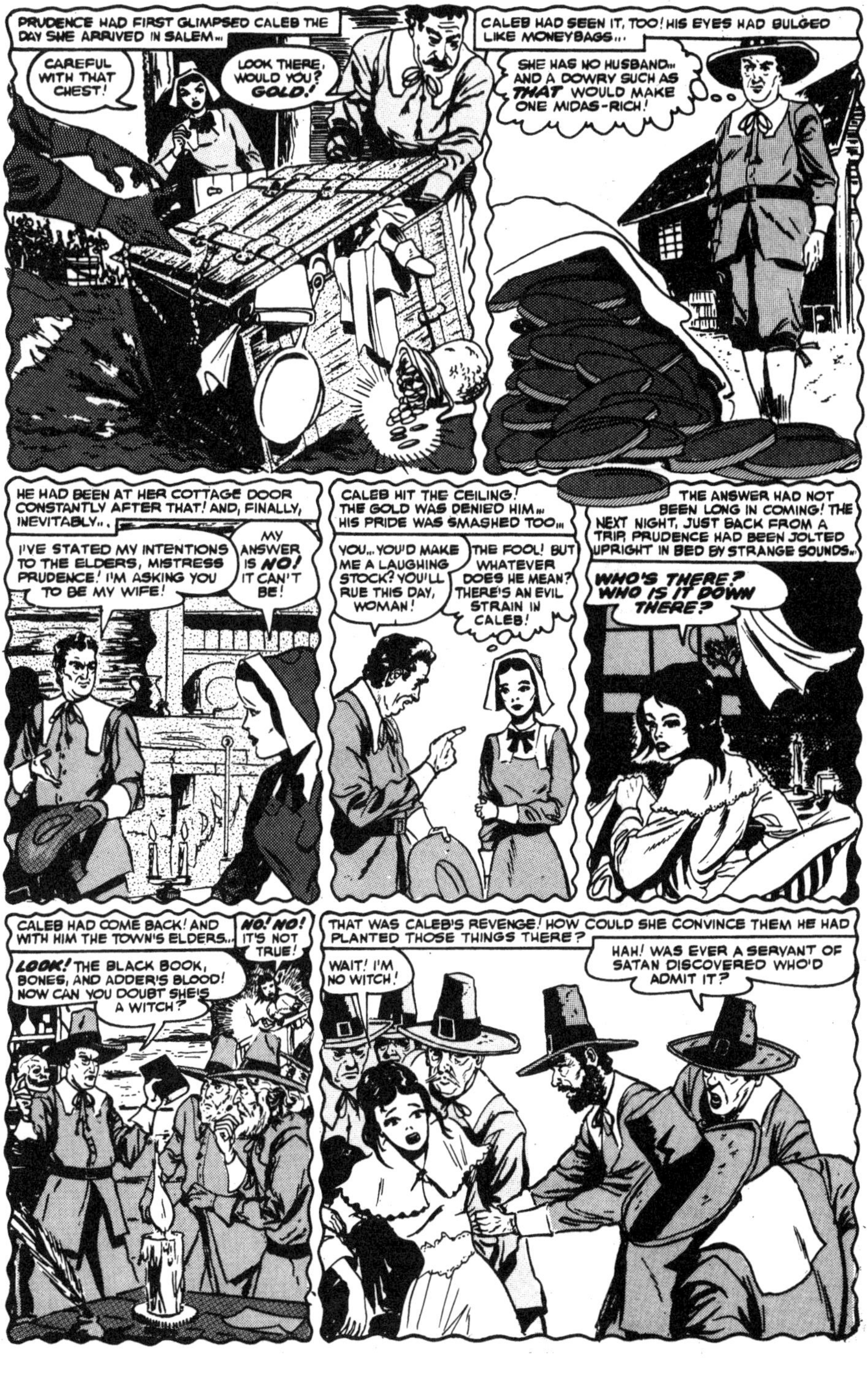
PRUDENCE HAD FIRST GLIMPSED CALEB THE DAY SHE ARRIVED IN SALEM...
CAREFUL WITH THAT CHEST!
LOOK THERE, WOULD YOU? GOLD!
CALEB HAD SEEN IT, TOO! HIS EYES HAD BULGED LIKE MONEYBAGS...
SHE HAS NO HUSBAND... AND A DOWRY SUCH AS THAT WOULD MAKE ONE MIDAS-RICH!
HE HAD BEEN AT HER COTTAGE DOOR CONSTANTLY AFTER THAT! AND, FINALLY, INEVITABLY...
I'VE STATED MY INTENTIONS TO THE ELDERS, MISTRESS PRUDENCE! I'M ASKING YOU TO BE MY WIFE!
MY ANSWER IS NO! IT CAN'T BE!
CALEB HIT THE CEILING! THE GOLD WAS DENIED HIM... HIS PRIDE WAS SMASHED TOO...
YOU... YOU'D MAKE ME A LAUGHING STOCK? YOU'LL RUE THIS DAY, WOMAN!
THE FOOL! BUT WHATEVER DOES HE MEAN? THERE'S AN EVIL STRAIN IN CALEB!
THE ANSWER HAD NOT BEEN LONG IN COMING! THE NEXT NIGHT, JUST BACK FROM A TRIP, PRUDENCE HAD BEEN JOLTED UPRIGHT IN BED BY STRANGE SOUNDS...
WHO'S THERE? WHO IS IT DOWN THERE?
CALEB HAD COME BACK! AND WITH HIM THE TOWN'S ELDERS...
NO! NO! IT'S NOT TRUE!
LOOK! THE BLACK BOOK, BONES, AND ADDER'S BLOOD! NOW CAN YOU DOUBT SHE'S A WITCH?
THAT WAS CALEB'S REVENGE! HOW COULD SHE CONVINCE THEM HE HAD PLANTED THOSE THINGS THERE?
WAIT! I'M NO WITCH!
HAH! WAS EVER A SERVANT OF SATAN DISCOVERED WHO'D ADMIT IT?

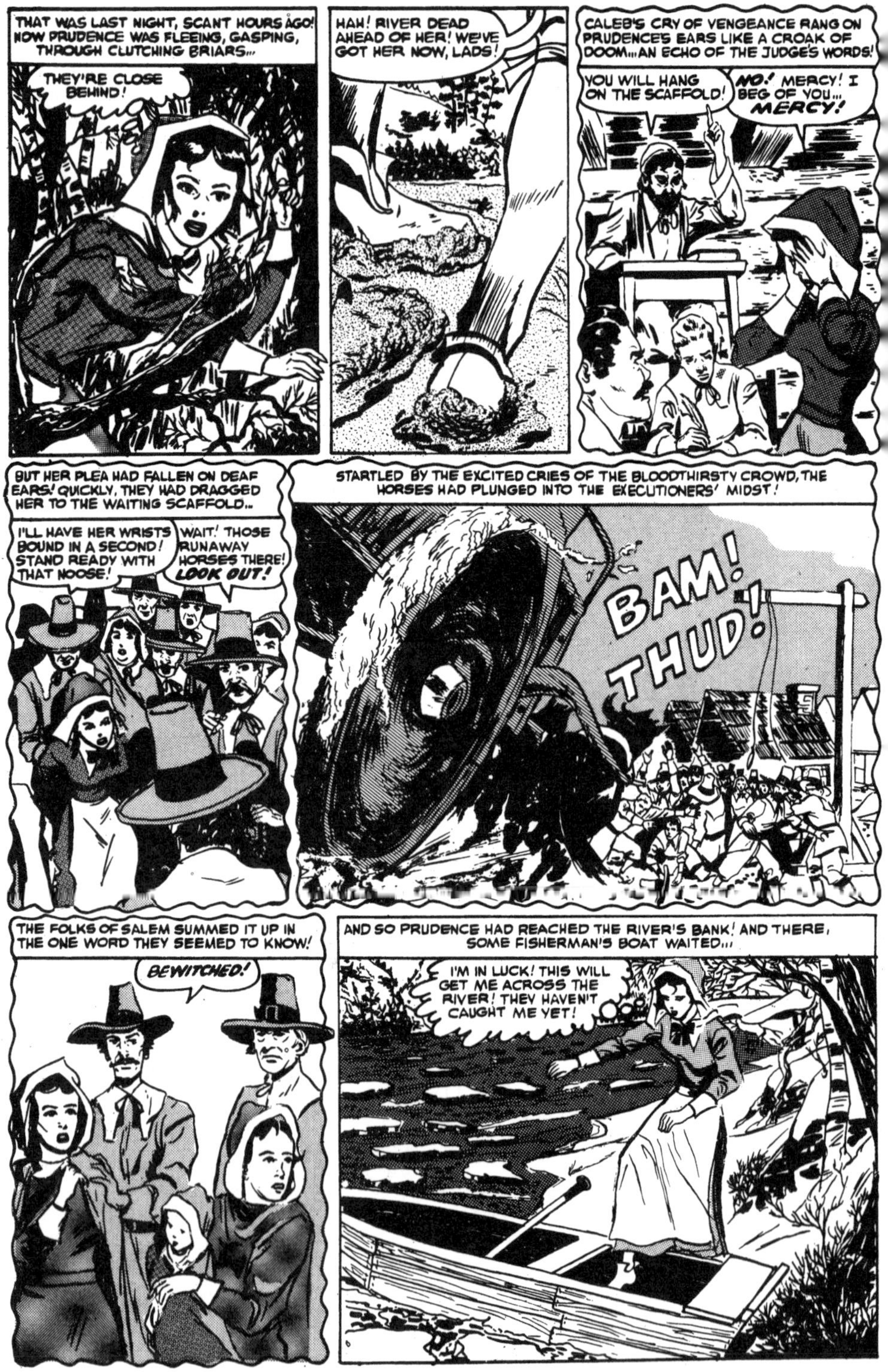
THAT WAS LAST NIGHT, SCANT HOURS AGO! NOW PRUDENCE WAS FLEEING, GASPING, THROUGH CLUTCHING BRIARS...
THEY'RE CLOSE BEHIND!
HAH! RIVER DEAD AHEAD OF HER! WE'VE GOT HER NOW, LADS!
CALEB'S CRY OF VENGEANCE RANG ON PRUDENCE'S EARS LIKE A CROAK OF DOOM... AN ECHO OF THE JUDGE'S WORDS!
YOU WILL HANG ON THE SCAFFOLD!
NO! MERCY! I BEG OF YOU... MERCY!
BUT HER PLEA HAD FALLEN ON DEAF EARS! QUICKLY, THEY HAD DRAGGED HER TO THE WAITING SCAFFOLD..
I'LL HAVE HER WRISTS BOUND IN A SECOND! STAND READY WITH THAT NOOSE!
WAIT! THOSE RUNAWAY HORSES THERE! LOOK OUT!
STARTLED BY THE EXCITED CRIES OF THE BLOODTHIRSTY CROWD, THE HORSES HAD PLUNGED INTO THE EXECUTIONERS' MIDST!
BAM! THUD!
THE FOLKS OF SALEM SUMMED IT UP IN THE ONE WORD THEY SEEMED TO KNOW!
BEWITCHED!
AND SO PRUDENCE HAD REACHED THE RIVER'S BANK! AND THERE, SOME FISHERMAN'S BOAT WAITED...
I'M IN LUCK! THIS WILL GET ME ACROSS THE RIVER! THEY HAVEN'T CAUGHT ME YET!

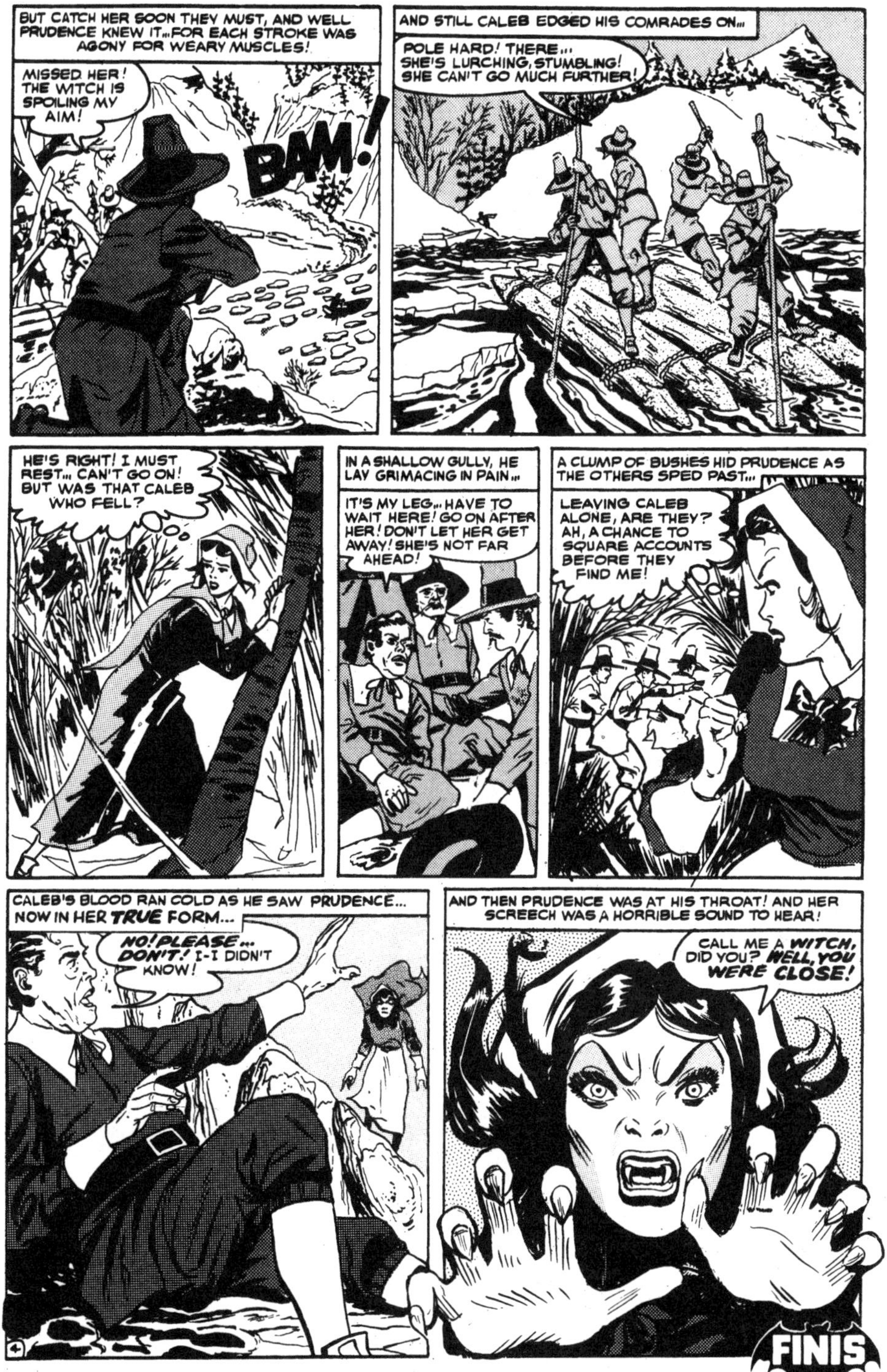
BUT CATCH HER SOON THEY MUST, AND WELL PRUDENCE KNEW IT... FOR EACH STROKE WAS AGONY FOR WEARY MUSCLES!
MISSED HER! THE WITCH IS SPOILING MY AIM!
BAM!
AND STILL CALEB EDGED HIS COMRADES ON...
POLE HARD! THERE... SHE'S LURCHING, STUMBLING! SHE CAN'T GO MUCH FURTHER!
HE'S RIGHT! I MUST REST... CAN'T GO ON! BUT WAS THAT CALEB WHO FELL?
IN A SHALLOW GULLY, HE LAY GRIMACING IN PAIN...
IT'S MY LEG... HAVE TO WAIT HERE! GO ON AFTER HER! DON'T LET HER GET AWAY! SHE'S NOT FAR AHEAD!
A CLUMP OF BUSHES HID PRUDENCE AS THE OTHERS SPED PAST...
LEAVING CALEB ALONE, ARE THEY? AH, A CHANCE TO SQUARE ACCOUNTS BEFORE THEY FIND ME!
CALEB'S BLOOD RAN COLD AS HE SAW PRUDENCE... NOW IN HER TRUE FORM...
NO! PLEASE... DON'T! I-I DIDN'T KNOW!
AND THEN PRUDENCE WAS AT HIS THROAT! AND HER SCREECH WAS A HORRIBLE SOUND TO HEAR!
CALL ME A WITCH, DID YOU? WELL, YOU WERE CLOSE!
4
FINIS

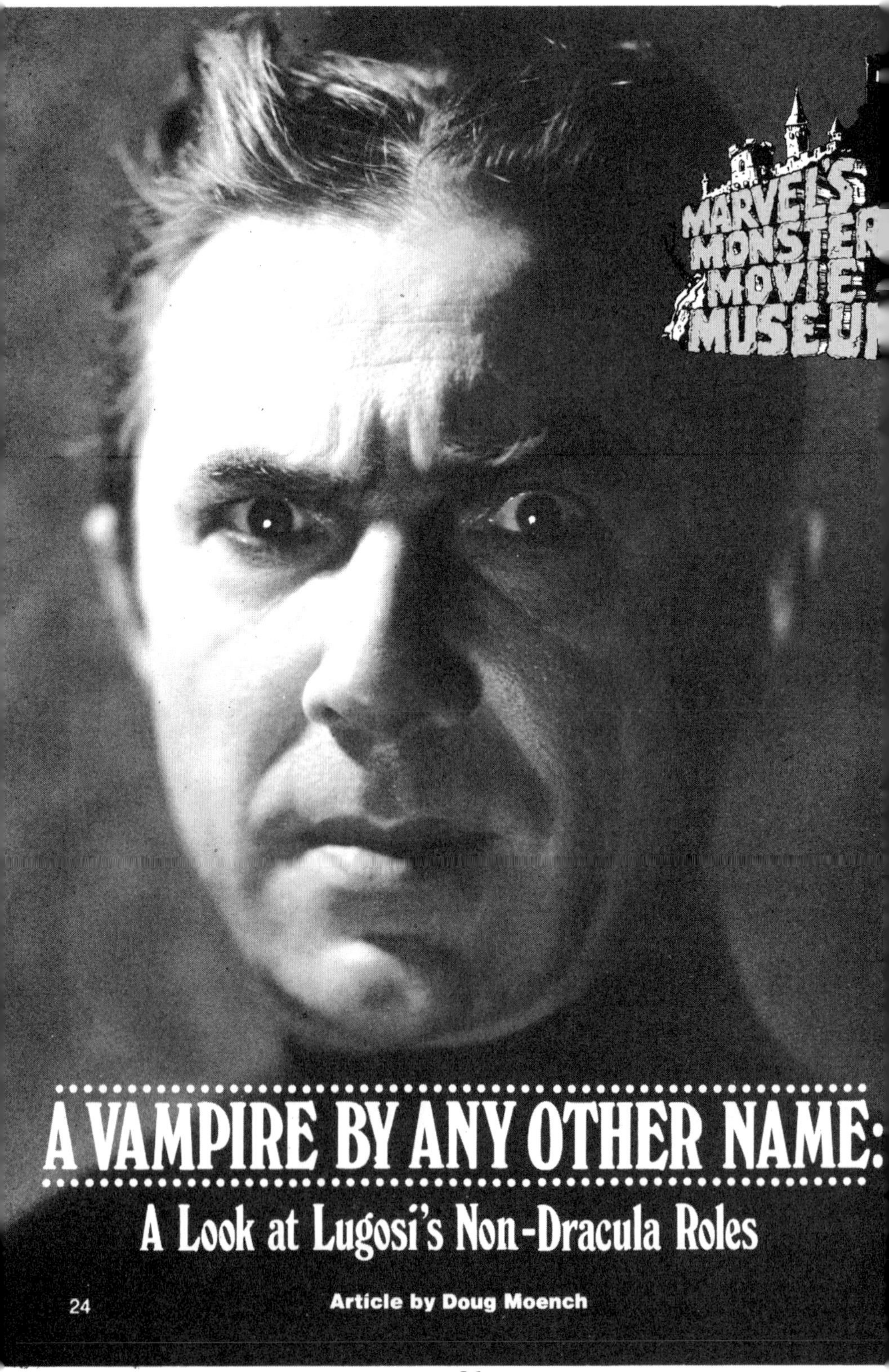
MARVEL'S MONSTER MOVIE MUSEUM

A VAMPIRE BY ANY OTHER NAME:

A Look at Lugosi's Non-Dracula Roles

Article by Doug Moench

Sharp stakes and rancid garlic weren't the only things ever to plague the nearly unflappable Count Dracula. Following the triumphant success of Universal Pictures' 1931 *Dracula*, the redoubtable Count found himself stymied by a blockade of interlocking legal hassles, poor planning, low budgets, lack of faith, and sheer unadulterated studio idiocy.

And since, at the time, the name of Dracula was synonymous with Lugosi, poor Bela was faced with the same obstacles. As revealed by the Lugosi/Dracula article in DRACULA LIVES #3 (if you're good, and say your prayers, and the wolfbane is blooming, it might still be on sale), Bela was destined to impersonate the mythic figure of Count Dracula — on film — only twice during the course of his otherwise eventful career. And that's the long (*Abbott and Costello Meet Frankenstein*) and the short (*Dracula*) of it.

But Lugosi possessed an incomparable personality and physical aspect, attributes which were acutely conducive to evoking the sinister malevolence of nocturnal predators. It was *inevitable* that he would essay other vampire roles — roles which, if not the real thing, were at least blood-brothers to his most renowned portrayal.

Excluding two brief instances of Disney-animated Lugosian vampires (*Mickey's Gala Premiere* and *Fantasia*, the latter allegedly drawn from actual modeling sessions with Lugosi himself), there were six non-Dracula vampire roles in the Lugosi canon. Some of these featured vampires which might very well have been Dracula operating under an alias, the better to suit his devious machinations; the rest changed names to protect the guilty.

Chronologically, then, follow the rebounding night-fiends:

Four years after *Dracula*, in 1935, we find that director Tod Browning has gravitated over to the more prestigious MGM studios. Browning was now at the zenith of his directorial prowess and, ostensibly because the Dracula character was the exclusive property of Universal Pictures, decided to regress back to his roots for the basis of his pending MGM vampire offering. In this case, his roots happened to be planted in the 1927 silent, *London After Midnight*, in which Browning directed the versatile Lon Chaney, Sr., through a triple role of ersatz vampire, civilian vampire-squasher, and policeman. Remaking the film under the title of *Mark of the Vampire*, Browning cast a hammy Lionel Barrymore as the civilian vampire-nemesis, Lionel Atwill as the cop, and Lugosi as the bogus vampire.

Still held in some esteem by film buffs, the most severe criticism leveled against *Mark of the Vampire* is the fact that Lugosi is largely wasted in the part of a virtually mute vampire who (aha!) isn't really a vampire at all. It's one those depressingly draggy things wherein cast and crew do their contrived best to convince you that genuine ghosts are indeed haunting the decrepit gothic mansion on the seacliff, and then pull the groan-eliciting whammy of revealing that it was the jealous son-in-law under a freshly-laundered sheet all along. Had you fooled, eh?

To satisfy the unimaginative realists, the phony ghost trappings of white sheets and tape-recorded moans are replaced in *Mark of the Vampire* by a hypodermic needle which siphons blood from various corpses to simulate

MARK OF THE VAMPIRE. Lugosi was a phony creature of the night.

vampiric murders. Lugosi, it turns out in the end, is merely an actor hired to portray a vampire, thereby furthering the schemes and displacing any suspicion of the actual and non-supernatural villain.

Just as the name Dracula was derived by Bram Stoker from the Slavic term "dracul" meaning devil, Lugosi is given the name Count *Mora*, as in "death" (mortuary, moratorium, morgue, mortician, mortgage, etc.), to validate his macabre doings in *Mark of the Vampire*. Count Mora's counterpart in the earlier *London After*

Midnight was named "Mooney," hardly an impressive cognomen. In *Mark of the Vampire*, Lugosi is joined by Carol Borland who plays his daughter (and another make-believe vampire) named Luna. The character corresponding with Luna in the silent *London After Midnight* was "Looney," and since Luna refers of course to the moon, we must keep in mind the fact that incidence of mental derangement is always logged higher on nights of the full moon. You see how everything falls neatly into place?

Remember, a few paragraphs back, the allusion to Lugosi being a virtually mute vampire? Well, that's because Bela *did* get to say his one short piece near the denouement. The ruse is up and, as the audience threatens to slash the screen with flattened popcorn boxes, we learn that Lugosi is not a vampire after all, but a mere actor, a charlatan mocking his performance in *Dracula*. Debasement of debasements! But here's how Bela explained it: "This vampire business has given me a great idea for a new act. Did you watch me? I gave all of me. I was greater than any *real* vampire!"

We beg to differ, but neither do we wish to completely disparage either Lugosi's individual performance or *Mark of the Vampire* as a whole. Aside from the "natural explanation of supernatural phenomena" schtick, the script is quite adequate — almost exemplary for its time. Written by Guy Endore (who, you may remember, was the author of the gothic novel *Werewo of Paris*) and Bernard Schubert, it thankfully avoids th pitfall Browning and scripter Garrett Fort succumbed in *Dracula*, emerging as a bonafide movie rather than statically filmed stage play. *Mark of the Vampire* make excellent use of exterior scenes (the movie is set in th contemporary — 1935 then — Balkan-sequestere village of Visoka in Czechoslavakia), and is graced wi more fluidly cinematic camerawork than is characterist of Browning. Replete with peasants fleeing sunset le they be apprehended by nefarious vampires and oth nightgaunt permutations, *Mark of the Vampire* distills sufficiently tight essence of mood and foreboding. Th the most charitable thing one can say for Lugosi hobbled performance is that he tried his best to be hea through a figurative mouth gag is a commentary not c Lugosi, but on Tod Browning and his inexplicab insistence that audiences could not swallow the conce of a real vampire. After all, he'd directed one only fo years earlier in *Dracula*.

That brings us up to Lugosi's second non-Dracul vampire film, the 1941 Producers Releasing Corporatio feature, *The Devil Bat*. Perhaps we're hedging a bit her as Lugosi does not actually portray a vampire but, at th opposite gradient of the miscreant spectrum, a archetypal mad scientist named Dr. Paul Carruthers wh weans several specimens of colossally-proportione

COLLECTOR'S ITEM. An autographed photo of Bela Lugosi.

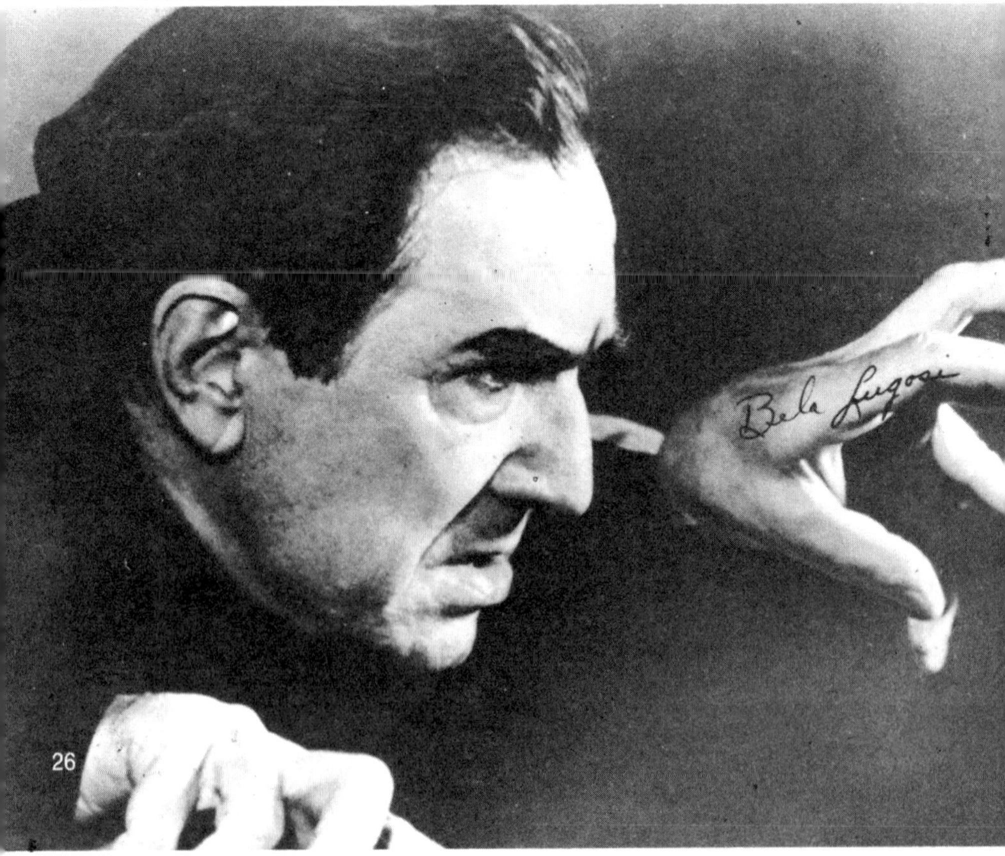
Bela Lugosi
26

ampire bats to serve as the middle men in his dreary spree of murders. He surreptitiously smears a little ab'll-do-ya bat-attracting substance on the throats of whomever he wishes killed. The bats catch the scent nd — presto — glom onto poor slobs who should've realized their body odor couldn't have been *that* bad. The film, exhibiting at least *some* consideration for its audience, mercifully ends as Lugosi inadvertently slops some of the come-hither fragrance on his own person whilst the bats happen to be nose-twitchingly free. Scrumptious.

We could say *The Devil Bat* is a minor and inauspicious film crippled by a destitute production budget ... but we'd prefer to say only that it stinks.

THE DEVIL BAT. Murder by vampire bat was the basis of this 1941 film.

The third item on our itinerary isn't much better — or worse. Also released in '41, *Spooks Run Wild* is a boringly tame offering from Monogram, a studio notorious for cheapie quickies and other sundry items. Lugosi, playing a stage magician by the name of Nardo, becomes embroiled in the strained antics of the East Side Kids (sort of a low-budget Dead End Kids/Bowery Boys social club) who momentarily mistake the prestidigitator for a mad killer currently on the loose. We're definitely guilty of hedging here, because the only resemblance to Dracula or vampires in this film is the fact that Lugosi is attired in his midnight-black satin cape. This one should be missed at all costs, even if it's sandwiched between a triple bill with *Citizen Kane* and *The Godfather*.

Now we come to *Return of the Vampire*, the fourth Lugosi-vampire film on our list, and it's a minor-grade goodie from Columbia, circa 1943. This one, if not for Universal's retention of the Dracula rights, evinces indications that it might possibly have been a sequel to the original *Dracula*. Forbidden the Dracula name and attendant mystique, Columbia dubbed Lugosi's vampiric character Armand Tesla and did (almost) the best under prevailing circumstances. After dying and rising from his grave as a vampire, Tesla is spiked through the heart with an iron stake wielded by two sentinels of altruism, an old guy and a young girl. Then along comes the blitz of World War II which blows Tesla's crypt wide open.

RETURN OF THE VAMPIRE. Lugosi as Armand Tesla.

Two unwitting Civil Defense volunteers in the guise of "comic relief" and *deus ex machina* wander by and extract the stake from Tesla's exposed corpse — subsequently fleeing in exaggerated terror when the corpse returns to life, or, at least, úndeath. Now Tesla's back in circulation; he conscripts the services of his former lackey, Andreas Obry (played by Matt Willis) who, incidentally, happens to be a werewolf on the side. Together, they set out to inflict vengeance upon the one surviving (young girl) altruist who had wielded that iron

RETURN OF THE VAMPIRE. One of Lugosi's best vampire films.

27

89

stake. But just as Tesla manages to inveigle his way into his former murderess' home and all is proceeding according to plan, irony strikes, couched in poetic justice. Another bomb (it was a bomb, remember, which opened Tesla's crypt, thereby providing for his resurrection) strikes, knocking Tesla for a cold loop into oblivion. When he awakens, he finds himself outside in the midst of getting a severe sunburn with his female foe hovering over him, anxious to do an encore with the stake. He dies, and disintegrates.

While Lugosi's matchless charisma is exerted in full force here, *Return of the Vampire* suffers a plethora of debilities — not the least of which are negligible production values and vacuous performances on the part of the other players. Nevertheless, a worthwhile film for Lugosi adherents. It might be mentioned that *Return of the Vampire's* director, Lew Landers, was also responsible for another Lugosi chiller (in a team-up with Boris Karloff), *The Raven.*

OLD MOTHER RILEY MEETS THE VAMPIRE. The title was mercifully changed to My Son, the Vampire in America.

THE RAVEN. Lugosi appeared with Boris Karloff in this chiller.

Cut to England, 1952. Lugosi is sadly near the end of his career and his life, and they have to go and pick him up with something like *Old Mother Riley Meets the Vampire*, an ineffectual stab at horror comedy which would have drawn nothing but sneers from Abbott and Costello. Finally released in America in 1964, under the equally insipid title, *My Son, the Vampire*, it is at once a lesson in dismal film-making and a soporific to soothe nerves jangled by *Sesame Street* and *Lassie* reruns. Lugosi plays a megalomaniac bent on dominating the world if only his delusions of being a vampire don't interfere. He spends his days asleep in a two-pillow coffin, rising at night to vociferously vow the total annihilation of Earth's combined defenses. (A study

of Hitler as a vampire?) His global *putsch*, however, is to be accomplished by preposterous scientific methods and his actual consumption of blood is only inferred. He seems whacko enough to drink the stuff, but we never see it and, if we did, it'd probably come by the six-pack and not the pulsing vein. The cruelest ignominy of all is that Lugosi's expansive campaign is snuffed at the wick by the irascible and doughty old Mother Riley, in conjunction with the local constabulary, during a hackneyed shootout finale. Lugosi is *arrested!*

Lugosi's sixth and final association with vampiric roles outside of the Dracula characterization is a tragic epitaph and it's chiselled: *Plan Nine from Outer Space.* We're straddling the hedge again, as Lugosi only *looks* like a vampire; he's actually a somnambulistic "Ghoul Man" created by a repercussion of outer space invaders' plan number nine. While most film freaks are relieved to have been spared the other eight, there are some who regard this film with a cultishly reverent attitude. After all, it was made in the year of Lugosi's death (1956, but not theatrically released until '59) and marks his final film appearance in any role. And besides, they say, the flick's so bad it's good — sort of like *The Manster* or Roger Corman's 36-hour masterpiece, *Little Shop of Horrors.*

MY SON THE VAMPIRE. Lugosi and director Alex Gordon on the set.

But let's not make excuses; the film is a prime exponent of unmitigated dreck, saved from total mediocrity only by virtue of its utter worthlessness. The only conceivable notion for seeking this film out might be to assuage rising masochistic tendencies and other aberrant proclivities. In other words, to indulge in punishment. Is there *any* redeeming factor to be found anywhere in *Plan Nine from Outer Space*, any subliminal interest to it at all, you ask? Well, you can see some excerpted (stolen) spliced scenes of Lugosi from the original *Dracula*. And you can chortle over the lame attempts to disguise the

THE BLACK CAT. Lugosi as the Cat's henchman.

That Lugosi is still universally remembered as the ubiquitous Count Dracula powerfully attests to the impact engendered by his single serious film performance in that role. It's a role which will forever associate his memory with vampires, superceding the estimable talents displayed in non-vampire films such as *The Raven, The Black Cat, Chandu the Magician, Murders in the Rue Morgue, Ninotchka,* and a host of others.

It's a fact which can hardly be repudiated: Bela Lugosi was Dracula.

CHANDU THE MAGICIAN.
Lugosi on the side of the angels.

FINIS

MURDERS IN THE RUE MORGUE. The Edgar Allan Poe classic.

fact that Lugosi was available for only the initial portion of the film (the rest of the time they employed an extra who perpetually held the cape drawn across his face). And, if you really want to, you can glimpse Carol Borland again (remember Luna?) in a vapid role which might have served as the progenitor for Carolyn Jones' Morticia on *The Addams Family*.

But that's about it.

In summation, then, it appears that Bela Lugosi's career was not as distinguished by vampire roles as posterity (and nostalgia-steeped memory) would have it. There was *Dracula, Mark of the Vampire,* and *Return of the Vampire*. The rest, with the possible exception of *Abbott and Costello Meet Frankenstein* (and this might be discounted as essentially a comedy), are bleak travesties.

There are worlds beyond our own.
Some are wondrous to behold.
Others are terrible to imagine.
So if the vampires of our
world are things to be feared . . .

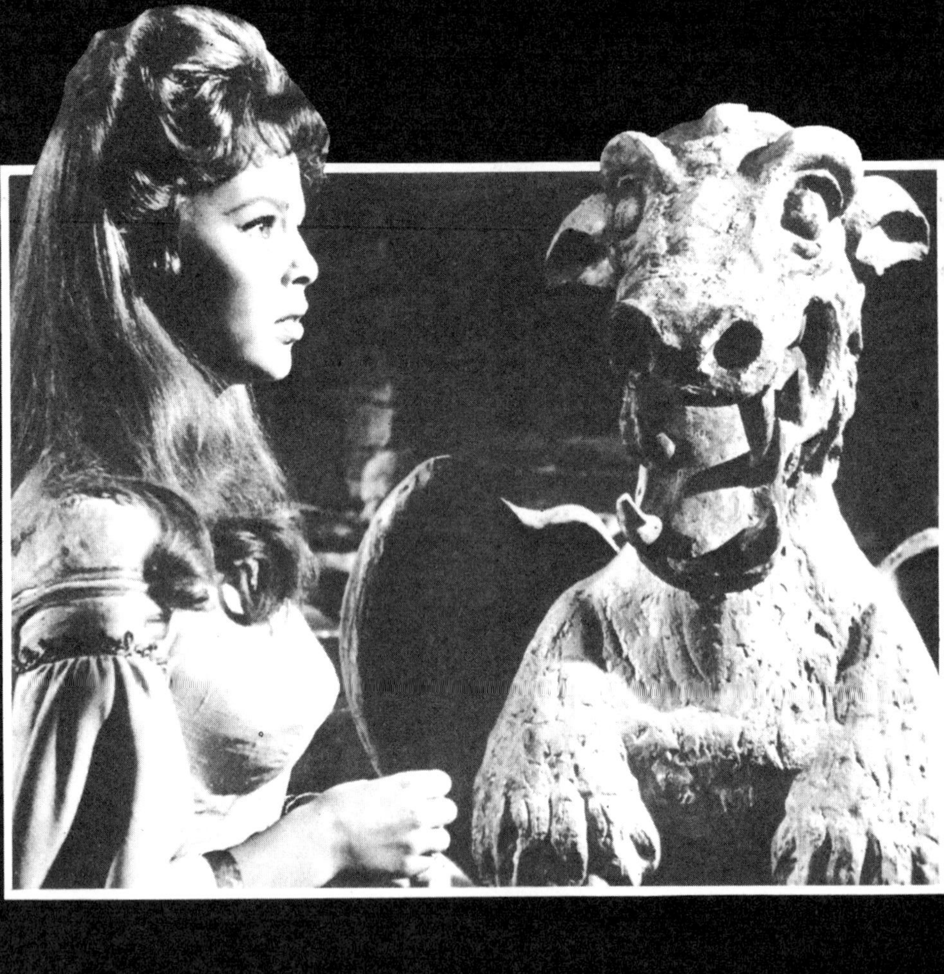

. . . what of the blood-preyers of other, alien dimensions? And, more to the point, how does one fight *them*?

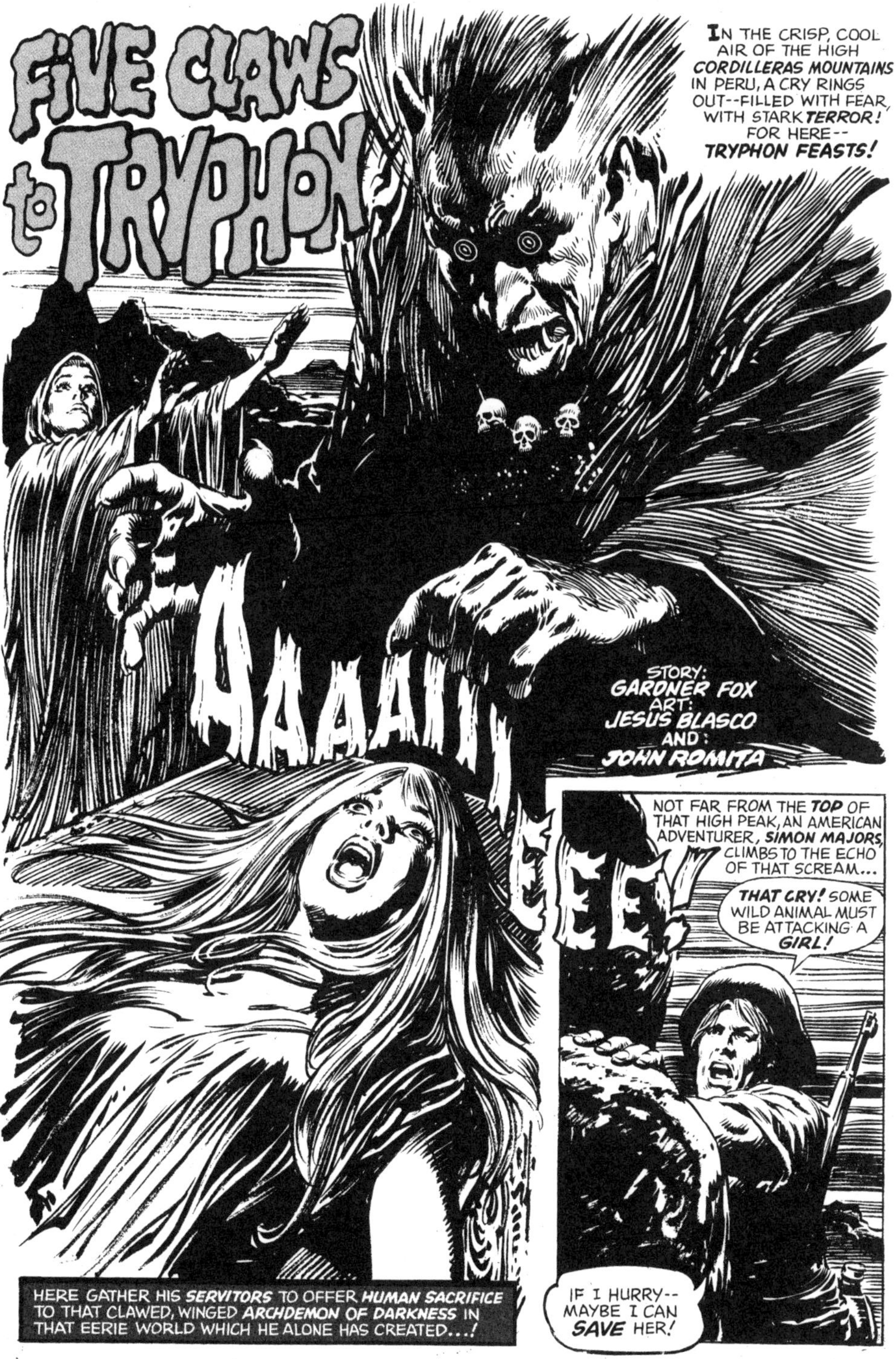
FIVE CLAWS to TRYPHON
IN THE CRISP, COOL AIR OF THE HIGH CORDILLERAS MOUNTAINS IN PERU, A CRY RINGS OUT--FILLED WITH FEAR, WITH STARK TERROR! FOR HERE-- TRYPHON FEASTS!
AAAAIIEEE!
STORY: GARDNER FOX ART: JESUS BLASCO AND: JOHN ROMITA
HERE GATHER HIS SERVITORS TO OFFER HUMAN SACRIFICE TO THAT CLAWED, WINGED ARCHDEMON OF DARKNESS IN THAT EERIE WORLD WHICH HE ALONE HAS CREATED...!
NOT FAR FROM THE TOP OF THAT HIGH PEAK, AN AMERICAN ADVENTURER, SIMON MAJORS, CLIMBS TO THE ECHO OF THAT SCREAM...
THAT CRY! SOME WILD ANIMAL MUST BE ATTACKING A GIRL!
IF I HURRY-- MAYBE I CAN SAVE HER!

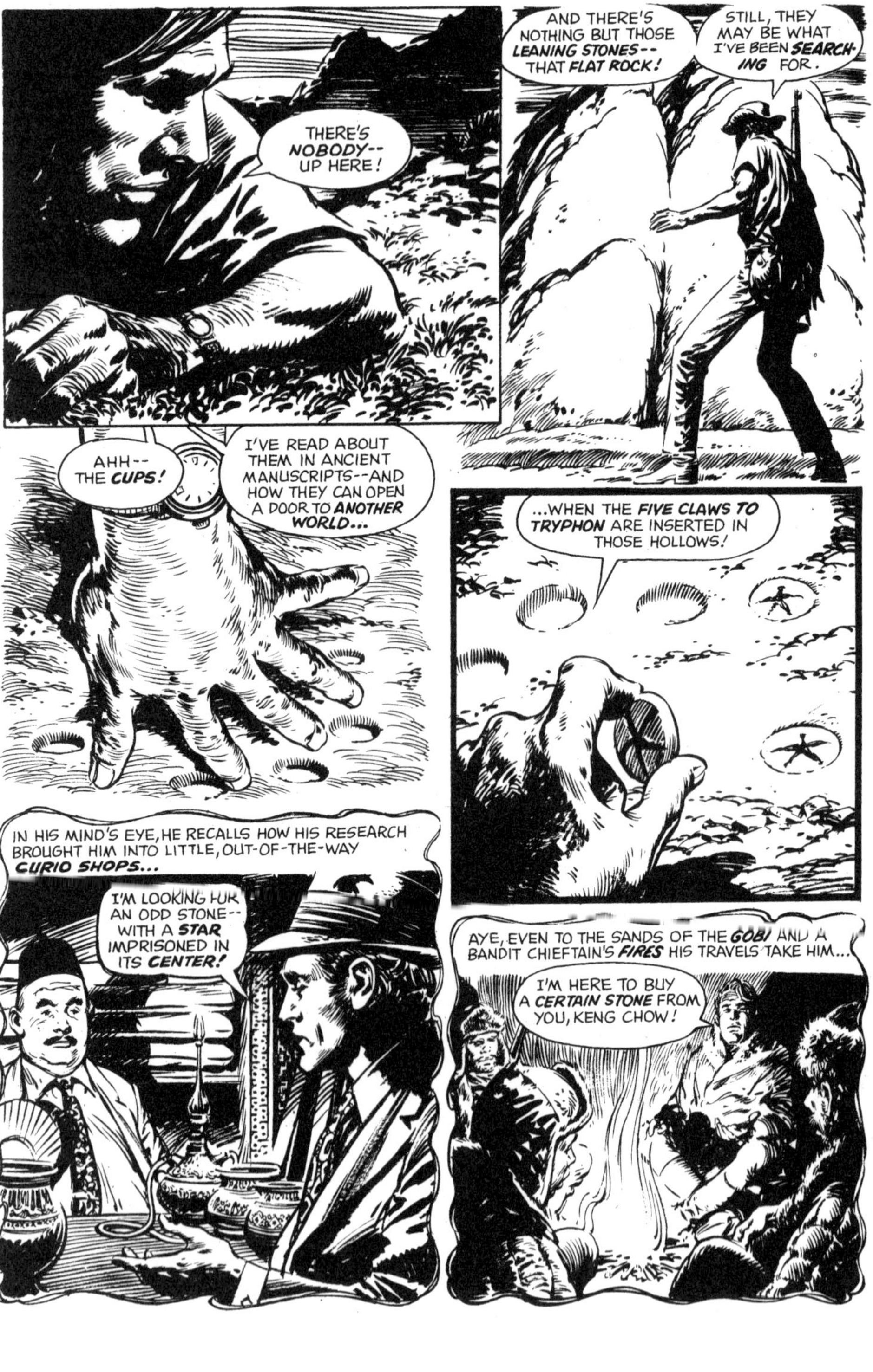
THERE'S NOBODY-- UP HERE!
AND THERE'S NOTHING BUT THOSE LEANING STONES-- THAT FLAT ROCK!
STILL, THEY MAY BE WHAT I'VE BEEN SEARCHING FOR.
AHH-- THE CUPS!
I'VE READ ABOUT THEM IN ANCIENT MANUSCRIPTS--AND HOW THEY CAN OPEN A DOOR TO ANOTHER WORLD...
...WHEN THE FIVE CLAWS TO TRYPHON ARE INSERTED IN THOSE HOLLOWS!
IN HIS MIND'S EYE, HE RECALLS HOW HIS RESEARCH BROUGHT HIM INTO LITTLE, OUT-OF-THE-WAY CURIO SHOPS...
I'M LOOKING FOR AN ODD STONE-- WITH A STAR IMPRISONED IN ITS CENTER!
AYE, EVEN TO THE SANDS OF THE GOBI AND A BANDIT CHIEFTAIN'S FIRES HIS TRAVELS TAKE HIM...
I'M HERE TO BUY A CERTAIN STONE FROM YOU, KENG CHOW!

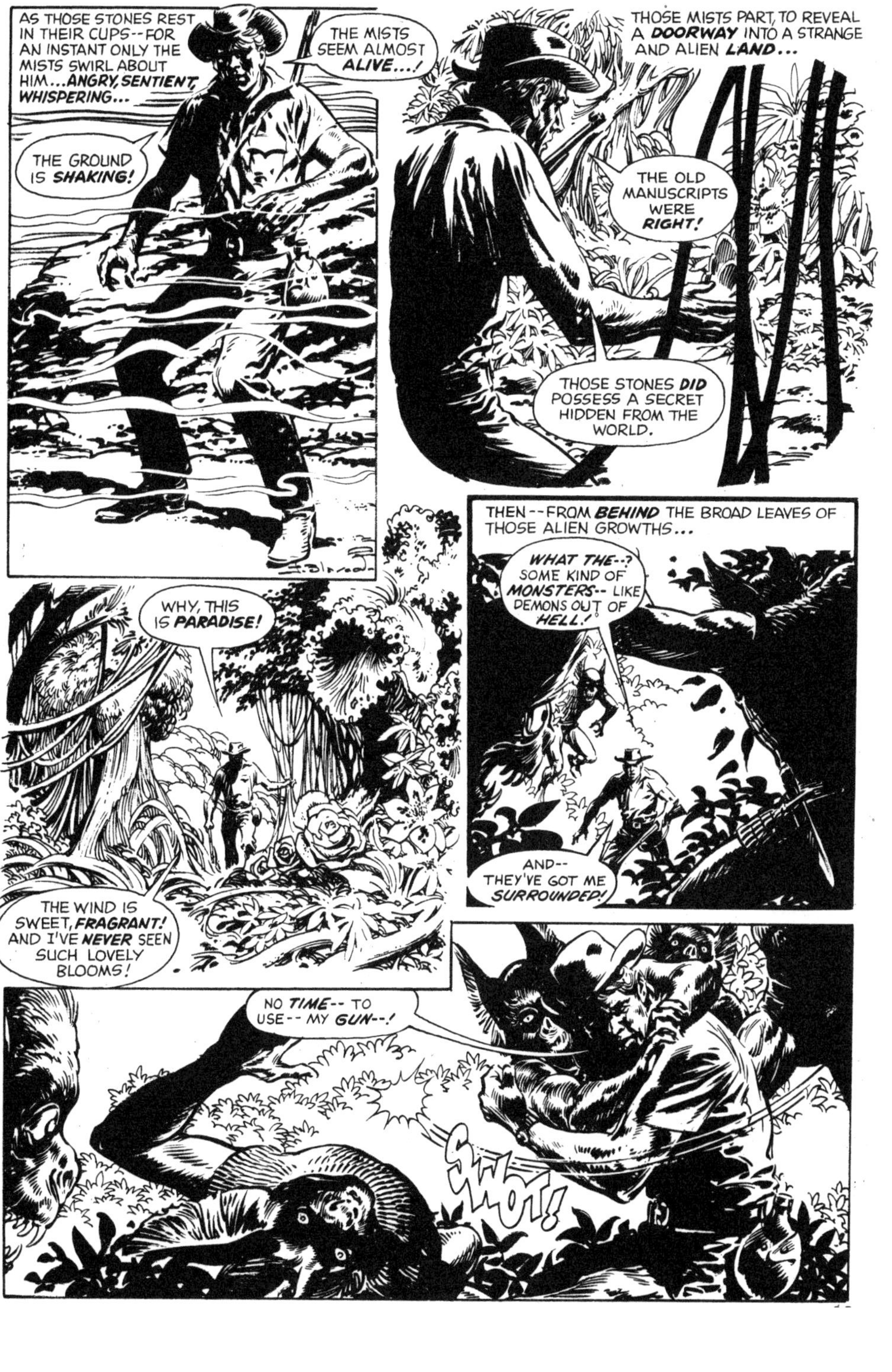
AS THOSE STONES REST IN THEIR CUPS--FOR AN INSTANT ONLY THE MISTS SWIRL ABOUT HIM...ANGRY, SENTIENT, WHISPERING...
THE MISTS SEEM ALMOST ALIVE...!
THE GROUND IS SHAKING!
THOSE MISTS PART, TO REVEAL A DOORWAY INTO A STRANGE AND ALIEN LAND...
THE OLD MANUSCRIPTS WERE RIGHT!
THOSE STONES DID POSSESS A SECRET HIDDEN FROM THE WORLD.
WHY, THIS IS PARADISE!
THE WIND IS SWEET, FRAGRANT! AND I'VE NEVER SEEN SUCH LOVELY BLOOMS!
THEN--FROM BEHIND THE BROAD LEAVES OF THOSE ALIEN GROWTHS...
WHAT THE--? SOME KIND OF MONSTERS-- LIKE DEMONS OUT OF HELL!
AND-- THEY'VE GOT ME SURROUNDED!
NO TIME-- TO USE-- MY GUN--!
SWOT!

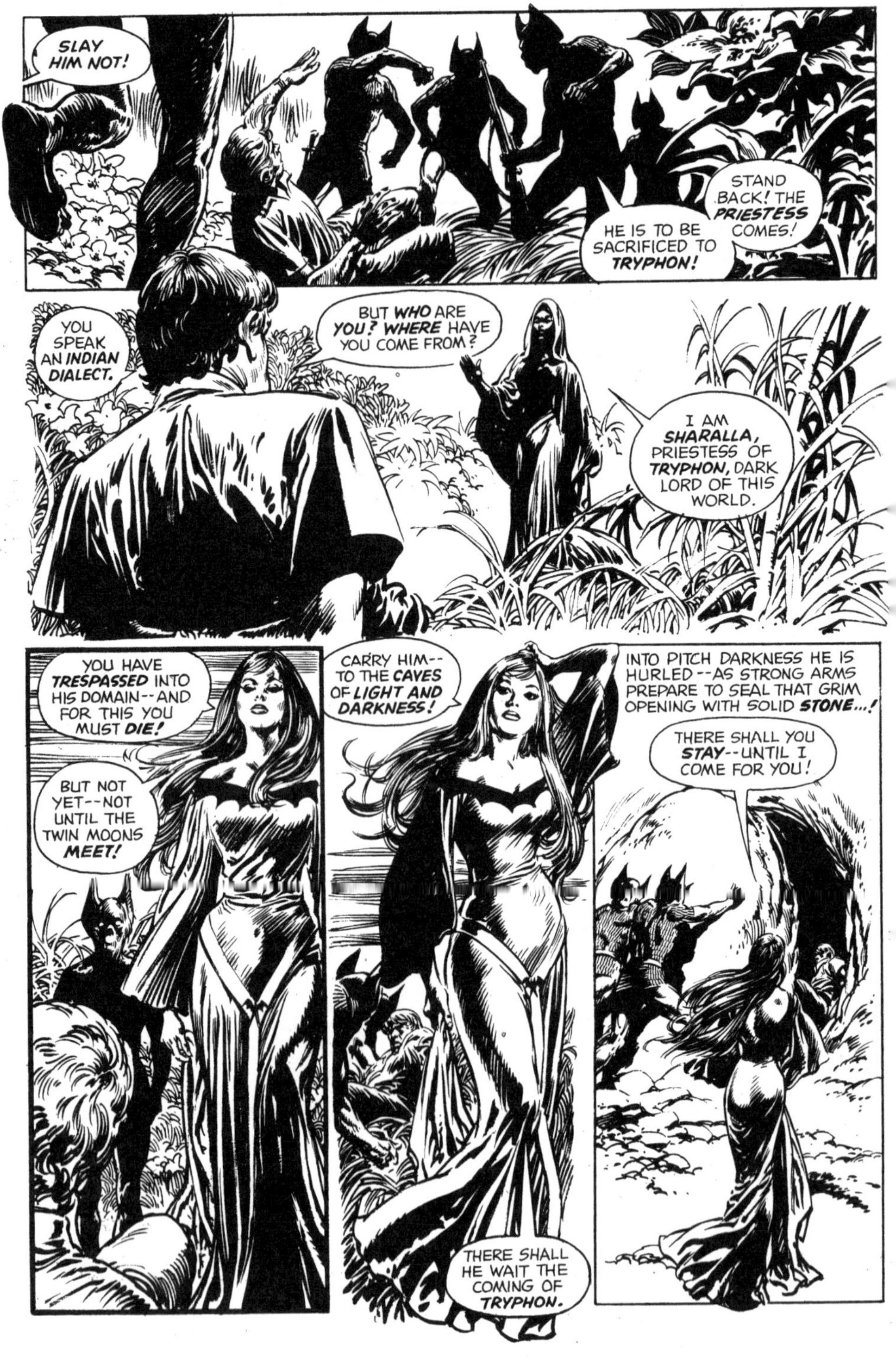
SLAY HIM NOT!
STAND BACK! THE PRIESTESS COMES!
HE IS TO BE SACRIFICED TO TRYPHON!
YOU SPEAK AN INDIAN DIALECT.
BUT WHO ARE YOU? WHERE HAVE YOU COME FROM?
I AM SHARALLA, PRIESTESS OF TRYPHON, DARK LORD OF THIS WORLD.
YOU HAVE TRESPASSED INTO HIS DOMAIN--AND FOR THIS YOU MUST DIE!
BUT NOT YET--NOT UNTIL THE TWIN MOONS MEET!
CARRY HIM--TO THE CAVES OF LIGHT AND DARKNESS!
THERE SHALL HE WAIT THE COMING OF TRYPHON.
INTO PITCH DARKNESS HE IS HURLED--AS STRONG ARMS PREPARE TO SEAL THAT GRIM OPENING WITH SOLID STONE...!
THERE SHALL YOU STAY--UNTIL I COME FOR YOU!

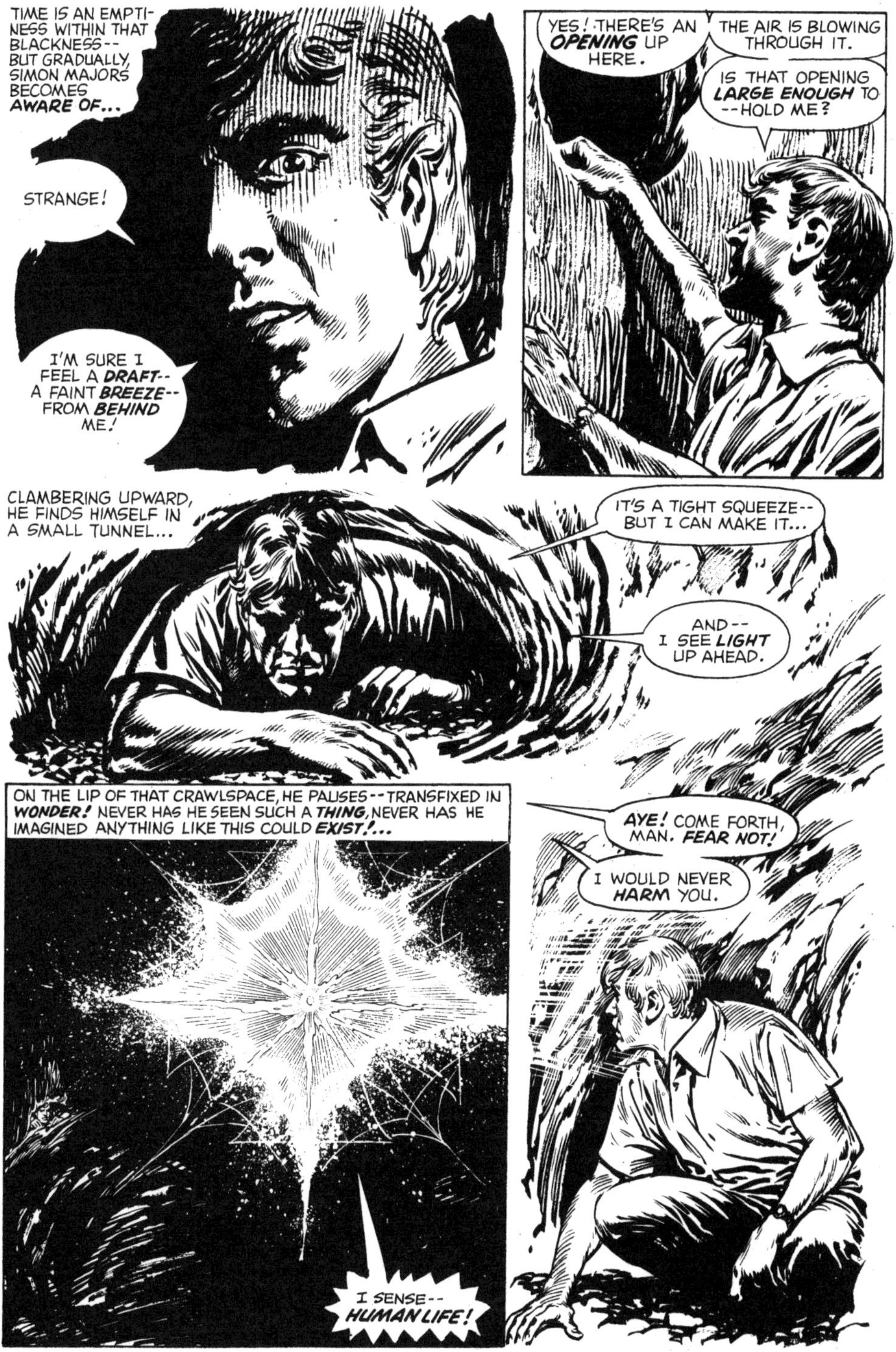
TIME IS AN EMPTINESS WITHIN THAT BLACKNESS-- BUT GRADUALLY, SIMON MAJORS BECOMES AWARE OF...
STRANGE!
I'M SURE I FEEL A DRAFT-- A FAINT BREEZE-- FROM BEHIND ME!
YES! THERE'S AN OPENING UP HERE.
THE AIR IS BLOWING THROUGH IT.
IS THAT OPENING LARGE ENOUGH TO --HOLD ME?
CLAMBERING UPWARD, HE FINDS HIMSELF IN A SMALL TUNNEL...
IT'S A TIGHT SQUEEZE-- BUT I CAN MAKE IT...
AND-- I SEE LIGHT UP AHEAD.
ON THE LIP OF THAT CRAWLSPACE, HE PAUSES--TRANSFIXED IN WONDER! NEVER HAS HE SEEN SUCH A THING, NEVER HAS HE IMAGINED ANYTHING LIKE THIS COULD EXIST!...
I SENSE-- HUMAN LIFE!
AYE! COME FORTH, MAN. FEAR NOT!
I WOULD NEVER HARM YOU.

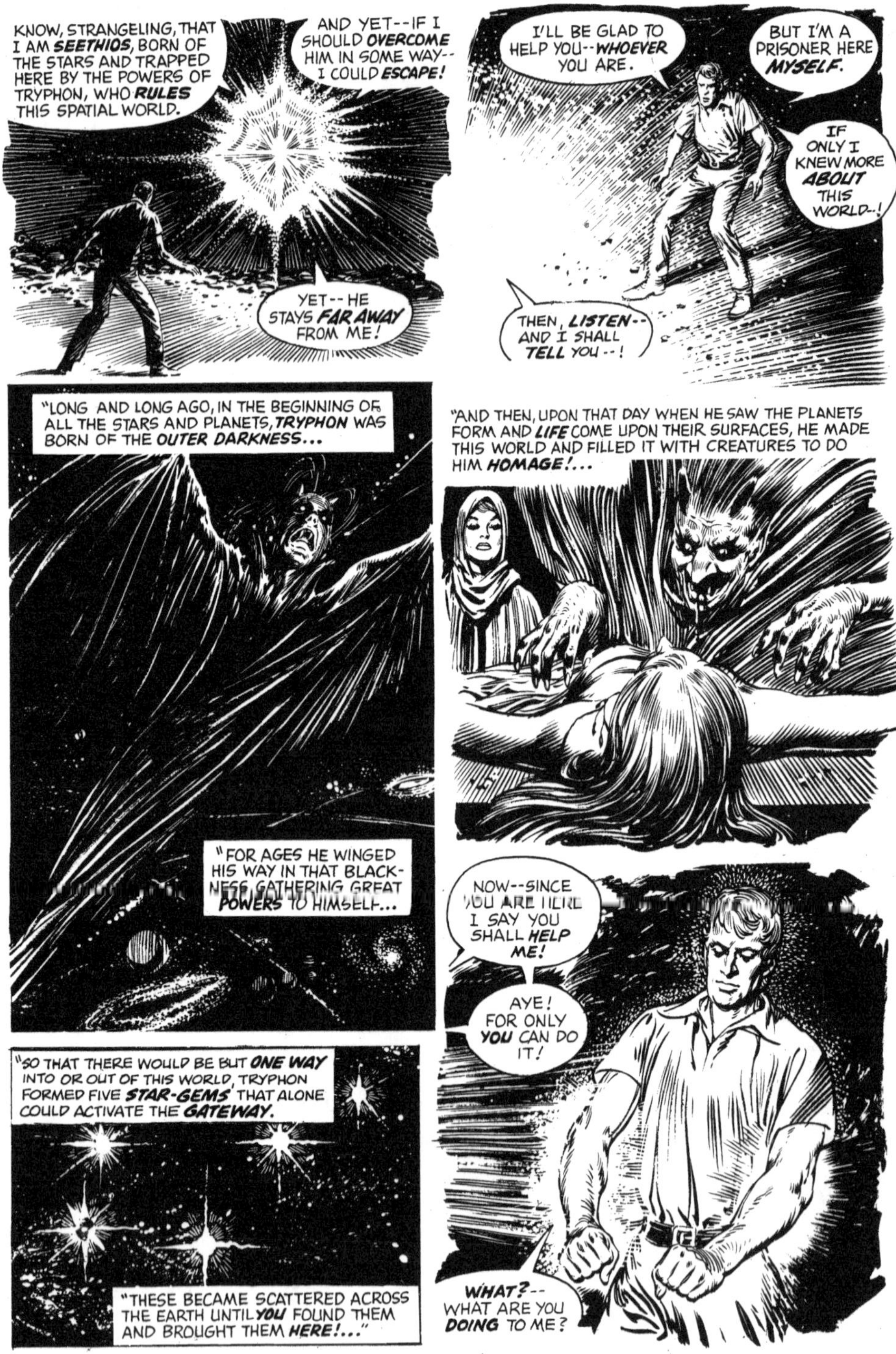
KNOW, STRANGELING, THAT I AM SEETHIOS, BORN OF THE STARS AND TRAPPED HERE BY THE POWERS OF TRYPHON, WHO RULES THIS SPATIAL WORLD.
AND YET--IF I SHOULD OVERCOME HIM IN SOME WAY--I COULD ESCAPE!
YET--HE STAYS FAR AWAY FROM ME!
I'LL BE GLAD TO HELP YOU--WHOEVER YOU ARE.
BUT I'M A PRISONER HERE MYSELF.
IF ONLY I KNEW MORE ABOUT THIS WORLD--!
THEN, LISTEN--AND I SHALL TELL YOU--!
"LONG AND LONG AGO, IN THE BEGINNING OF ALL THE STARS AND PLANETS, TRYPHON WAS BORN OF THE OUTER DARKNESS...
"FOR AGES HE WINGED HIS WAY IN THAT BLACKNESS GATHERING GREAT POWERS TO HIMSELF...
"AND THEN, UPON THAT DAY WHEN HE SAW THE PLANETS FORM AND LIFE COME UPON THEIR SURFACES, HE MADE THIS WORLD AND FILLED IT WITH CREATURES TO DO HIM HOMAGE!...
"SO THAT THERE WOULD BE BUT ONE WAY INTO OR OUT OF THIS WORLD, TRYPHON FORMED FIVE STAR-GEMS THAT ALONE COULD ACTIVATE THE GATEWAY.
"THESE BECAME SCATTERED ACROSS THE EARTH UNTIL YOU FOUND THEM AND BROUGHT THEM HERE!..."
NOW--SINCE YOU ARE HERE I SAY YOU SHALL HELP ME!
AYE! FOR ONLY YOU CAN DO IT!
WHAT?--WHAT ARE YOU DOING TO ME?

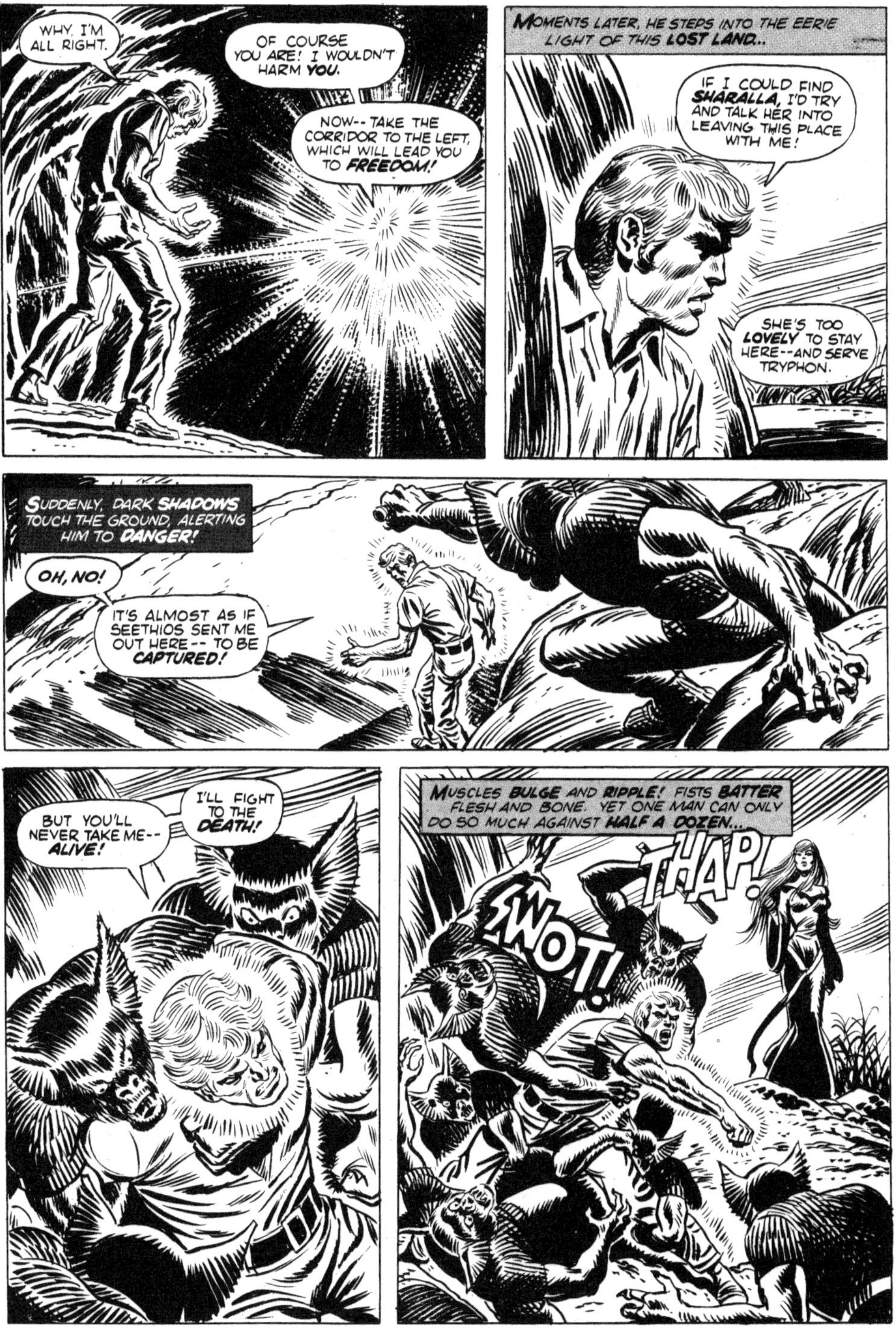
WHY, I'M ALL RIGHT.
OF COURSE YOU ARE! I WOULDN'T HARM YOU.
NOW-- TAKE THE CORRIDOR TO THE LEFT, WHICH WILL LEAD YOU TO FREEDOM!
MOMENTS LATER, HE STEPS INTO THE EERIE LIGHT OF THIS LOST LAND..
IF I COULD FIND SHARALLA, I'D TRY AND TALK HER INTO LEAVING THIS PLACE WITH ME!
SHE'S TOO LOVELY TO STAY HERE--AND SERVE TRYPHON.
SUDDENLY, DARK SHADOWS TOUCH THE GROUND, ALERTING HIM TO DANGER!
OH, NO!
IT'S ALMOST AS IF SEETHIOS SENT ME OUT HERE-- TO BE CAPTURED!
BUT YOU'LL NEVER TAKE ME-- ALIVE!
I'LL FIGHT TO THE DEATH!
MUSCLES BULGE AND RIPPLE! FISTS BATTER FLESH AND BONE. YET ONE MAN CAN ONLY DO SO MUCH AGAINST HALF A DOZEN...
THAP!
SWOT!

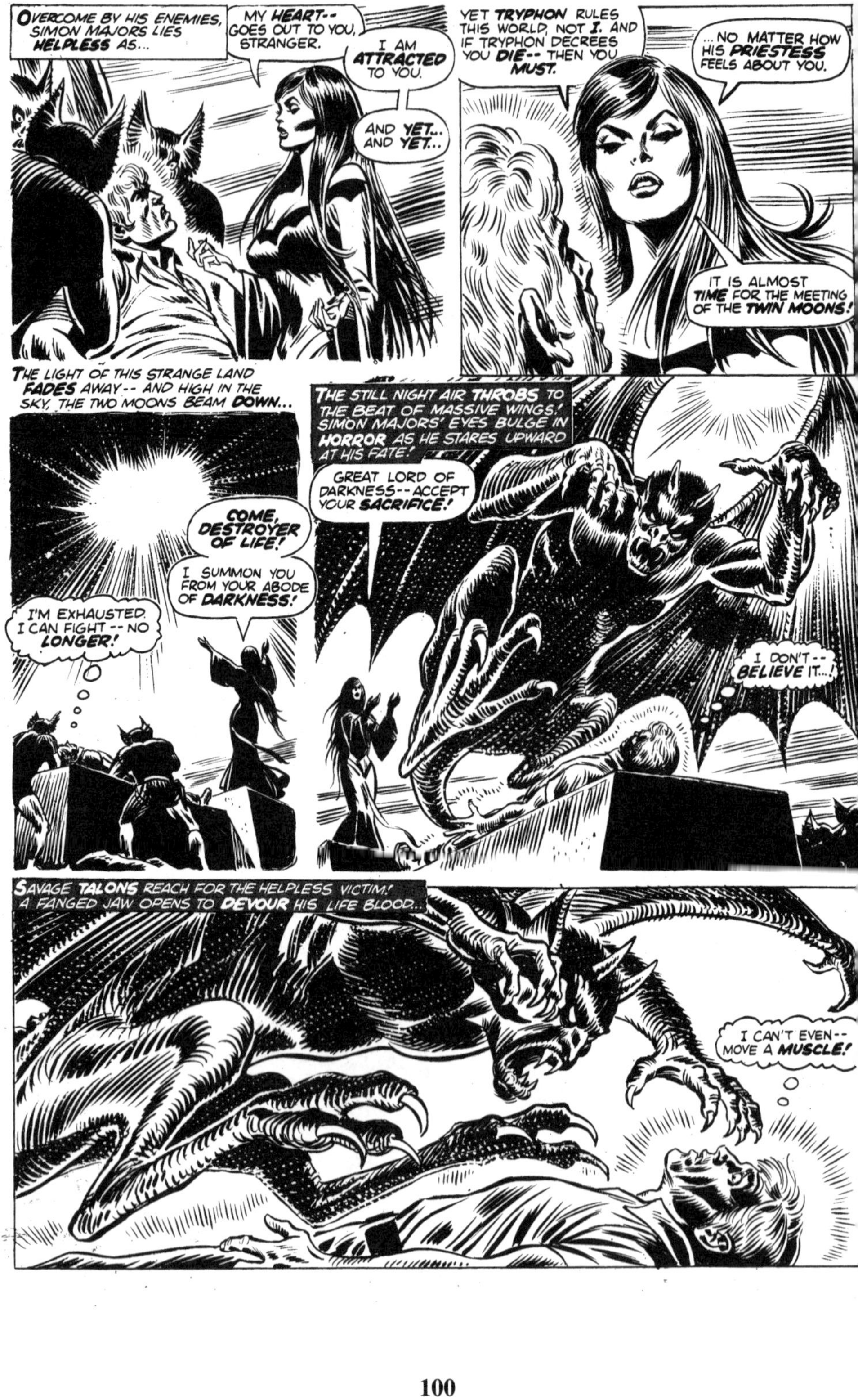
OVERCOME BY HIS ENEMIES, SIMON MAJORS LIES HELPLESS AS...
MY HEART-- GOES OUT TO YOU, STRANGER.
I AM ATTRACTED TO YOU.
AND YET... AND YET...
YET TRYPHON RULES THIS WORLD, NOT I. AND IF TRYPHON DECREES YOU DIE-- THEN YOU MUST.
...NO MATTER HOW HIS PRIESTESS FEELS ABOUT YOU.
IT IS ALMOST TIME FOR THE MEETING OF THE TWIN MOONS!
THE LIGHT OF THIS STRANGE LAND FADES AWAY-- AND HIGH IN THE SKY, THE TWO MOONS BEAM DOWN...
COME, DESTROYER OF LIFE!
I SUMMON YOU FROM YOUR ABODE OF DARKNESS!
I'M EXHAUSTED. I CAN FIGHT -- NO LONGER!
THE STILL NIGHT AIR THROBS TO THE BEAT OF MASSIVE WINGS! SIMON MAJORS' EYES BULGE IN HORROR AS HE STARES UPWARD AT HIS FATE!
GREAT LORD OF DARKNESS--ACCEPT YOUR SACRIFICE!
I DON'T -- BELIEVE IT...!
SAVAGE TALONS REACH FOR THE HELPLESS VICTIM! A FANGED JAW OPENS TO DEVOUR HIS LIFE BLOOD...
I CAN'T EVEN-- MOVE A MUSCLE!

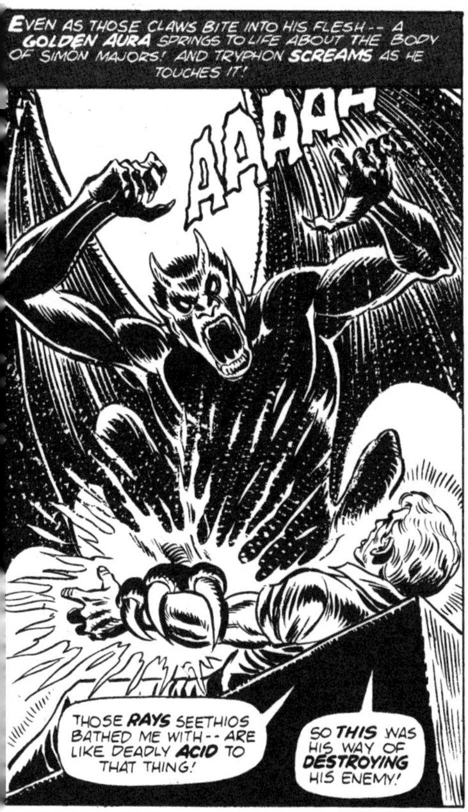
EVEN AS THOSE CLAWS BITE INTO HIS FLESH -- A GOLDEN AURA SPRINGS TO LIFE ABOUT THE BODY OF SIMON MAJORS! AND TRYPHON SCREAMS AS HE TOUCHES IT!
AAAAH
THOSE RAYS SEETHIOS BATHED ME WITH -- ARE LIKE DEADLY ACID TO THAT THING!
SO THIS WAS HIS WAY OF DESTROYING HIS ENEMY!

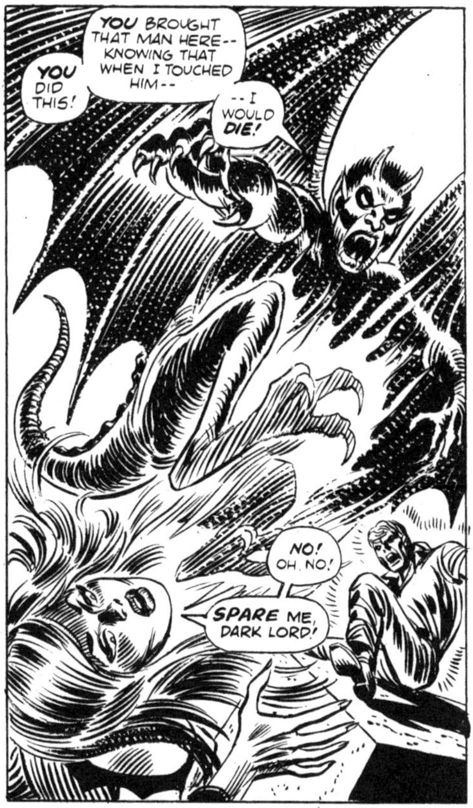
YOU DID THIS!
YOU BROUGHT THAT MAN HERE -- KNOWING THAT WHEN I TOUCHED HIM --
-- I WOULD DIE!
NO! OH, NO!
SPARE ME, DARK LORD!

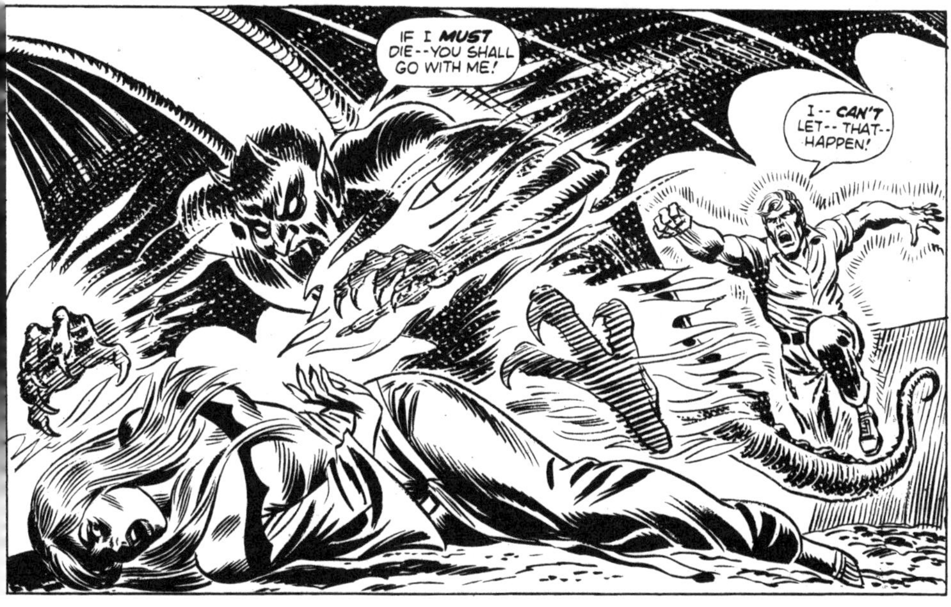
IF I MUST DIE -- YOU SHALL GO WITH ME!
I -- CAN'T LET -- THAT -- HAPPEN!

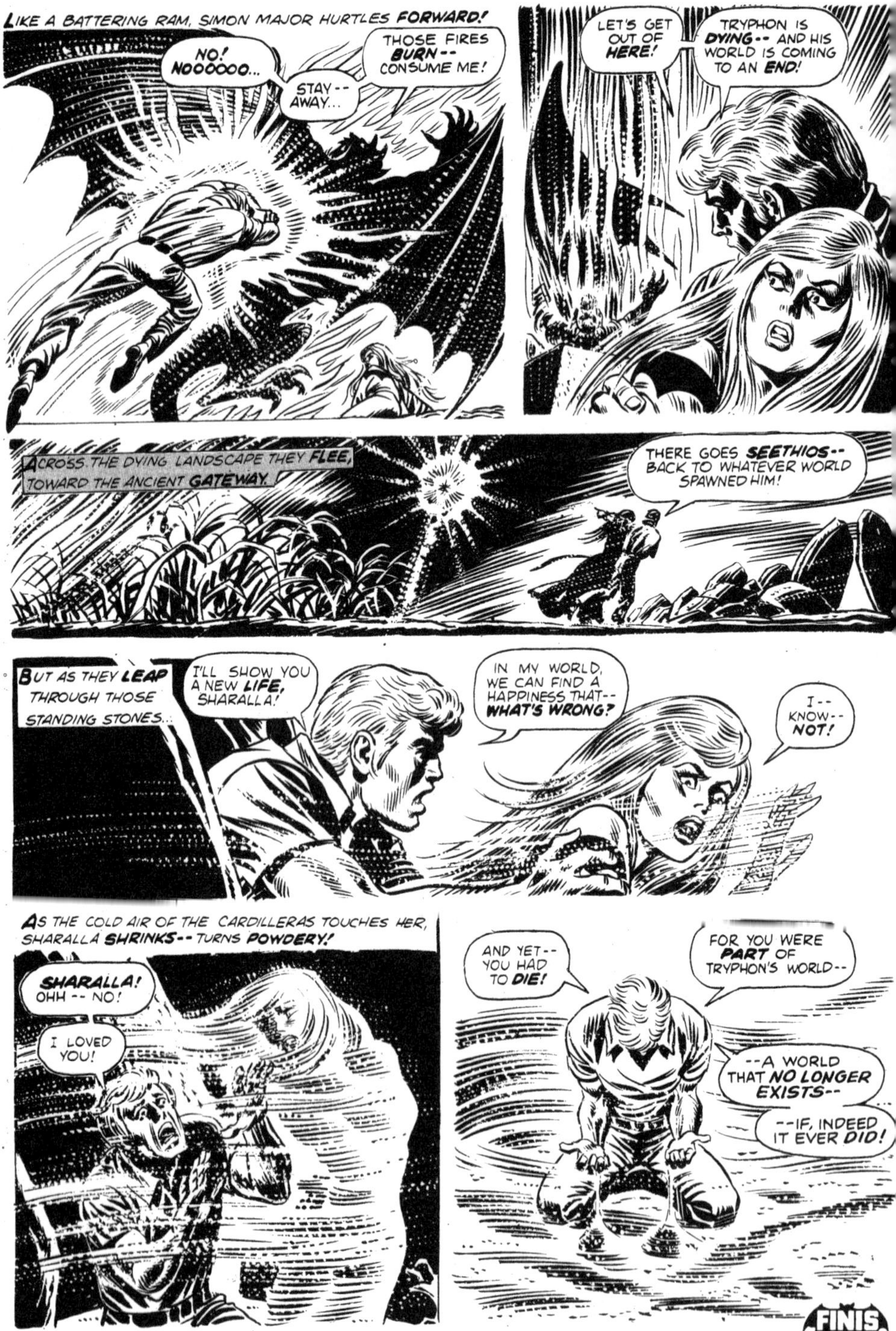
LIKE A BATTERING RAM, SIMON MAJOR HURTLES FORWARD!
NO! NOOOOOO...
STAY-- AWAY...
THOSE FIRES BURN-- CONSUME ME!
LET'S GET OUT OF HERE!
TRYPHON IS DYING-- AND HIS WORLD IS COMING TO AN END!
ACROSS THE DYING LANDSCAPE THEY FLEE, TOWARD THE ANCIENT GATEWAY.
THERE GOES SEETHIOS-- BACK TO WHATEVER WORLD SPAWNED HIM!
BUT AS THEY LEAP THROUGH THOSE STANDING STONES...
I'LL SHOW YOU A NEW LIFE, SHARALLA!
IN MY WORLD, WE CAN FIND A HAPPINESS THAT-- WHAT'S WRONG?
I-- KNOW-- NOT!
AS THE COLD AIR OF THE CARDILLERAS TOUCHES HER, SHARALLA SHRINKS-- TURNS POWDERY!
SHARALLA! OHH -- NO!
I LOVED YOU!
AND YET-- YOU HAD TO DIE!
FOR YOU WERE PART OF TRYPHON'S WORLD--
--A WORLD THAT NO LONGER EXISTS--
--IF, INDEED IT EVER DID!
FINIS

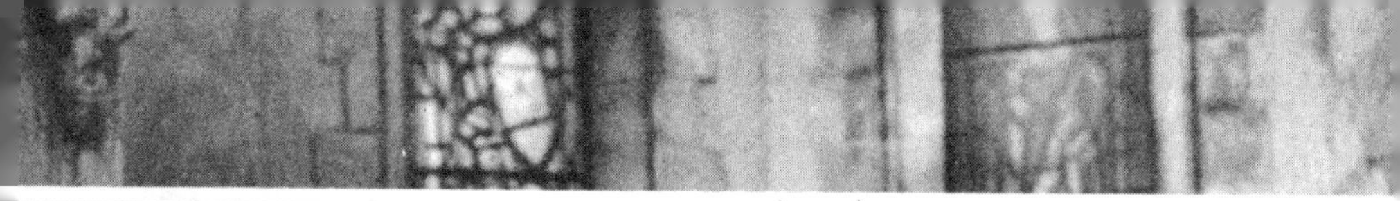

a Generation of Vampires:

art Two of A Five-Part Study of Montague Summers' THE VAMPIRE—HIS KITH AND KIN

Article by Chris Claremont

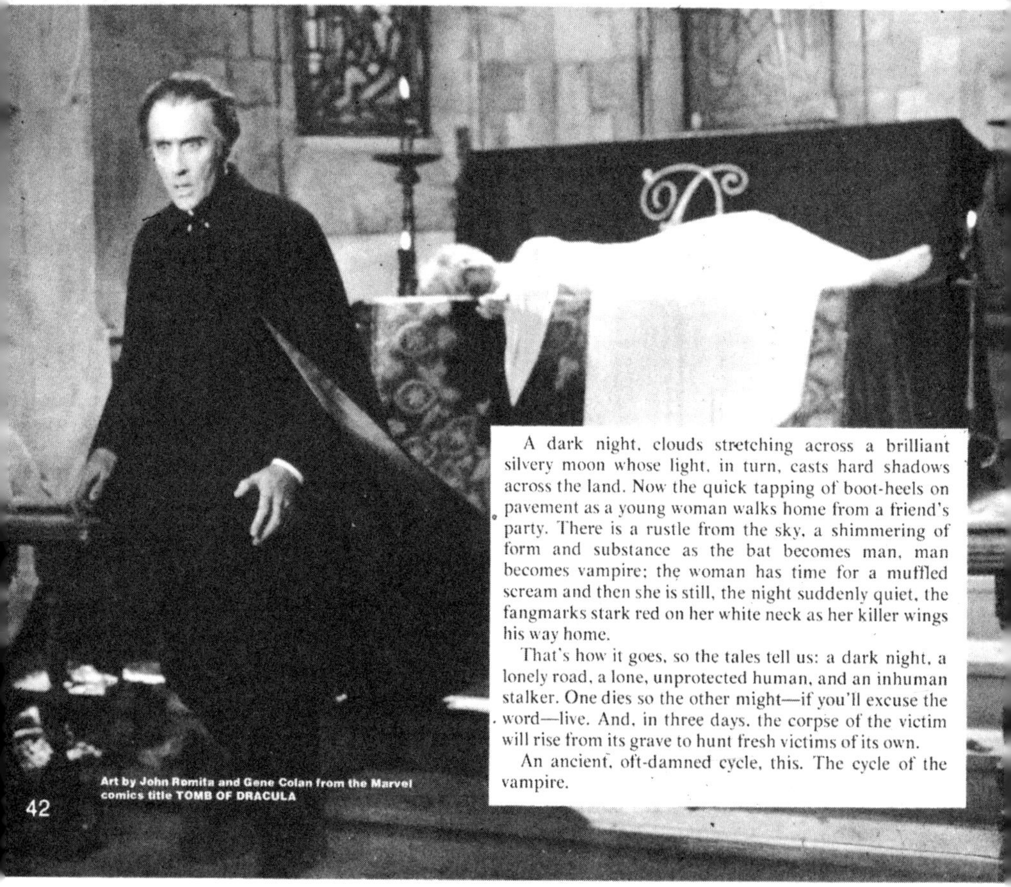

A dark night, clouds stretching across a brilliant silvery moon whose light, in turn, casts hard shadows across the land. Now the quick tapping of boot-heels on pavement as a young woman walks home from a friend's party. There is a rustle from the sky, a shimmering of form and substance as the bat becomes man, man becomes vampire; the woman has time for a muffled scream and then she is still, the night suddenly quiet, the fangmarks stark red on her white neck as her killer wings his way home.

That's how it goes, so the tales tell us: a dark night, a lonely road, a lone, unprotected human, and an inhuman stalker. One dies so the other might—if you'll excuse the word—live. And, in three days, the corpse of the victim will rise from its grave to hunt fresh victims of its own.

An ancient, oft-damned cycle, this. The cycle of the vampire.

Art by John Romita and Gene Colan from the Marvel comics title TOMB OF DRACULA

How did it begin? Where did the first vampire come from? Ever wonder about that? We know how this disease spreads and how to treat it—if you can call an execution a treatment; it's like cauterizing a wound; you begin to wonder if the cure isn't as bad as, or even worse than, the disease; but I digress—we don't know its ultimate cause.

Like so many other things in life, we can only guess, and hope we're right. Or pray we're wrong.

The vampire is supposed to be the penultimate daemonic force, chief honcho of the Satannic hierarchy, surpassed in power only by the Devil himself. When alive, he was a person who, to quote Summers' book, "...led a life of more than ordinary immorality and unbridled wickedness; a man of foul, gross and selfish passions, of evil ambitions, delighting in cruelty and blood." He was probably a highly-experienced adept of the Black Arts (a modern Thoth-Amon, for the Robert E. Howard freaks among us—and if you're not a REH fan, SAVAGE TALES #2, now on sale, will convert you!), a man whose twisted hates and desires kept pushing him on to greater and greater feats of depravity and murder, even after death. Such a man could easily come back from the grave, to wreak vengeance on those who might have crossed him in life.

Or the vampire might not be a man at all. He can be the offspring of a union between the Devil and a human witch—a Satannic variation of the legendary trysts between the Olympian gods and mortal women; indeed, part of the old medieval mythos is that the halfbreed born of this match—à la Rosemary's Baby—will be the Anti-Christ, the one who will lead the forces of Hell against those of Heaven at Armageddon.

If so, there may be a lot more to our night-winged friends than meets the eye.

There's another way a mortal man can find himself condemned to the vampiric path, a way that strikes a little closer to home than adept warlock/witches or trysting demons. It is said that a man who dies excommunicate can become a vampire.

Excommunication. It's an archaic word today, more at home in a creaking Errol Flynn epic wherein he takes on Basil Rathbone and the Spanish Navy, in that order, and creams them all, than in the technic hubbub of our modern, enlightened society. It's tucked away with those other best-selling giggle words: possession and exorcism. Like organized religion itself, it seems, many pay the word lip service and few really take it seriously.

Five hundred years ago, it could mean life and death.

Simply put, excommunication is an exile from the body of the "Holy Mother Church"—any church, oriental or occidental—the Catholics just seem to do it more publicly than most—and in a very real sense, the excommunicate becomes one of the living dead. He lives, yet to those around him he does not exist. He has no family, no friends, no rights; he is denied all sacraments of the Church. Should he die excommunicate, he cannot be buried on consecrated ground. And he dies already condemned before God; he has no chance to plead his case and try for Heaven. He must go to Hell. He cannot pass Go; he cannot collect his two hundred dollars (OUCH!).

Ideally, the only people hit with this ultimate punishment should have been those who truly deserved it, people whose actions while alive put them totally beyond the morality of human society. People like Gilles de Rais or

Vlad Tepes or Elisabeth Ba'thory; or their more modern counterpart, Heinrich Himmler and his late unlamented Austrian boss. As I said, this is the ultimate punishment the Church can levy on a soul; it was not intended to be meted out carelessly. Ever.

Men being men and all-too-fallible, it didn't always work out that way. As a U.S. Senator once said, "Extremism in the defense of virtue is no vice"; and what greater virtue could there be to defend than the virtue of God, right? Suffice to say, the Inquisition went about its work with a vengeance seldom rivaled since, outside of Washington Redskin title play-offs. People were bounced out for personal reasons, angering the wrong prelate at the wrong time, or political ones. Getting excommunicated became a fact of life for Henry II of England; he bought the Pope off both times. Henry VIII ignored the Pope and started his own church, and as far as anyone knows, both monarchs are still in their tombs.

If it were only a word, to be taken as lightly as we take much of life today, it wouldn't matter so much.

If it were only a word . . .

Almost a thousand years ago—1031 A.D., to be precise, during the so-called "Truce of God"—a French noble was excommunicated for "...his ceaseless rapine and unprecedented murders, his evil examples of a lewd and licentious life, his blasphemies and infidelity..."

104

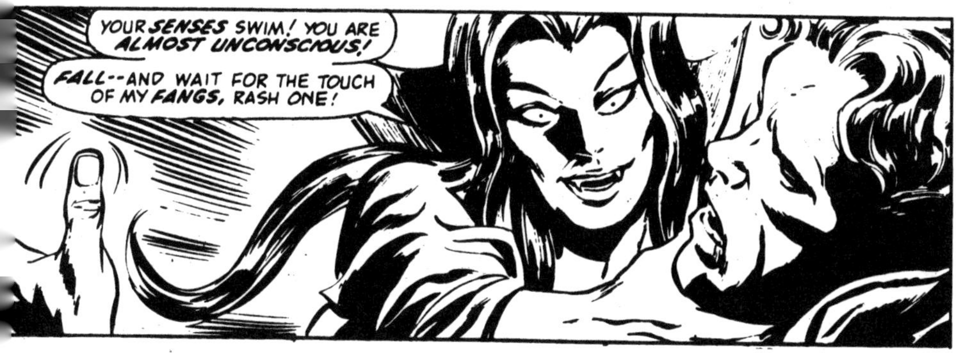
YOUR SENSES SWIM! YOU ARE ALMOST UNCONSCIOUS!
FALL--AND WAIT FOR THE TOUCH OF MY FANGS, RASH ONE!

The local Bishop intended this drastic step as an example to the other nobles of the district to cool it, or else. His gamble payed off far better than he'd dreamed.

Shortly after his excommunication, the Baron died in a midnight skirmish. His friends, expecting the Bishop to rescind his order and forgive the Baron, prepared an elaborate, formal, proper funeral, intending to bury their lord in the vault of his ancestors—hallowed ground. Then all would be well between his soul and the Church.

Not so. The Bishop refused to rescind his excommunication and he forbade their planned funeral. The Baron was damned and damned he would stay. So the Baron's men marched into the city and interred their lord in his tomb by force of arms, carefully sealing the sepulchre after them.

The next morning, the body was found naked in the market square, badly bruised and banged about, as if it had been violently thrown from its tomb. Yet, the tomb was untouched, the seals unbroken, the mortar still fresh and in place. Angry and confused, the soldiers interred their lord a second time, sealing the church itself this time, as well as the sepulchre; no one would enter the church this night.

No one did. And the Baron was found crumpled in the square just after daybreak, his body more smashed than before, the church and tomb still locked up tight.

The Baron's men were nothing if not determined. They tried to bury their lord five times, all told, and each time the corpse was found in the square the next morning. Finally, they took the hint and slipped away with their lord, burying the shattered, rotting carcass deep in some lonely patch of ground far removed from the holy soil.

There are other stories like this one, some of them witnessed, some heresay. And there are variations where the spirit of some dead soul was seen to leave the church during High Mass, to huddle fearfully in the nave until the service was over before returning to its coffin. These stories, too, have their witnesses.

For the curious, there was a well-known, extremely grisly rule of thumb one could follow to determine whether an interred corpse was excommunicate or not—and, by association, vampiric or not. Sanctified corpses decayed in a normal fashion; excommunicated ones didn't. There are cases of bodies being exhumed after they'd been in the ground a number of years—easily time enough for a once-proud manform to decay—only to find the corpse in perfect condition, looking as if it had just been laid to rest and not been down better than half a decade. And there are witnessed cases of a damned corpse abruptly disintegrating into dust at the precise moment its excommunication was lifted and its soul restored to God's grace.

A freak accident, some voice murmurs: hysterical superstition. Once, yes; twice, probably—especially over a period of centuries—but not a score or two of times, scattered across the length and bredth of Europe. There's too much there, the accounts too precise and similar, to dismiss them all with a smart quip and an airy gesture.

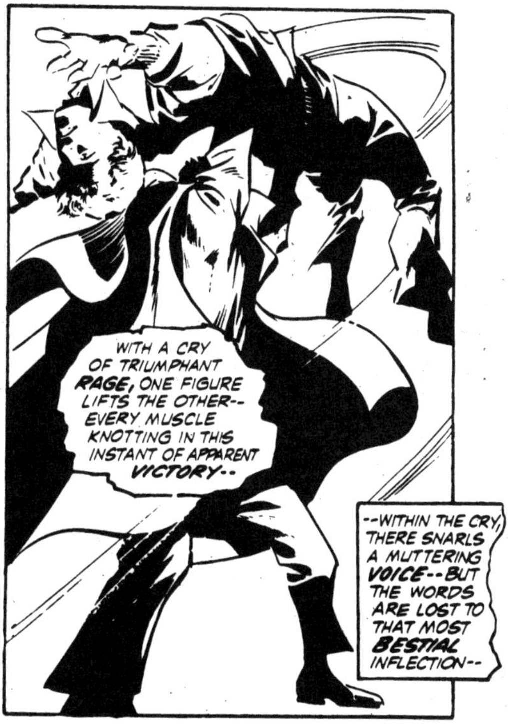
WITH A CRY OF TRIUMPHANT RAGE, ONE FIGURE LIFTS THE OTHER-- EVERY MUSCLE KNOTTING IN THIS INSTANT OF APPARENT VICTORY--
--WITHIN THE CRY, THERE SNARLS A MUTTERING VOICE--BUT THE WORDS ARE LOST TO THAT MOST BESTIAL INFLECTION--

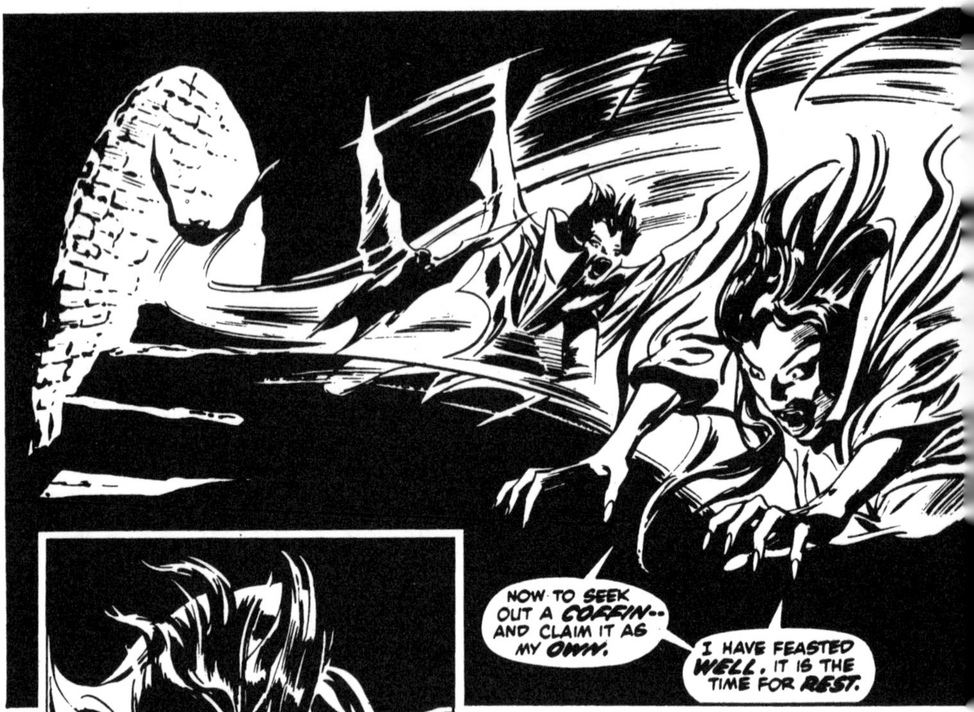
NOW TO SEEK OUT A COFFIN-- AND CLAIM IT AS MY OWN.
I HAVE FEASTED WELL, IT IS THE TIME FOR REST.

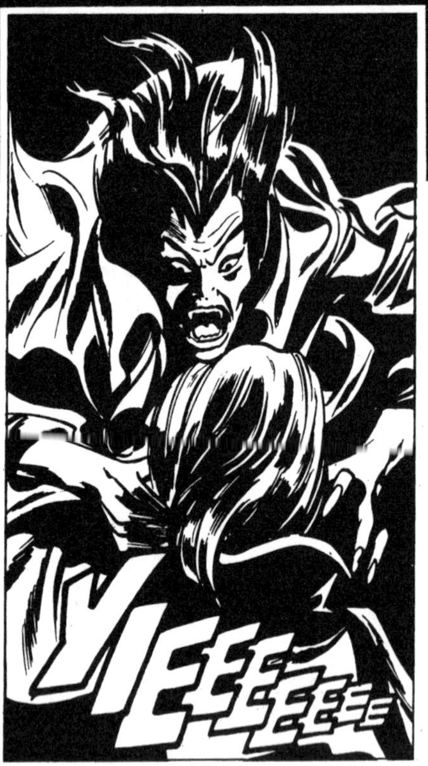

It is an easy step from here to the start of the vampire legend. Think a moment. If an excommunicated corpse —an evil man in life to have merited such a punishment —can be perfectly preserved after death, can it not also return to life, or a semblance of it? Especially if this corpse were that of a demon mage, an adept. It's easy to scoff now, reading this in a warm cozy house or apartment, your only worries how to survive the year without being mugged or over-taxed. But, just for a moment, put yourself in the place of some eleventh-century serf huddling in the damp, freezing darkness of his hut. A great forest is nearby, filled with hunting things, the castles nearby are filled with hunting men; you and your wife are poor, starving, illiterate; young people growing terribly old in a few brutally quick years. You are fair game for any knight eager to test a new sword, any hungry wolf or angry bear.

If something went bump in the darkness outside your door, would you open it and look to see what was there? Or would you huddle by the weak, not-very-warm fire with your family, cross in one hand, quater-staff in the other? Think it over before you answer.

And if someone whispered, "What's out there?", wouldn't it be so very easy to whisper in return: "Vampyr!"

Wouldn't it?

Next time, if you're still around and interested, we'll go into what you might find if you open that door and stick your dumb head out. More fool you.

Peace, brother. And pleasant dreams.

FINIS

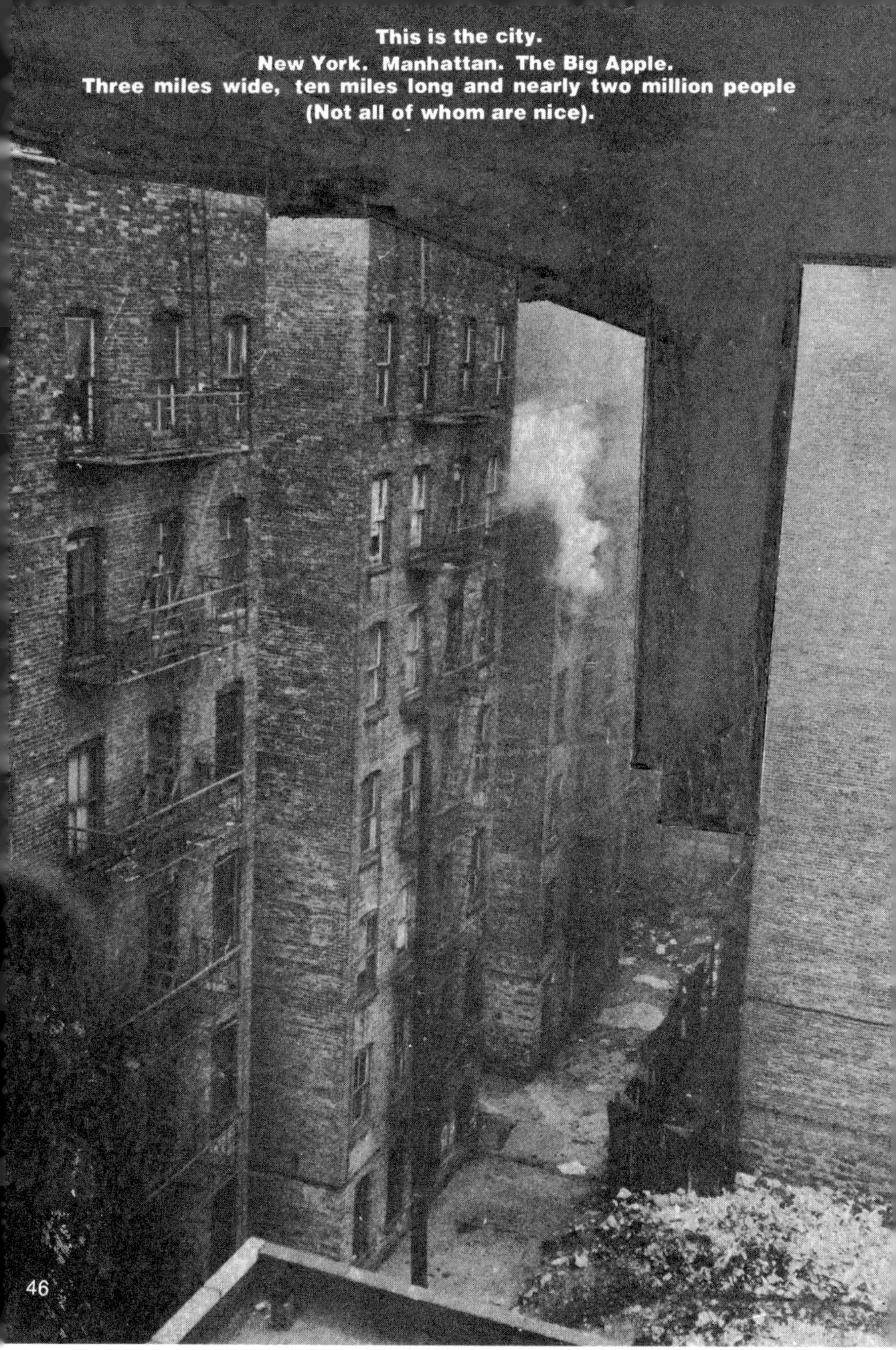
This is the city.
New York. Manhattan. The Big Apple.
Three miles wide, ten miles long and nearly two million people
(Not all of whom are nice).
46

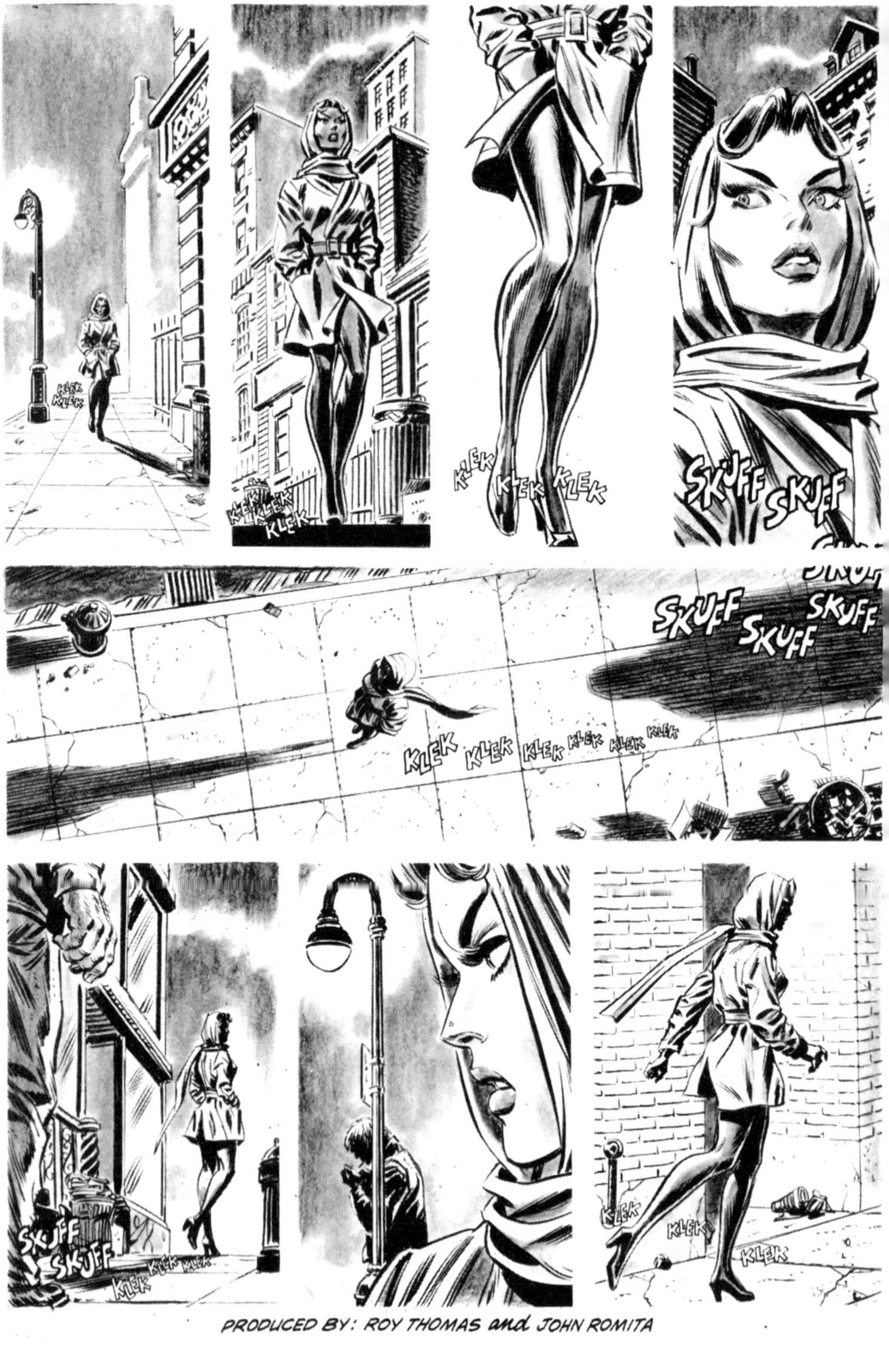
KLEK KLEK
KLEK KLEK KLEK
KLEK KLEK KLEK
SKUFF SKUFF
SKUFF SKUFF SKUFF
KLEK KLEK KLEK KLEK KLEK KLEK
SKUFF SKUFF
KLEK KLEK KLEK
KLEK KLEK KLEK

PRODUCED BY: ROY THOMAS and JOHN ROMITA

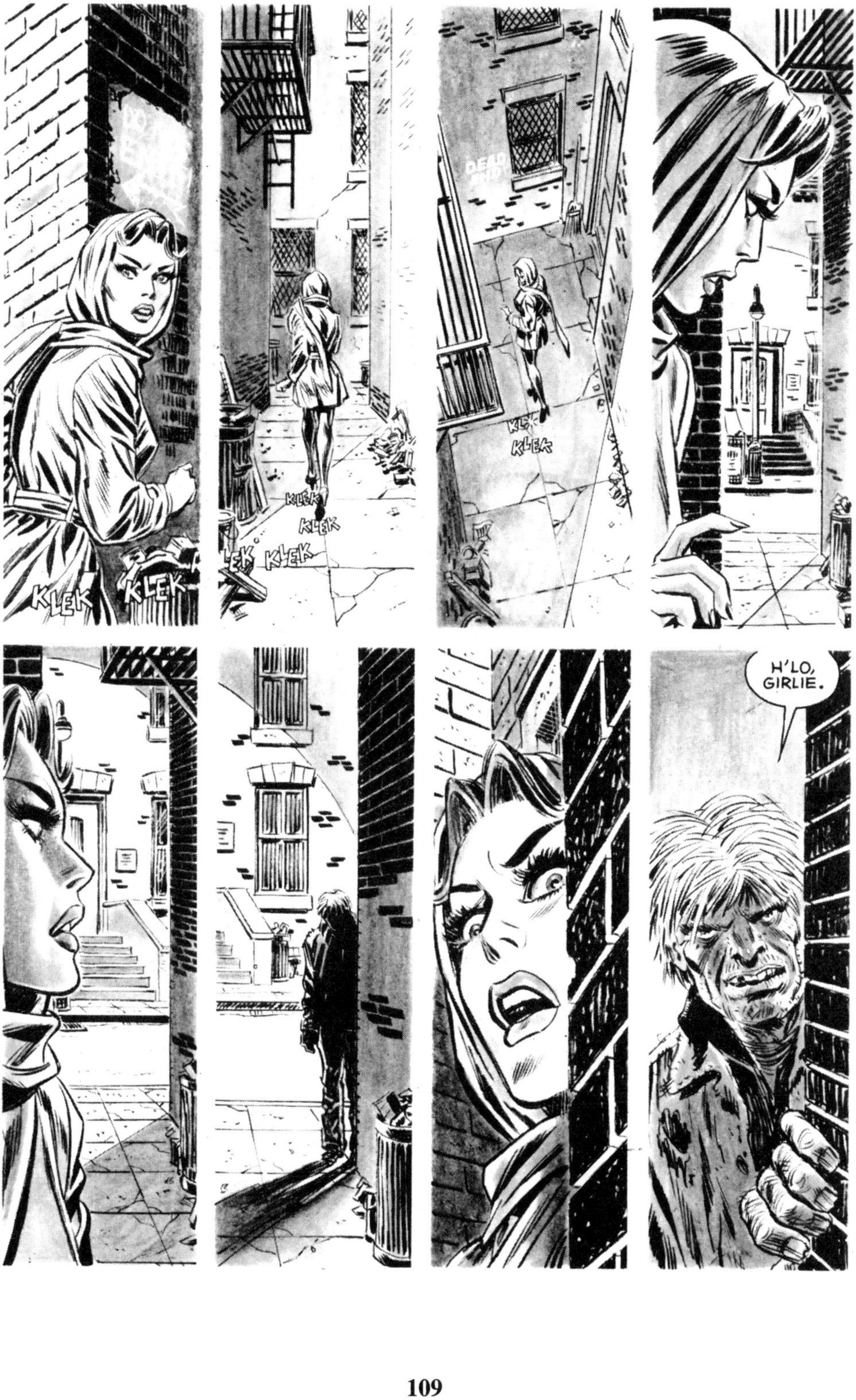
KLEK
KLEK
KLEK
KLEK
KLEK
KLEK
DEAD END
KLEK
KLEK
H'LO, GIRLIE.

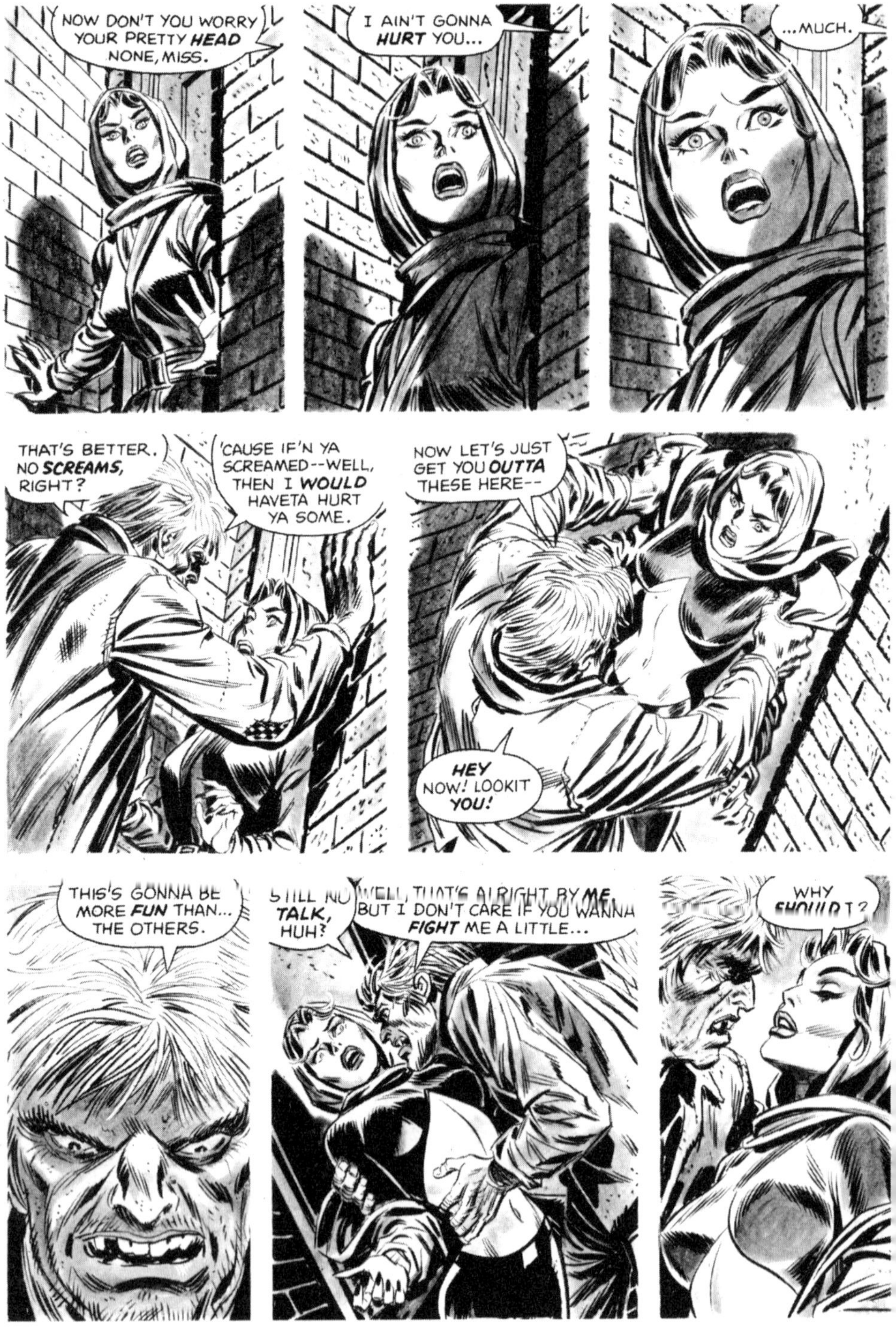
NOW DON'T YOU WORRY YOUR PRETTY HEAD NONE, MISS.
I AIN'T GONNA HURT YOU...
...MUCH.
THAT'S BETTER. NO SCREAMS, RIGHT?
'CAUSE IF'N YA SCREAMED--WELL, THEN I WOULD HAVETA HURT YA SOME.
NOW LET'S JUST GET YOU OUTTA THESE HERE--
HEY NOW! LOOKIT YOU!
THIS'S GONNA BE MORE FUN THAN... THE OTHERS.
STILL NO TALK, HUH?
WELL, THAT'S ALRIGHT BY ME, BUT I DON'T CARE IF YOU WANNA FIGHT ME A LITTLE...
WHY SHOULD I?

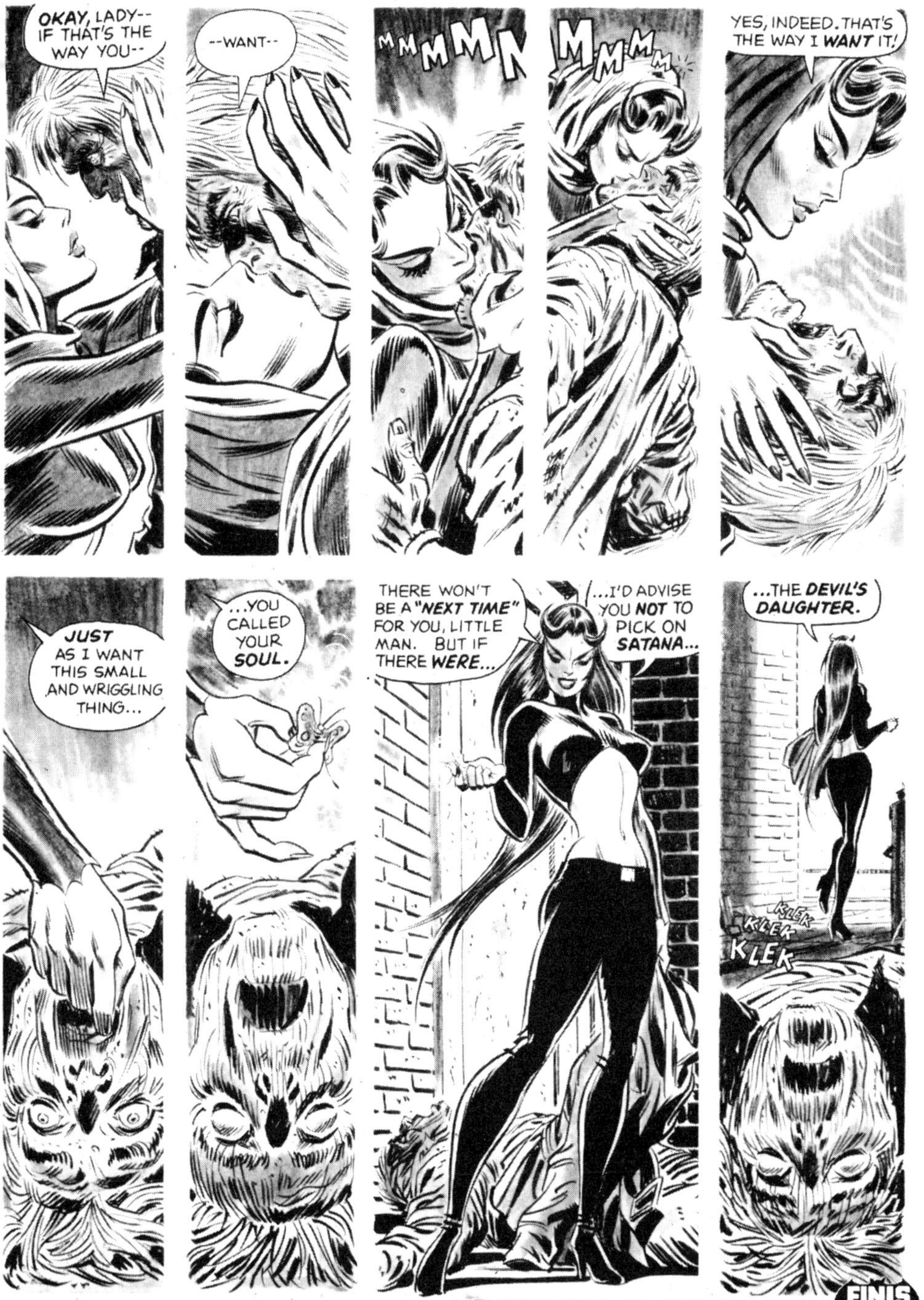
OKAY, LADY-- IF THAT'S THE WAY YOU--
--WANT--
MMMMM
MMMMM
YES, INDEED. THAT'S THE WAY I WANT IT!
JUST AS I WANT THIS SMALL AND WRIGGLING THING...
...YOU CALLED YOUR SOUL.
THERE WON'T BE A "NEXT TIME" FOR YOU, LITTLE MAN. BUT IF THERE WERE...
...I'D ADVISE YOU NOT TO PICK ON SATANA...
...THE DEVIL'S DAUGHTER.
KLEK KLEK KLEK
FINIS
COMING NEXT ISSUE: A FEATURE-LENGTH SPECTACULAR STARRING SATANA THE DEVIL'S DAUGHTER!
TM

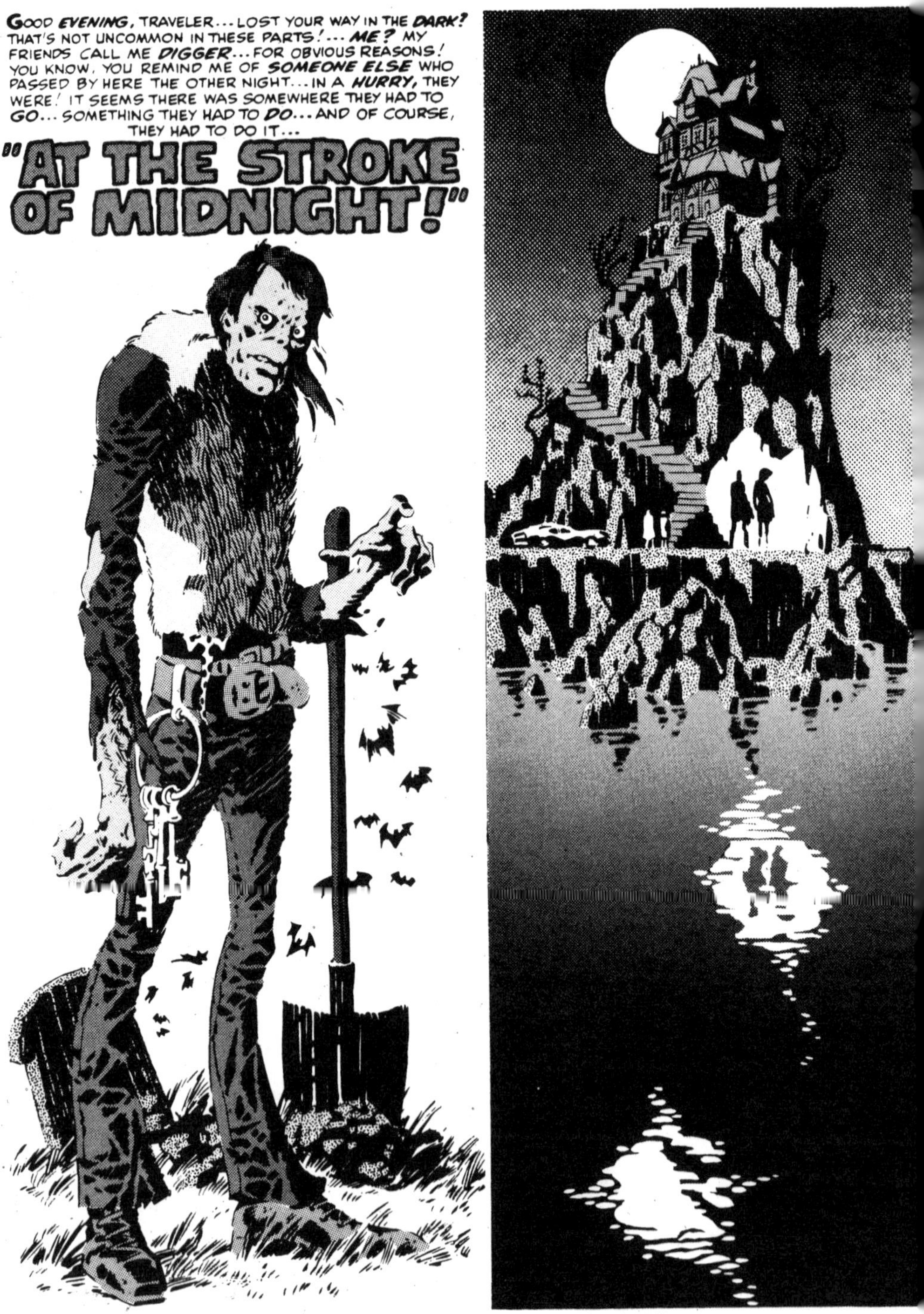
GOOD EVENING, TRAVELER... LOST YOUR WAY IN THE DARK? THAT'S NOT UNCOMMON IN THESE PARTS!... ME? MY FRIENDS CALL ME DIGGER... FOR OBVIOUS REASONS! YOU KNOW, YOU REMIND ME OF SOMEONE ELSE WHO PASSED BY HERE THE OTHER NIGHT... IN A HURRY, THEY WERE! IT SEEMS THERE WAS SOMEWHERE THEY HAD TO GO... SOMETHING THEY HAD TO DO... AND OF COURSE, THEY HAD TO DO IT...
"AT THE STROKE OF MIDNIGHT!"
WRITTEN AND ILLUSTRATED BY JIM STERANKO

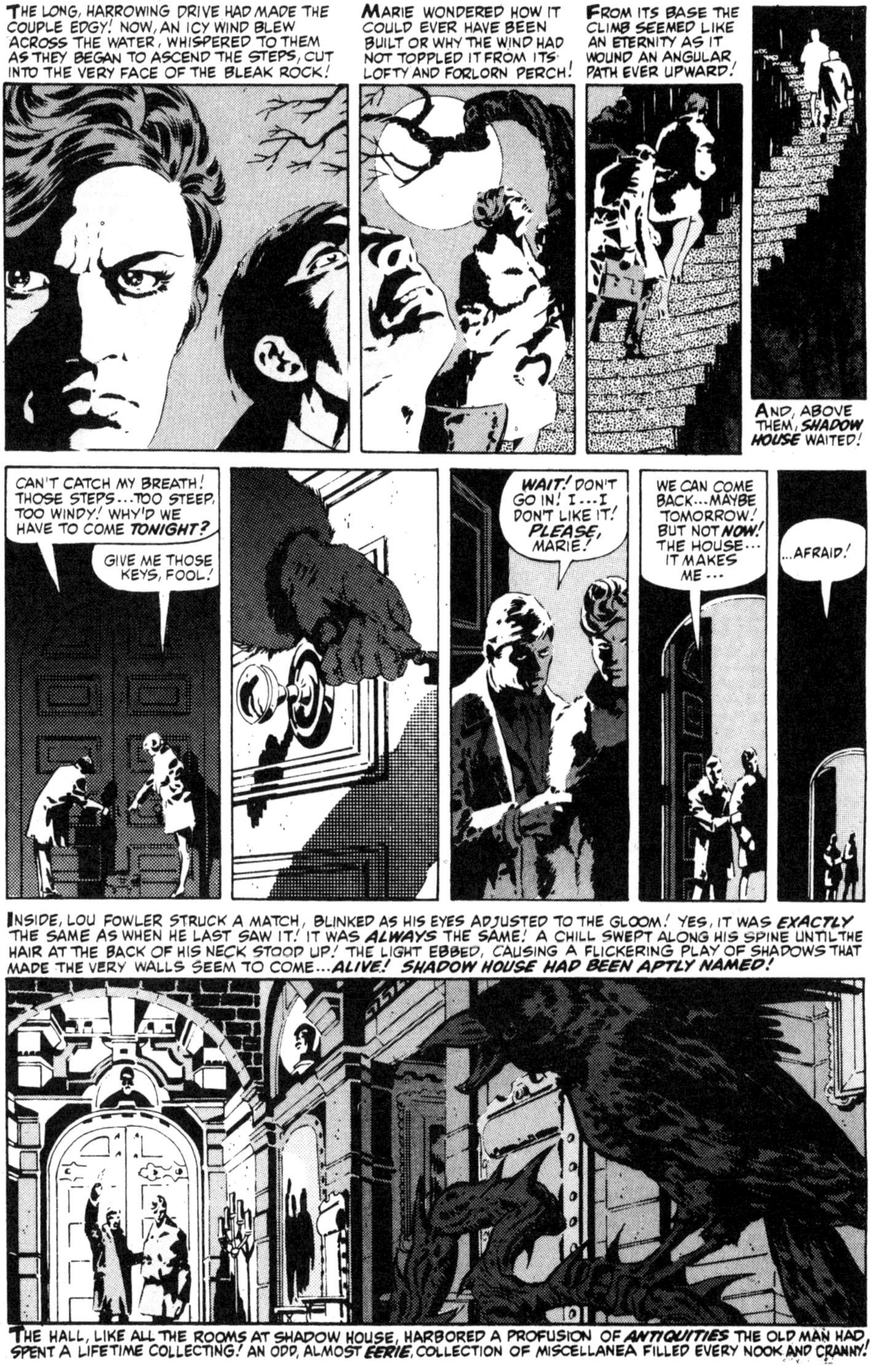
THE LONG, HARROWING DRIVE HAD MADE THE COUPLE EDGY! NOW, AN ICY WIND BLEW ACROSS THE WATER, WHISPERED TO THEM AS THEY BEGAN TO ASCEND THE STEPS, CUT INTO THE VERY FACE OF THE BLEAK ROCK!
MARIE WONDERED HOW IT COULD EVER HAVE BEEN BUILT OR WHY THE WIND HAD NOT TOPPLED IT FROM ITS LOFTY AND FORLORN PERCH!
FROM ITS BASE THE CLIMB SEEMED LIKE AN ETERNITY AS IT WOUND AN ANGULAR PATH EVER UPWARD!
AND, ABOVE THEM, SHADOW HOUSE WAITED!
CAN'T CATCH MY BREATH! THOSE STEPS...TOO STEEP, TOO WINDY! WHY'D WE HAVE TO COME TONIGHT?
GIVE ME THOSE KEYS, FOOL!
WAIT! DON'T GO IN! I...I DON'T LIKE IT! PLEASE, MARIE!
WE CAN COME BACK...MAYBE TOMORROW! BUT NOT NOW! THE HOUSE... IT MAKES ME...
...AFRAID!
INSIDE, LOU FOWLER STRUCK A MATCH, BLINKED AS HIS EYES ADJUSTED TO THE GLOOM! YES, IT WAS EXACTLY THE SAME AS WHEN HE LAST SAW IT! IT WAS ALWAYS THE SAME! A CHILL SWEPT ALONG HIS SPINE UNTIL THE HAIR AT THE BACK OF HIS NECK STOOD UP! THE LIGHT EBBED, CAUSING A FLICKERING PLAY OF SHADOWS THAT MADE THE VERY WALLS SEEM TO COME...ALIVE! SHADOW HOUSE HAD BEEN APTLY NAMED!
THE HALL, LIKE ALL THE ROOMS AT SHADOW HOUSE, HARBORED A PROFUSION OF ANTIQUITIES THE OLD MAN HAD SPENT A LIFETIME COLLECTING! AN ODD, ALMOST EERIE, COLLECTION OF MISCELLANEA FILLED EVERY NOOK AND CRANNY!

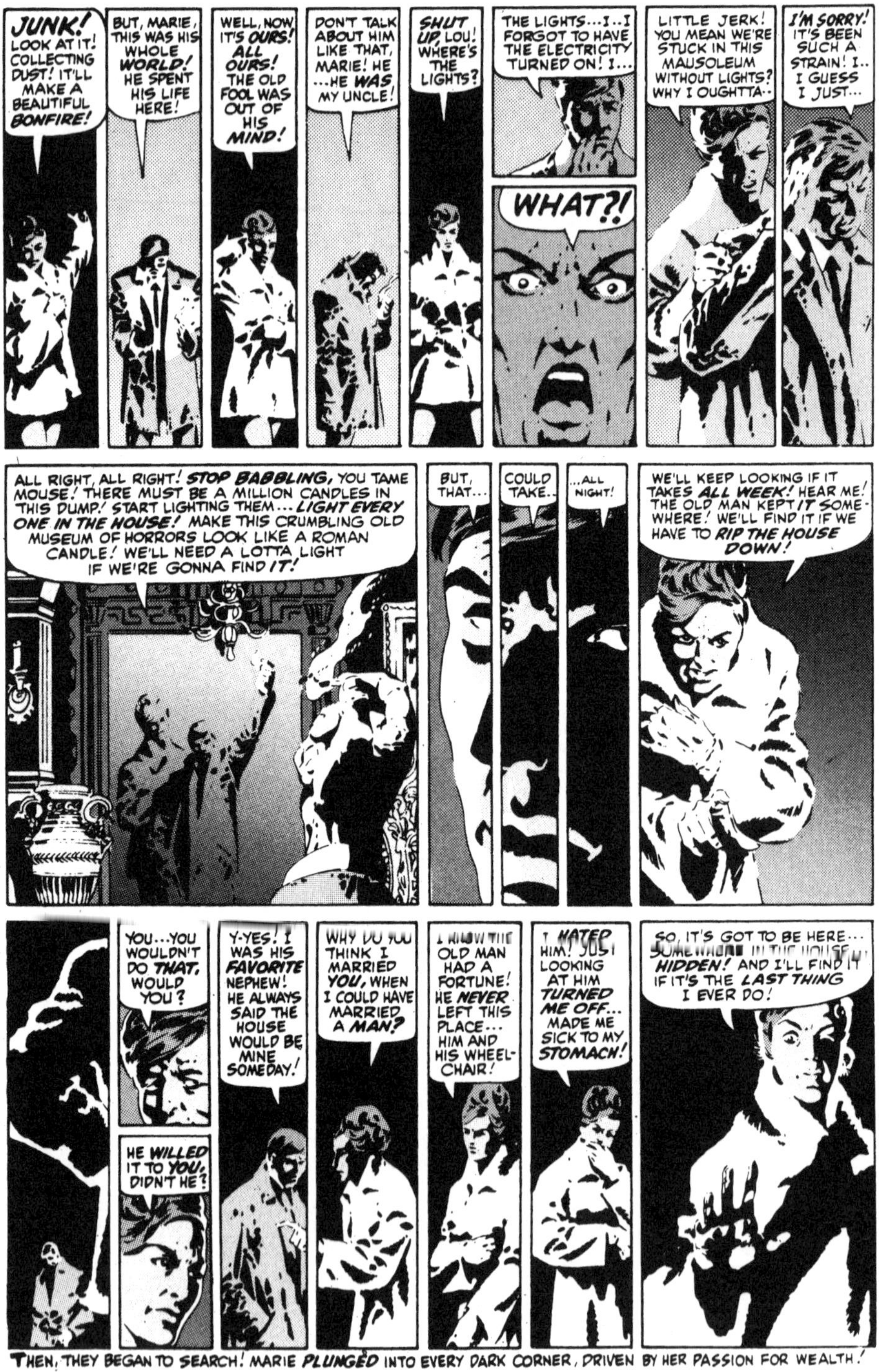
JUNK! LOOK AT IT! COLLECTING DUST! IT'LL MAKE A BEAUTIFUL BONFIRE!
BUT, MARIE, THIS WAS HIS WHOLE WORLD! HE SPENT HIS LIFE HERE!
WELL, NOW IT'S OURS! ALL OURS! THE OLD FOOL WAS OUT OF HIS MIND!
DON'T TALK ABOUT HIM LIKE THAT, MARIE! HE ...HE WAS MY UNCLE!
SHUT UP, LOU! WHERE'S THE LIGHTS?
THE LIGHTS...I...I FORGOT TO HAVE THE ELECTRICITY TURNED ON! I...
WHAT?!
LITTLE JERK! YOU MEAN WE'RE STUCK IN THIS MAUSOLEUM WITHOUT LIGHTS? WHY I OUGHTTA--
I'M SORRY! IT'S BEEN SUCH A STRAIN! I... I GUESS I JUST...
ALL RIGHT, ALL RIGHT! STOP BABBLING, YOU TAME MOUSE! THERE MUST BE A MILLION CANDLES IN THIS DUMP! START LIGHTING THEM... LIGHT EVERY ONE IN THE HOUSE! MAKE THIS CRUMBLING OLD MUSEUM OF HORRORS LOOK LIKE A ROMAN CANDLE! WE'LL NEED A LOTTA LIGHT IF WE'RE GONNA FIND IT!
BUT, THAT...
COULD TAKE...
...ALL NIGHT!
WE'LL KEEP LOOKING IF IT TAKES ALL WEEK! HEAR ME! THE OLD MAN KEPT IT SOMEWHERE! WE'LL FIND IT IF WE HAVE TO RIP THE HOUSE DOWN!
YOU...YOU WOULDN'T DO THAT, WOULD YOU?
HE WILLED IT TO YOU, DIDN'T HE?
Y-YES! I WAS HIS FAVORITE NEPHEW! HE ALWAYS SAID THE HOUSE WOULD BE MINE SOMEDAY!
THINK I MARRIED YOU, WHEN I COULD HAVE MARRIED A MAN?
OLD MAN HAD A FORTUNE! HE NEVER LEFT THIS PLACE... HIM AND HIS WHEELCHAIR!
I HATED HIM! JUST LOOKING AT HIM TURNED ME OFF... MADE ME SICK TO MY STOMACH!
SO, IT'S GOT TO BE HERE...
HIDDEN! AND I'LL FIND IT IF IT'S THE LAST THING I EVER DO!
THEN, THEY BEGAN TO SEARCH! MARIE PLUNGED INTO EVERY DARK CORNER, DRIVEN BY HER PASSION FOR WEALTH!

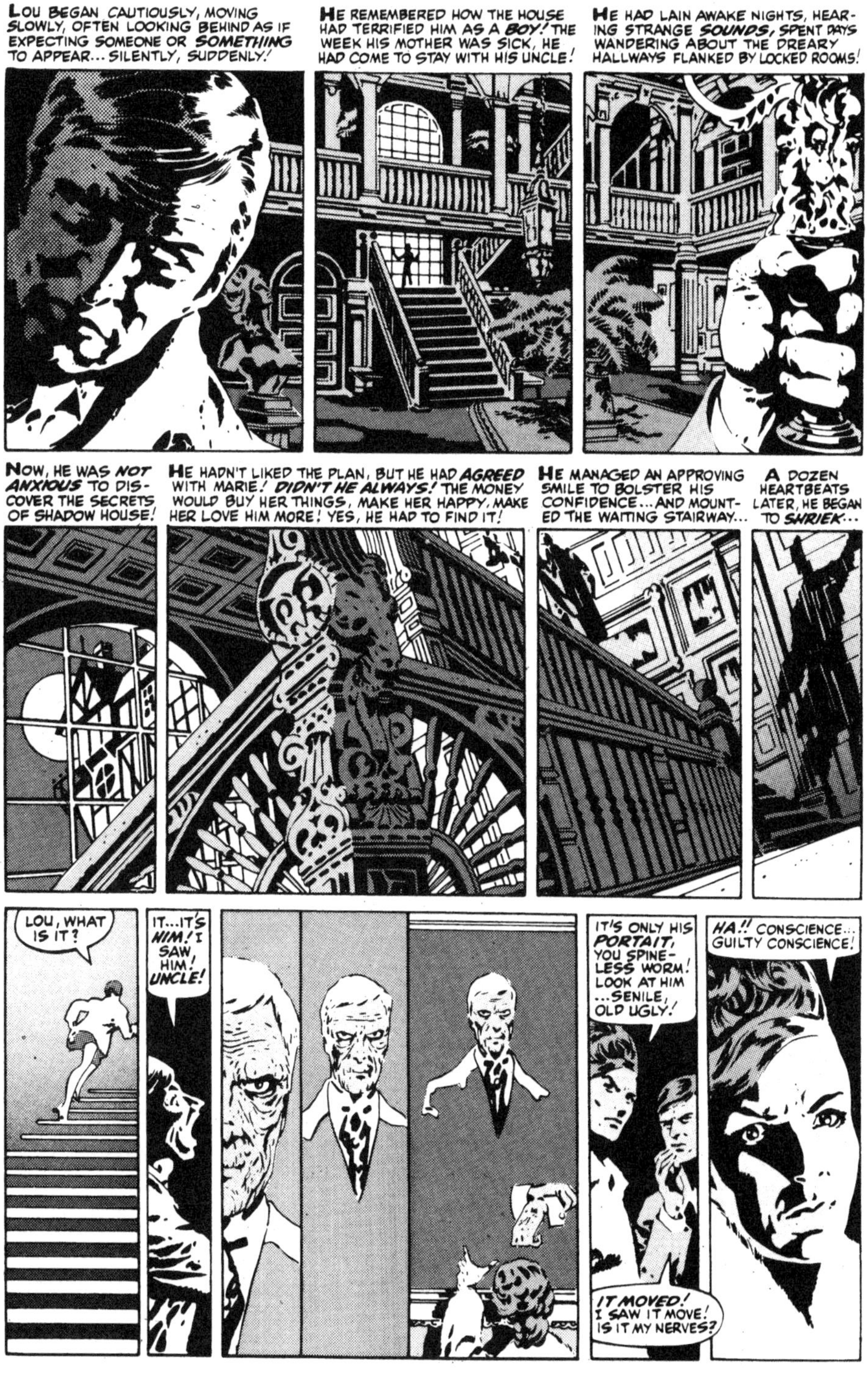
LOU BEGAN CAUTIOUSLY, MOVING SLOWLY, OFTEN LOOKING BEHIND AS IF EXPECTING SOMEONE OR SOMETHING TO APPEAR... SILENTLY, SUDDENLY!
HE REMEMBERED HOW THE HOUSE HAD TERRIFIED HIM AS A BOY! THE WEEK HIS MOTHER WAS SICK, HE HAD COME TO STAY WITH HIS UNCLE!
HE HAD LAIN AWAKE NIGHTS, HEARING STRANGE SOUNDS, SPENT DAYS WANDERING ABOUT THE DREARY HALLWAYS FLANKED BY LOCKED ROOMS!
NOW, HE WAS NOT ANXIOUS TO DISCOVER THE SECRETS OF SHADOW HOUSE!
HE HADN'T LIKED THE PLAN, BUT HE HAD AGREED WITH MARIE! DIDN'T HE ALWAYS! THE MONEY WOULD BUY HER THINGS, MAKE HER HAPPY, MAKE HER LOVE HIM MORE! YES, HE HAD TO FIND IT!
HE MANAGED AN APPROVING SMILE TO BOLSTER HIS CONFIDENCE... AND MOUNTED THE WAITING STAIRWAY...
A DOZEN HEARTBEATS LATER, HE BEGAN TO SHRIEK...
LOU, WHAT IS IT?
IT...IT'S HIM! I SAW HIM! UNCLE!
IT'S ONLY HIS PORTAIT, YOU SPINELESS WORM! LOOK AT HIM ...SENILE, OLD UGLY!
IT MOVED! I SAW IT MOVE! IS IT MY NERVES?
HA!! CONSCIENCE... GUILTY CONSCIENCE!

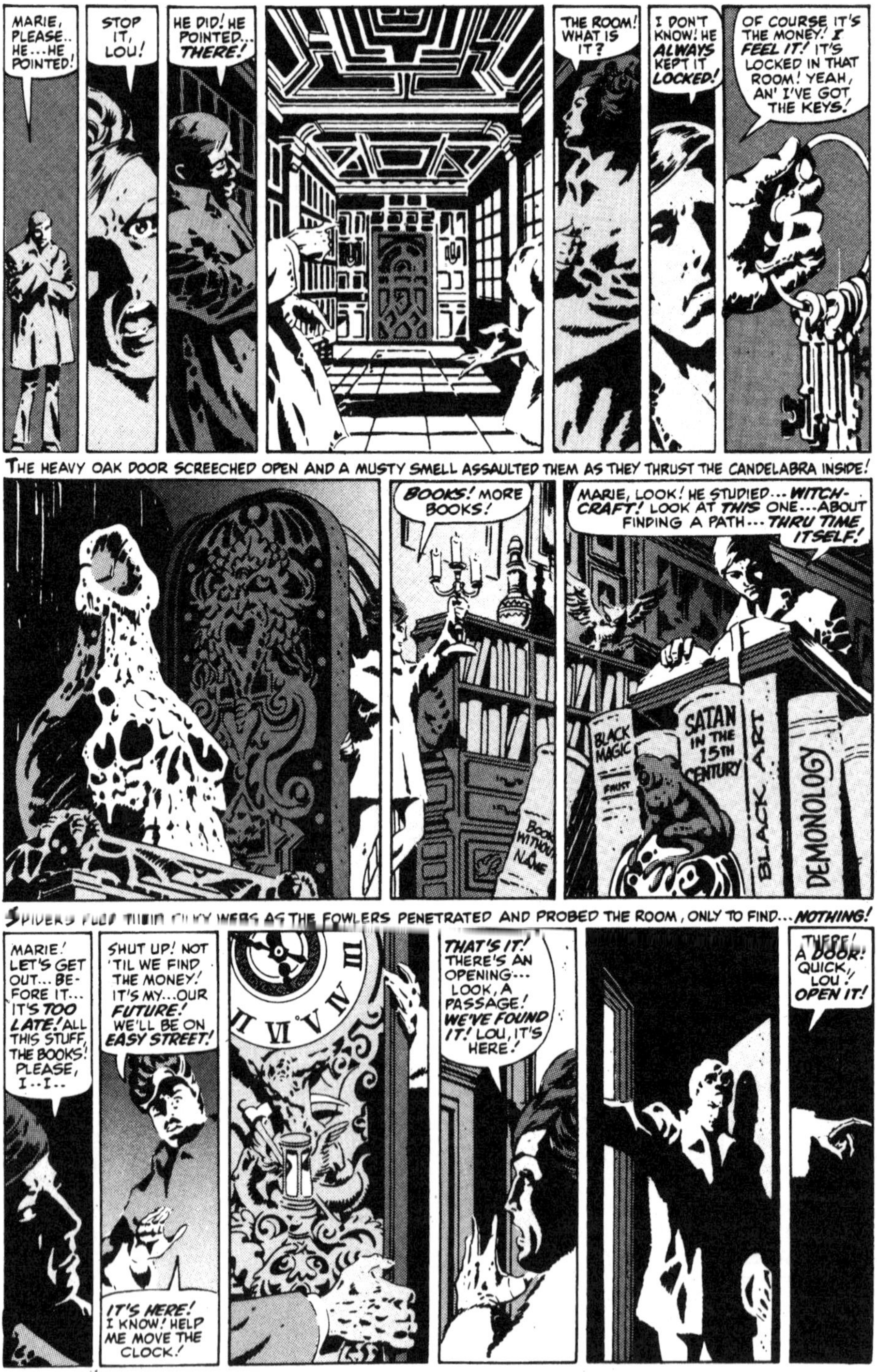
MARIE, PLEASE.. HE...HE POINTED!
STOP IT, LOU!
HE DID! HE POINTED... THERE!
THE ROOM! WHAT IS IT?
I DON'T KNOW! HE ALWAYS KEPT IT LOCKED!
OF COURSE IT'S THE MONEY! I FEEL IT! IT'S LOCKED IN THAT ROOM! YEAH, AN' I'VE GOT THE KEYS!
THE HEAVY OAK DOOR SCREECHED OPEN AND A MUSTY SMELL ASSAULTED THEM AS THEY THRUST THE CANDELABRA INSIDE!
BOOKS! MORE BOOKS!
MARIE, LOOK! HE STUDIED... WITCH-CRAFT! LOOK AT THIS ONE... ABOUT FINDING A PATH... THRU TIME ITSELF!
BLACK MAGIC
FAUST
SATAN IN THE 15TH CENTURY
BLACK ART
DEMONOLOGY
WEBS AS THE FOWLERS PENETRATED AND PROBED THE ROOM, ONLY TO FIND... NOTHING!
MARIE! LET'S GET OUT... BE-FORE IT... IT'S TOO LATE! ALL THIS STUFF, THE BOOKS! PLEASE, I--I--
SHUT UP! NOT 'TIL WE FIND THE MONEY! IT'S MY...OUR FUTURE! WE'LL BE ON EASY STREET!
IT'S HERE! I KNOW! HELP ME MOVE THE CLOCK!
THAT'S IT! THERE'S AN OPENING--- LOOK, A PASSAGE! WE'VE FOUND IT! LOU, IT'S HERE!
THERE! A DOOR! QUICK, LOU! OPEN IT!

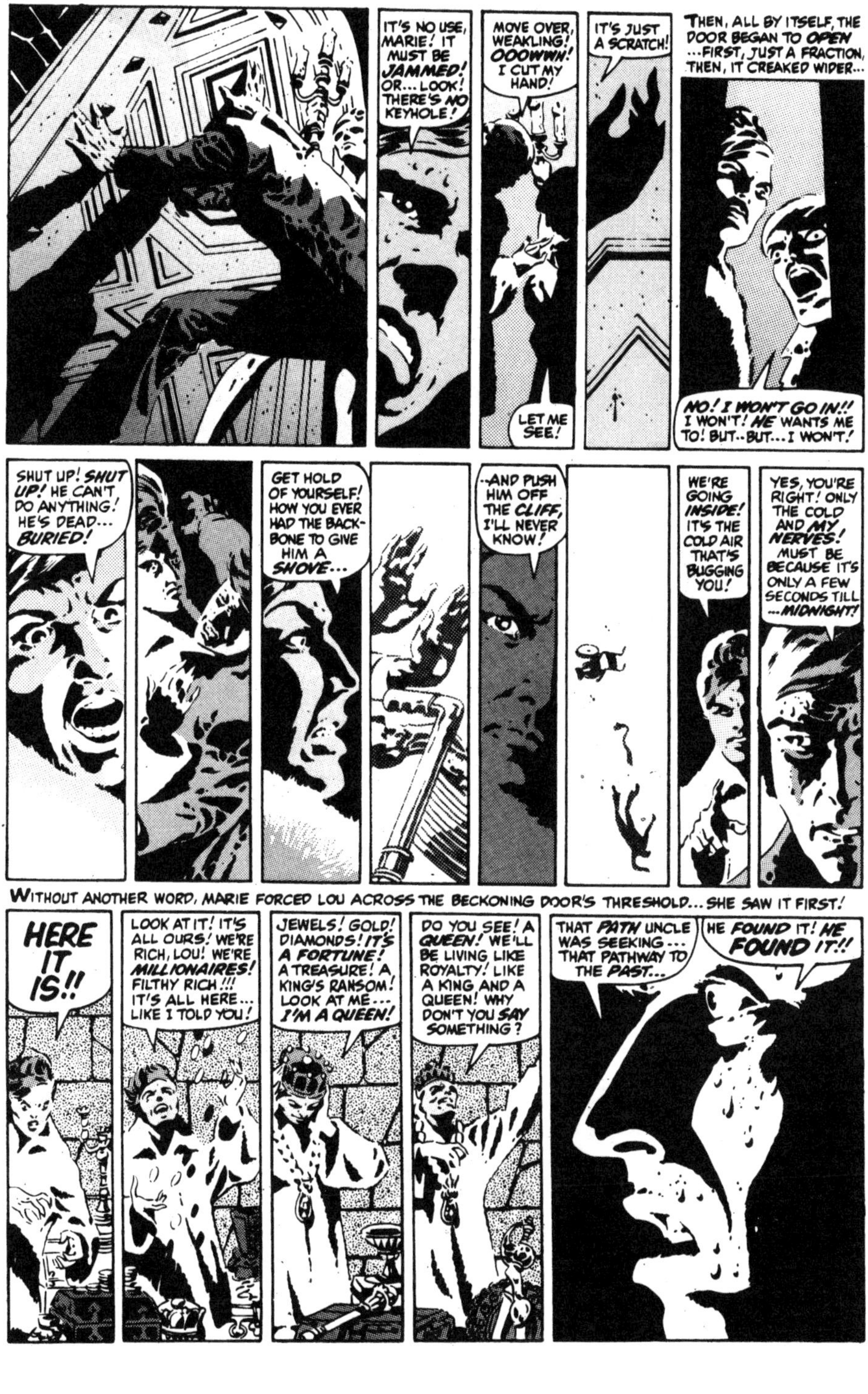
IT'S NO USE, MARIE! IT MUST BE JAMMED! OR... LOOK! THERE'S NO KEYHOLE!
MOVE OVER, WEAKLING! OOOWWN! I CUT MY HAND!
LET ME SEE!
IT'S JUST A SCRATCH!
THEN, ALL BY ITSELF, THE DOOR BEGAN TO OPEN ...FIRST, JUST A FRACTION, THEN, IT CREAKED WIDER...
NO! I WON'T GO IN!! I WON'T! HE WANTS ME TO! BUT.. BUT... I WON'T!
SHUT UP! SHUT UP! HE CAN'T DO ANYTHING! HE'S DEAD... BURIED!
GET HOLD OF YOURSELF! HOW YOU EVER HAD THE BACK-BONE TO GIVE HIM A SHOVE...
--AND PUSH HIM OFF THE CLIFF, I'LL NEVER KNOW!
WE'RE GOING INSIDE! IT'S THE COLD AIR THAT'S BUGGING YOU!
YES, YOU'RE RIGHT! ONLY THE COLD AND MY NERVES! MUST BE BECAUSE IT'S ONLY A FEW SECONDS TILL ...MIDNIGHT!
WITHOUT ANOTHER WORD, MARIE FORCED LOU ACROSS THE BECKONING DOOR'S THRESHOLD... SHE SAW IT FIRST!
HERE IT IS!!
LOOK AT IT! IT'S ALL OURS! WE'RE RICH, LOU! WE'RE MILLIONAIRES! FILTHY RICH!!! IT'S ALL HERE... LIKE I TOLD YOU!
JEWELS! GOLD! DIAMONDS! IT'S A FORTUNE! A TREASURE! A KING'S RANSOM! LOOK AT ME... I'M A QUEEN!
DO YOU SEE! A QUEEN! WE'LL BE LIVING LIKE ROYALTY! LIKE A KING AND A QUEEN! WHY DON'T YOU SAY SOMETHING?
THAT PATH UNCLE WAS SEEKING... THAT PATHWAY TO THE PAST...
HE FOUND IT! HE FOUND IT!!

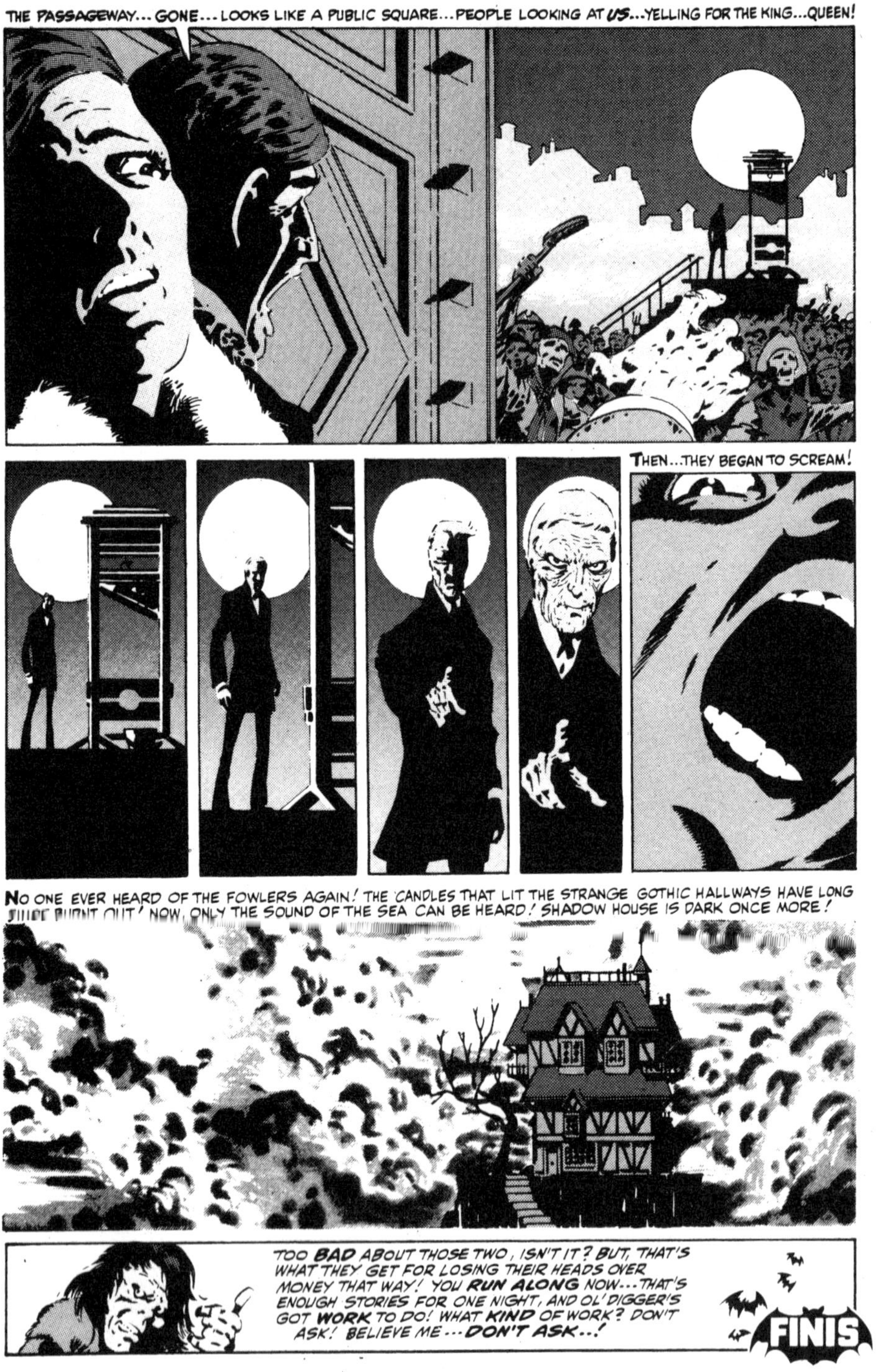

THE PASSAGEWAY... GONE... LOOKS LIKE A PUBLIC SQUARE... PEOPLE LOOKING AT US... YELLING FOR THE KING... QUEEN!
THEN... THEY BEGAN TO SCREAM!
NO ONE EVER HEARD OF THE FOWLERS AGAIN! THE CANDLES THAT LIT THE STRANGE GOTHIC HALLWAYS HAVE LONG SINCE BURNT OUT! NOW, ONLY THE SOUND OF THE SEA CAN BE HEARD! SHADOW HOUSE IS DARK ONCE MORE!
TOO BAD ABOUT THOSE TWO, ISN'T IT? BUT, THAT'S WHAT THEY GET FOR LOSING THEIR HEADS OVER MONEY THAT WAY! YOU RUN ALONG NOW... THAT'S ENOUGH STORIES FOR ONE NIGHT, AND OL' DIGGER'S GOT WORK TO DO! WHAT KIND OF WORK? DON'T ASK! BELIEVE ME... DON'T ASK...!
FINIS

Survival. So important to us. So many and varied the means we use to insure it. Case-in-point: Hodiah Twist, who survives a battered existence by retreating into a fantasy world of foggy nights and old mysteries.

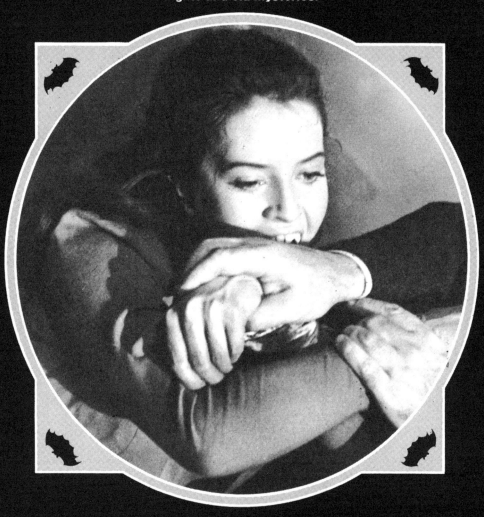

Survival. So important to us. So many and varied the means we use to insure it. Cases-in-point: Madam Angela and the delicate young ladies who "live" with her . . . !

60

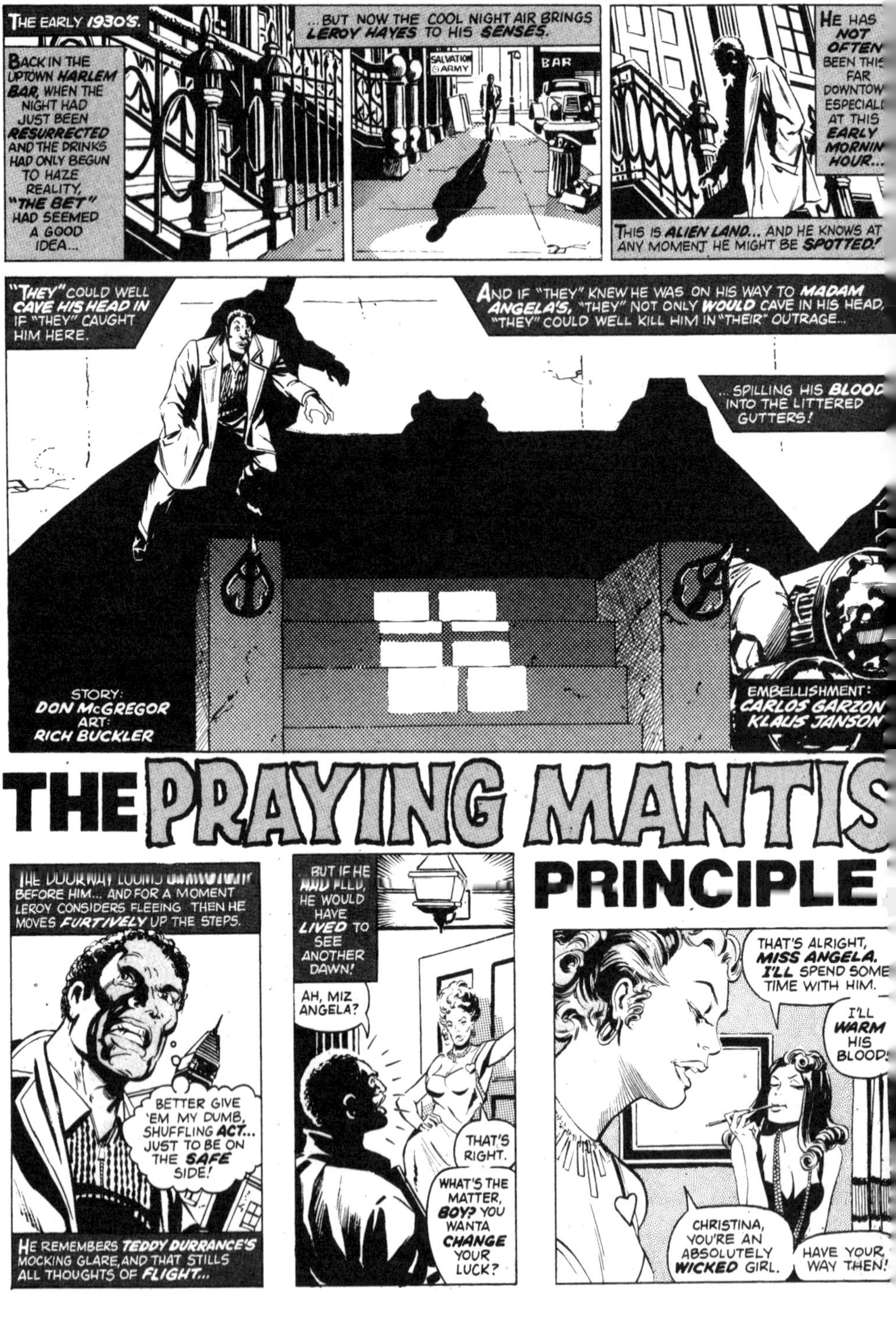
THE EARLY 1930'S.
BACK IN THE UPTOWN HARLEM BAR, WHEN THE NIGHT HAD JUST BEEN RESURRECTED AND THE DRINKS HAD ONLY BEGUN TO HAZE REALITY, "THE BET" HAD SEEMED A GOOD IDEA...
...BUT NOW THE COOL NIGHT AIR BRINGS LEROY HAYES TO HIS SENSES.
SALVATION ARMY
BAR
HE HAS NOT OFTEN BEEN THIS FAR DOWNTOWN ESPECIALLY AT THIS EARLY MORNING HOUR...
THIS IS ALIEN LAND... AND HE KNOWS AT ANY MOMENT HE MIGHT BE SPOTTED!
"THEY" COULD WELL CAVE HIS HEAD IN IF "THEY" CAUGHT HIM HERE.
AND IF "THEY" KNEW HE WAS ON HIS WAY TO MADAM ANGELA'S, "THEY" NOT ONLY WOULD CAVE IN HIS HEAD, "THEY" COULD WELL KILL HIM IN "THEIR" OUTRAGE...
...SPILLING HIS BLOOD INTO THE LITTERED GUTTERS!
STORY: DON McGREGOR
ART: RICH BUCKLER
EMBELLISHMENT: CARLOS GARZON KLAUS JANSON
THE PRAYING MANTIS PRINCIPLE
THE DOORWAY LOOMS BEFORE HIM... AND FOR A MOMENT LEROY CONSIDERS FLEEING THEN HE MOVES FURTIVELY UP THE STEPS.
BETTER GIVE 'EM MY DUMB, SHUFFLING ACT... JUST TO BE ON THE SAFE SIDE!
HE REMEMBERS TEDDY DURRANCE'S MOCKING GLARE, AND THAT STILLS ALL THOUGHTS OF FLIGHT...
BUT IF HE HAD FLED, HE WOULD HAVE LIVED TO SEE ANOTHER DAWN!
AH, MIZ ANGELA?
THAT'S RIGHT.
WHAT'S THE MATTER, BOY? YOU WANTA CHANGE YOUR LUCK?
THAT'S ALRIGHT, MISS ANGELA. I'LL SPEND SOME TIME WITH HIM.
I'LL WARM HIS BLOOD!
CHRISTINA, YOU'RE AN ABSOLUTELY WICKED GIRL.
HAVE YOUR WAY THEN!

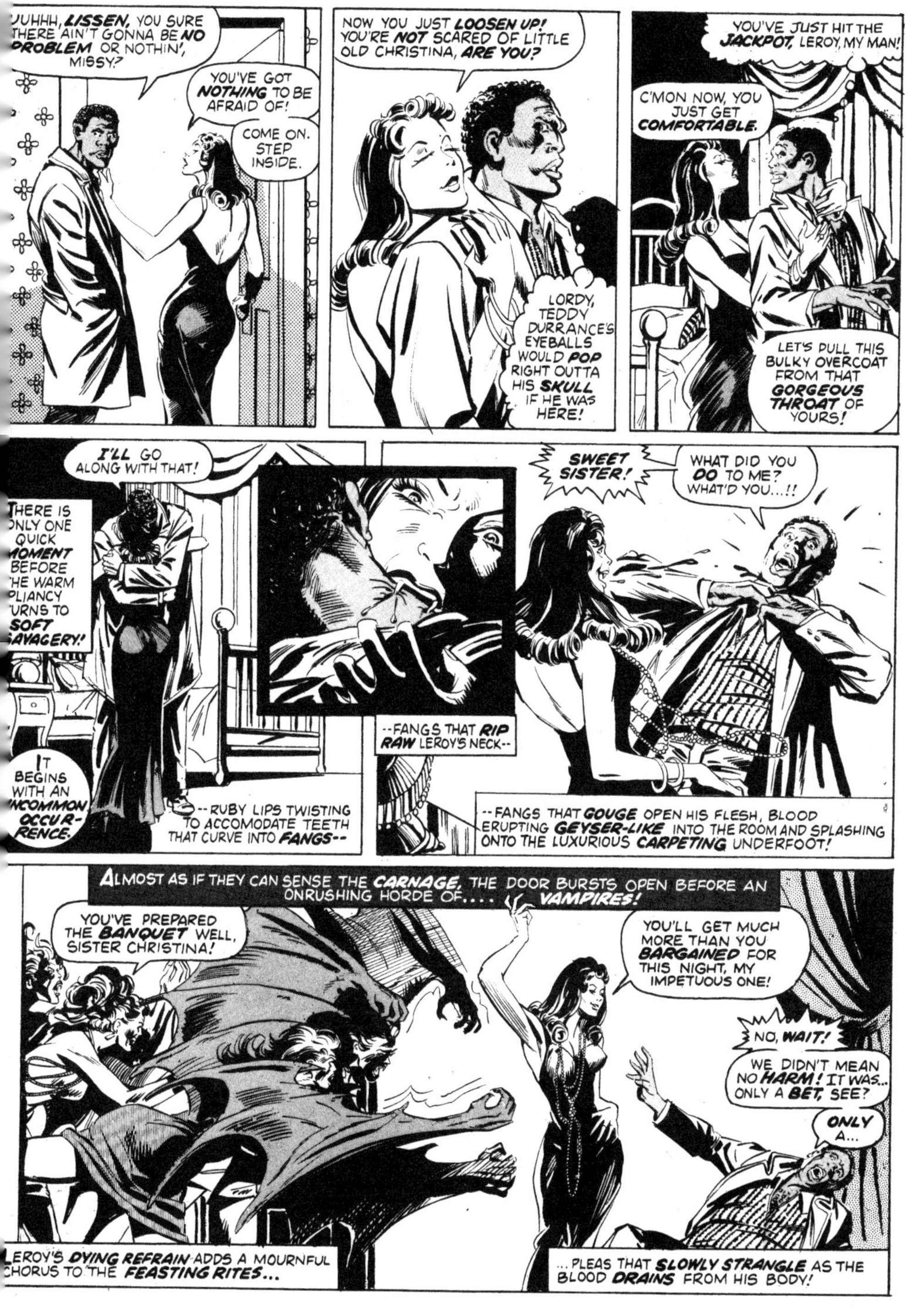
UHHH, LISSEN, YOU SURE THERE AIN'T GONNA BE NO PROBLEM OR NOTHIN', MISSY?
YOU'VE GOT NOTHING TO BE AFRAID OF!
COME ON. STEP INSIDE.
NOW YOU JUST LOOSEN UP! YOU'RE NOT SCARED OF LITTLE OLD CHRISTINA, ARE YOU?
LORDY, TEDDY DURRANCE'S EYEBALLS WOULD POP RIGHT OUTTA HIS SKULL IF HE WAS HERE!
YOU'VE JUST HIT THE JACKPOT, LEROY, MY MAN!
C'MON NOW, YOU JUST GET COMFORTABLE.
LET'S PULL THIS BULKY OVERCOAT FROM THAT GORGEOUS THROAT OF YOURS!
I'LL GO ALONG WITH THAT!
THERE IS ONLY ONE QUICK MOMENT BEFORE THE WARM PLIANCY TURNS TO SOFT SAVAGERY!
IT BEGINS WITH AN UNCOMMON OCCURRENCE.
--RUBY LIPS TWISTING TO ACCOMODATE TEETH THAT CURVE INTO FANGS--
--FANGS THAT RIP RAW LEROY'S NECK--
SWEET SISTER!
WHAT DID YOU DO TO ME? WHAT'D YOU...!!
--FANGS THAT GOUGE OPEN HIS FLESH, BLOOD ERUPTING GEYSER-LIKE INTO THE ROOM AND SPLASHING ONTO THE LUXURIOUS CARPETING UNDERFOOT!
ALMOST AS IF THEY CAN SENSE THE CARNAGE, THE DOOR BURSTS OPEN BEFORE AN ONRUSHING HORDE OF.... VAMPIRES!
YOU'VE PREPARED THE BANQUET WELL, SISTER CHRISTINA!
YOU'LL GET MUCH MORE THAN YOU BARGAINED FOR THIS NIGHT, MY IMPETUOUS ONE!
NO, WAIT!
WE DIDN'T MEAN NO HARM! IT WAS... ONLY A BET, SEE?
ONLY A...
LEROY'S DYING REFRAIN ADDS A MOURNFUL CHORUS TO THE FEASTING RITES...
...PLEAS THAT SLOWLY STRANGLE AS THE BLOOD DRAINS FROM HIS BODY!

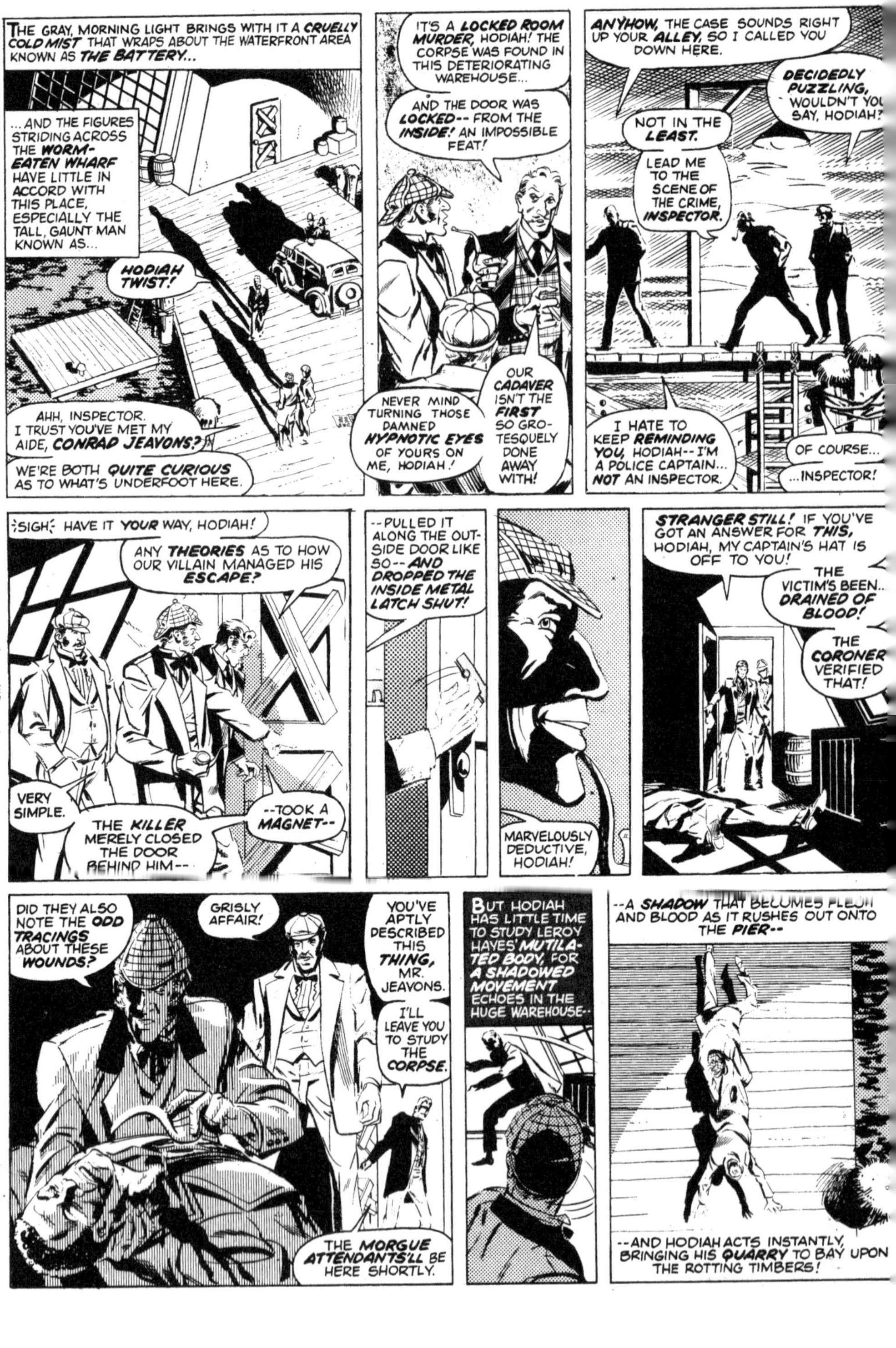
THE GRAY, MORNING LIGHT BRINGS WITH IT A CRUELLY COLD MIST THAT WRAPS ABOUT THE WATERFRONT AREA KNOWN AS THE BATTERY...
...AND THE FIGURES STRIDING ACROSS THE WORM-EATEN WHARF HAVE LITTLE IN ACCORD WITH THIS PLACE, ESPECIALLY THE TALL, GAUNT MAN KNOWN AS...
HODIAH TWIST!
AHH, INSPECTOR. I TRUST YOU'VE MET MY AIDE, CONRAD JEAVONS?
WE'RE BOTH QUITE CURIOUS AS TO WHAT'S UNDERFOOT HERE.
IT'S A LOCKED ROOM MURDER, HODIAH! THE CORPSE WAS FOUND IN THIS DETERIORATING WAREHOUSE...
AND THE DOOR WAS LOCKED-- FROM THE INSIDE! AN IMPOSSIBLE FEAT!
NEVER MIND TURNING THOSE DAMNED HYPNOTIC EYES OF YOURS ON ME, HODIAH!
OUR CADAVER ISN'T THE FIRST SO GRO-TESQUELY DONE AWAY WITH!
ANYHOW, THE CASE SOUNDS RIGHT UP YOUR ALLEY, SO I CALLED YOU DOWN HERE.
DECIDEDLY PUZZLING, WOULDN'T YOU SAY, HODIAH?
NOT IN THE LEAST.
LEAD ME TO THE SCENE OF THE CRIME, INSPECTOR.
I HATE TO KEEP REMINDING YOU, HODIAH-- I'M A POLICE CAPTAIN... NOT AN INSPECTOR.
OF COURSE...
...INSPECTOR!
SIGH HAVE IT YOUR WAY, HODIAH!
ANY THEORIES AS TO HOW OUR VILLAIN MANAGED HIS ESCAPE?
VERY SIMPLE.
THE KILLER MERELY CLOSED THE DOOR BEHIND HIM--
--TOOK A MAGNET--
--PULLED IT ALONG THE OUT-SIDE DOOR LIKE SO-- AND DROPPED THE INSIDE METAL LATCH SHUT!
MARVELOUSLY DEDUCTIVE, HODIAH!
STRANGER STILL! IF YOU'VE GOT AN ANSWER FOR THIS, HODIAH, MY CAPTAIN'S HAT IS OFF TO YOU!
THE VICTIM'S BEEN.. DRAINED OF BLOOD!
THE CORONER VERIFIED THAT!
DID THEY ALSO NOTE THE ODD TRACINGS ABOUT THESE WOUNDS?
GRISLY AFFAIR!
YOU'VE APTLY DESCRIBED THIS THING, MR. JEAVONS.
I'LL LEAVE YOU TO STUDY THE CORPSE.
THE MORGUE ATTENDANTS'LL BE HERE SHORTLY.
BUT HODIAH HAS LITTLE TIME TO STUDY LEROY HAYES' MUTILA-TED BODY, FOR A SHADOWED MOVEMENT ECHOES IN THE HUGE WAREHOUSE--
--A SHADOW THAT BECOMES FLESH AND BLOOD AS IT RUSHES OUT ONTO THE PIER--
--AND HODIAH ACTS INSTANTLY, BRINGING HIS QUARRY TO BAY UPON THE ROTTING TIMBERS!

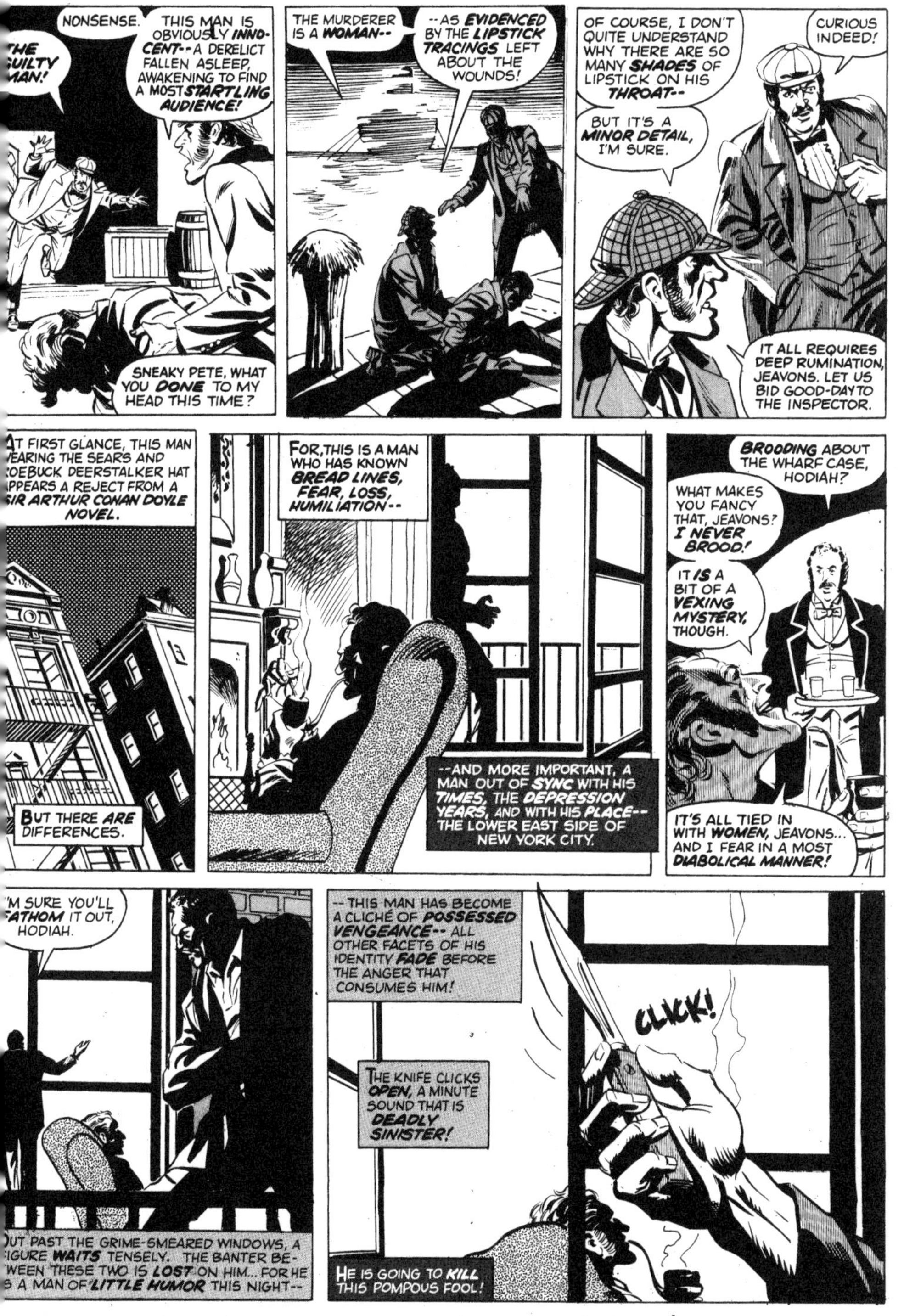
THE GUILTY MAN!
NONSENSE.
THIS MAN IS OBVIOUSLY INNOCENT--A DERELICT FALLEN ASLEEP, AWAKENING TO FIND A MOST STARTLING AUDIENCE!
SNEAKY PETE, WHAT YOU DONE TO MY HEAD THIS TIME?
THE MURDERER IS A WOMAN--
--AS EVIDENCED BY THE LIPSTICK TRACINGS LEFT ABOUT THE WOUNDS!
OF COURSE, I DON'T QUITE UNDERSTAND WHY THERE ARE SO MANY SHADES OF LIPSTICK ON HIS THROAT--
BUT IT'S A MINOR DETAIL, I'M SURE.
CURIOUS INDEED!
IT ALL REQUIRES DEEP RUMINATION, JEAVONS. LET US BID GOOD-DAY TO THE INSPECTOR.
AT FIRST GLANCE, THIS MAN WEARING THE SEARS AND ROEBUCK DEERSTALKER HAT APPEARS A REJECT FROM A SIR ARTHUR CONAN DOYLE NOVEL.
BUT THERE ARE DIFFERENCES.
FOR, THIS IS A MAN WHO HAS KNOWN BREAD LINES, FEAR, LOSS, HUMILIATION--
--AND MORE IMPORTANT, A MAN OUT OF SYNC WITH HIS TIMES, THE DEPRESSION YEARS, AND WITH HIS PLACE--THE LOWER EAST SIDE OF NEW YORK CITY.
BROODING ABOUT THE WHARF CASE, HODIAH?
WHAT MAKES YOU FANCY THAT, JEAVONS? I NEVER BROOD!
IT IS A BIT OF A VEXING MYSTERY, THOUGH.
IT'S ALL TIED IN WITH WOMEN, JEAVONS... AND I FEAR IN A MOST DIABOLICAL MANNER!
I'M SURE YOU'LL FATHOM IT OUT, HODIAH.
OUT PAST THE GRIME-SMEARED WINDOWS, A FIGURE WAITS TENSELY. THE BANTER BETWEEN THESE TWO IS LOST ON HIM... FOR HE IS A MAN OF LITTLE HUMOR THIS NIGHT--
--THIS MAN HAS BECOME A CLICHÉ OF POSSESSED VENGEANCE--ALL OTHER FACETS OF HIS IDENTITY FADE BEFORE THE ANGER THAT CONSUMES HIM!
THE KNIFE CLICKS OPEN, A MINUTE SOUND THAT IS DEADLY SINISTER!
CLICK!
HE IS GOING TO KILL THIS POMPOUS FOOL!

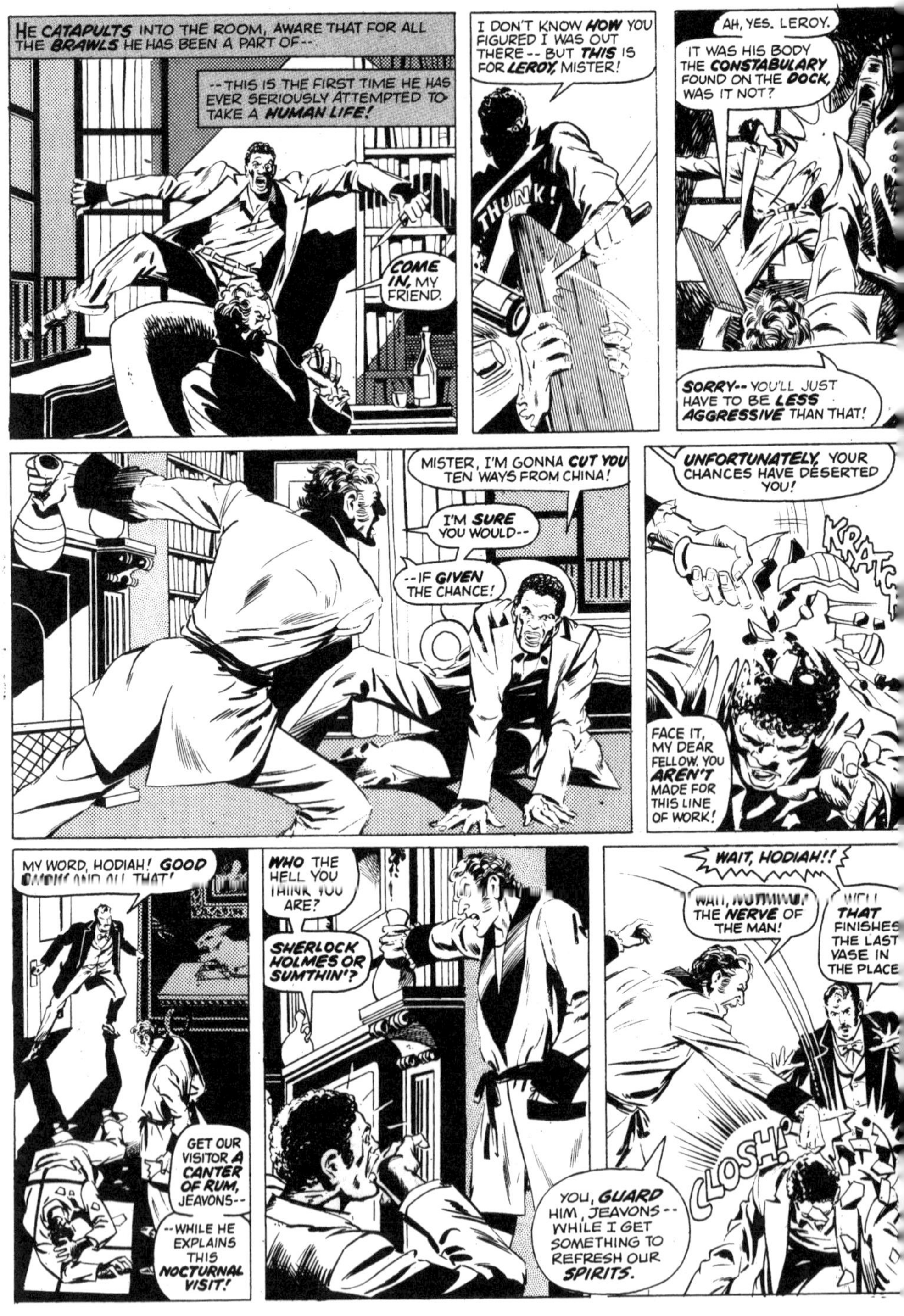
HE CATAPULTS INTO THE ROOM, AWARE THAT FOR ALL THE BRAWLS HE HAS BEEN A PART OF--
--THIS IS THE FIRST TIME HE HAS EVER SERIOUSLY ATTEMPTED TO TAKE A HUMAN LIFE!
COME IN, MY FRIEND.
I DON'T KNOW HOW YOU FIGURED I WAS OUT THERE -- BUT THIS IS FOR LEROY, MISTER!
THUNK!
AH, YES. LEROY.
IT WAS HIS BODY THE CONSTABULARY FOUND ON THE DOCK, WAS IT NOT?
SORRY-- YOU'LL JUST HAVE TO BE LESS AGGRESSIVE THAN THAT!
MISTER, I'M GONNA CUT YOU TEN WAYS FROM CHINA!
I'M SURE YOU WOULD--
--IF GIVEN THE CHANCE!
UNFORTUNATELY, YOUR CHANCES HAVE DESERTED YOU!
KRATCH
FACE IT, MY DEAR FELLOW. YOU AREN'T MADE FOR THIS LINE OF WORK!
MY WORD, HODIAH! GOOD
GET OUR VISITOR A CANTER OF RUM, JEAVONS--
--WHILE HE EXPLAINS THIS NOCTURNAL VISIT!
WHO THE HELL YOU THINK YOU ARE?
SHERLOCK HOLMES OR SUMTHIN'?
YOU, GUARD HIM, JEAVONS -- WHILE I GET SOMETHING TO REFRESH OUR SPIRITS.
WAIT, HODIAH!!
THE NERVE OF THE MAN!
THAT FINISHES THE LAST VASE IN THE PLACE
CLOSH!

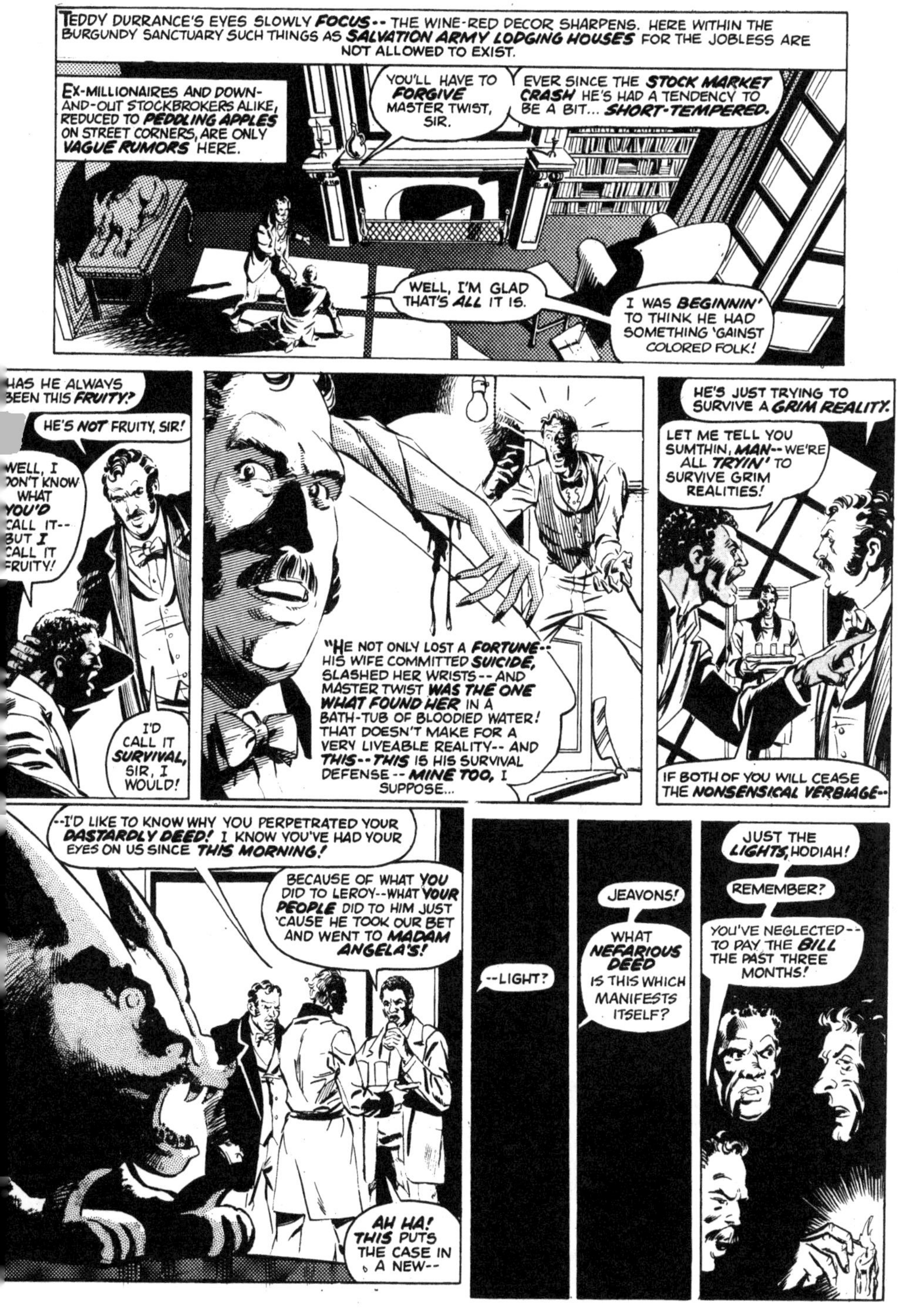
TEDDY DURRANCE'S EYES SLOWLY FOCUS-- THE WINE-RED DECOR SHARPENS. HERE WITHIN THE BURGUNDY SANCTUARY SUCH THINGS AS SALVATION ARMY LODGING HOUSES FOR THE JOBLESS ARE NOT ALLOWED TO EXIST.
EX-MILLIONAIRES AND DOWN-AND-OUT STOCKBROKERS ALIKE, REDUCED TO PEDDLING APPLES ON STREET CORNERS, ARE ONLY VAGUE RUMORS HERE.
YOU'LL HAVE TO FORGIVE MASTER TWIST, SIR.
EVER SINCE THE STOCK MARKET CRASH HE'S HAD A TENDENCY TO BE A BIT... SHORT-TEMPERED.
WELL, I'M GLAD THAT'S ALL IT IS.
I WAS BEGINNIN' TO THINK HE HAD SOMETHING 'GAINST COLORED FOLK!
HAS HE ALWAYS BEEN THIS FRUITY?
HE'S NOT FRUITY, SIR!
WELL, I DON'T KNOW WHAT YOU'D CALL IT-- BUT I CALL IT FRUITY!
I'D CALL IT SURVIVAL, SIR, I WOULD!
"HE NOT ONLY LOST A FORTUNE-- HIS WIFE COMMITTED SUICIDE, SLASHED HER WRISTS-- AND MASTER TWIST WAS THE ONE WHAT FOUND HER IN A BATH-TUB OF BLOODIED WATER! THAT DOESN'T MAKE FOR A VERY LIVEABLE REALITY-- AND THIS--THIS IS HIS SURVIVAL DEFENSE-- MINE TOO, I SUPPOSE...
HE'S JUST TRYING TO SURVIVE A GRIM REALITY.
LET ME TELL YOU SUMTHIN, MAN-- WE'RE ALL TRYIN' TO SURVIVE GRIM REALITIES!
IF BOTH OF YOU WILL CEASE THE NONSENSICAL VERBIAGE--
--I'D LIKE TO KNOW WHY YOU PERPETRATED YOUR DASTARDLY DEED! I KNOW YOU'VE HAD YOUR EYES ON US SINCE THIS MORNING!
BECAUSE OF WHAT YOU DID TO LEROY--WHAT YOUR PEOPLE DID TO HIM JUST 'CAUSE HE TOOK OUR BET AND WENT TO MADAM ANGELA'S!
AH HA! THIS PUTS THE CASE IN A NEW--
--LIGHT?
JEAVONS!
WHAT NEFARIOUS DEED IS THIS WHICH MANIFESTS ITSELF?
JUST THE LIGHTS, HODIAH!
REMEMBER?
YOU'VE NEGLECTED-- TO PAY THE BILL THE PAST THREE MONTHS!

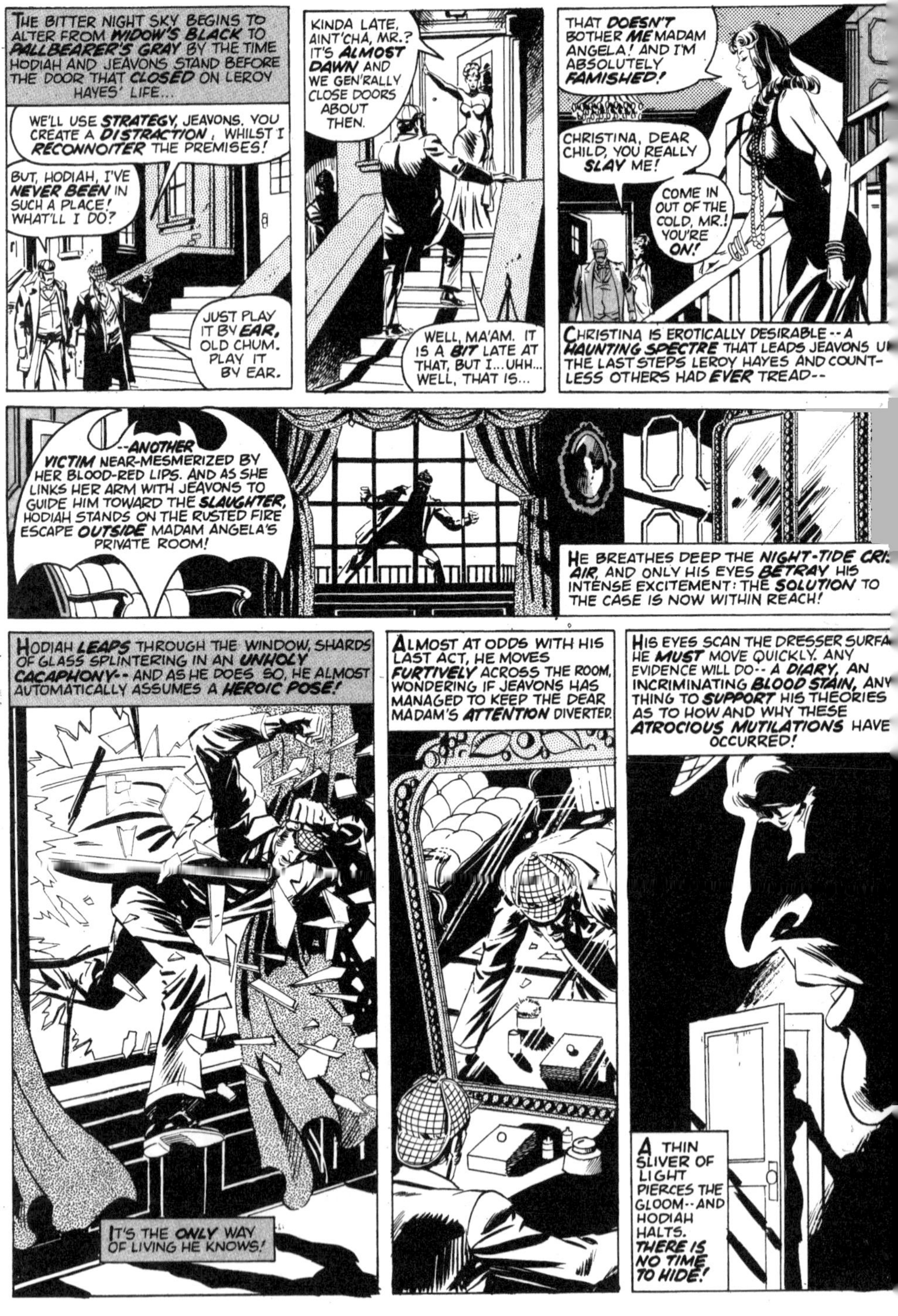
THE BITTER NIGHT SKY BEGINS TO ALTER FROM WIDOW'S BLACK TO PALLBEARER'S GRAY BY THE TIME HODIAH AND JEAVONS STAND BEFORE THE DOOR THAT CLOSED ON LEROY HAYES' LIFE...
WE'LL USE STRATEGY, JEAVONS. YOU CREATE A DISTRACTION, WHILST I RECONNOITER THE PREMISES!
BUT, HODIAH, I'VE NEVER BEEN IN SUCH A PLACE! WHAT'LL I DO?
JUST PLAY IT BY EAR, OLD CHUM. PLAY IT BY EAR.
KINDA LATE, AINT'CHA, MR.? IT'S ALMOST DAWN AND WE GEN'RALLY CLOSE DOORS ABOUT THEN.
WELL, MA'AM. IT IS A BIT LATE AT THAT, BUT I...UHH... WELL, THAT IS...
THAT DOESN'T BOTHER ME MADAM ANGELA! AND I'M ABSOLUTELY FAMISHED!
CHRISTINA, DEAR CHILD, YOU REALLY SLAY ME!
COME IN OUT OF THE COLD, MR.! YOU'RE ON!
CHRISTINA IS EROTICALLY DESIRABLE -- A HAUNTING SPECTRE THAT LEADS JEAVONS U THE LAST STEPS LEROY HAYES AND COUNTLESS OTHERS HAD EVER TREAD--
--ANOTHER VICTIM NEAR-MESMERIZED BY HER BLOOD-RED LIPS. AND AS SHE LINKS HER ARM WITH JEAVONS TO GUIDE HIM TOWARD THE SLAUGHTER, HODIAH STANDS ON THE RUSTED FIRE ESCAPE OUTSIDE MADAM ANGELA'S PRIVATE ROOM!
HE BREATHES DEEP THE NIGHT-TIDE CRI AIR, AND ONLY HIS EYES BETRAY HIS INTENSE EXCITEMENT: THE SOLUTION TO THE CASE IS NOW WITHIN REACH!
HODIAH LEAPS THROUGH THE WINDOW, SHARDS OF GLASS SPLINTERING IN AN UNHOLY CACAPHONY-- AND AS HE DOES SO, HE ALMOST AUTOMATICALLY ASSUMES A HEROIC POSE!
IT'S THE ONLY WAY OF LIVING HE KNOWS!
ALMOST AT ODDS WITH HIS LAST ACT, HE MOVES FURTIVELY ACROSS THE ROOM, WONDERING IF JEAVONS HAS MANAGED TO KEEP THE DEAR MADAM'S ATTENTION DIVERTED.
HIS EYES SCAN THE DRESSER SURFA HE MUST MOVE QUICKLY. ANY EVIDENCE WILL DO-- A DIARY, AN INCRIMINATING BLOOD STAIN, ANY THING TO SUPPORT HIS THEORIES AS TO HOW AND WHY THESE ATROCIOUS MUTILATIONS HAVE OCCURRED!
A THIN SLIVER OF LIGHT PIERCES THE GLOOM-- AND HODIAH HALTS. THERE IS NO TIME TO HIDE!

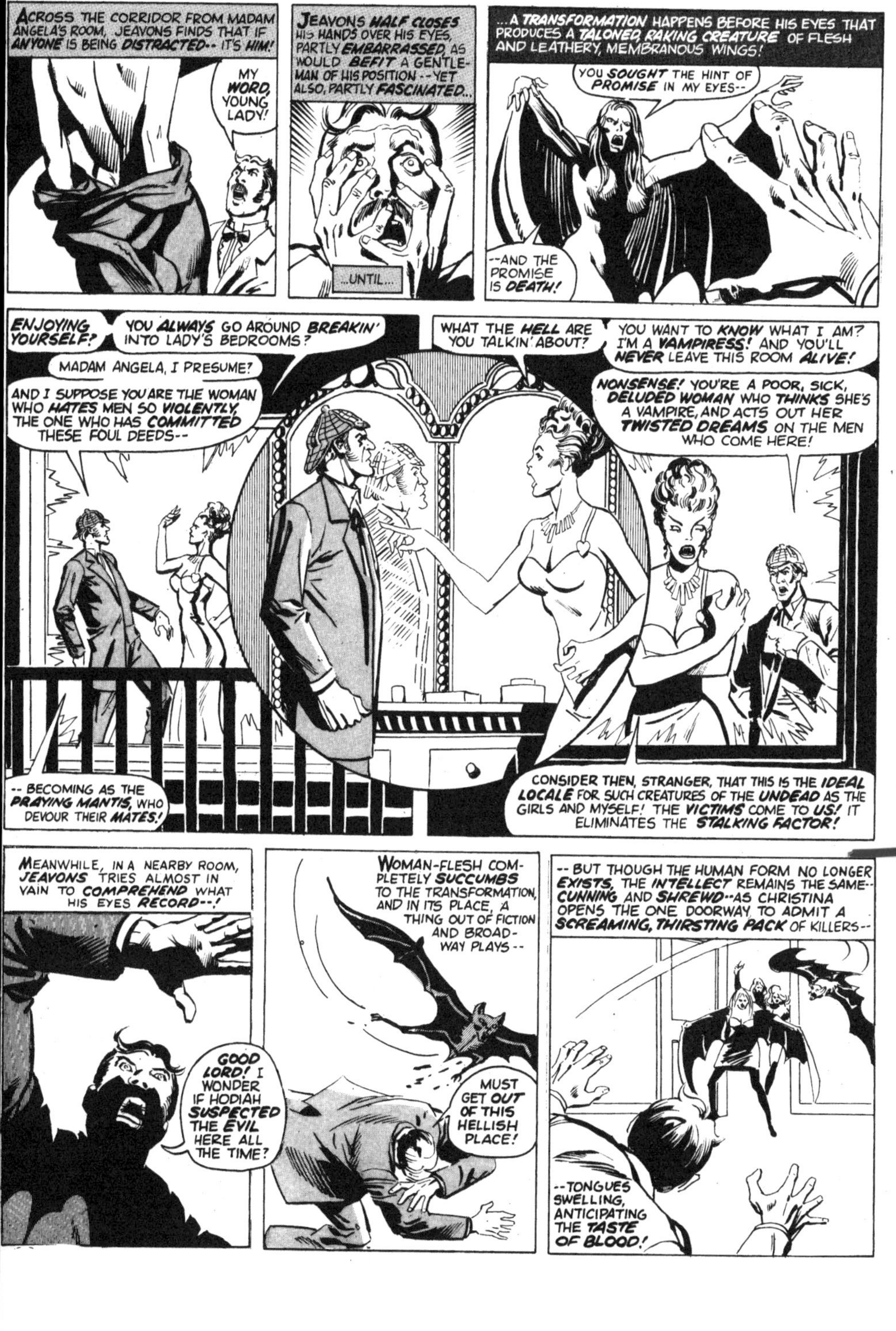
ACROSS THE CORRIDOR FROM MADAM ANGELA'S ROOM, JEAVONS FINDS THAT IF ANYONE IS BEING DISTRACTED-- IT'S HIM!
MY WORD, YOUNG LADY!
JEAVONS HALF CLOSES HIS HANDS OVER HIS EYES, PARTLY EMBARRASSED, AS WOULD BEFIT A GENTLEMAN OF HIS POSITION --YET ALSO, PARTLY FASCINATED...
...UNTIL...
...A TRANSFORMATION HAPPENS BEFORE HIS EYES THAT PRODUCES A TALONED, RAKING CREATURE OF FLESH AND LEATHERY, MEMBRANOUS WINGS!
YOU SOUGHT THE HINT OF PROMISE IN MY EYES--
--AND THE PROMISE IS DEATH!
ENJOYING YOURSELF?
YOU ALWAYS GO AROUND BREAKIN' INTO LADY'S BEDROOMS?
MADAM ANGELA, I PRESUME?
AND I SUPPOSE YOU ARE THE WOMAN WHO HATES MEN SO VIOLENTLY, THE ONE WHO HAS COMMITTED THESE FOUL DEEDS--
-- BECOMING AS THE PRAYING MANTIS, WHO DEVOUR THEIR MATES!
WHAT THE HELL ARE YOU TALKIN' ABOUT?
YOU WANT TO KNOW WHAT I AM? I'M A VAMPIRESS! AND YOU'LL NEVER LEAVE THIS ROOM ALIVE!
NONSENSE! YOU'RE A POOR, SICK, DELUDED WOMAN WHO THINKS SHE'S A VAMPIRE, AND ACTS OUT HER TWISTED DREAMS ON THE MEN WHO COME HERE!
CONSIDER THEN, STRANGER, THAT THIS IS THE IDEAL LOCALE FOR SUCH CREATURES OF THE UNDEAD AS THE GIRLS AND MYSELF! THE VICTIMS COME TO US! IT ELIMINATES THE STALKING FACTOR!
MEANWHILE, IN A NEARBY ROOM, JEAVONS TRIES ALMOST IN VAIN TO COMPREHEND WHAT HIS EYES RECORD--!
GOOD LORD! I WONDER IF HODIAH SUSPECTED THE EVIL HERE ALL THE TIME?
WOMAN-FLESH COMPLETELY SUCCUMBS TO THE TRANSFORMATION, AND IN ITS PLACE, A THING OUT OF FICTION AND BROADWAY PLAYS --
MUST GET OUT OF THIS HELLISH PLACE!
-- BUT THOUGH THE HUMAN FORM NO LONGER EXISTS, THE INTELLECT REMAINS THE SAME-- CUNNING AND SHREWD--AS CHRISTINA OPENS THE ONE DOORWAY, TO ADMIT A SCREAMING, THIRSTING PACK OF KILLERS--
--TONGUES SWELLING, ANTICIPATING THE TASTE OF BLOOD!

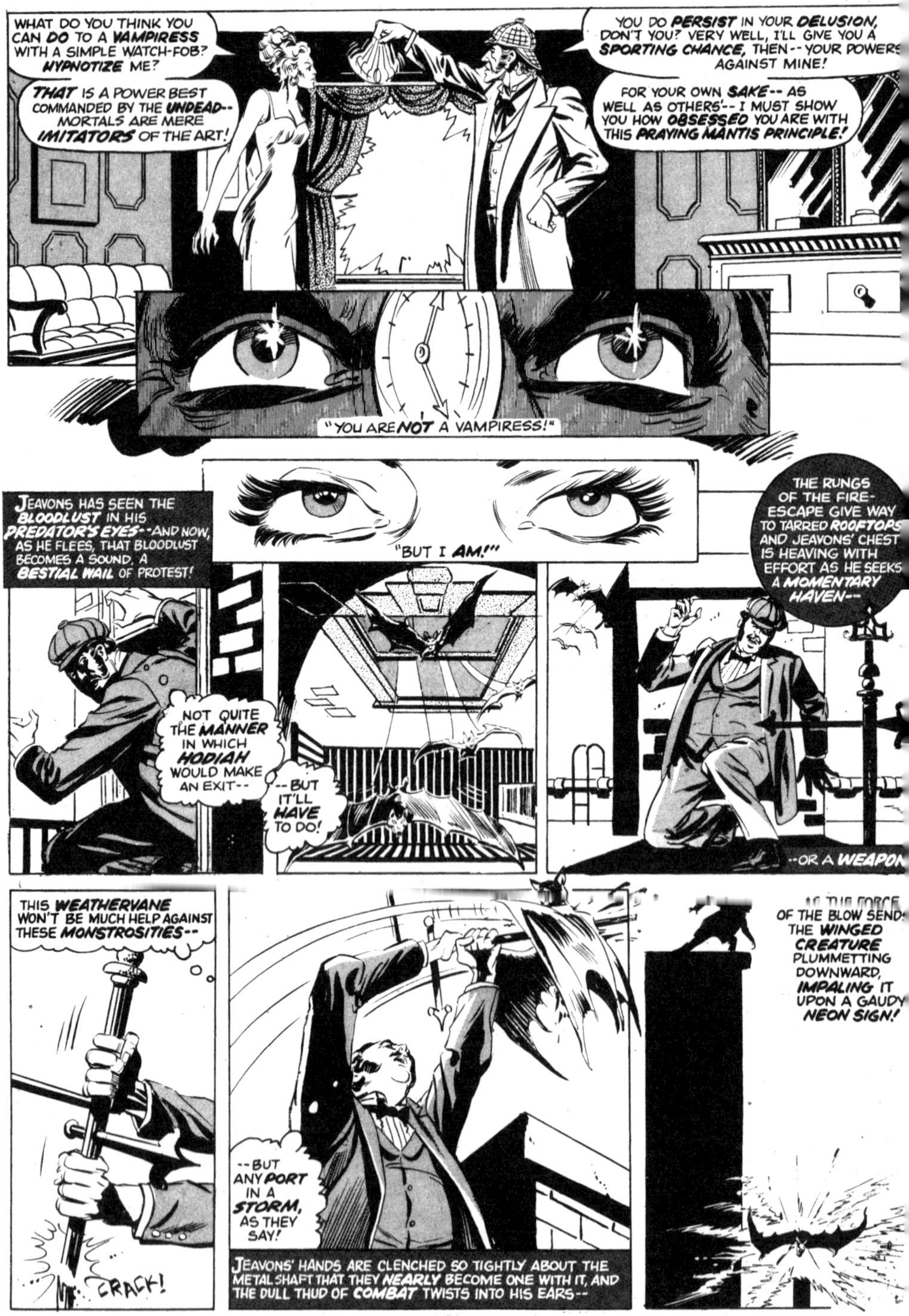
WHAT DO YOU THINK YOU CAN DO TO A VAMPIRESS WITH A SIMPLE WATCH-FOB? HYPNOTIZE ME?
THAT IS A POWER BEST COMMANDED BY THE UNDEAD-- MORTALS ARE MERE IMITATORS OF THE ART!
YOU DO PERSIST IN YOUR DELUSION, DON'T YOU? VERY WELL, I'LL GIVE YOU A SPORTING CHANCE, THEN--YOUR POWERS AGAINST MINE!
FOR YOUR OWN SAKE-- AS WELL AS OTHERS'-- I MUST SHOW YOU HOW OBSESSED YOU ARE WITH THIS PRAYING MANTIS PRINCIPLE!
"YOU ARE NOT A VAMPIRESS!"
"BUT I AM!"
JEAVONS HAS SEEN THE BLOODLUST IN HIS PREDATOR'S EYES--AND NOW, AS HE FLEES, THAT BLOODLUST BECOMES A SOUND, A BESTIAL WAIL OF PROTEST!
NOT QUITE THE MANNER IN WHICH HODIAH WOULD MAKE AN EXIT--
--BUT IT'LL HAVE TO DO!
THE RUNGS OF THE FIRE-ESCAPE GIVE WAY TO TARRED ROOFTOPS AND JEAVONS' CHEST IS HEAVING WITH EFFORT AS HE SEEKS A MOMENTARY HAVEN--
--OR A WEAPON
THIS WEATHERVANE WON'T BE MUCH HELP AGAINST THESE MONSTROSITIES--
CRACK!
--BUT ANY PORT IN A STORM, AS THEY SAY!
JEAVONS' HANDS ARE CLENCHED SO TIGHTLY ABOUT THE METAL SHAFT THAT THEY NEARLY BECOME ONE WITH IT, AND THE DULL THUD OF COMBAT TWISTS INTO HIS EARS--
OF THE BLOW SENDS THE WINGED CREATURE PLUMMETTING DOWNWARD, IMPALING IT UPON A GAUDY NEON SIGN!

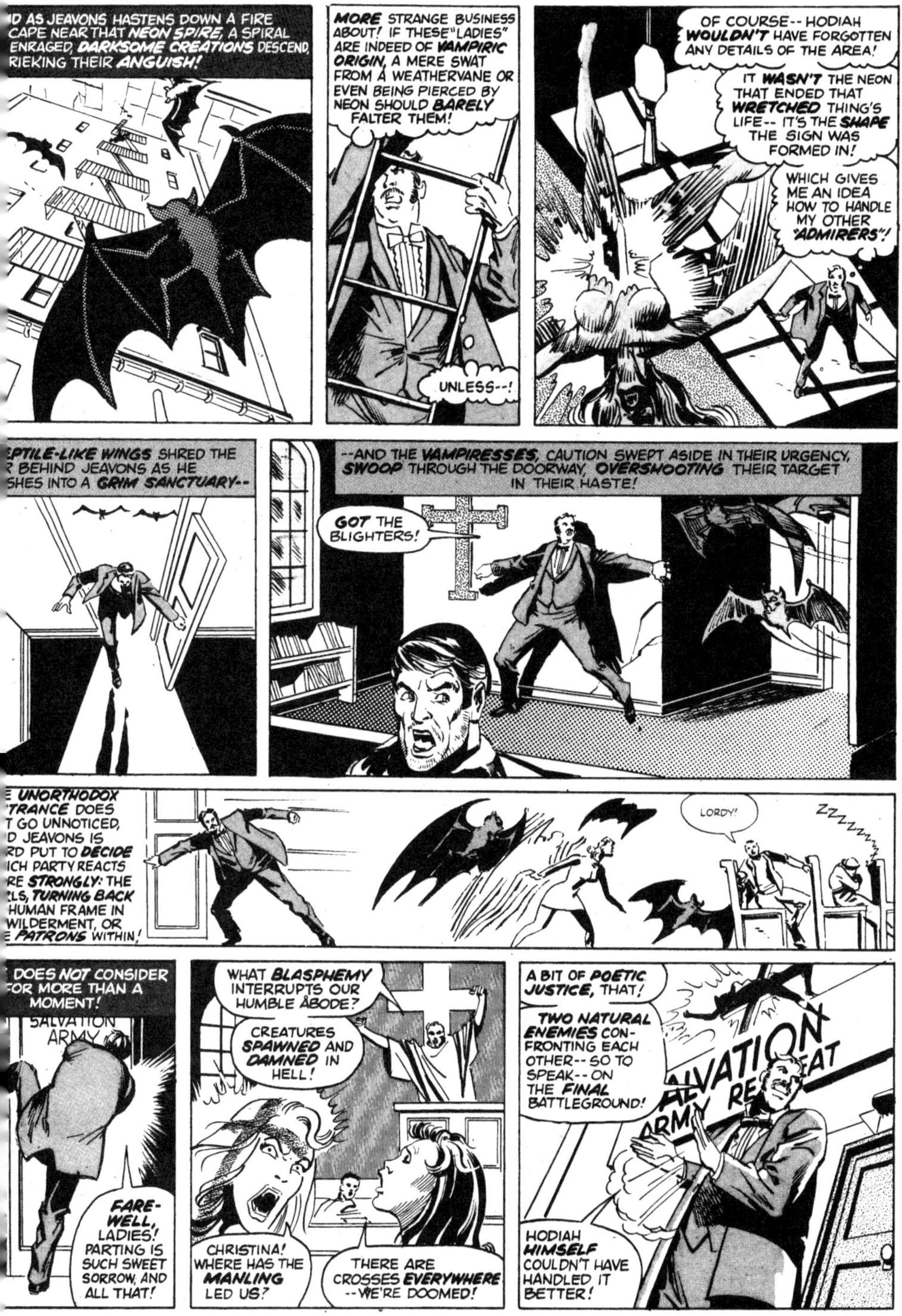

ID AS JEAVONS HASTENS DOWN A FIRE CAPE NEAR THAT NEON SPIRE, A SPIRAL ENRAGED, DARKSOME CREATIONS DESCEND, RIEKING THEIR ANGUISH!
MORE STRANGE BUSINESS ABOUT! IF THESE "LADIES" ARE INDEED OF VAMPIRIC ORIGIN, A MERE SWAT FROM A WEATHERVANE OR EVEN BEING PIERCED BY NEON SHOULD BARELY FALTER THEM!
UNLESS--!
OF COURSE-- HODIAH WOULDN'T HAVE FORGOTTEN ANY DETAILS OF THE AREA!
IT WASN'T THE NEON THAT ENDED THAT WRETCHED THING'S LIFE-- IT'S THE SHAPE THE SIGN WAS FORMED IN!
WHICH GIVES ME AN IDEA HOW TO HANDLE MY OTHER "ADMIRERS"!
EPTILE-LIKE WINGS SHRED THE R BEHIND JEAVONS AS HE SHES INTO A GRIM SANCTUARY--
--AND THE VAMPIRESSES, CAUTION SWEPT ASIDE IN THEIR URGENCY, SWOOP THROUGH THE DOORWAY, OVERSHOOTING THEIR TARGET IN THEIR HASTE!
GOT THE BLIGHTERS!
E UNORTHODOX TRANCE DOES T GO UNNOTICED, D JEAVONS IS RD PUT TO DECIDE ICH PARTY REACTS RE STRONGLY: THE LS, TURNING BACK HUMAN FRAME IN WILDERMENT, OR E PATRONS WITHIN!
LORDY!
ZZZZZZZ
DOES NOT CONSIDER FOR MORE THAN A MOMENT!
SALVATION ARMY
FARE-WELL, LADIES! PARTING IS SUCH SWEET SORROW, AND ALL THAT!
WHAT BLASPHEMY INTERRUPTS OUR HUMBLE ABODE?
CREATURES SPAWNED AND DAMNED IN HELL!
CHRISTINA! WHERE HAS THE MANLING LED US?
THERE ARE CROSSES EVERYWHERE --WE'RE DOOMED!
A BIT OF POETIC JUSTICE, THAT!
TWO NATURAL ENEMIES CON-FRONTING EACH OTHER-- SO TO SPEAK-- ON THE FINAL BATTLEGROUND!
SALVATION ARMY RETREAT
HODIAH HIMSELF COULDN'T HAVE HANDLED IT BETTER!

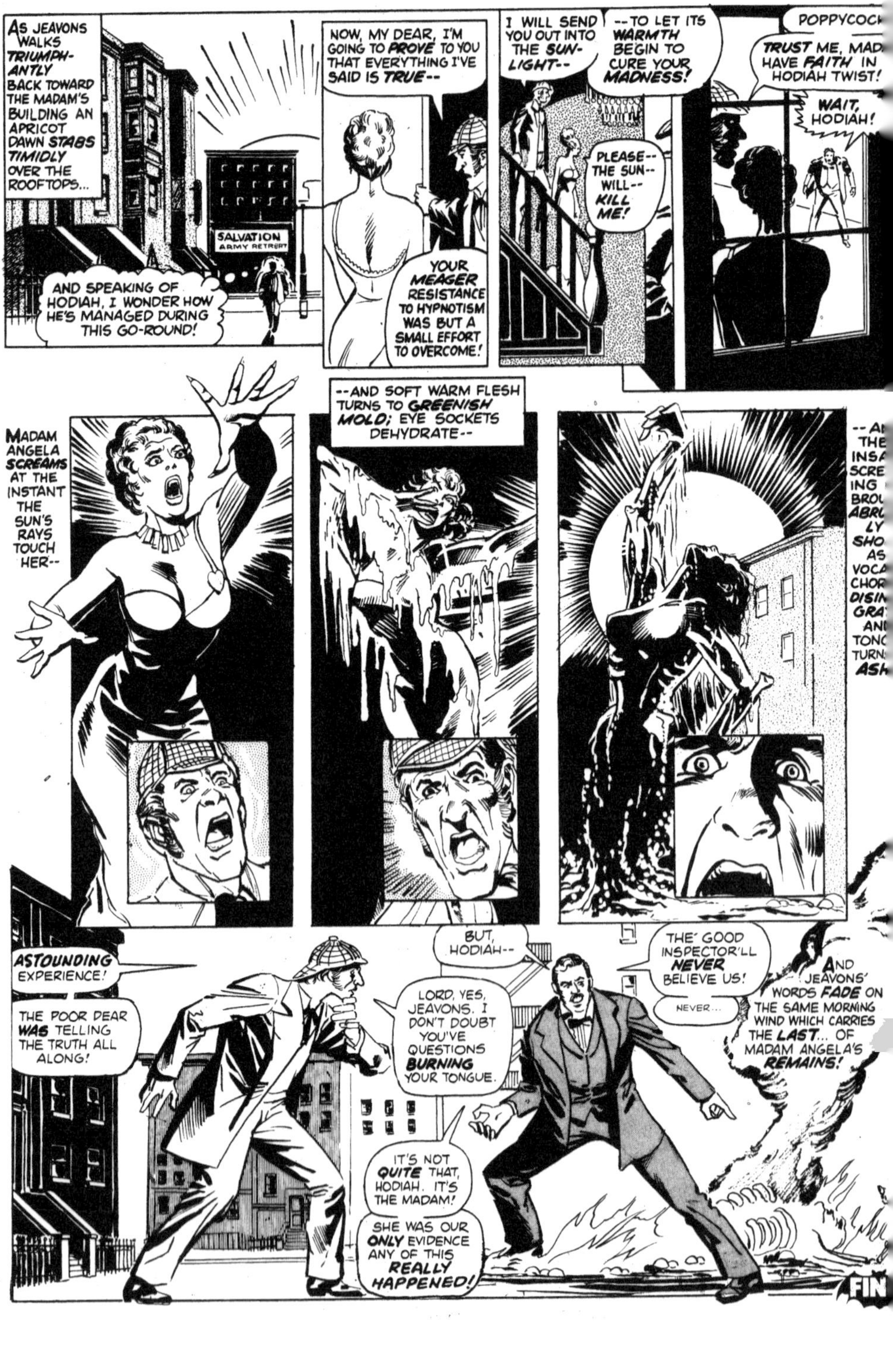
AS JEAVONS WALKS TRIUMPHANTLY BACK TOWARD THE MADAM'S BUILDING AN APRICOT DAWN STABS TIMIDLY OVER THE ROOFTOPS...
SALVATION ARMY RETREAT
AND SPEAKING OF HODIAH, I WONDER HOW HE'S MANAGED DURING THIS GO-ROUND!
NOW, MY DEAR, I'M GOING TO PROVE TO YOU THAT EVERYTHING I'VE SAID IS TRUE--
YOUR MEAGER RESISTANCE TO HYPNOTISM WAS BUT A SMALL EFFORT TO OVERCOME!
I WILL SEND YOU OUT INTO THE SUN-LIGHT--
--TO LET ITS WARMTH BEGIN TO CURE YOUR MADNESS!
PLEASE-- THE SUN-- WILL-- KILL ME!
POPPYCOCK
TRUST ME, MAD HAVE FAITH IN HODIAH TWIST!
WAIT, HODIAH!
MADAM ANGELA SCREAMS AT THE INSTANT THE SUN'S RAYS TOUCH HER--
--AND SOFT WARM FLESH TURNS TO GREENISH MOLD; EYE SOCKETS DEHYDRATE--
--AI THE INSA SCRE ING BROU ABRU LY SHO AS VOCA CHOR DISIN GRA AN TONG TURN ASH
ASTOUNDING EXPERIENCE!
THE POOR DEAR WAS TELLING THE TRUTH ALL ALONG!
BUT, HODIAH--
LORD, YES, JEAVONS. I DON'T DOUBT YOU'VE QUESTIONS BURNING YOUR TONGUE.
THE GOOD INSPECTOR'LL NEVER BELIEVE US!
NEVER...
IT'S NOT QUITE THAT, HODIAH. IT'S THE MADAM!
SHE WAS OUR ONLY EVIDENCE ANY OF THIS REALLY HAPPENED!
AND JEAVONS' WORDS FADE ON THE SAME MORNING WIND WHICH CARRIES THE LAST... OF MADAM ANGELA'S REMAINS!
FIN

VAMPIRE TALES FEATURE PAGE

This year has seen Marvel Comics enter the "horror" magazine field and revitalize said field. But some twenty years ago, E.C. Comics attempted the same thing and produced a hefty handful of terror masterpieces. These classics from the 1950's have been recently brought to the screen, first in TALES FROM THE CRYPT and now in . . .

THE VAULT OF HORROR

VAULT OF HORROR is the second in a series of horror films to be released by Cinerama based on the old E.C. Comics stories, the first being TALES FROM THE CRYPT (directed by Freddie Francis). VAULT OF HORROR—directed by Roy Ward—is similar both in structure and style to TALES FROM THE CRYPT. However, this time five men explore their nightmares and fantasies in an underground *vault*—hence the title. At the end of their explorations, they discover that their dreams are, in fact, reality. The five selected tales are connected by use of this central theme.

"Midnight Mess," the first of these varied sketches, is a suspense-filled tale of vampirism set in the "olde English countryside." It proves emphatically that one should never scoff at local superstitions. Roger, a young gentleman of modest means, arrives in a small out-of-the-way village intent on murdering his sister who has been left the entire family fortune and finds himself in the midst of a banquet for *vampires.* Daniel Massey does an excellent job as the irreverent brother. Anna Massey is *haunting* in the role of his favored sister. The vampires at the banquet, and especially the head waiter, will not easily be forgotten as they go through their nighttime festivities.

Second, and least interesting, is a short tale entitled "Bargain in Death". This little vignette focuses on an attempted life insurance fraud in which a man is buried alive only to fall into the hands of a couple of unscrupulous body snatchers. Michael Craig does a very good job creating the illusion that he is suffocating inside the

VAULT OF HORROR. Anna Massey invites her brother to town for a drink—on him, of course.

coffin and there are some tense moments while the viewer wonders if the coffin will be opened in time.

The third offering, "This Trick'll Kill You," was a favorite of mine. A British husband/wife magic team (Sebastian and Inez) are in India scouting up some new acts for their show. They come across a "simple" peasant girl with a wonderful magic rope. Unfortunately, the rope has a mind of its own, and when Inez and Sebastian try to take it away from the girl they find their own lives imperiled. The tale successfully captures the "threat" of the mysterious East and all roles are well developed by the actors: Curt Jergens (Sebastian), Dawn Addams (Inez), Jasima Hilton (Indian Girl), and Ishaq Bux (Fakir).

Fourth, "The Neat Job," is one of the best known and most widely imitated of the E.C. classics. Because it's so well-known, its segment is hard pressed to retain any sense of suspense. I guessed the climax almost at the start. The tale depicts the macabre retribution a mistreated wife inflicts upon a tyranical husband. The director, understanding the problems of over-exposure inherent in this tale, tried to circumvent them by adding a dimension of comedy. Thus he cast Terry-Thomas and Glynis Johns as the ill-fated couple. However, even these multi-talented pros couldn't add enough vitality to the sketch to clear away the clichés.

"Drawn and Quartered" was last, longest, and best. Mixing Voodoo and the occult, it's guaranteed to tingle your spine and leave you spellbound at its conclusion. The theme, once again, is injustice and eventual retribution focusing on a young, semi-irrational, impoverished artist living on a South Seas island. He discovers that his art representatives in England are selling his paintings at exhorbitant prices and not passing any profits along to him. Moore seeks out a Voodoo man and is given the ability to paint death. Upon his arrival in London, a series of horrifying accidents occur which will haunt your dreams for months. Denholm Elliot, Terrence Alexander, John Witty play the unfortunate victims of Moore, played by Tom Baker.

VAULT OF HORROR is a fine example of the horror genre, offering over tones of humor for a singular and unique flavor in the story-telling. In short, I recommend it.

— Carla Joseph

There seems to be some sort of community mind at work in the vast Marvel empire. No sooner had we put the finishing touches on this issue's introduction of Satana, than we received a call from our vituperating Los Angeles correspondent Mark Evanier asking if we had seen a flick called "Daughters of Satan." We hadn't, but why didn't he "do a review of it for the issue of VAMPIRE TALES in which you introduced your own, indubitably superior version of the devil's daughter? Why do you think I called, you blood-sucking bastion of comic bookery? If I waited for you to assign a review, I'd starve to death!"

Is it any wonder we love _Mark_ every bit as much as _he_ loved . . .

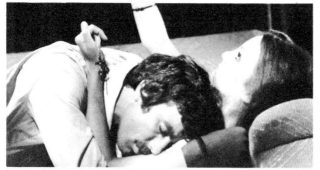

The Daughters of Satan

DAUGHTERS OF SATAN. Under a sinister influence, Barra Grant tries to kill her husband, played by Tom Selleck.

Marvel wants a five-hundred-word review of DAUGHTERS OF SATAN, that turkey of a movie that is making the rounds again—apparently because everyone in his right mind refused to see it the first time out. But how to write five hundred words on a film that anyone with the smallest particle of intelligence (such as this reviewer) simply *must* walk out on? As of forty-eight minutes into this "movie" (loose interpretation of the word "movie" there) virtually nothing happened—except that the more tastful members of the audience had made their way to the lobby and beyond.

It all begins with some unidentified Oriental girl being tortured in a cave somewhere. Then, the "plot" (very loose interpretation of the word "plot" there) switches to a Manila art shoppe where a handsome young American, who looks like Fernando Lamas, buys a witch-burning painting that reminds him of his wife. The Lamas look-a-like is not at all uprising. This movie was produced by C. Aubrey Schenk and, in C. Aubrey Schenk movies, *everyone* looks like Fernando Lamas, including the women. If you're ever entrapped into sitting through a C. Aubrey Schenk movie, poor soul, watch and see if this reviewer isn't right.

The art connoisseur takes the painting home to his wife, who is strangely repulsed by it—and it isn't the only repulsive picture around, you can bet! There then follows a long period during which absolutely nothing happens. This is the highlight of the "movie," as it turns out.

Finally, something happens—apart from the audience's continuing exodus: The couple's house gets two new boarders—an old lady and a dog who not only resemble Fernando Lamas, they also resemble an old lady and a dog in the aforementioned painting. Then, a Filipino bandido shows up and disappears.

By the time these thrilling plot developments have taken place, though, it is forty-eight minutes into the "film" and not even the most heartless editor could expect his film reviewer to sit through another second.

So, if Marvel wants five hundred words about DAUGHTER OF SATAN, they'll be disappointed. All we could come up with was the twenty-eight that follow, take 'em or leave 'em . . . unbearable, ridiculous, boring, tedious, weary, lethargic, insipid, dull, vapid, monotonous, stereotyped, uninteresting, tired, prosaic, colorless, flat, humdrum, characterless, insipid, lifeless, stale, hackneyed, spiritless, trite, wooden, unexciting, interminable, and the ever-popular *lousy!*

In case you haven't guessed . . . this is not a very good movie.

—Mark Evanier

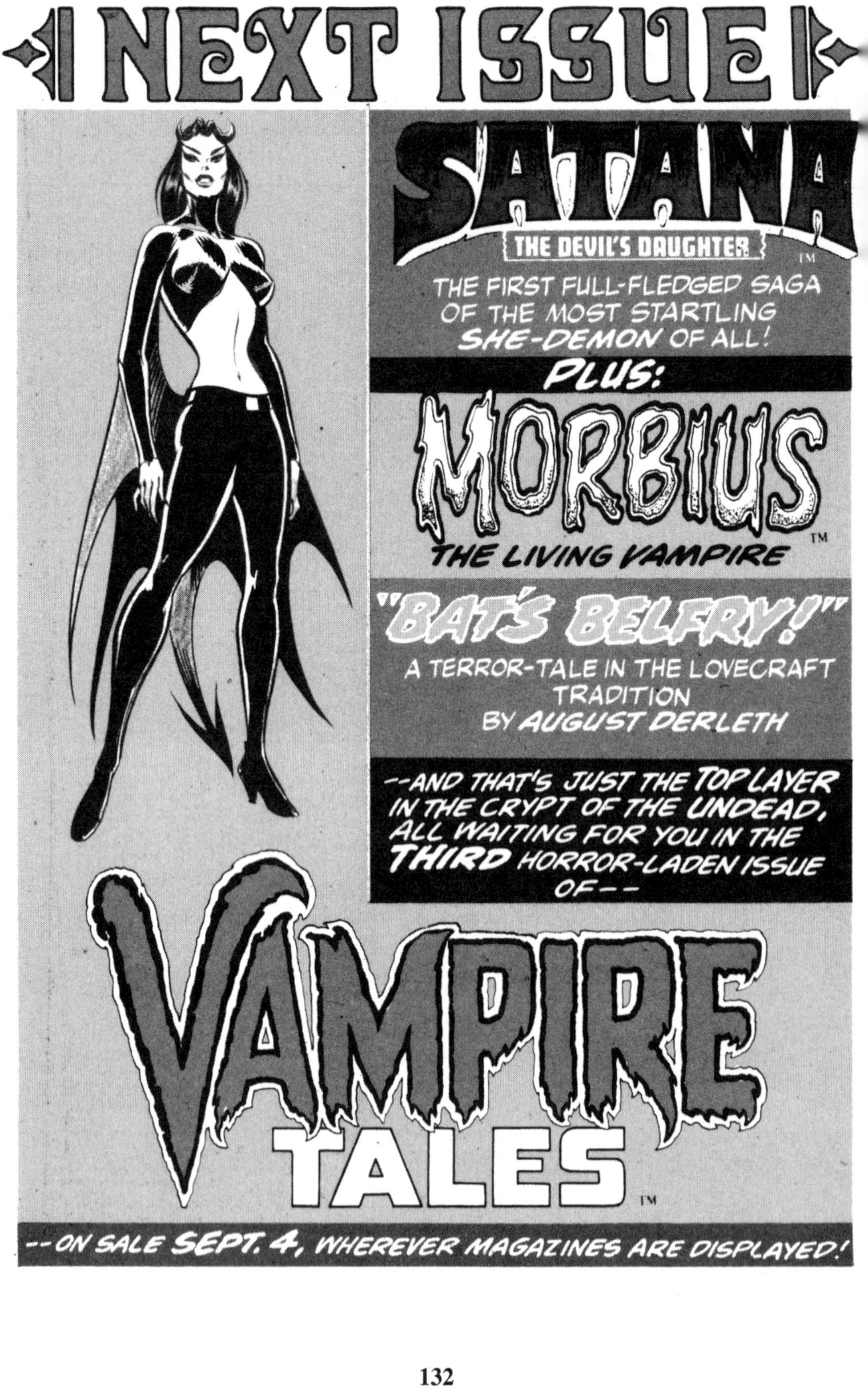
NEXT ISSUE
SATANA
THE DEVIL'S DAUGHTER
TM
THE FIRST FULL-FLEDGED SAGA OF THE MOST STARTLING SHE-DEMON OF ALL!
PLUS:
MORBIUS
TM
THE LIVING VAMPIRE
"BAT'S BELFRY!"
A TERROR-TALE IN THE LOVECRAFT TRADITION BY AUGUST DERLETH
--AND THAT'S JUST THE TOP LAYER IN THE CRYPT OF THE UNDEAD, ALL WAITING FOR YOU IN THE THIRD HORROR-LADEN ISSUE OF--
VAMPIRE TALES
TM
--ON SALE SEPT. 4, WHEREVER MAGAZINES ARE DISPLAYED!

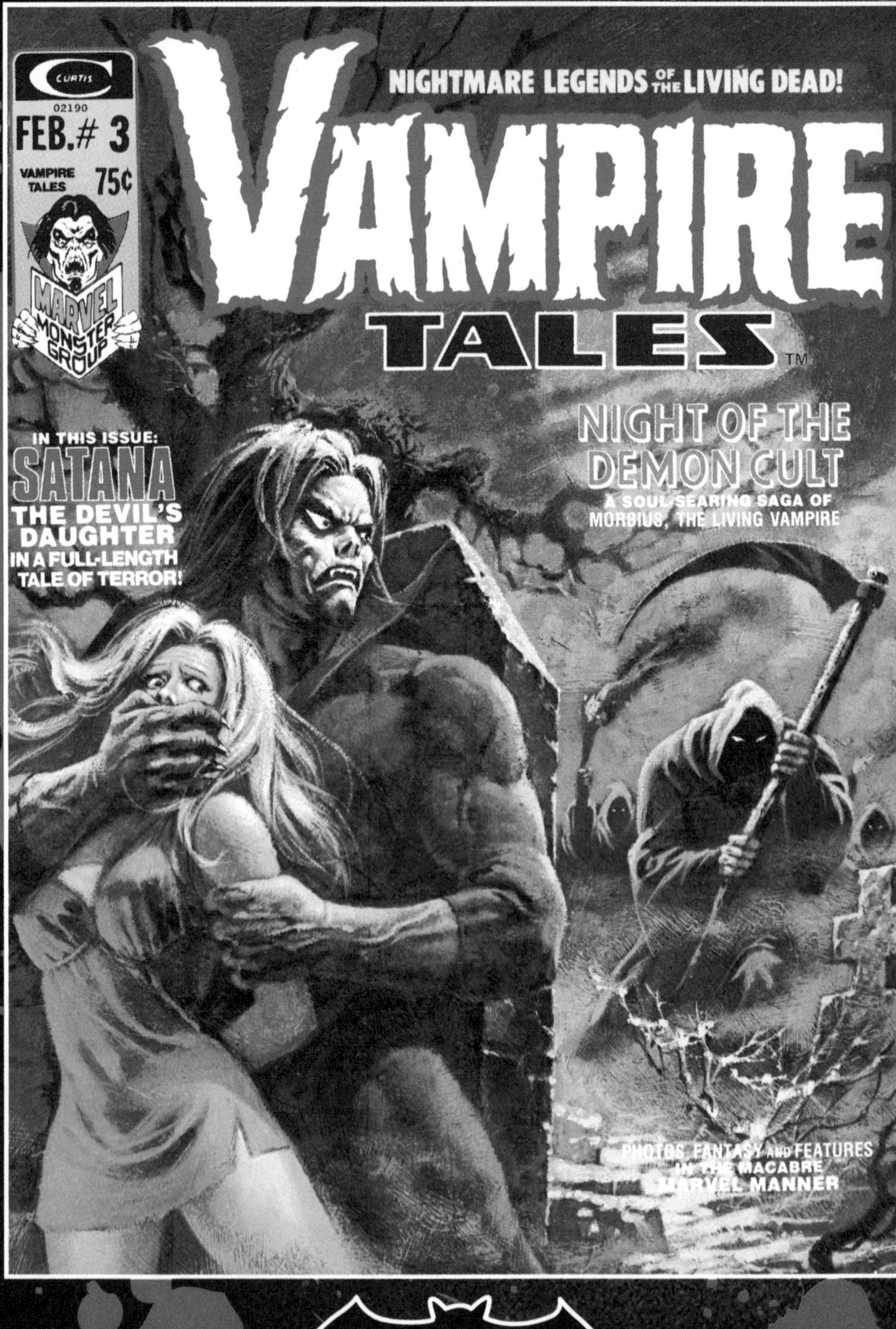
CURTIS
02190
FEB. # 3
VAMPIRE TALES 75¢
MARVEL MONSTER GROUP
NIGHTMARE LEGENDS OF THE LIVING DEAD!
VAMPIRE
TALES TM
NIGHT OF THE DEMON CULT
A SOUL-SEARING SAGA OF MORBIUS, THE LIVING VAMPIRE
IN THIS ISSUE:
SATANA
THE DEVIL'S DAUGHTER
IN A FULL-LENGTH TALE OF TERROR!
PHOTOS, FANTASY AND FEATURES IN THE MACABRE MARVEL MANNER

THREE

BRUARY 1974

STAN LEE presents

VAMPIRE TALES

table of contents

ROY THOMAS
Editor

MARV WOLFMAN
Associate Editor

JOHN VERPOORTEN & MURRAY FRIEDMAN
Production

Contributing Editors: GERRY CONWAY, TONY ISABELLA
DON McGREGOR, CARLA JOSEPH

Artists This Issue: RICH BUCKLER, VICENTE IBENEZ
CARMINE INFANTINO, KLAUS JANSON, PABLO MARCOS,
ESTEBAN MAROTO, PAUL REINMAN, JOHN ROMITA,
MARIE SEVERIN

Writers This Issue: CHRIS CLAREMONT, GERRY CONWAY,
TONY ISABELLA, RUSS JONES, CARLA JOSEPH, STAN LEE,
DON McGREGOR, BHOB STEWART

LUIS DOMINGUEZ   Technical Advisor: LORD RUTHVEN

VAMPIRE TALES is published by MARVEL COMICS GROUP, OFFICE OF PUBLICATION: 575 Madison
Avenue, New York, N.Y. 10022. Published Quarterly. Copyright © 1973 by Marvel Comics Group, a
division of Cadence Industries Corporation. All rights reserved 575 Madison Avenue, New York, N.Y.
Vol. 1, No. 3, Feb. 1974 issue. Price 75¢ per copy in the U.S. and Canada. No similarity between
any of the names, characters, persons and/or institutions in this magazine with those of any living or
dead person or institution is intended, and any such similarity which may exist is purely coincidental.

This is the city—Los Angeles, *California*. It's a city of dreams and a city of constant changes. One such change: Grauman's Chinese Theatre no longer exists. A new owner has changed its famous name to Mann's Chinese Theatre. And though there are those who protest this change, it will doubtless take hold as so many other changes have.

Another change—a small, ominous one—an addition to the ranks of those who populate this city. Her name is *Satana* and she is the *Devil's Daughter*. Her father looks at her new home and he *smiles*.

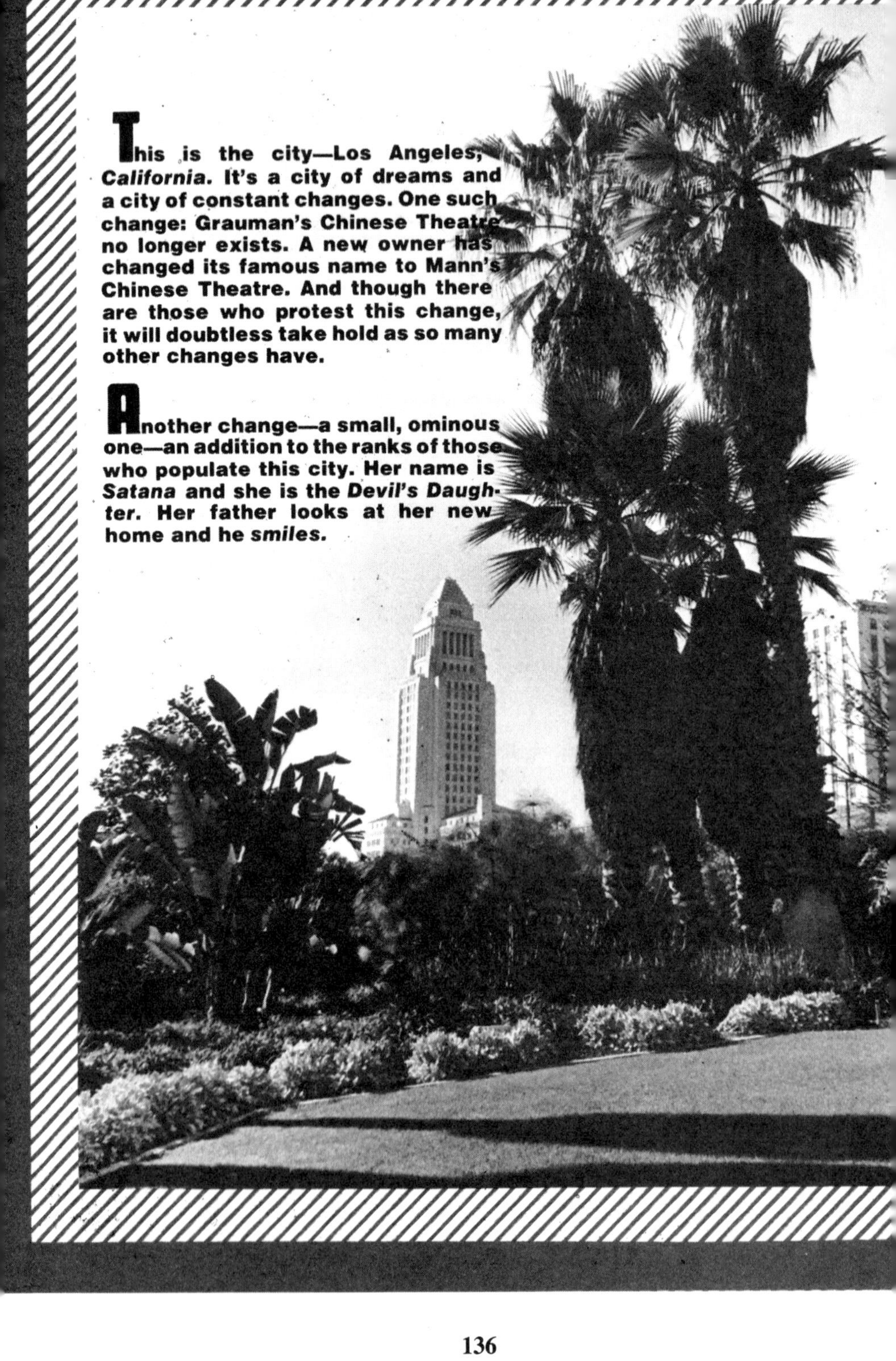

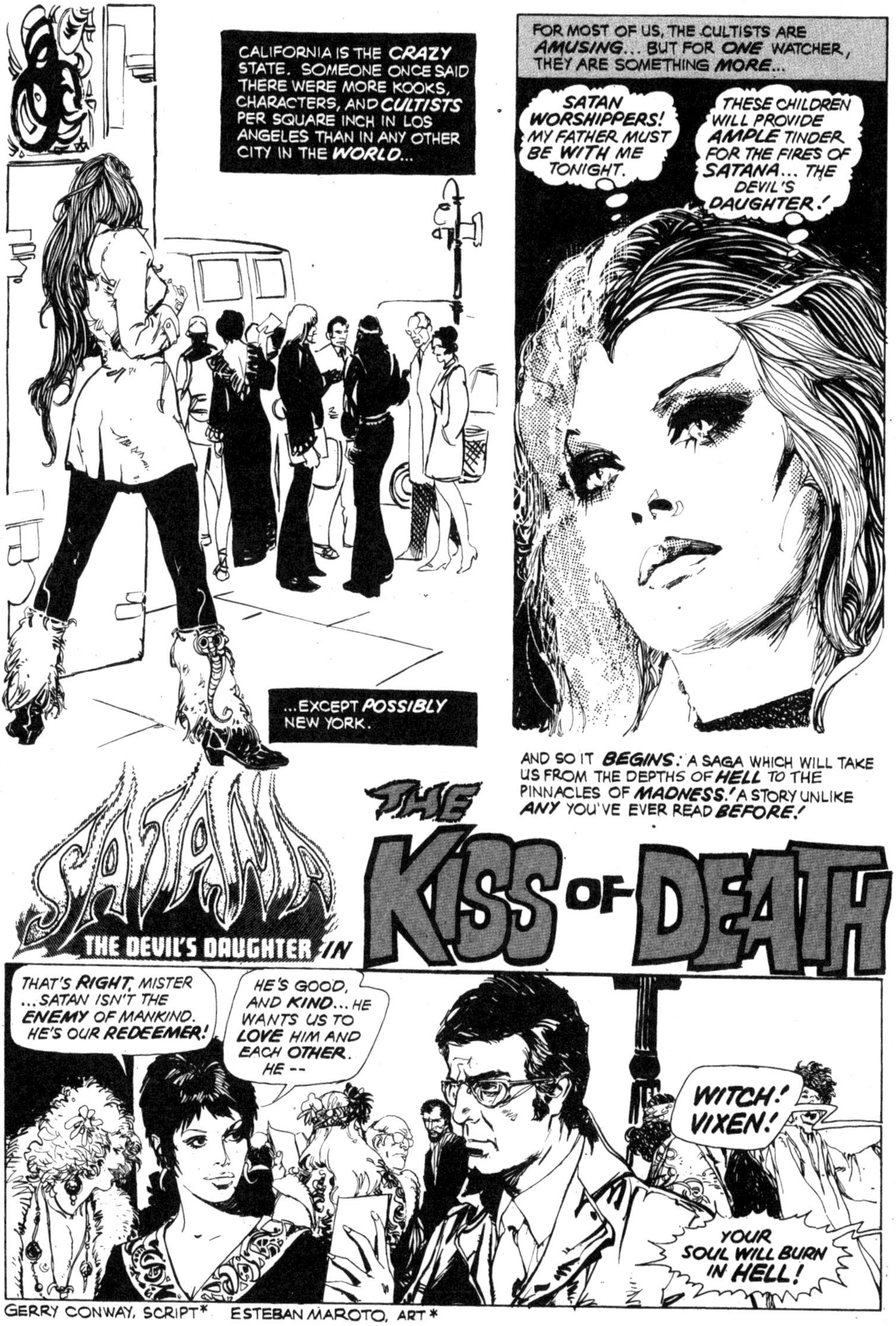
CALIFORNIA IS THE CRAZY STATE. SOMEONE ONCE SAID THERE WERE MORE KOOKS, CHARACTERS, AND CULTISTS PER SQUARE INCH IN LOS ANGELES THAN IN ANY OTHER CITY IN THE WORLD...
...EXCEPT POSSIBLY NEW YORK.
FOR MOST OF US, THE CULTISTS ARE AMUSING... BUT FOR ONE WATCHER, THEY ARE SOMETHING MORE...
SATAN WORSHIPPERS! MY FATHER MUST BE WITH ME TONIGHT.
THESE CHILDREN WILL PROVIDE AMPLE TINDER FOR THE FIRES OF SATANA... THE DEVIL'S DAUGHTER!
AND SO IT BEGINS: A SAGA WHICH WILL TAKE US FROM THE DEPTHS OF HELL TO THE PINNACLES OF MADNESS! A STORY UNLIKE ANY YOU'VE EVER READ BEFORE!
SATANA
THE DEVIL'S DAUGHTER IN
THE KISS OF DEATH
THAT'S RIGHT, MISTER ...SATAN ISN'T THE ENEMY OF MANKIND. HE'S OUR REDEEMER!
HE'S GOOD, AND KIND... HE WANTS US TO LOVE HIM AND EACH OTHER. HE --
WITCH! VIXEN!
YOUR SOUL WILL BURN IN HELL!

GERRY CONWAY, SCRIPT* ESTEBAN MAROTO, ART*

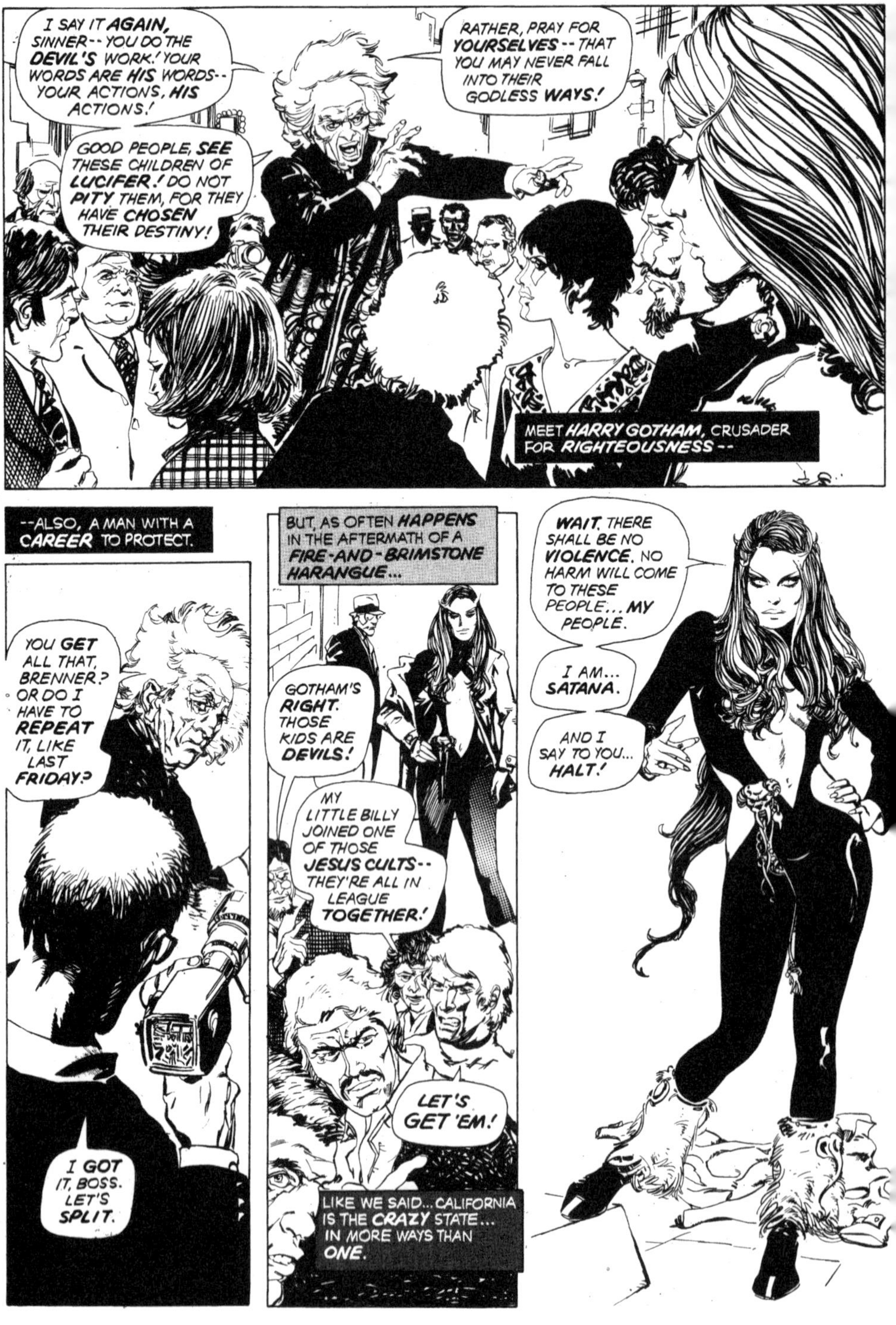
I SAY IT AGAIN, SINNER-- YOU DO THE DEVIL'S WORK! YOUR WORDS ARE HIS WORDS-- YOUR ACTIONS, HIS ACTIONS!
GOOD PEOPLE, SEE THESE CHILDREN OF LUCIFER! DO NOT PITY THEM, FOR THEY HAVE CHOSEN THEIR DESTINY!
RATHER, PRAY FOR YOURSELVES-- THAT YOU MAY NEVER FALL INTO THEIR GODLESS WAYS!
MEET HARRY GOTHAM, CRUSADER FOR RIGHTEOUSNESS--
--ALSO, A MAN WITH A CAREER TO PROTECT.
YOU GET ALL THAT, BRENNER? OR DO I HAVE TO REPEAT IT, LIKE LAST FRIDAY?
I GOT IT, BOSS. LET'S SPLIT.
BUT, AS OFTEN HAPPENS IN THE AFTERMATH OF A FIRE-AND-BRIMSTONE HARANGUE...
GOTHAM'S RIGHT. THOSE KIDS ARE DEVILS!
MY LITTLE BILLY JOINED ONE OF THOSE JESUS CULTS-- THEY'RE ALL IN LEAGUE TOGETHER!
LET'S GET 'EM!
LIKE WE SAID... CALIFORNIA IS THE CRAZY STATE... IN MORE WAYS THAN ONE.
WAIT. THERE SHALL BE NO VIOLENCE. NO HARM WILL COME TO THESE PEOPLE... MY PEOPLE.
I AM... SATANA.
AND I SAY TO YOU... HALT!

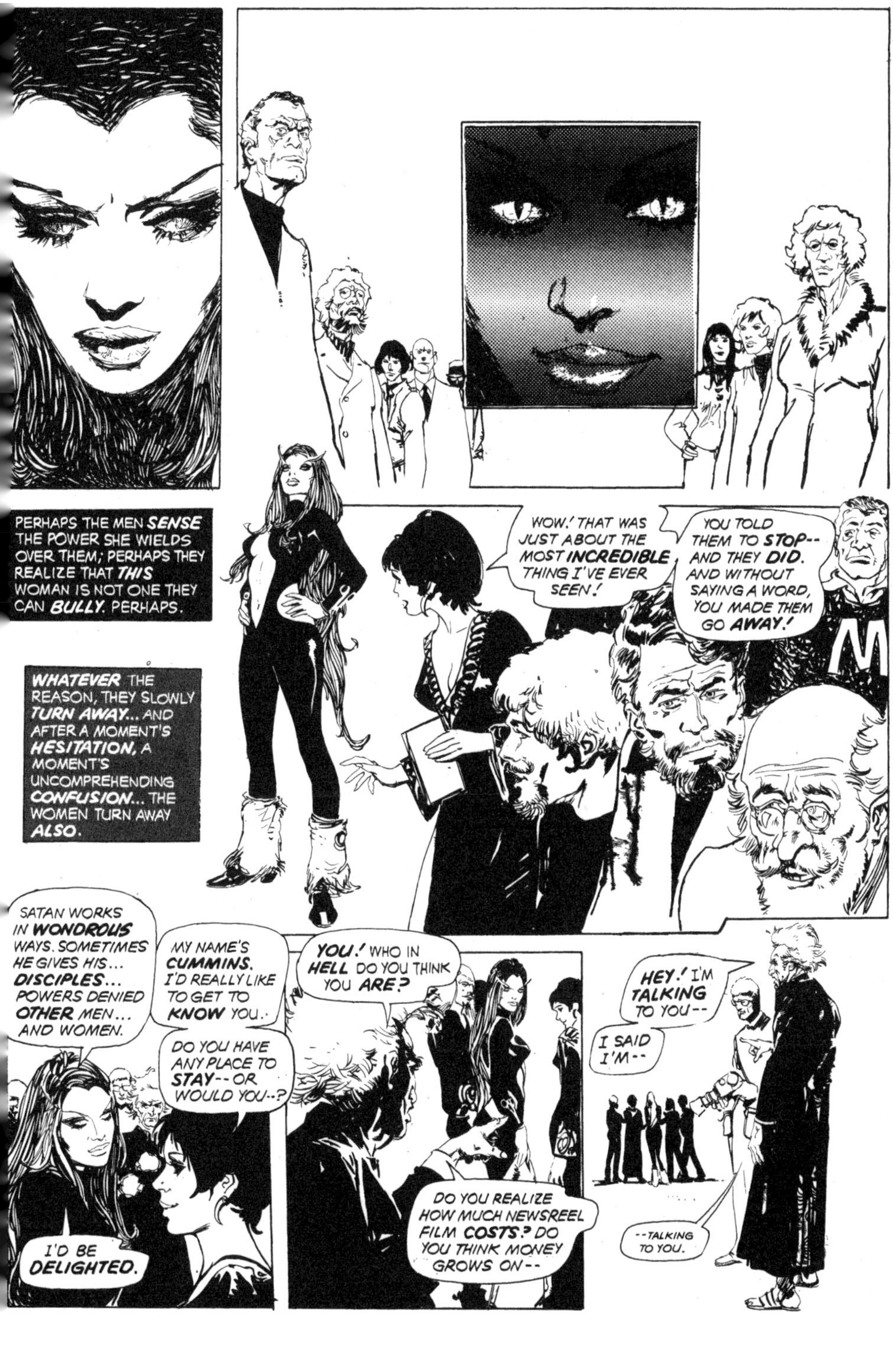
PERHAPS THE MEN SENSE THE POWER SHE WIELDS OVER THEM; PERHAPS THEY REALIZE THAT THIS WOMAN IS NOT ONE THEY CAN BULLY. PERHAPS.
WHATEVER THE REASON, THEY SLOWLY TURN AWAY... AND AFTER A MOMENT'S HESITATION, A MOMENT'S UNCOMPREHENDING CONFUSION... THE WOMEN TURN AWAY ALSO.
WOW! THAT WAS JUST ABOUT THE MOST INCREDIBLE THING I'VE EVER SEEN!
YOU TOLD THEM TO STOP-- AND THEY DID. AND WITHOUT SAYING A WORD, YOU MADE THEM GO AWAY!
SATAN WORKS IN WONDROUS WAYS. SOMETIMES HE GIVES HIS... DISCIPLES... POWERS DENIED OTHER MEN... AND WOMEN.
MY NAME'S CUMMINS. I'D REALLY LIKE TO GET TO KNOW YOU.
DO YOU HAVE ANY PLACE TO STAY--OR WOULD YOU--?
I'D BE DELIGHTED.
YOU! WHO IN HELL DO YOU THINK YOU ARE?
DO YOU REALIZE HOW MUCH NEWSREEL FILM COSTS? DO YOU THINK MONEY GROWS ON--
HEY! I'M TALKING TO YOU--
I SAID I'M--
--TALKING TO YOU.

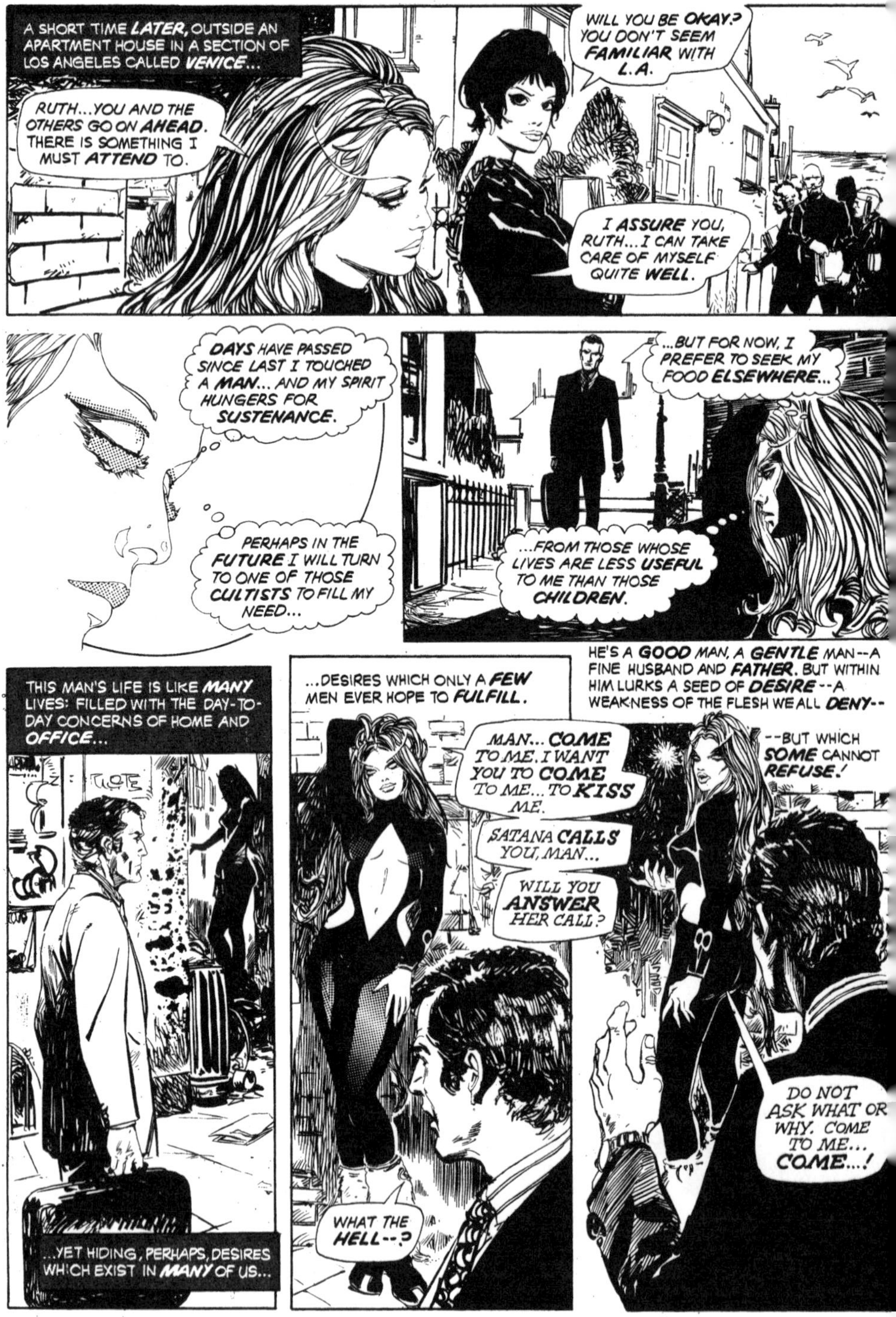
A SHORT TIME LATER, OUTSIDE AN APARTMENT HOUSE IN A SECTION OF LOS ANGELES CALLED VENICE...
RUTH... YOU AND THE OTHERS GO ON AHEAD. THERE IS SOMETHING I MUST ATTEND TO.
WILL YOU BE OKAY? YOU DON'T SEEM FAMILIAR WITH L.A.
I ASSURE YOU, RUTH... I CAN TAKE CARE OF MYSELF QUITE WELL.
DAYS HAVE PASSED SINCE LAST I TOUCHED A MAN... AND MY SPIRIT HUNGERS FOR SUSTENANCE.
PERHAPS IN THE FUTURE I WILL TURN TO ONE OF THOSE CULTISTS TO FILL MY NEED...
...BUT FOR NOW, I PREFER TO SEEK MY FOOD ELSEWHERE...
...FROM THOSE WHOSE LIVES ARE LESS USEFUL TO ME THAN THOSE CHILDREN.
THIS MAN'S LIFE IS LIKE MANY LIVES: FILLED WITH THE DAY-TO-DAY CONCERNS OF HOME AND OFFICE...
...YET HIDING, PERHAPS, DESIRES WHICH EXIST IN MANY OF US...
...DESIRES WHICH ONLY A FEW MEN EVER HOPE TO FULFILL.
MAN... COME TO ME. I WANT YOU TO COME TO ME... TO KISS ME.
SATANA CALLS YOU, MAN...
WILL YOU ANSWER HER CALL?
WHAT THE HELL--?
HE'S A GOOD MAN, A GENTLE MAN--A FINE HUSBAND AND FATHER. BUT WITHIN HIM LURKS A SEED OF DESIRE--A WEAKNESS OF THE FLESH WE ALL DENY--
--BUT WHICH SOME CANNOT REFUSE.!
DO NOT ASK WHAT OR WHY. COME TO ME... COME...!

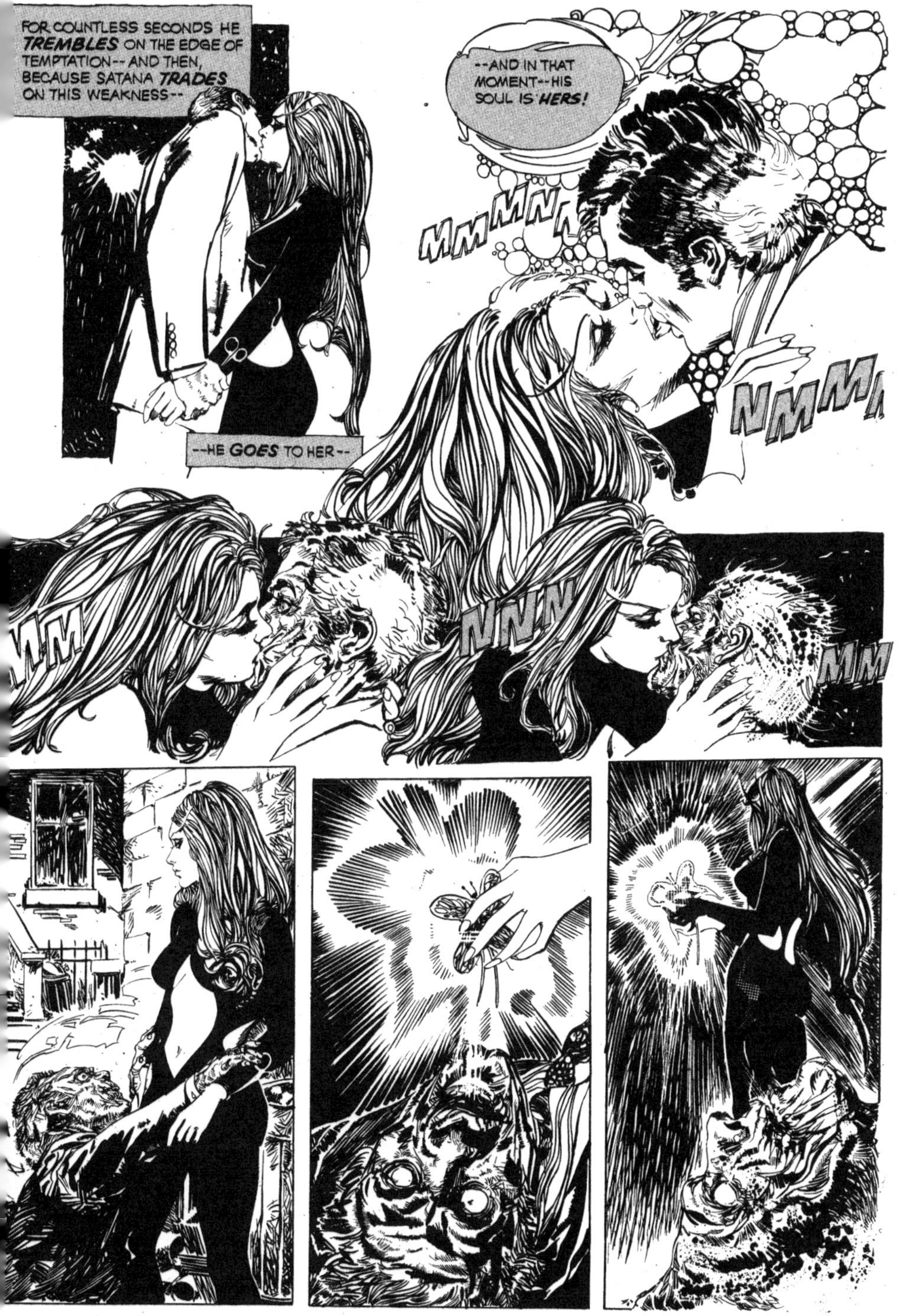
FOR COUNTLESS SECONDS HE TREMBLES ON THE EDGE OF TEMPTATION-- AND THEN, BECAUSE SATANA TRADES ON THIS WEAKNESS--
--HE GOES TO HER--
--AND IN THAT MOMENT--HIS SOUL IS HERS!
MMMMNN
NMMM
MM
NNN
MM

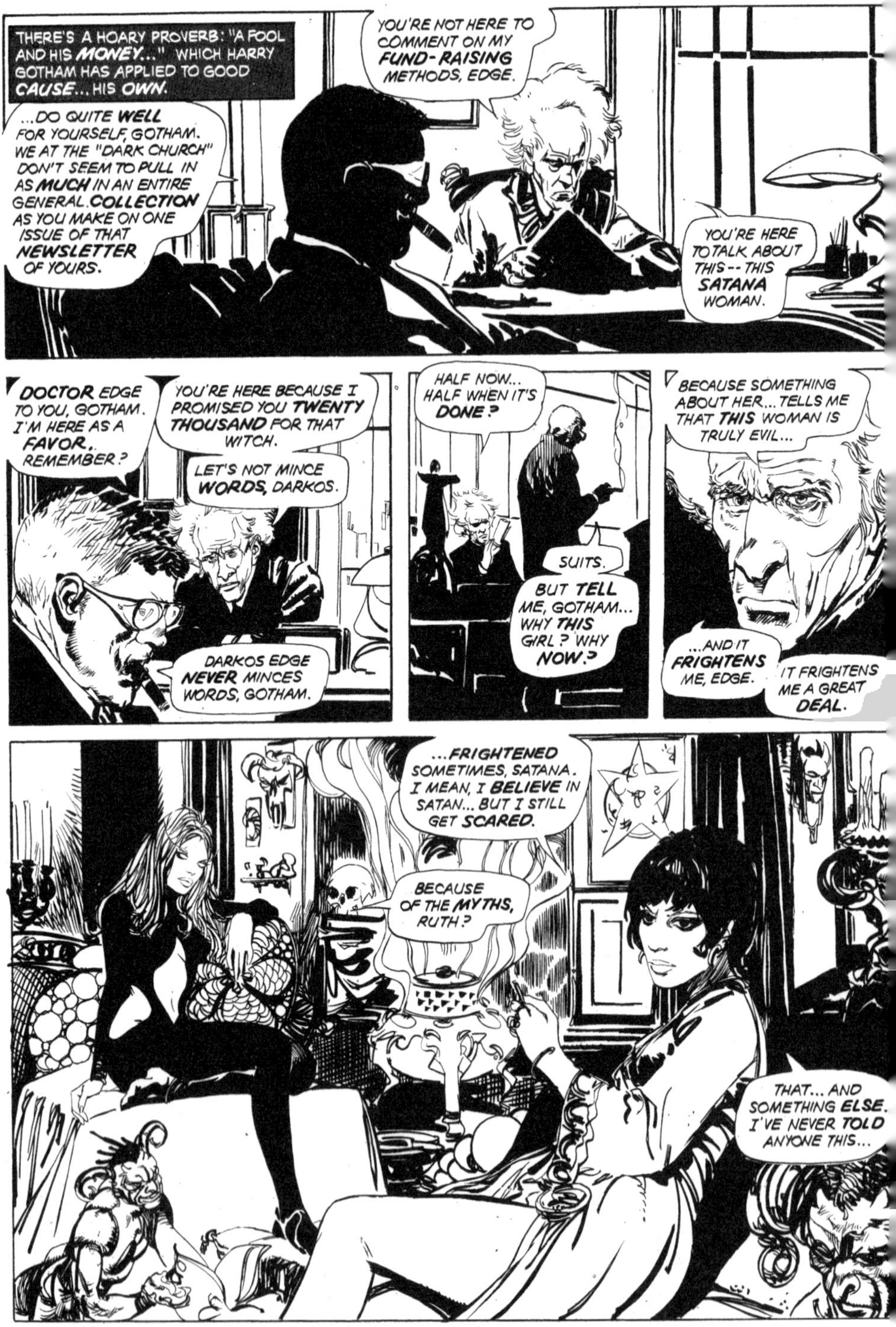
THERE'S A HOARY PROVERB: "A FOOL AND HIS MONEY..." WHICH HARRY GOTHAM HAS APPLIED TO GOOD CAUSE... HIS OWN.
...DO QUITE WELL FOR YOURSELF, GOTHAM. WE AT THE "DARK CHURCH" DON'T SEEM TO PULL IN AS MUCH IN AN ENTIRE GENERAL COLLECTION AS YOU MAKE ON ONE ISSUE OF THAT NEWSLETTER OF YOURS.
YOU'RE NOT HERE TO COMMENT ON MY FUND-RAISING METHODS, EDGE.
YOU'RE HERE TO TALK ABOUT THIS--THIS SATANA WOMAN.
DOCTOR EDGE TO YOU, GOTHAM. I'M HERE AS A FAVOR, REMEMBER?
YOU'RE HERE BECAUSE I PROMISED YOU TWENTY THOUSAND FOR THAT WITCH.
LET'S NOT MINCE WORDS, DARKOS.
DARKOS EDGE NEVER MINCES WORDS, GOTHAM.
HALF NOW... HALF WHEN IT'S DONE?
SUITS.
BUT TELL ME, GOTHAM... WHY THIS GIRL? WHY NOW?
BECAUSE SOMETHING ABOUT HER... TELLS ME THAT THIS WOMAN IS TRULY EVIL...
...AND IT FRIGHTENS ME, EDGE.
IT FRIGHTENS ME A GREAT DEAL.
...FRIGHTENED SOMETIMES, SATANA. I MEAN, I BELIEVE IN SATAN... BUT I STILL GET SCARED.
BECAUSE OF THE MYTHS, RUTH?
THAT... AND SOMETHING ELSE. I'VE NEVER TOLD ANYONE THIS...

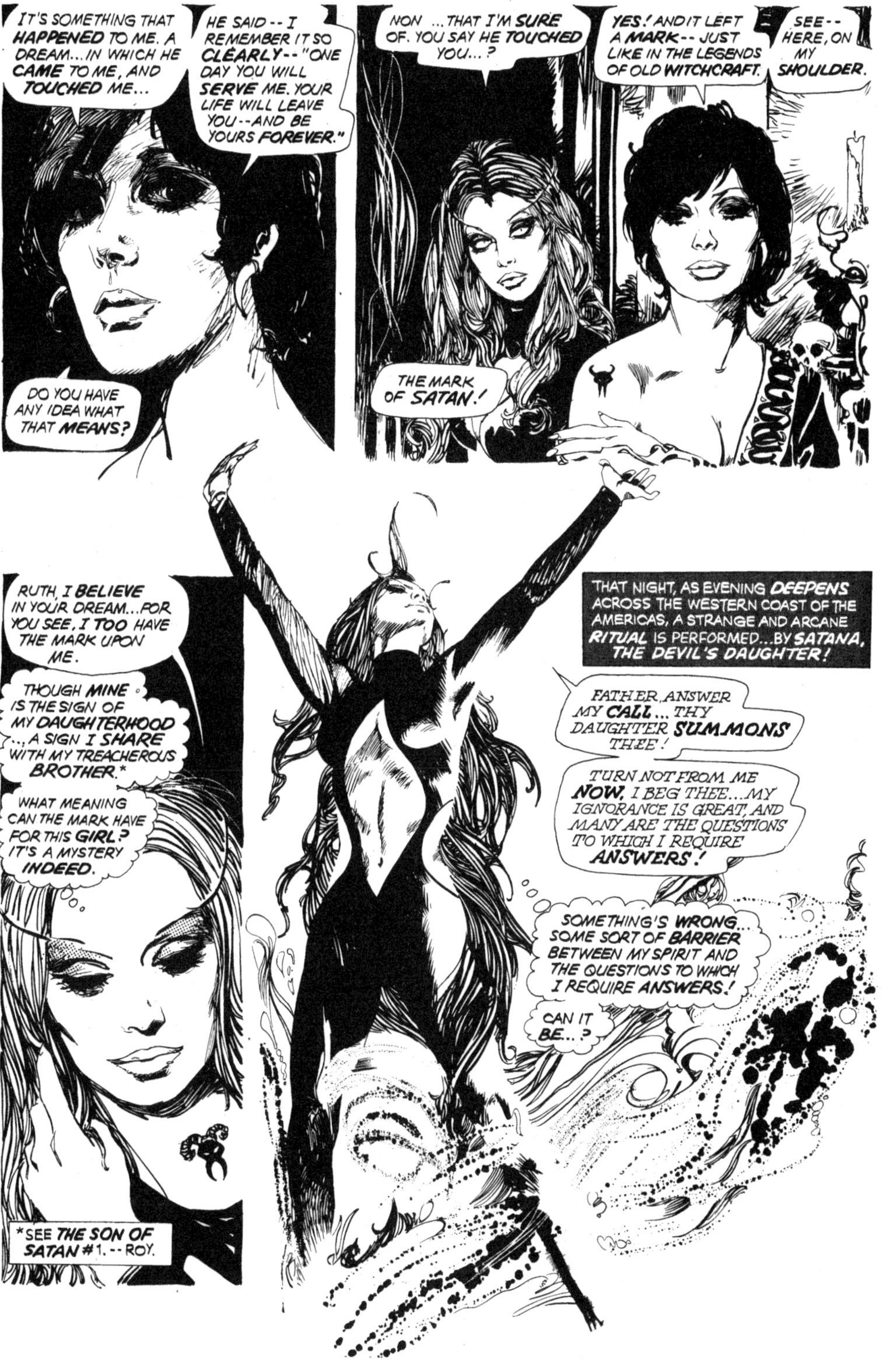
IT'S SOMETHING THAT HAPPENED TO ME. A DREAM... IN WHICH HE CAME TO ME, AND TOUCHED ME...
HE SAID -- I REMEMBER IT SO CLEARLY -- "ONE DAY YOU WILL SERVE ME. YOUR LIFE WILL LEAVE YOU -- AND BE YOURS FOREVER."
DO YOU HAVE ANY IDEA WHAT THAT MEANS?
NON ... THAT I'M SURE OF. YOU SAY HE TOUCHED YOU...?
YES! AND IT LEFT A MARK -- JUST LIKE IN THE LEGENDS OF OLD WITCHCRAFT.
SEE -- HERE, ON MY SHOULDER.
THE MARK OF SATAN!
RUTH, I BELIEVE IN YOUR DREAM... FOR YOU SEE, I TOO HAVE THE MARK UPON ME.
THOUGH MINE IS THE SIGN OF MY DAUGHTERHOOD ... A SIGN I SHARE WITH MY TREACHEROUS BROTHER.*
WHAT MEANING CAN THE MARK HAVE FOR THIS GIRL? IT'S A MYSTERY INDEED.
*SEE THE SON OF SATAN #1. -- ROY.
THAT NIGHT, AS EVENING DEEPENS ACROSS THE WESTERN COAST OF THE AMERICAS, A STRANGE AND ARCANE RITUAL IS PERFORMED... BY SATANA, THE DEVIL'S DAUGHTER!
FATHER, ANSWER MY CALL ... THY DAUGHTER SUMMONS THEE!
TURN NOT FROM ME NOW, I BEG THEE... MY IGNORANCE IS GREAT, AND MANY ARE THE QUESTIONS TO WHICH I REQUIRE ANSWERS!
SOMETHING'S WRONG... SOME SORT OF BARRIER BETWEEN MY SPIRIT AND THE QUESTIONS TO WHICH I REQUIRE ANSWERS!
CAN IT BE...?

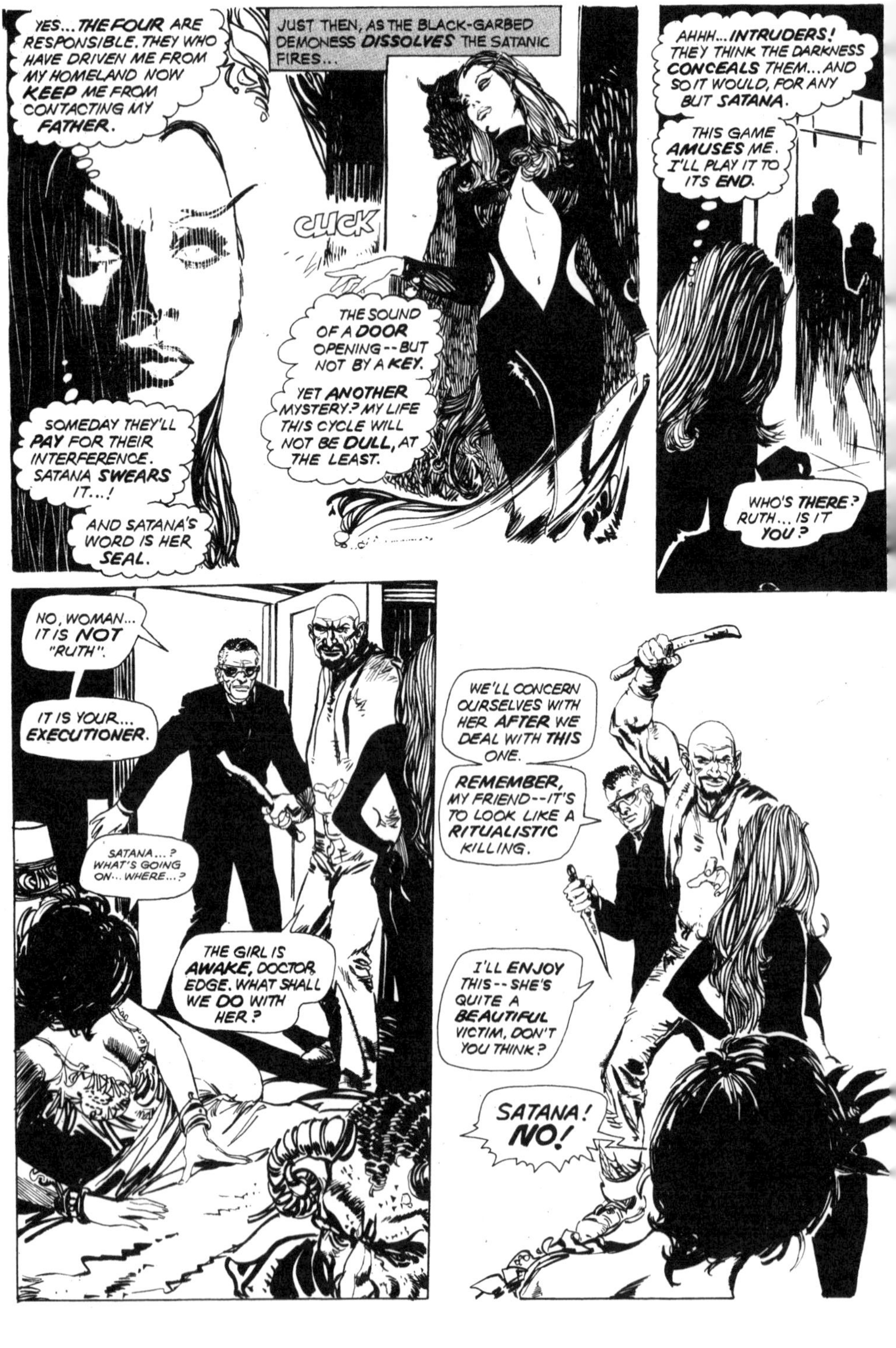
YES... THE FOUR ARE RESPONSIBLE. THEY WHO HAVE DRIVEN ME FROM MY HOMELAND NOW KEEP ME FROM CONTACTING MY FATHER.
SOMEDAY THEY'LL PAY FOR THEIR INTERFERENCE. SATANA SWEARS IT...!
AND SATANA'S WORD IS HER SEAL.
JUST THEN, AS THE BLACK-GARBED DEMONESS DISSOLVES THE SATANIC FIRES...
CLICK
THE SOUND OF A DOOR OPENING -- BUT NOT BY A KEY.
YET ANOTHER MYSTERY? MY LIFE THIS CYCLE WILL NOT BE DULL, AT THE LEAST.
AHHH... INTRUDERS! THEY THINK THE DARKNESS CONCEALS THEM... AND SO IT WOULD, FOR ANY BUT SATANA.
THIS GAME AMUSES ME. I'LL PLAY IT TO ITS END.
WHO'S THERE? RUTH... IS IT YOU?
NO, WOMAN... IT IS NOT "RUTH".
IT IS YOUR... EXECUTIONER.
SATANA...? WHAT'S GOING ON... WHERE...?
THE GIRL IS AWAKE, DOCTOR EDGE. WHAT SHALL WE DO WITH HER?
WE'LL CONCERN OURSELVES WITH HER AFTER WE DEAL WITH THIS ONE.
REMEMBER, MY FRIEND--IT'S TO LOOK LIKE A RITUALISTIC KILLING.
I'LL ENJOY THIS -- SHE'S QUITE A BEAUTIFUL VICTIM, DON'T YOU THINK?
SATANA! NO!

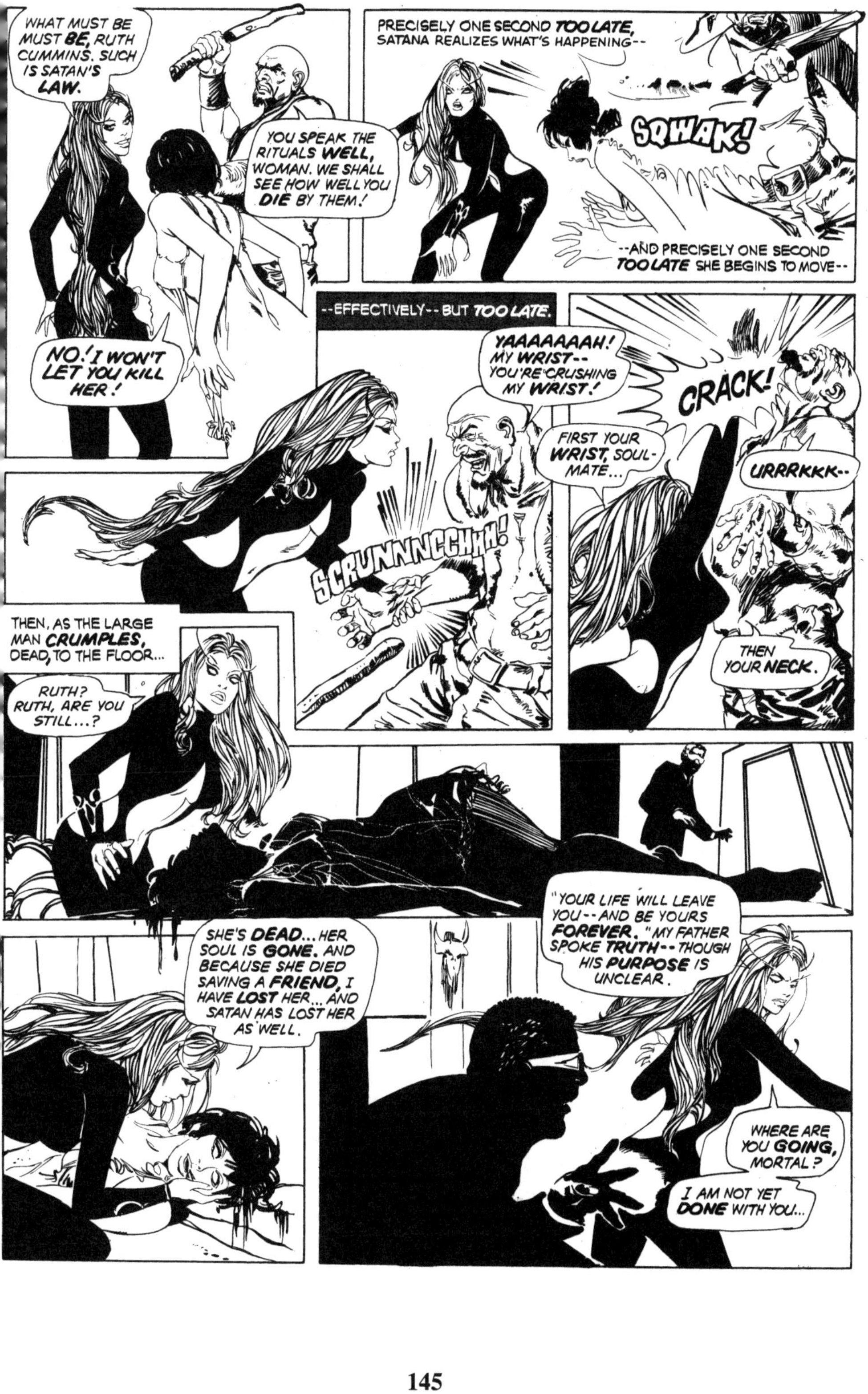
WHAT MUST BE MUST BE, RUTH CUMMINS. SUCH IS SATAN'S LAW.
YOU SPEAK THE RITUALS WELL, WOMAN. WE SHALL SEE HOW WELL YOU DIE BY THEM!
NO! I WON'T LET YOU KILL HER!
PRECISELY ONE SECOND TOO LATE, SATANA REALIZES WHAT'S HAPPENING--
SQWAK!
--AND PRECISELY ONE SECOND TOO LATE SHE BEGINS TO MOVE--
--EFFECTIVELY--BUT TOO LATE.
YAAAAAAAH! MY WRIST-- YOU'RE CRUSHING MY WRIST!
SCRUNNNCCHHH!
CRACK!
FIRST YOUR WRIST, SOUL-MATE...
URRRKKK--
THEN YOUR NECK.
THEN, AS THE LARGE MAN CRUMPLES, DEAD, TO THE FLOOR...
RUTH? RUTH, ARE YOU STILL...?
SHE'S DEAD... HER SOUL IS GONE. AND BECAUSE SHE DIED SAVING A FRIEND, I HAVE LOST HER... AND SATAN HAS LOST HER AS WELL.
"YOUR LIFE WILL LEAVE YOU--AND BE YOURS FOREVER." MY FATHER SPOKE TRUTH--THOUGH HIS PURPOSE IS UNCLEAR.
WHERE ARE YOU GOING, MORTAL?
I AM NOT YET DONE WITH YOU...

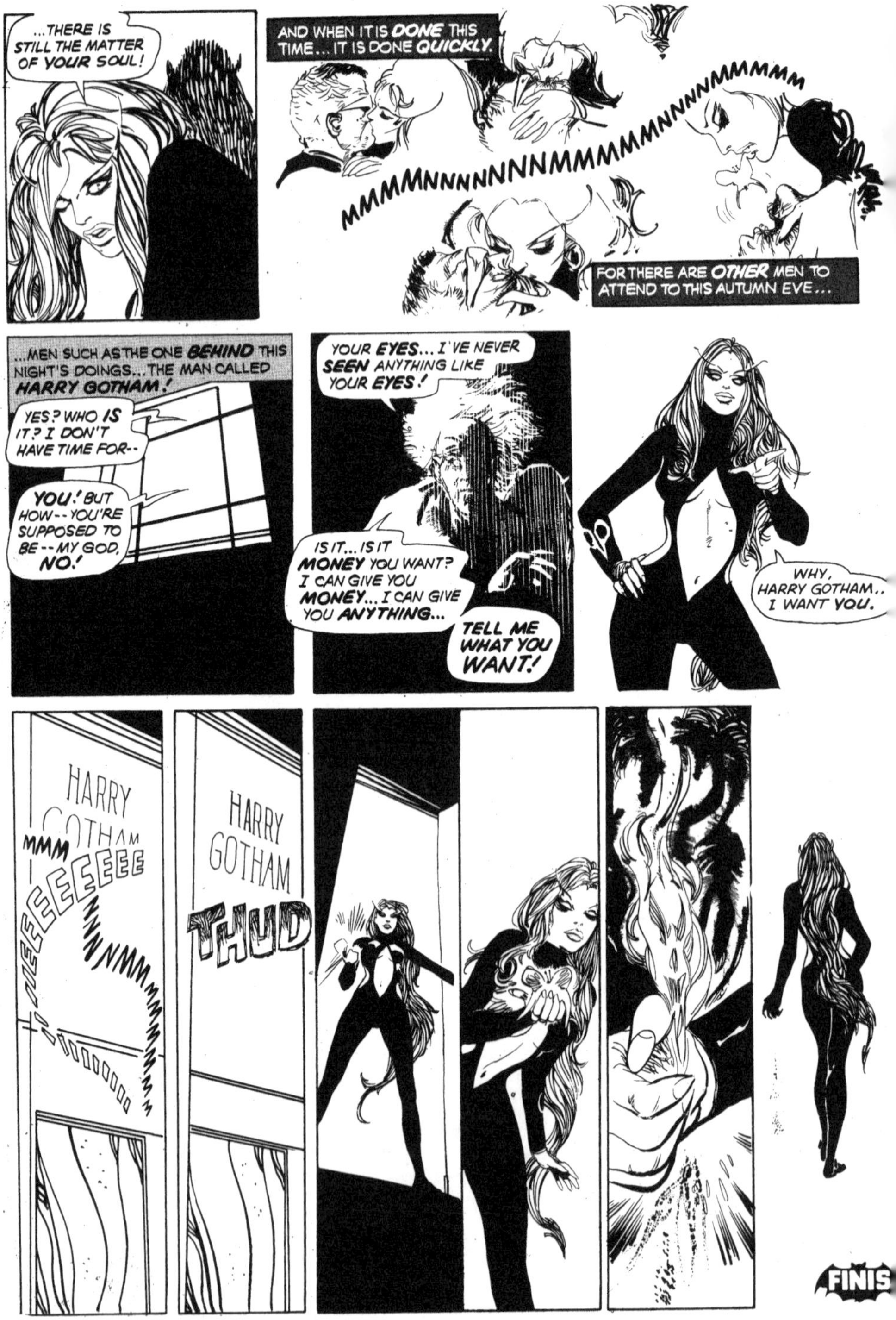
...THERE IS STILL THE MATTER OF YOUR SOUL!
AND WHEN IT IS DONE THIS TIME... IT IS DONE QUICKLY.
MMMMNNNNNNNNMMMMMMNNNNNMMMMMM
FOR THERE ARE OTHER MEN TO ATTEND TO THIS AUTUMN EVE...
...MEN SUCH AS THE ONE BEHIND THIS NIGHT'S DOINGS... THE MAN CALLED HARRY GOTHAM!
YES? WHO IS IT? I DON'T HAVE TIME FOR--
YOU! BUT HOW--YOU'RE SUPPOSED TO BE--MY GOD, NO!
YOUR EYES... I'VE NEVER SEEN ANYTHING LIKE YOUR EYES!
IS IT... IS IT MONEY YOU WANT? I CAN GIVE YOU MONEY... I CAN GIVE YOU ANYTHING...
TELL ME WHAT YOU WANT!
WHY, HARRY GOTHAM.. I WANT YOU.
HARRY GOTHAM
MMM
EEEEEEE
NNNMMMMMM
HARRY GOTHAM
THUD
FINIS

The "B" movies: **low-priced dreams playing in neighborhood theaters, two for a dime with a cartoon and a serial chapter—in a time when a dime went much further than it does today.**

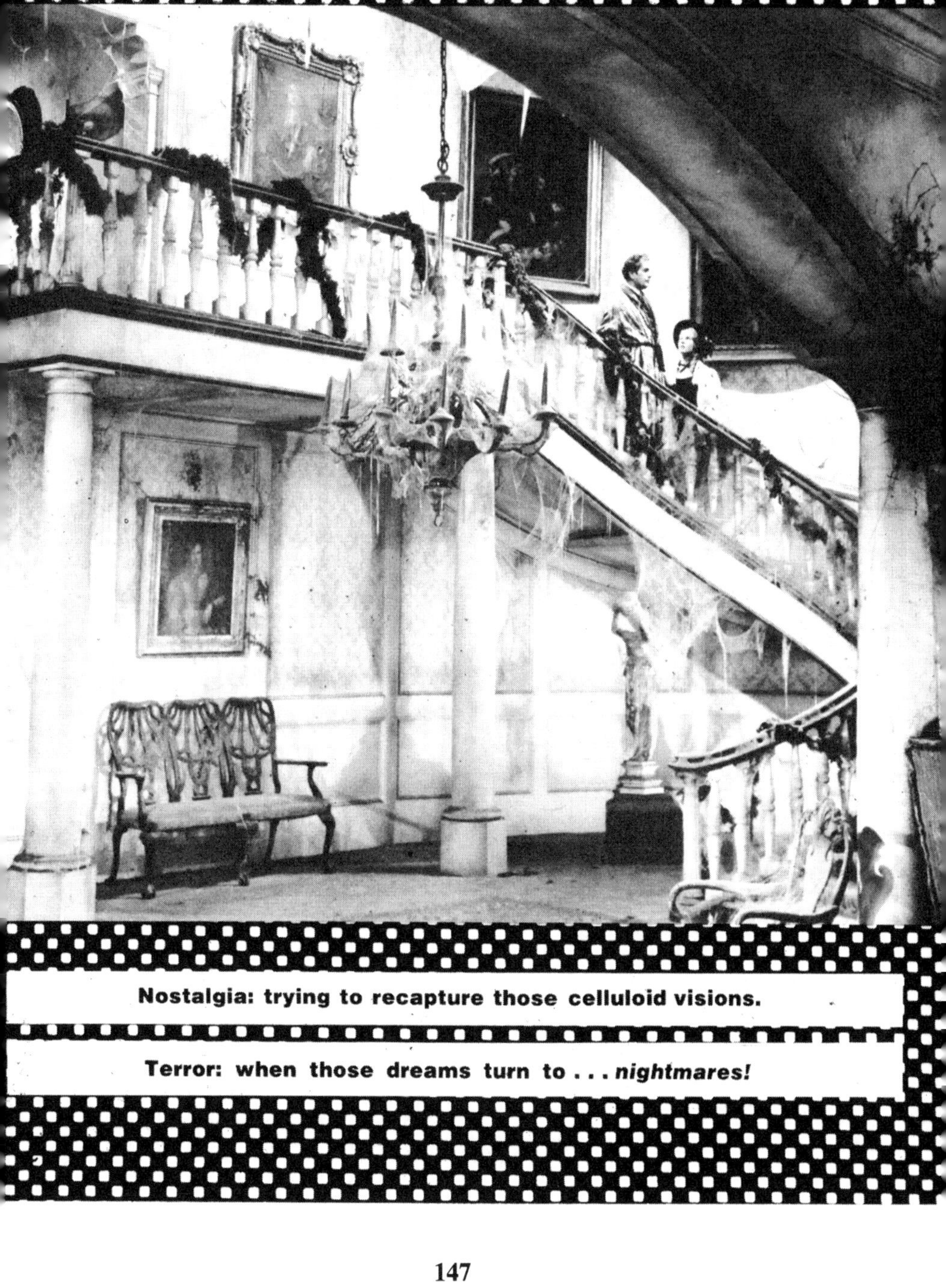

Nostalgia: trying to recapture those celluloid visions.

Terror: when those dreams turn to . . . *nightmares!*

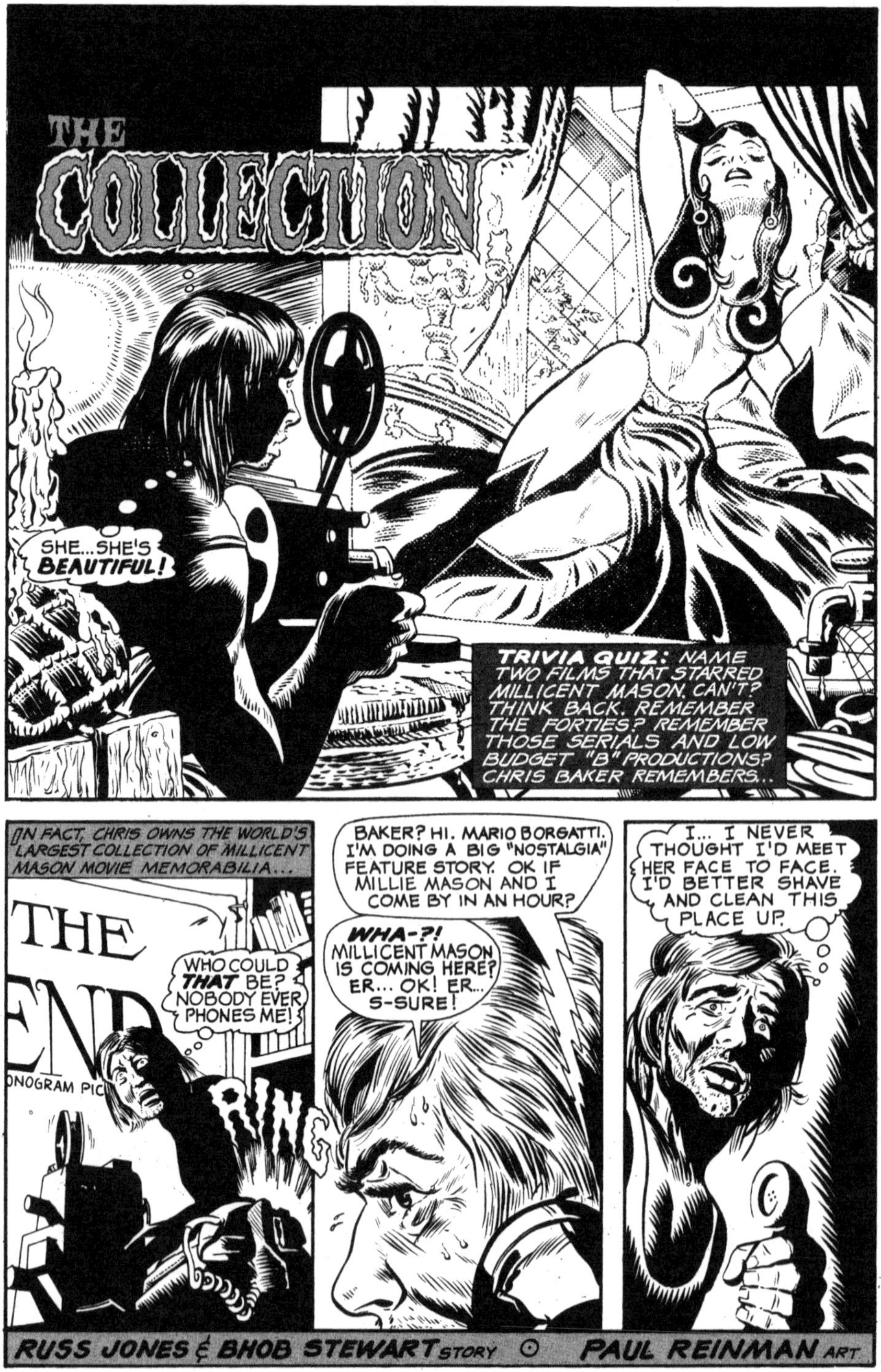
THE COLLECTION
SHE...SHE'S BEAUTIFUL!
TRIVIA QUIZ: NAME TWO FILMS THAT STARRED MILLICENT MASON. CAN'T? THINK BACK. REMEMBER THE FORTIES? REMEMBER THOSE SERIALS AND LOW BUDGET "B" PRODUCTIONS? CHRIS BAKER REMEMBERS...
IN FACT, CHRIS OWNS THE WORLD'S LARGEST COLLECTION OF MILLICENT MASON MOVIE MEMORABILIA...
THE
WHO COULD THAT BE? NOBODY EVER PHONES ME!
RING
BAKER? HI. MARIO BORGATTI. I'M DOING A BIG "NOSTALGIA" FEATURE STORY. OK IF MILLIE MASON AND I COME BY IN AN HOUR?
WHA-?! MILLICENT MASON IS COMING HERE? ER... OK! ER... S-SURE!
I... I NEVER THOUGHT I'D MEET HER FACE TO FACE. I'D BETTER SHAVE AND CLEAN THIS PLACE UP.
RUSS JONES & BHOB STEWART STORY
PAUL REINMAN ART

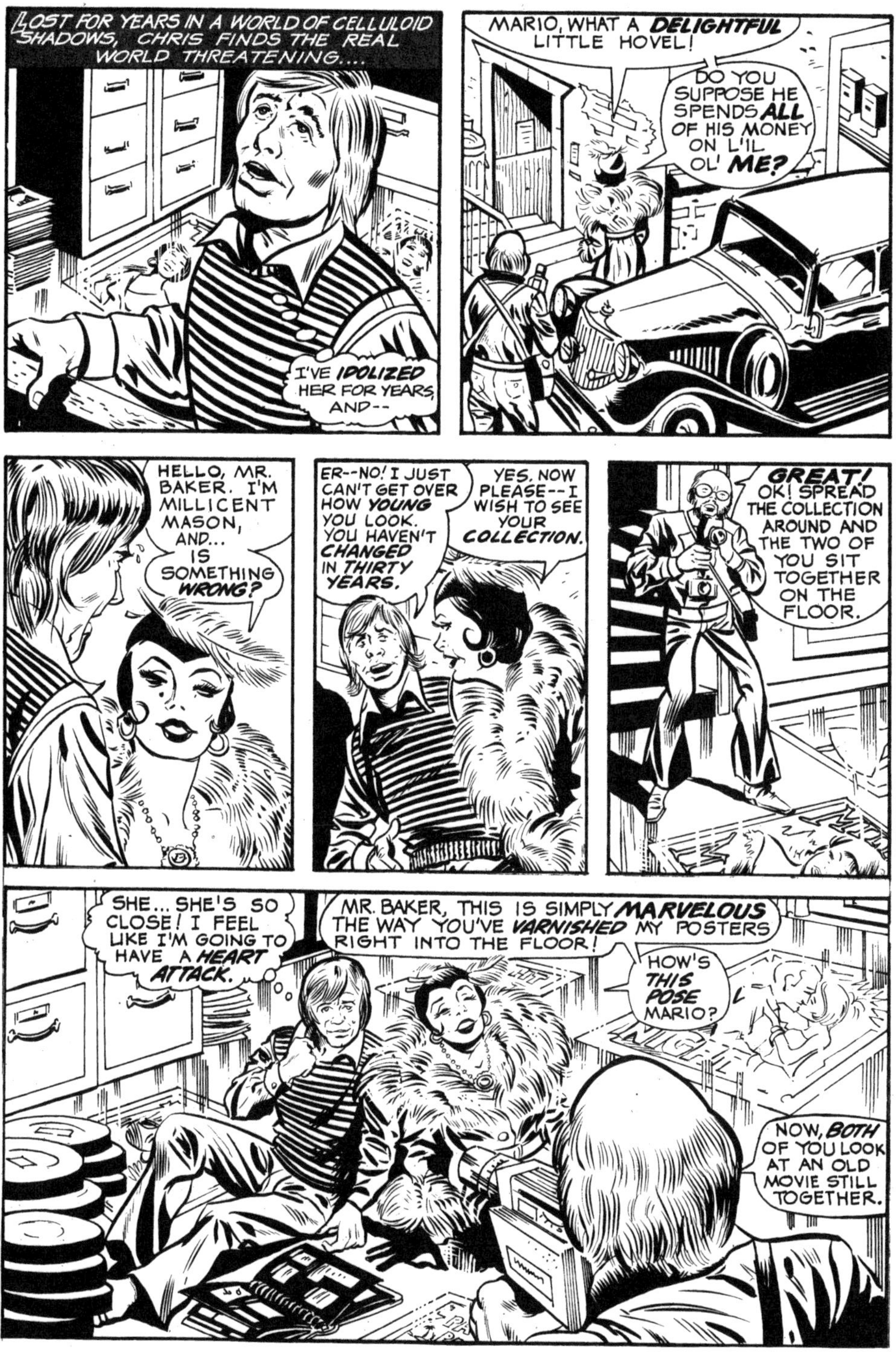
LOST FOR YEARS IN A WORLD OF CELLULOID SHADOWS, CHRIS FINDS THE REAL WORLD THREATENING....
I'VE IDOLIZED HER FOR YEARS, AND--
MARIO, WHAT A DELIGHTFUL LITTLE HOVEL!
DO YOU SUPPOSE HE SPENDS ALL OF HIS MONEY ON L'IL OL' ME?
HELLO, MR. BAKER. I'M MILLICENT MASON, AND... IS SOMETHING WRONG?
ER--NO! I JUST CAN'T GET OVER HOW YOUNG YOU LOOK. YOU HAVEN'T CHANGED IN THIRTY YEARS.
YES, NOW PLEASE--I WISH TO SEE YOUR COLLECTION.
GREAT! OK! SPREAD THE COLLECTION AROUND AND THE TWO OF YOU SIT TOGETHER ON THE FLOOR.
SHE... SHE'S SO CLOSE! I FEEL LIKE I'M GOING TO HAVE A HEART ATTACK.
MR. BAKER, THIS IS SIMPLY MARVELOUS THE WAY YOU'VE VARNISHED MY POSTERS RIGHT INTO THE FLOOR!
HOW'S THIS POSE MARIO?
NOW, BOTH OF YOU LOOK AT AN OLD MOVIE STILL TOGETHER.

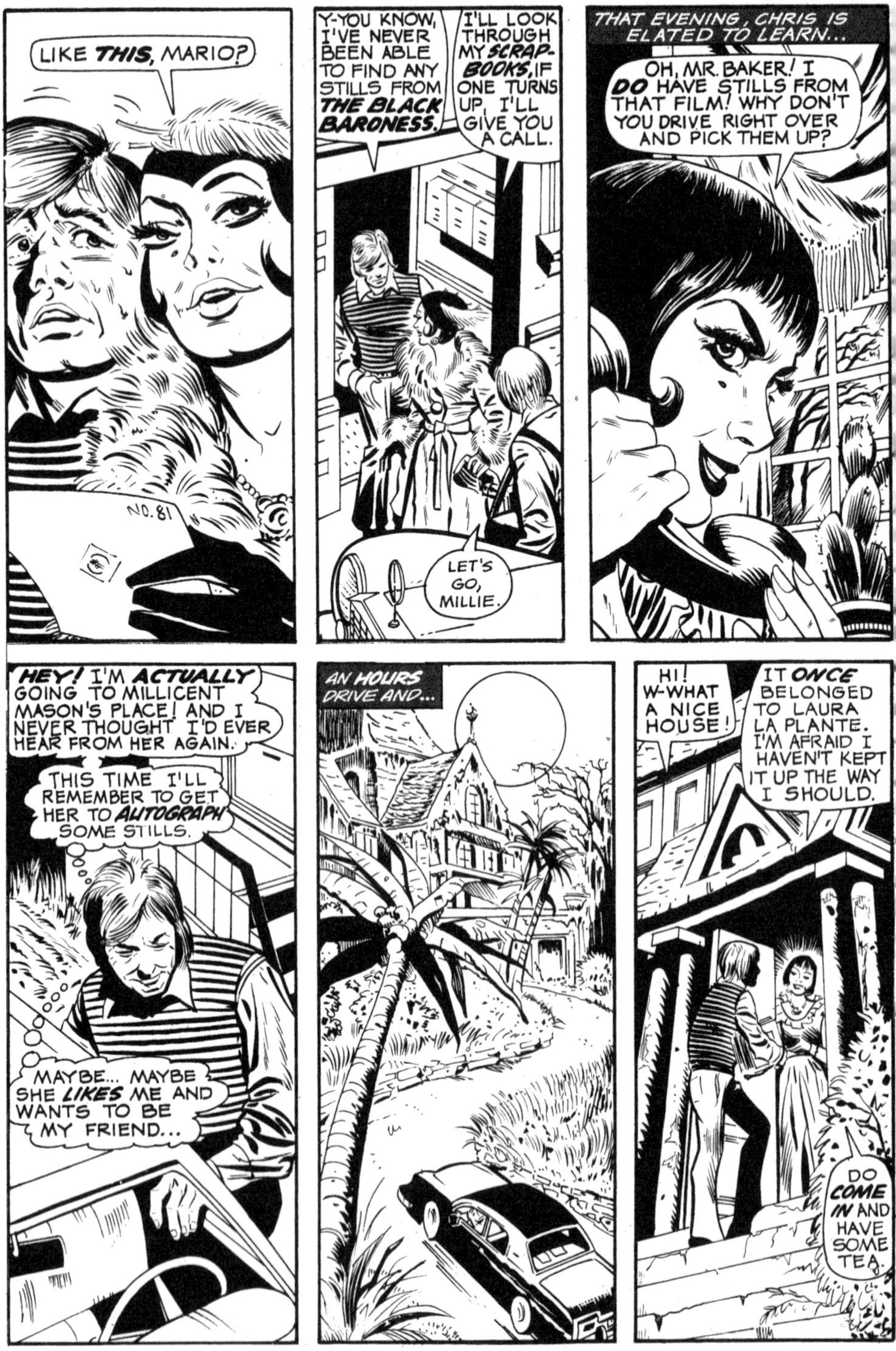

LIKE **THIS**, MARIO?
NO. 81
Y-YOU KNOW, I'VE NEVER BEEN ABLE TO FIND ANY STILLS FROM **THE BLACK BARONESS.**
I'LL LOOK THROUGH MY **SCRAP-BOOKS**, IF ONE TURNS UP, I'LL GIVE YOU A CALL.
LET'S GO, MILLIE.
THAT EVENING, CHRIS IS ELATED TO LEARN...
OH, MR. BAKER! I **DO** HAVE STILLS FROM THAT FILM! WHY DON'T YOU DRIVE RIGHT OVER AND PICK THEM UP?
HEY! I'M **ACTUALLY** GOING TO MILLICENT MASON'S PLACE! AND I NEVER THOUGHT I'D EVER HEAR FROM HER AGAIN.
THIS TIME I'LL REMEMBER TO GET HER TO **AUTOGRAPH** SOME STILLS.
MAYBE... MAYBE SHE **LIKES** ME AND WANTS TO BE MY FRIEND...
AN **HOURS** DRIVE AND...
HI! W-WHAT A NICE HOUSE!
IT **ONCE** BELONGED TO LAURA LA PLANTE. I'M AFRAID I HAVEN'T KEPT IT UP THE WAY I SHOULD.
DO **COME IN** AND HAVE SOME TEA.

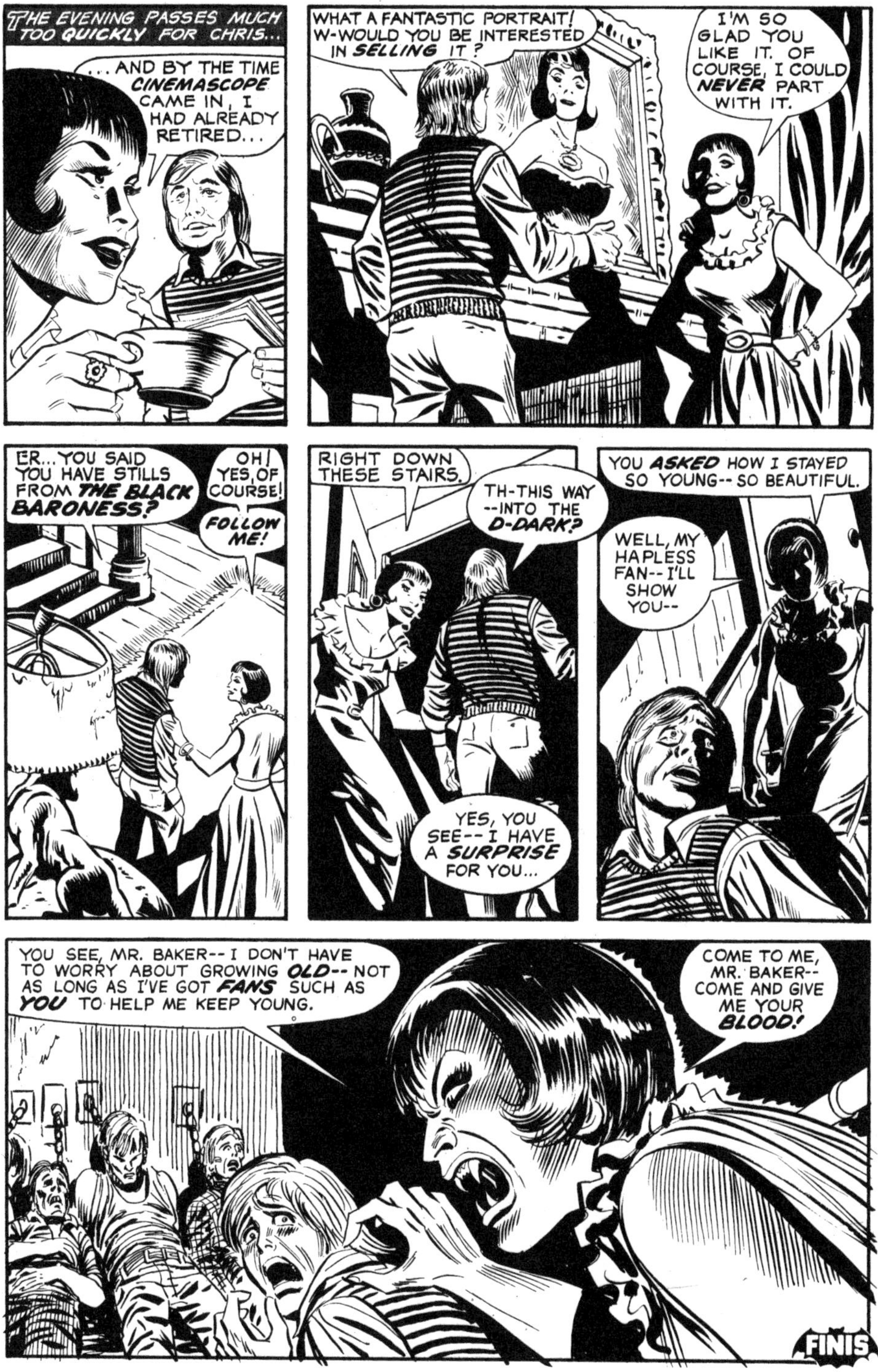
THE EVENING PASSES MUCH TOO QUICKLY FOR CHRIS...
...AND BY THE TIME CINEMASCOPE CAME IN, I HAD ALREADY RETIRED...
WHAT A FANTASTIC PORTRAIT! W-WOULD YOU BE INTERESTED IN SELLING IT?
I'M SO GLAD YOU LIKE IT. OF COURSE, I COULD NEVER PART WITH IT.
ER...YOU SAID YOU HAVE STILLS FROM THE BLACK BARONESS?
OH! YES, OF COURSE!
FOLLOW ME!
RIGHT DOWN THESE STAIRS.
TH-THIS WAY --INTO THE D-DARK?
YES, YOU SEE--I HAVE A SURPRISE FOR YOU...
YOU ASKED HOW I STAYED SO YOUNG--SO BEAUTIFUL.
WELL, MY HAPLESS FAN--I'LL SHOW YOU--
YOU SEE, MR. BAKER--I DON'T HAVE TO WORRY ABOUT GROWING OLD--NOT AS LONG AS I'VE GOT FANS SUCH AS YOU TO HELP ME KEEP YOUNG.
COME TO ME, MR. BAKER-- COME AND GIVE ME YOUR BLOOD!
FINIS

Vampyr.

As we've said, it's a name to conjure with, whether you're a starving serf trying to eke out a living for you and your family on the fringe of some Great Forest, bound body and soul to the local baron who owns your land, your house and, probably, you — or a modern member of the middleclass, still struggling to live, still hungry, still scared as you find yourself braving the terrors of our "modern" age — the junkies and the muggers — bound body and soul to the local bank.

That's reality. Of a sort. Your reality, pilgrim. But what of Bram Stoker's reality? Or Montague Summer's? Bela Lugosi's or Christopher Lee's? Suppose the dream-things these men wrote of and portrayed weren't dreams. Just suppose . . .

Ever wonder what a true vampire's supposed to look like?

He's a tall man, generally — and always a man; there's almost no mention of the female side of the clan — his features gaunt with a desperate, unhuman hunger, twisted into a hideous travesty of what is human and decent in Man, his eyes gleaming a feral, Hellborn red. And yet, despite his appearance of near-starvation, the vampire i incredibly strong, credited — in some places — with th strength of at least ten *strong* men and with speed tha could easily outstrip the wind.

When he has fed, his manic lust for blood sated for time, his body may become puffed or bloated — like som great leech; or some corpse that has lain too many days i the hot sun. His skin is deathly pale and it can burn wit the fire of a red-hot coal, or with the equally painful col of an Arctic night. His lips have color, though, a deep glistening red; and he has very fine teeth, well-formed an as white as his skin. The canine teeth are especially wel formed, much longer than are usually found in Man, muc sharper — teeth well-suited to a hunting carnivore

In some places, the vampire is said to have only on nostril; in others, a sharp point on the end of his tongue like the sting of a bee. His palms may be downy with hai the nails curved and crooked, scarred with ingrained clot of black blood. And he has *bad breath* — with a vengeanc — his stench is the stench of the death-house, the charne pit, the corpse-strewn battlefield; some say it is the stencl of Hell itself, and to breathe it is to sentence oneself to

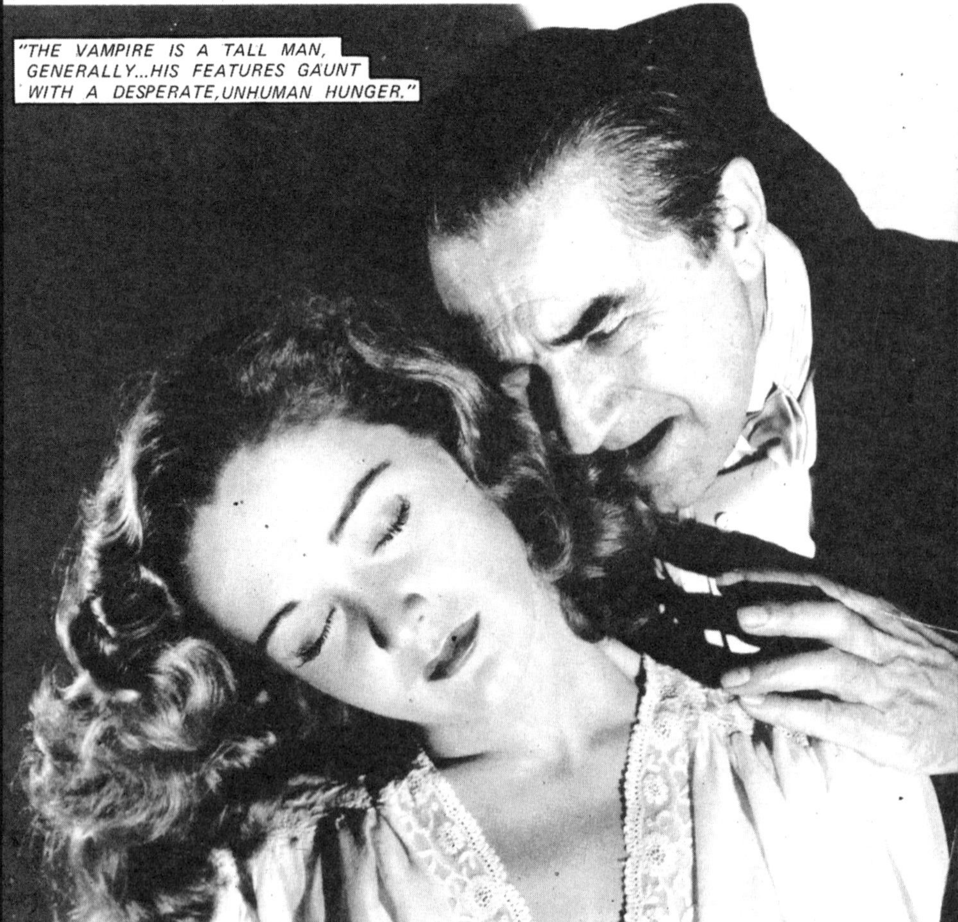

"THE VAMPIRE IS A TALL MAN, GENERALLY...HIS FEATURES GAUNT WITH A DESPERATE,UNHUMAN HUNGER."

horrible, lingering death.

There's a story told about a Black Forest (Bavaria) witch, sentenced to be burned at the stake for her foul crimes. She looked into the face of her jailer and said, "I will pay you." And she breathed into his face.

The jailer was dead in a week. Of leprosy.

Well, pilgrim; you're out of your hovel now, no good trying to sneak back in. And here we are, faithfully scrivening the third installment of our cautious excursion into Montague Summers' renowned book, *The Vampire: His Kith & Kin.*

For the unenlightened among you, Summers' book is about vampires and vampiric lore — and a lot of other things besides; Summers digresses like a man getting paid by the word — it's a good book (better if you're fluent in Greek, Latin, French, German, Italian, plus a little Hebrew; he doesn't translate too many of his source quotes) and if these articles pique your interest enough to find a copy for yourself, the book's just been re-issued by — take notes,

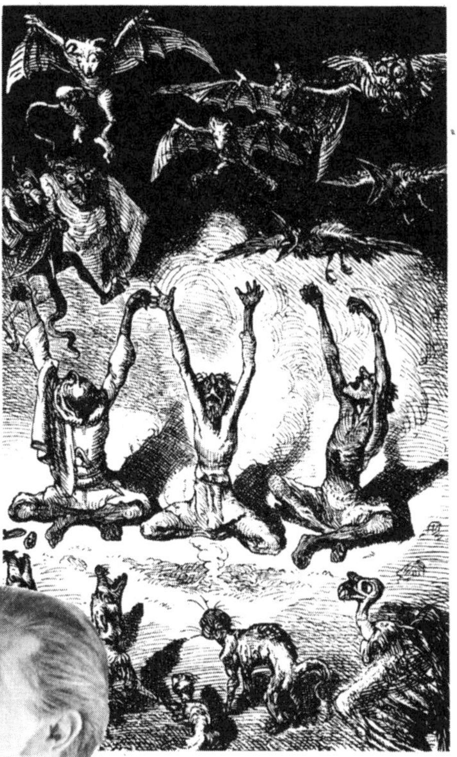

THE BAITAL--AN INDIAN VARIETY OF VAMPIRE.

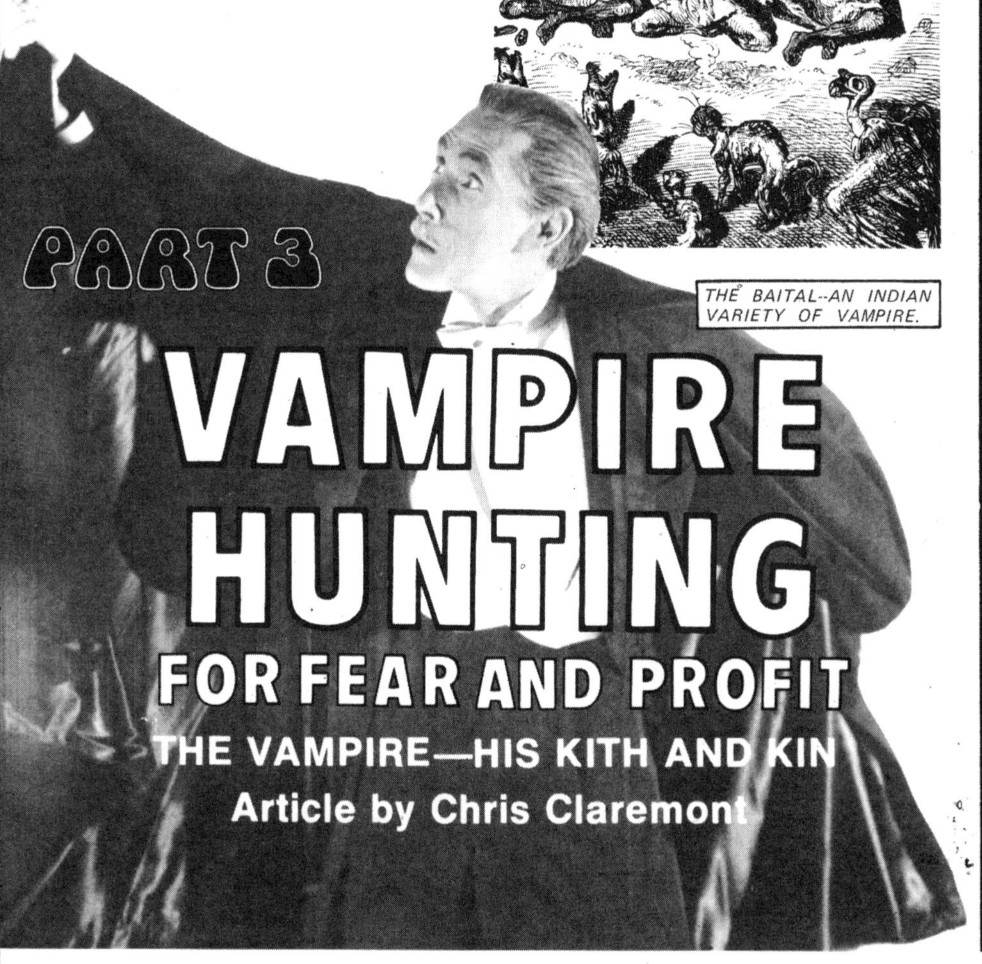

PART 3

VAMPIRE HUNTING

FOR FEAR AND PROFIT

THE VAMPIRE—HIS KITH AND KIN

Article by Chris Claremont

25

bunkies – University Books, Inc, of New Hyde Park, New York; at the sum of $7.95 (pre-inflation). It's steep, sure, but what isn't these days, and it's a better deal than many of the other vampire-fact books flitting about right now.

Enough free advertising, already. Back to work . . .

Legends and folk-tales name other ways to identify a vampire. Anyone who was severely deformed, physically, was suspected of carrying the vampiric curse; the more grotesque the deformity, the stronger the suspicions (and in those times, suspicion was all that was needed to convict, the sentence generally death – sometimes mutilation – carried out immediately; there was no appeal). *Chorea*, often called *St. Vitus' Dance*, (a nervous disorder characterized by an uncontrollable jerking of the extremities) was a sign of vampirism and/or daemonic possession; these people, too, were quickly dealt with.

In some parts of the Balkans, especially Greece, people with blue eyes were suspected of bearing the curse (which knocks yet another country off this author's European travel itinerary); in many other countries in Eastern Europe, those with a particular shade of red hair get the axe. For is not red, the executioners say, the color of Cain's hair, and of Judas Iscariot's? And there is a tradition in Serbia, Bulgaria and Rumania, that there exist red-headed vampires known as the *Children of Judas*, who kill their victims with one bite, or kiss, which drains that victim's blood in a single draught. "The poisoned flesh of the victim is wounded with the Devil's stigmata," Summers goes on to say, "three hideous scars shaped thus, signifying the thirty pieces of silver, the price of blood."

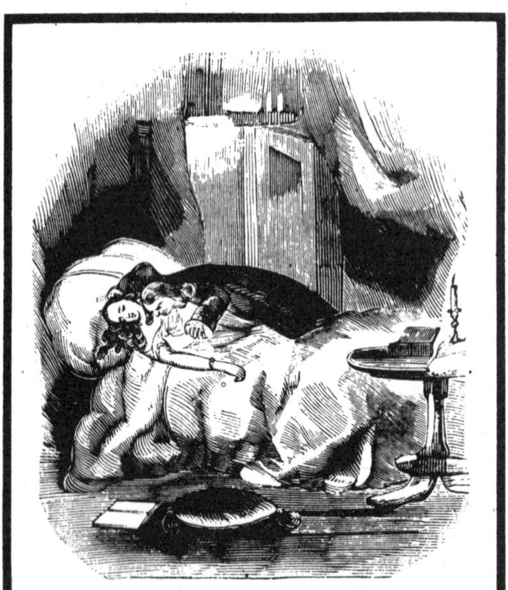

VARNEY THE VAMPIRE--FROM VICTORIAN LITERATURE.

Which brings us to the *how* of it all. The vampiric b

The vampire bites his prey, most often on the thr penetrating the jugular vein – which lies near the sur of the skin. The legends say that anyone born with te already formed is destined to become a vampire. victim remains in a trance-like sleep throughout all and generally wakes up the next day feeling totally was and very weak, very tired; unable to get out of bed, una to move.

There is sexual element in all this, as anyone who has given or received a love-bite – or hickey – can test Summers spends a few pages talking about it: "Under stress of strong sexual emotion when love is closely with pain there is often an overwhelming tendency to the partner of the act . . . This curious biting is referre in literature from Plautus to Dryden to the Ara *Perfumed Gardens*, to the *Kama Sutra* (a whole cha devoted to it). Among the Slavic nations, biting amorous embraces is quite common; and, in Sicily, pea woman have been known to have kissed their child violently, before biting them and sucking their blood w the child wails in pain. All this in the name of l

Does this mean all of us carry the vampiric c locked deep within the DNA structure of our genes? some don't have it locked quite as securely as others, it might slip free on occasion – say, *a propos* of werewo at the full moon? Or is it nothing more than a ger atavism, a throwback to the time when Man killed as other carnivores hunting the prehistoric plains did, with teeth, going for the neck and the quick kill? Like m things about us, this kill instinct has mellowed over aeons and mutated into something completely differ

Who can say?

The vampire is a creature of the night, and, if follows the cinematic history of Dracula as told by Ham Films, one sees that exposure to direct sunlight will him. Indeed, the film legend, itself derived from B Stoker's novel, *Dracula*, goes on to state that the vam must spend each day in a trance-like state, a coma, repo on soil from the grave in which he was buried.

Buried.

Now *that's* an intriguing word. Because, regardles which legend one believes, they all agree on one point: body has to die before it can resurrect itself – o resurrected by Lucifer – as a vampire. And dead bodie sealed in coffins, the coffins buried, usually six feet do the height of a tall man.

Question, posed by Dom Augustin Calmet (a n French theologian and Renaissance expert in vampiric l how does he get out?

First off, the vampire's got about 72 cubic feet of sitting on the lid of his coffin (assuming dimension 6ft x 2ft x 6ft), not to mention the earth supporting, imprisoning, the other three sides. Not having to brea the vampire could probably dig his way out; but that w be a slow, arduous process, not to mention an obvious to any passer-by who cared to look at the sudden de sion in the gravesite. And, once out, he would be faced the problem of removing his coffin and finding somew to hide it from the sun, not to mention the problem finding sustenance for himself before the dawn catches in the open.

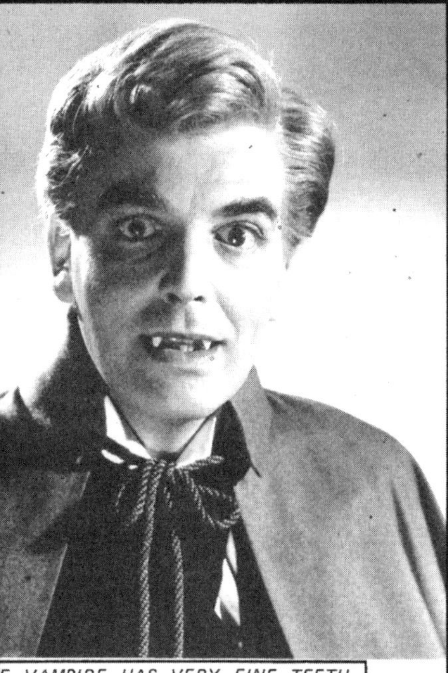

E VAMPIRE HAS VERY FINE TEETH, LL-FORMED AND AS WHITE AS HIS SKIN."

Of course, like Dracula, he could either have an above-ground sepulcher, or a couple of gypsy servants around to dig him up after he was buried. Dracula never lacked for assistance, either on the printed page or the silver screen. But for the average, garden-variety, poor/middleclass vampire, it isn't so easy. So, it was theorized that the vampire had the power to change its shape, into the form of another animal — a wolf or bat — or into that of an elemental wraith — a cloud of sentient smoke or fog — or, finally, like our much-respected mage of mages, Doctor Strange, he can become pure ectoplasm and slip out through the vast molecular spaces that make up each grain of earth, reforming himself on the outside into his own body, or possessing the body of a sympathetic human, one ripe for vampirism himself (an example, check your back issues for *The Terror That Stalked Castle Dracula* which appeared in *DRACULA LIVES #2)*.

Once the vampire gets out and begins killing, a new set of questions raise their hoary, demanding heads: how do you find the grave, and how do you kill the vampire? We'll take them both in turn.

In films, finding the beastie is fairly simple; just go looking for the nearest clifftop castle or ruined townhouse/manor house/abbey, poke around in the catacombs for a while, and . . . BINGO!

Oddly enough, in reality, it's not that much harder. As one of Summers' sources tells it: " '(You) select a young lad who is a pure maiden, that is to say, who . . . had never performed the sexual act. He is set upon a young stallion who has not yet mounted his first mare, who has never stumbled, and who must be coal-black without a speck of white; the stud is ridden into the cemetery (where the suspected vampire is believed to be interred) in and out of the graves and that grave over which the steed in spite of the graves and that grave over which the steed in spite of the blows — (dealt him) — refuses to pass is where the Vampire lies." The method is a sort of, how to catch a Unicorn, except in reverse.

Once found, of course, the Undead must be destroyed. Exposure to direct sunlight is one way; cremation is another, a favorite of Inquisitions the world over — but though it's a horrible way to go, the method has much to commend it to those desperate enough to use it; fire cleanses as it destroys and it destroys completely; nothing is left of the corpse save ashes and once those ashes are strewn on the winds, the vampire can never gather itself back together again.

There are other ways. The Chuwashe tribe of Finland nail the corpse to the coffin, while the Burmese tie the body's two big toes and two thumbs together. The Arabs tie only the feet; others tie the hands, some break the spine. In Dalmatia (a region of southwest Yugoslavia), the locals cut the corpse's hams (the part of the leg behind the knee) and then prick its whole body with pins.

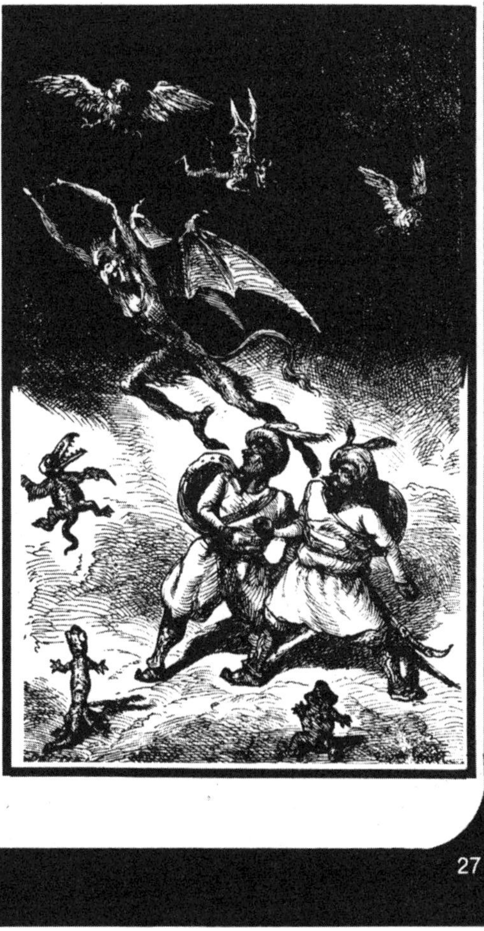

Like the saying goes, different strokes to different folks. Which brings us to the classic, approved method. The old stake-through-the-heart trick.

It's quite simple, really, brutal in its simplicity. All you have to do is pound a stake — carved from aspen or maple, though usually from hawthorn or whitethorn (aspen — the wood that formed the cross Jesus was nailed to — is the most sacred of the quartet; whitethorn was the wood used for His crown of thorns) — through the vampire's heart. Actually, it's not necessary to use a wooden stake at all; a consecrated dagger — a poniard that has been laid on an altar and ritually blessed by the local priest or bishop with all due-and-proper ceremony — will do just as well.

The most important thing to remember in all this is you only have one shot at the bull's-eye. The vampire must be impaled in one stroke, one stroke *only*; any more than one and the vampire will come alive again and we'll all be up that proverbial paddleless creek.

Once he's been staked out, the vampire killers must then cut off his head with a sharpened spade — for some reason a sword won't do.

So, finally, irrevocably (one hopes) the vampire is dead.

"THE VAMPIRE MUST SPEND EACH DAY IN A TRANCE-LIKE STATE, A COMA, REPOSING IN A COFFIN ON SOIL FROM THE GRAVE IN WHICH HE WAS BURIED."

Just bear in mind when you fight the bug beastie, o best beloved, that he's bigger, stronger, faster, tougher than you are; he's a shape-changer, a hypnotist and God knows what else; and when you do get a chance to zap him, you only get one and no more. Or you're quite dead.

Anyone willing to join van Helsing now?

See you next go 'round, pilgrims; and 'til then, walk softly through dark cemeteries and carry a sharp stake.

*Maple will do.

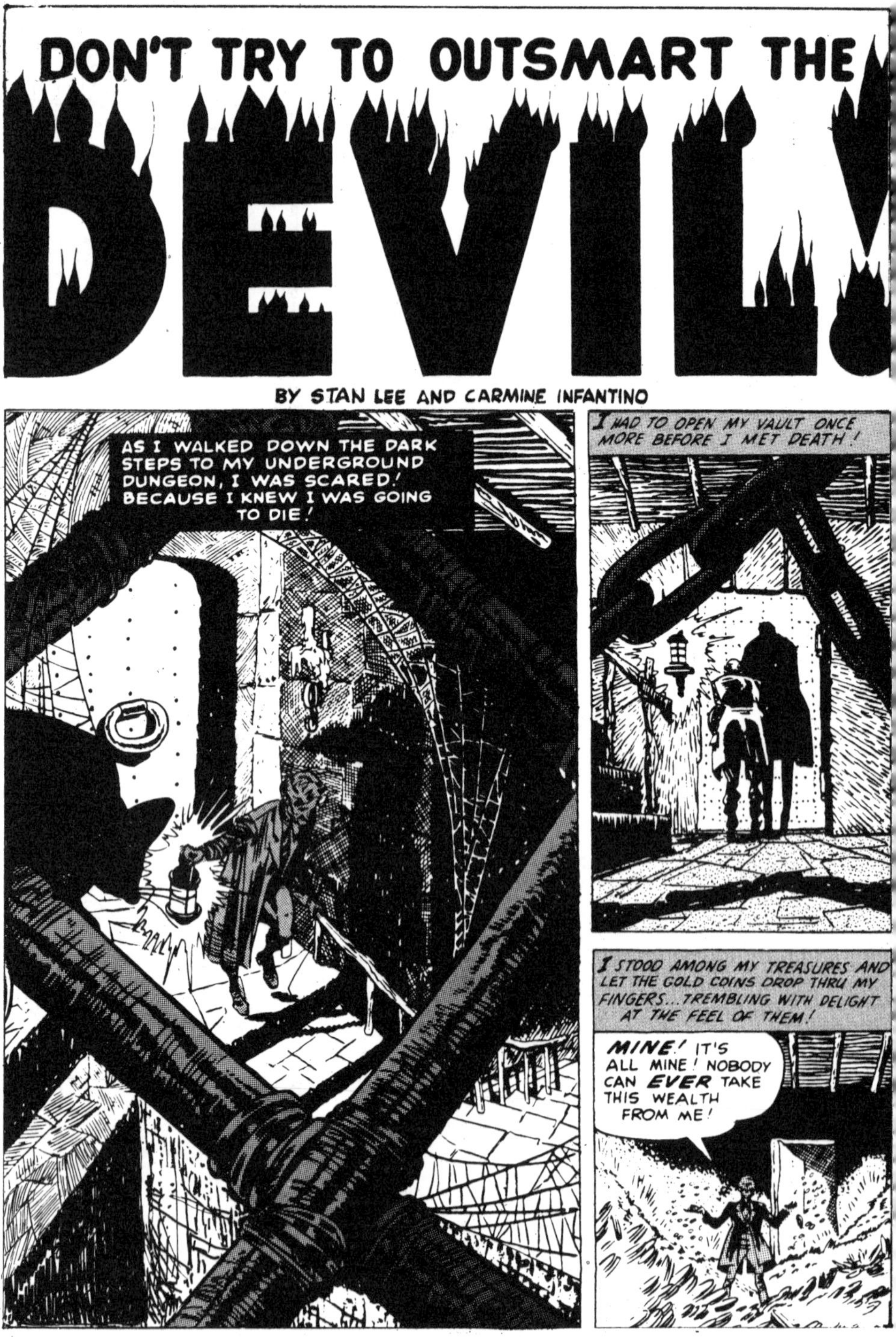
DON'T TRY TO OUTSMART THE
DEVIL!
BY STAN LEE AND CARMINE INFANTINO
AS I WALKED DOWN THE DARK STEPS TO MY UNDERGROUND DUNGEON, I WAS SCARED! BECAUSE I KNEW I WAS GOING TO DIE!
I HAD TO OPEN MY VAULT ONCE MORE BEFORE I MET DEATH!
I STOOD AMONG MY TREASURES AND LET THE GOLD COINS DROP THRU MY FINGERS... TREMBLING WITH DELIGHT AT THE FEEL OF THEM!
MINE! IT'S ALL MINE! NOBODY CAN EVER TAKE THIS WEALTH FROM ME!

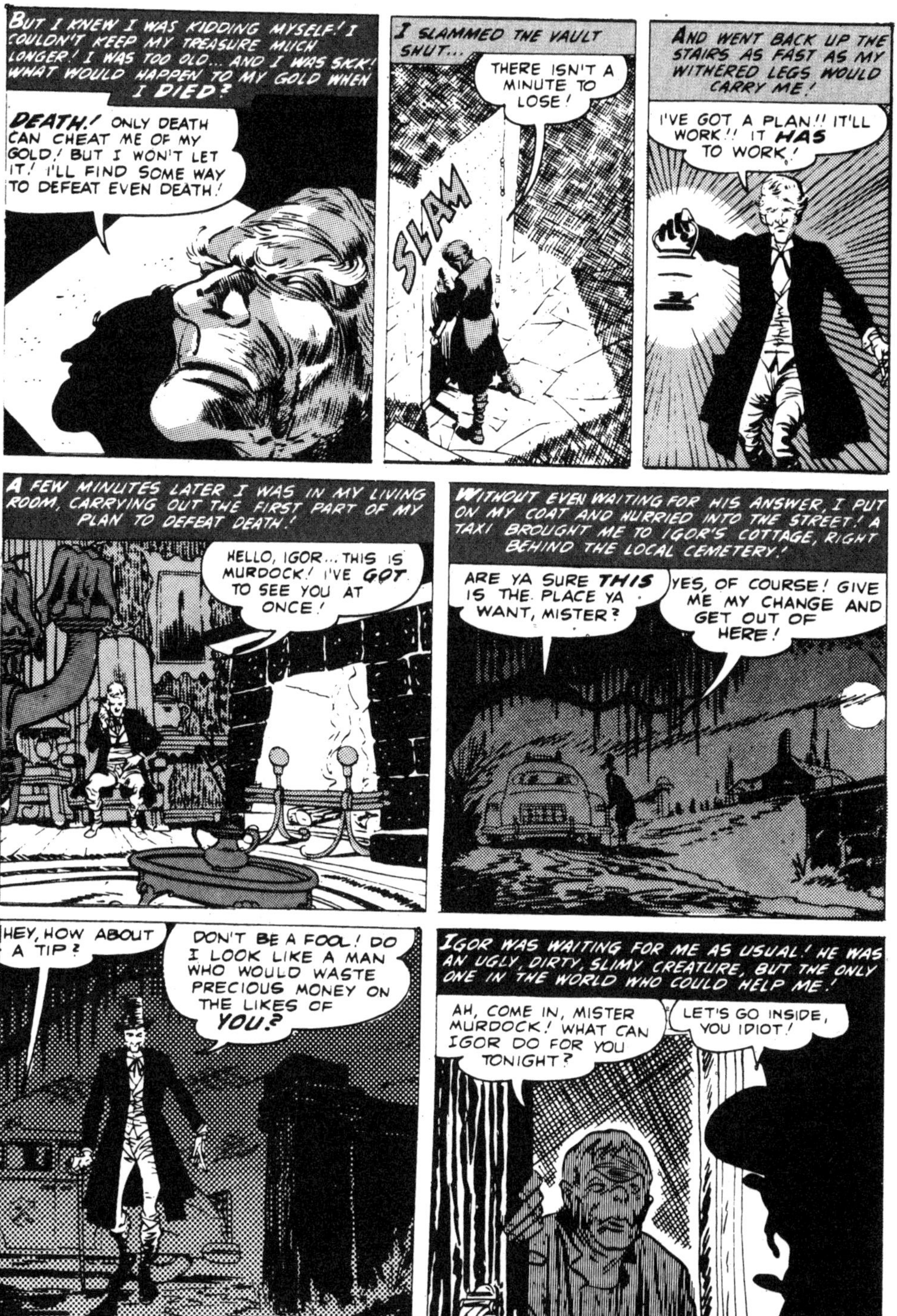
BUT I KNEW I WAS KIDDING MYSELF! I COULDN'T KEEP MY TREASURE MUCH LONGER! I WAS TOO OLD... AND I WAS SICK! WHAT WOULD HAPPEN TO MY GOLD WHEN I DIED?
DEATH! ONLY DEATH CAN CHEAT ME OF MY GOLD! BUT I WON'T LET IT! I'LL FIND SOME WAY TO DEFEAT EVEN DEATH!
I SLAMMED THE VAULT SHUT...
THERE ISN'T A MINUTE TO LOSE!
SLAM
AND WENT BACK UP THE STAIRS AS FAST AS MY WITHERED LEGS WOULD CARRY ME!
I'VE GOT A PLAN!! IT'LL WORK!! IT HAS TO WORK!
A FEW MINUTES LATER I WAS IN MY LIVING ROOM, CARRYING OUT THE FIRST PART OF MY PLAN TO DEFEAT DEATH!
HELLO, IGOR... THIS IS MURDOCK! I'VE GOT TO SEE YOU AT ONCE!
WITHOUT EVEN WAITING FOR HIS ANSWER, I PUT ON MY COAT AND HURRIED INTO THE STREET! A TAXI BROUGHT ME TO IGOR'S COTTAGE, RIGHT BEHIND THE LOCAL CEMETERY!
ARE YA SURE THIS IS THE PLACE YA WANT, MISTER?
YES, OF COURSE! GIVE ME MY CHANGE AND GET OUT OF HERE!
HEY, HOW ABOUT A TIP?
DON'T BE A FOOL! DO I LOOK LIKE A MAN WHO WOULD WASTE PRECIOUS MONEY ON THE LIKES OF YOU?
IGOR WAS WAITING FOR ME AS USUAL! HE WAS AN UGLY, DIRTY, SLIMY CREATURE, BUT THE ONLY ONE IN THE WORLD WHO COULD HELP ME!
AH, COME IN, MISTER MURDOCK! WHAT CAN IGOR DO FOR YOU TONIGHT?
LET'S GO INSIDE, YOU IDIOT!

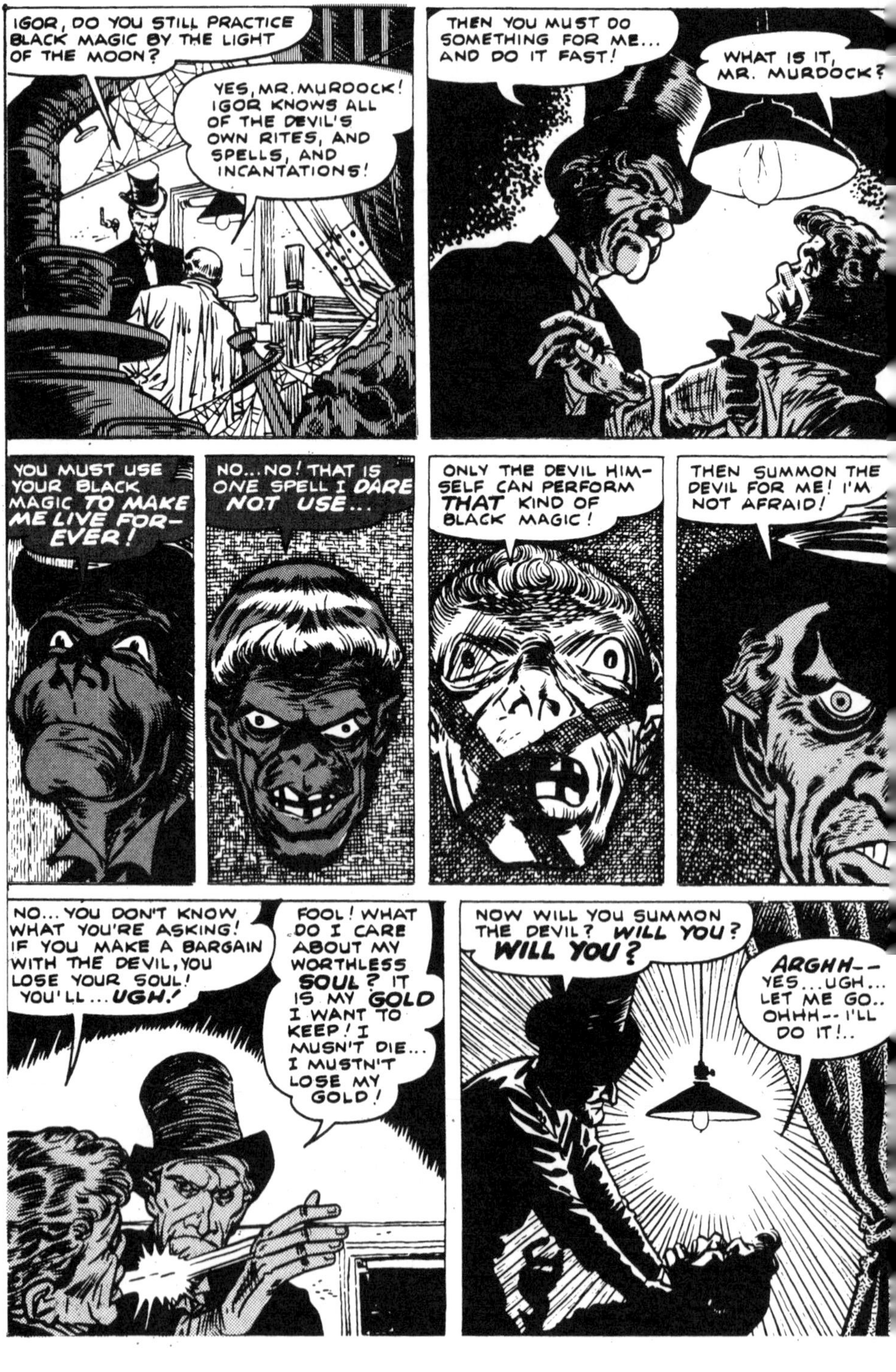
IGOR, DO YOU STILL PRACTICE BLACK MAGIC BY THE LIGHT OF THE MOON?
YES, MR. MURDOCK! IGOR KNOWS ALL OF THE DEVIL'S OWN RITES, AND SPELLS, AND INCANTATIONS!
THEN YOU MUST DO SOMETHING FOR ME... AND DO IT FAST!
WHAT IS IT, MR. MURDOCK?
YOU MUST USE YOUR BLACK MAGIC TO MAKE ME LIVE FOREVER!
NO... NO! THAT IS ONE SPELL I DARE NOT USE...
ONLY THE DEVIL HIMSELF CAN PERFORM THAT KIND OF BLACK MAGIC!
THEN SUMMON THE DEVIL FOR ME! I'M NOT AFRAID!
NO... YOU DON'T KNOW WHAT YOU'RE ASKING! IF YOU MAKE A BARGAIN WITH THE DEVIL, YOU LOSE YOUR SOUL! YOU'LL... UGH!
FOOL! WHAT DO I CARE ABOUT MY WORTHLESS SOUL? IT IS MY GOLD I WANT TO KEEP! I MUSN'T DIE... I MUSTN'T LOSE MY GOLD!
NOW WILL YOU SUMMON THE DEVIL? WILL YOU? WILL YOU?
ARGHH-- YES... UGH... LET ME GO.. OHHH-- I'LL DO IT!..

I STEPPED BACK TO CATCH MY BREATH! MY HEART WAS BEATING LIKE A TRIPHAMMER! I WAS GOING TO CHEAT DEATH! I KNEW IT! I FELT IT!

GIVE ME JUST A FEW MINUTES TO PREPARE THE RITUAL! IT ISN'T EASY TO SUMMON SATAN HIMSELF!

DON'T TAKE TOO LONG...OR I'LL THROTTLE YOU AGAIN!

IGOR STEPPED OUT OF HIS FILTHY SHACK AND MOTIONED ME TO FOLLOW!

COME!

WHERE ARE YOU LEADING ME, YOU UGLY DOLT?

IN ORDER TO SUMMON THE DEVIL, I MUST STAND OVER THE GRAVE OF AN EVIL MAN WHO HAS DIED! NOW MOVE BACK...WHILE I RECITE THE SATANIC CHANT!

AT LAST... AT LAST!!

AS IGOR BEGAN TO SAY THE MYSTIC WORDS, THE EARTH SEEMED TO RUMBLE AND THE NIGHT GREW EVEN DARKER! I WANTED TO SCREAM IN AGONY AT THE HORRIBLE SOUND OF THE DEVILISH INCANTATION!

SATANUS! BRUTANUS! FIRES BELOW! DEVILISH GLOW! TERRORS OF EVIL... HEAR ME, OH DEVIL...

SUDDENLY, THERE WAS A BLINDING FLASH WHICH BURNT THRU MY EYES UNTIL IT SCORCHED MY BRAIN ITSELF!

AND THEN, A DEEP THUNDEROUS ROAR WHICH MADE MY EARS RING WITH UNBEARABLE PAIN!

RRRR RRRR

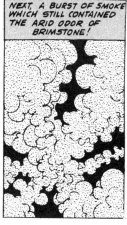

NEXT, A BURST OF SMOKE WHICH STILL CONTAINED THE ARID ODOR OF BRIMSTONE!

AND FINALLY, QUIET...THE UNNATURAL QUIETNESS OF DEATH..AND A LOOK OF AWE AND HORROR ON IGOR'S FACE!

HAIL, PRINCE OF EVIL!

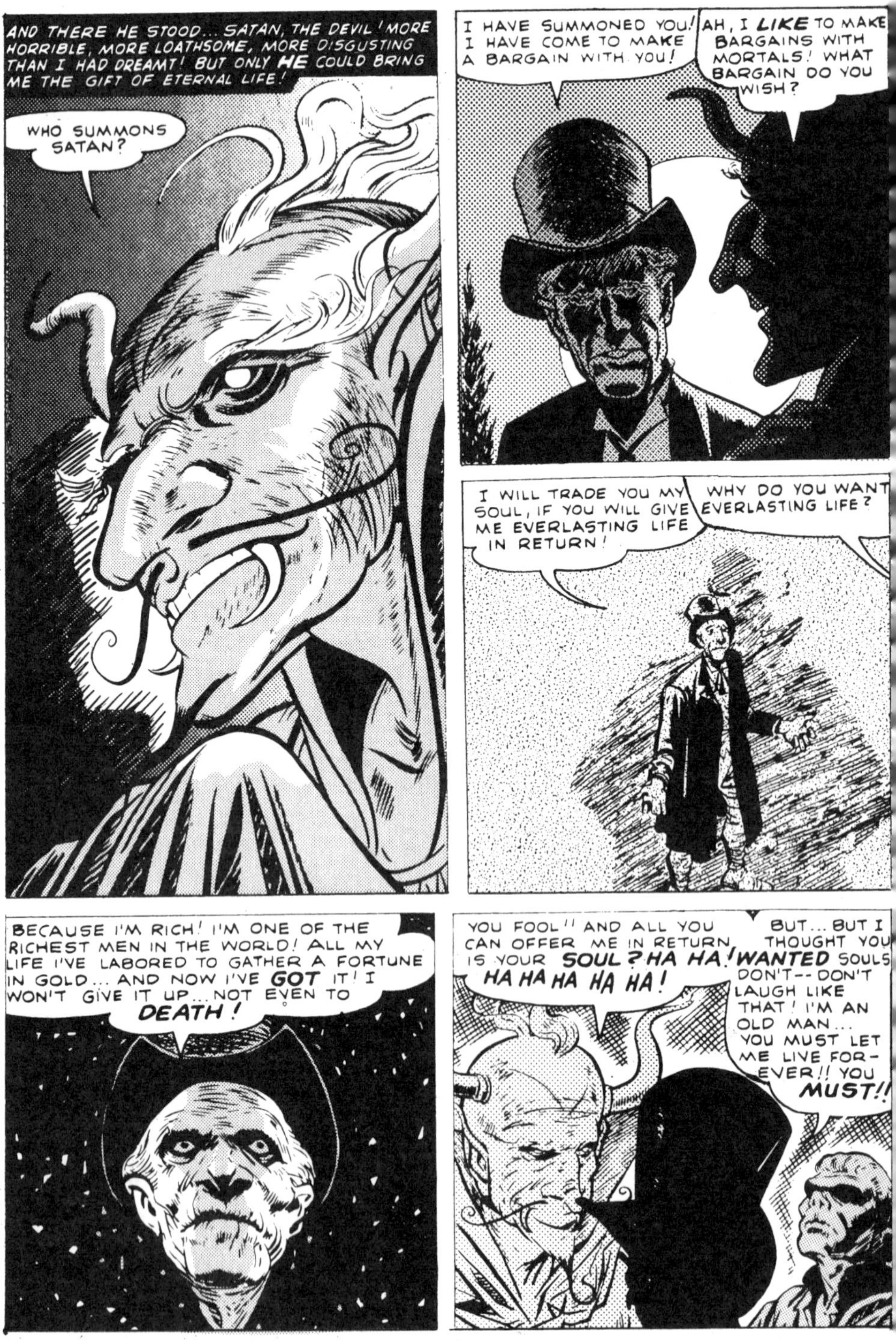
AND THERE HE STOOD... SATAN, THE DEVIL! MORE HORRIBLE, MORE LOATHSOME, MORE DISGUSTING THAN I HAD DREAMT! BUT ONLY HE COULD BRING ME THE GIFT OF ETERNAL LIFE!
WHO SUMMONS SATAN?
I HAVE SUMMONED YOU! I HAVE COME TO MAKE A BARGAIN WITH YOU!
AH, I LIKE TO MAKE BARGAINS WITH MORTALS! WHAT BARGAIN DO YOU WISH?
I WILL TRADE YOU MY SOUL, IF YOU WILL GIVE ME EVERLASTING LIFE IN RETURN!
WHY DO YOU WANT EVERLASTING LIFE?
BECAUSE I'M RICH! I'M ONE OF THE RICHEST MEN IN THE WORLD! ALL MY LIFE I'VE LABORED TO GATHER A FORTUNE IN GOLD... AND NOW I'VE GOT IT! I WON'T GIVE IT UP... NOT EVEN TO DEATH!
YOU FOOL!! AND ALL YOU CAN OFFER ME IN RETURN IS YOUR SOUL? HA HA! HA HA HA HA HA!
BUT... BUT I THOUGHT YOU WANTED SOULS! DON'T-- DON'T LAUGH LIKE THAT! I'M AN OLD MAN... YOU MUST LET ME LIVE FOREVER!! YOU MUST!!

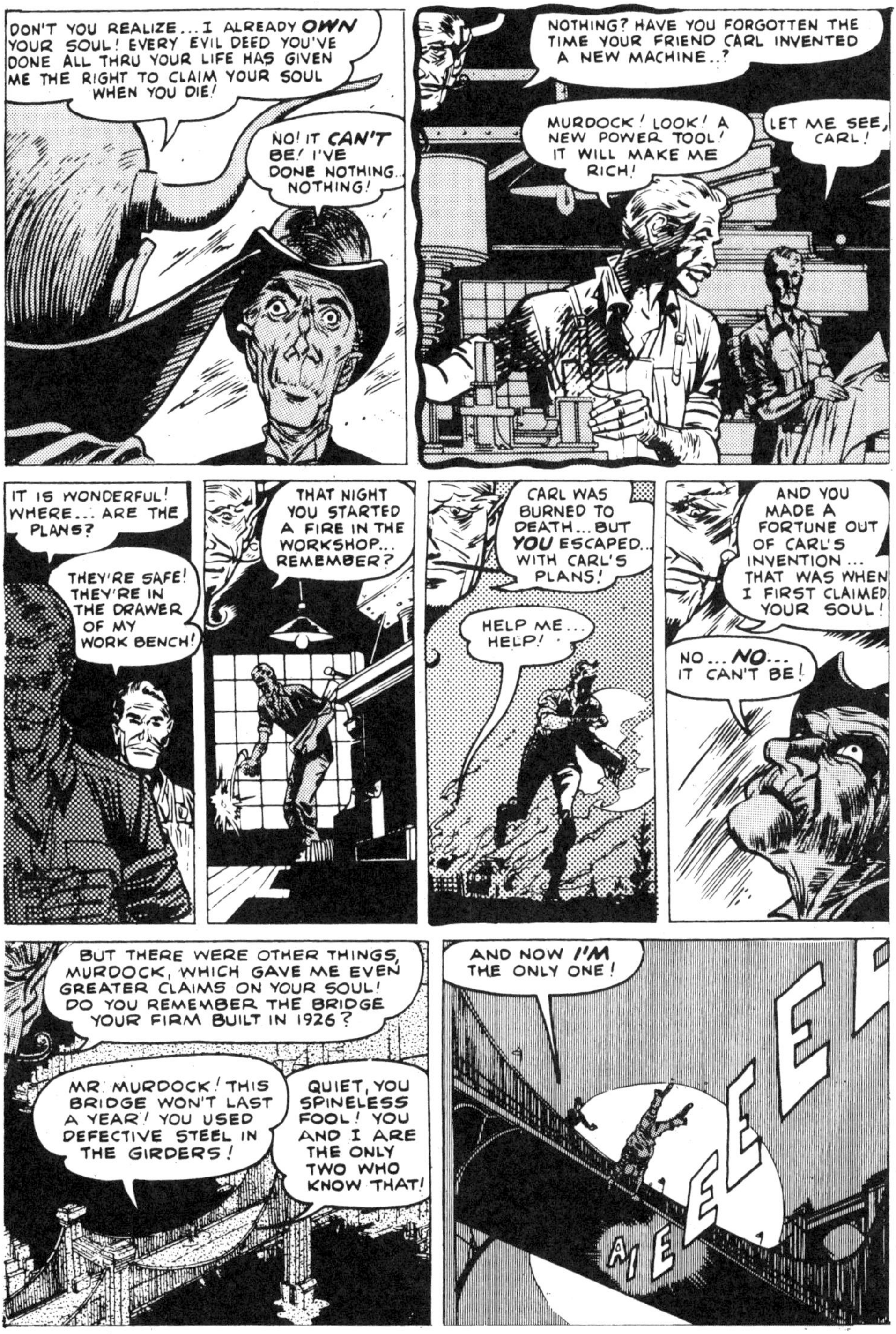
DON'T YOU REALIZE... I ALREADY OWN YOUR SOUL! EVERY EVIL DEED YOU'VE DONE ALL THRU YOUR LIFE HAS GIVEN ME THE RIGHT TO CLAIM YOUR SOUL WHEN YOU DIE!
NO! IT CAN'T BE! I'VE DONE NOTHING... NOTHING!
NOTHING? HAVE YOU FORGOTTEN THE TIME YOUR FRIEND CARL INVENTED A NEW MACHINE..?
MURDOCK! LOOK! A NEW POWER TOOL! IT WILL MAKE ME RICH!
LET ME SEE, CARL!
IT IS WONDERFUL! WHERE... ARE THE PLANS?
THEY'RE SAFE! THEY'RE IN THE DRAWER OF MY WORK BENCH!
THAT NIGHT YOU STARTED A FIRE IN THE WORKSHOP... REMEMBER?
CARL WAS BURNED TO DEATH... BUT YOU ESCAPED... WITH CARL'S PLANS!
HELP ME... HELP!
AND YOU MADE A FORTUNE OUT OF CARL'S INVENTION... THAT WAS WHEN I FIRST CLAIMED YOUR SOUL!
NO... NO... IT CAN'T BE!
BUT THERE WERE OTHER THINGS, MURDOCK, WHICH GAVE ME EVEN GREATER CLAIMS ON YOUR SOUL! DO YOU REMEMBER THE BRIDGE YOUR FIRM BUILT IN 1926?
MR. MURDOCK! THIS BRIDGE WON'T LAST A YEAR! YOU USED DEFECTIVE STEEL IN THE GIRDERS!
QUIET, YOU SPINELESS FOOL! YOU AND I ARE THE ONLY TWO WHO KNOW THAT!
AND NOW I'M THE ONLY ONE!
AIEEEEE

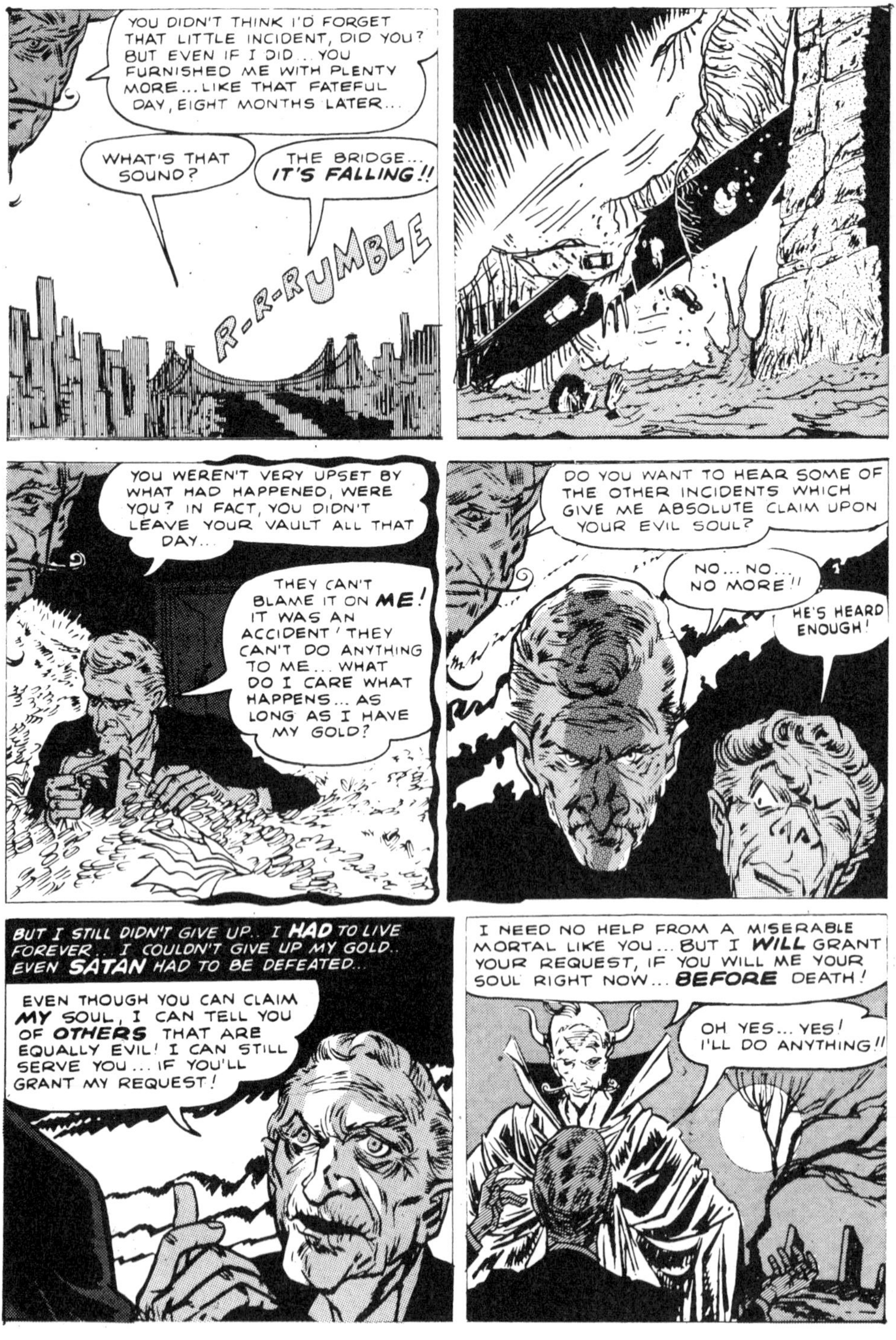
YOU DIDN'T THINK I'D FORGET THAT LITTLE INCIDENT, DID YOU? BUT EVEN IF I DID... YOU FURNISHED ME WITH PLENTY MORE... LIKE THAT FATEFUL DAY, EIGHT MONTHS LATER...
WHAT'S THAT SOUND?
THE BRIDGE... IT'S FALLING!!
R-R-RUMBLE
YOU WEREN'T VERY UPSET BY WHAT HAD HAPPENED, WERE YOU? IN FACT, YOU DIDN'T LEAVE YOUR VAULT ALL THAT DAY...
THEY CAN'T BLAME IT ON ME! IT WAS AN ACCIDENT! THEY CAN'T DO ANYTHING TO ME... WHAT DO I CARE WHAT HAPPENS... AS LONG AS I HAVE MY GOLD?
DO YOU WANT TO HEAR SOME OF THE OTHER INCIDENTS WHICH GIVE ME ABSOLUTE CLAIM UPON YOUR EVIL SOUL?
NO... NO... NO MORE!!
HE'S HEARD ENOUGH!
BUT I STILL DIDN'T GIVE UP.. I HAD TO LIVE FOREVER.. I COULDN'T GIVE UP MY GOLD.. EVEN SATAN HAD TO BE DEFEATED..
EVEN THOUGH YOU CAN CLAIM MY SOUL, I CAN TELL YOU OF OTHERS THAT ARE EQUALLY EVIL! I CAN STILL SERVE YOU... IF YOU'LL GRANT MY REQUEST!
I NEED NO HELP FROM A MISERABLE MORTAL LIKE YOU... BUT I WILL GRANT YOUR REQUEST, IF YOU WILL ME YOUR SOUL RIGHT NOW... BEFORE DEATH!
OH YES... YES! I'LL DO ANYTHING!!

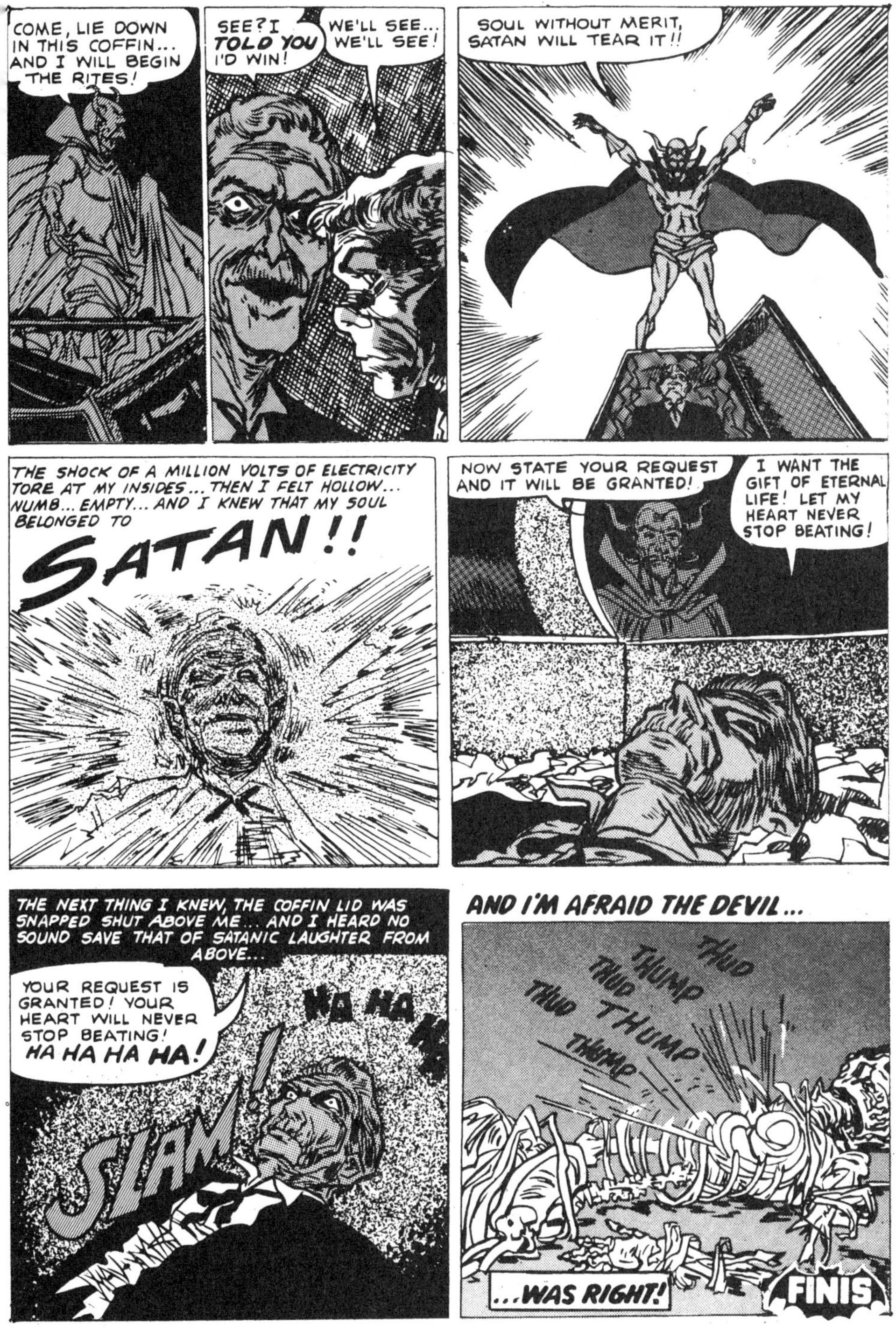
COME, LIE DOWN IN THIS COFFIN... AND I WILL BEGIN THE RITES!
SEE? I TOLD YOU I'D WIN!
WE'LL SEE... WE'LL SEE!
SOUL WITHOUT MERIT, SATAN WILL TEAR IT!!
THE SHOCK OF A MILLION VOLTS OF ELECTRICITY TORE AT MY INSIDES... THEN I FELT HOLLOW... NUMB... EMPTY... AND I KNEW THAT MY SOUL BELONGED TO
SATAN!!
NOW STATE YOUR REQUEST AND IT WILL BE GRANTED!
I WANT THE GIFT OF ETERNAL LIFE! LET MY HEART NEVER STOP BEATING!
THE NEXT THING I KNEW, THE COFFIN LID WAS SNAPPED SHUT ABOVE ME... AND I HEARD NO SOUND SAVE THAT OF SATANIC LAUGHTER FROM ABOVE...
YOUR REQUEST IS GRANTED! YOUR HEART WILL NEVER STOP BEATING! HA HA HA HA!
HA HA
SLAM!
AND I'M AFRAID THE DEVIL...
THUD
THUMP
THUD
THUD
THUMP
THUMP
...WAS RIGHT!
FINIS

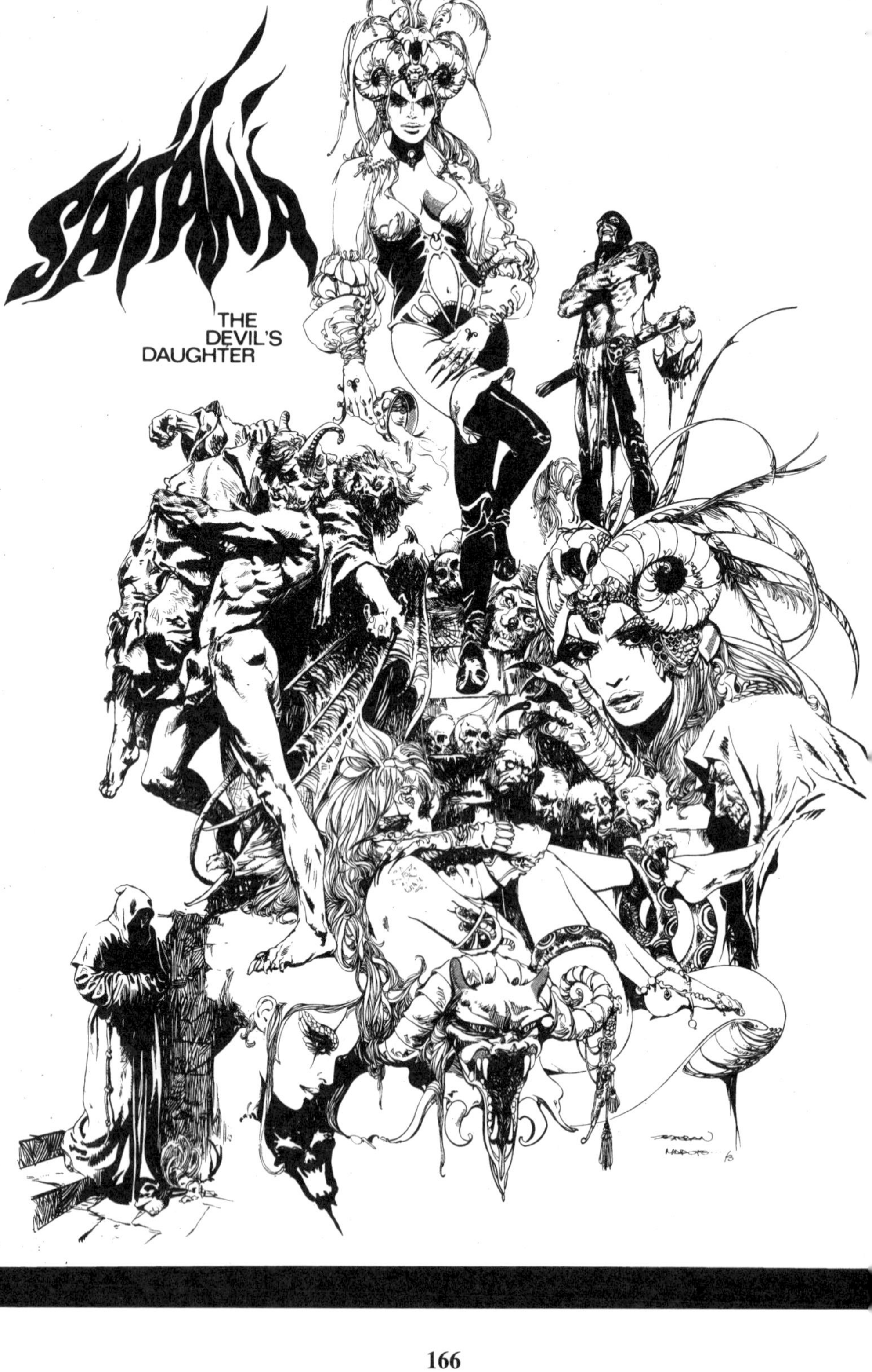
SATANA
THE DEVIL'S DAUGHTER

EDITORIAL NOTE: Last issue, in VAMPIRE TALES #2, we introduced a young lady by the name of Satana. She was beautiful, strong-willed, and a succubus. This issue, Satana is given her own full-length feature. And, in response to the many letters her premiere appearance generated, here's the story of the birth of Satana, as reported by Marvel's gal Friday/editorial assistant, Carla Joseph, who is beautiful, strong-willed, and, in her own way, as devastating as Satana. On behalf of Roy, Gerry, Marv, Don, and myself, I'd like to say: "Carla, we'll get you for this!"

EVERYTHING YOU ALWAYS WANTED TO KNOW ABOUT

SATANA *

(*But were too awestruck to ask)

Feature by CARLA JOSEPH

Dark-haired and shaggy Tony Isabella was sitting hunched over his desk in a corner of the Marvel editorial bullpen, housed in the plush new Marvel Comics offices on the sixth floor of 575 Madison Avenue. He was busily proofreading the latest issue of ASTONISHING TALES (featuring *It!*). Across from him, steadfast Don McGregor concentrated on JUNGLE ACTION (starring *the Black Panther*) while Marvel's Associate Editor, Marv Wolfman, was searching for his glasses so he could check out the printer's proofs on DRACULA LIVES! In the far corner, I was working on a reprint story for MY LOVE.

Tony'd been proofing *It* for two hours and was just about ready to hand it into the Production Department for final corrections. However, an outside thought had interrupted his concentration and he had to deal with it before he could finish the book. *It* is one of the books Tony writes, so the fact that some alien thought was interrupting his work annoyed him greatly. Tony drummed his fingers along the side of the desk, sat up, stretched, and swiveled his chair around so it faced me directly. There was madness in his eyes.

"Hey, Carla—when are you going to have that *Satana* article in? I wanted it last week!"

"Okay, Tony. I'll get to work on it first thing." That line had worked the last seven times I used it on him, so I hadn't expected this time to be any different.

"First thing when?"

"Hey, Tony," interjected Marv, "as associate editor of our giant-sized magazines, it's *my* responsibility to remind Carla that her Satana article is due. And, besides, I'm meaner and more obnoxious than you are."

"Not to mention bigger," added the dour, sandy-headed Scotsman, Don McGregor, who wasn't much taller than Tony, but enjoyed reminding the refugee from Cleveland that there was a difference.

"Very well, Marv. The honor is all yours. I'd rather read *It* anyway."

"Hey, Carla," shouted Marv, who bit through a pencil just to emphasize his words, "when are you going to have that Satana article in? I want it *soon!*"

"I'll write it this weekend, Marv."

"This weekend means *this* weekend! You understand?"

"Yes."

Jumbo John Verpoorten, Marvel's head of production, stuck his head into the Bullpen. "Hey, you guys, this isn't a coffee break—we'd like to see some pages proofed and ready for the corrections department!

"We're working on them, John," answered Don, who somehow reminds one of TV's Lt. Columbo. "I was just asking Marv about the Chinese migration into the jungles of southern Africa."

"The Chinese never migrated to southern Africa."

"They didn't?! Well, thanks, John. I'm glad I asked that question. Now I know for sure."

John withdrew muttering something about the things that jump out of small bottles of Scotch whiskey and everyone resumed work, except for Marv, who kept searching for his glasses ("Tony, are you sure you didn't mail my glasses to Doug Kenney with the CRAZY MAGAZINE rejection slip?"), and me—I started to think about *Satana* and the beautiful art job that Esteban Maroto* had done for Gerry Conway's script . . .

*Esteban Maroto Torres is one of Spain's greatest comic artists. His style has been one of the major influences of European comic publications. He first appeared in the United States in a Spanish publication imported to this country entitled *Five for Infinity*. During the past five years, Esteban's work has received more and more praise from comic fans and pros alike. He is noted for his sense of line and movement. His pages are complex tapestries of interactions rather than a linear series of events. Esteban is equally well known for his fine renderings of women. Put quite simply, his women are exquisite. They are lacking neither physical nor spiritual perfection. They are strong, commanding attention, and once seen, unforgettable.

*We now return you to our regularly scheduled article.

That previous Monday, the day that Esteban's artwork arrived, had started out universally disasterous for everyone. To begin with, it had been raining very hard. And, in August, that's always bad news. I had managed to knock over a night table and destroy my clock in a spastic attempt to turn off the alarm and had arrived at work to find a thick stack of "*last week's*" mail on my desk which had been delivered to our previous offices by mistake. Most of the mail seemed to be addressed to Roy Thomas, Marvel's enterprising editor and my boss. So I decided to sort the mail out in his office. A moment later Roy stomped into the office thoroughly drenched and mumbling about how taxi drivers should be shot if they didn't stop to pick up people in the rain.

"How's Jeanie?," I asked. I know Roy enjoys talking about his beautiful wife more than just about anything else, with one possible exception— writing pages for CONAN.

"Jeanie's fine. She's been accepted into Cornell Nursing School . . . Gosh - darn - dirty - no - good - sons - of - hacks!!!"

"Hacks! Did anyone call for me?" A bleary-eyed apparition peered into Roy's office. It was Gerry Conway, his eyes desperately trying to focus in on us as he swayed a little— his lack of balance accented by his lack of sleep. Roy and I stared at him, flabbergasted.

"Gerry, it's nine-thirty-two. . .What are you doing here at this hour? You're never up before one in the afternoon and you have a fit if anyone here calls you before two."

"That's because I need my beauty sleep," mumbled Gerry as he rubbed his eyes.

"So when do you start becoming beautiful?" queried Roy.

"When I reach sixty. . .You know I wouldn't be down here except John Verpoorten called me yesterday and said he needed some fast changes on a Spidey job I did that would involve changing the plot. He told me that if I wanted to make the changes myself, I'd have to be in here bright and early this morning. So here I am and you know what?—some mindless cretin mailed the story off to me last night! Got anything for me to do?" Gerry leaned against a wall for support. The early hours of the morning were too much for him.

"What a day this is going to be," remarked Roy as he sank into his chair.

"You can say that again," shouted the always excitable Marv as he rushed into Roy's office and pounded his fist on Roy's desk. "I get in early this morning to work on CRAZY and find the editorial that I wrote Friday isn't here."

"Maybe you took it home with you," offered Don McGregor. No one had even noticed him entering the office during Marv's fit of melodrama.

"I wouldn't do anything that stupid! Besides, if I had taken it home with me I would have worked on it over the weekend and not been forced to come in early on Monday to go over it. Something like that would be stupid beyond belief and— oh-my-God! I just remembered! I *did* take it home with me." Marv slouched down on the black couch in Roy's new office, desperately trying to keep from crying.

"And it isn't even ten o' clock," someone sighed.

"Hey! Why is everybody in Roy's office?" Tony Isabella had wandered in, disheveled as always.

"We're discussing the potential advantages of suicide. Want to participate?"

"No thanks, Dauntless Don McGregor."

"Why do I always get *nauseous* when he calls me that?"

"Hey folks! Here's something that looks interesting— it's a package of artwork from Spain— it's from Esteban Maroto."

"SATANA! IT'S SATANA!!!" Everyone crowded around Roy's desk while he fumbled with the wrappings.

"The way our luck's been running today, we'll probably find it's the wrong story," whined Marv.

"It isn't," snapped Roy as he began to unroll the pages. "Wee—ooooow! Will you look at *this!!!*"

Everyone began pushing and shoving to get a better look at the large pages of artwork Roy was holding open on his desk. Marv, who can switch instantaneously from abject pessimism to absolute optimism, took one look at the pages and began to sing.

We finished looking over the art. Roy put the pages down on his desk and leaned back in his chair. A long low whistle escaped him. It was reminiscent of the whistle that escaped Humphrey Bogart when Lauren Bacall left his room after uttering those immortal words in what has to be the all-time-greatest-seduction-scene-ever-recorded -on-film: "If you need me— just whistle . . ."

"She's dynamite," wailed Marv.

"Yeah," sighed Don.

"Ha-ha! I get to *write* her," smirked Gerry.

"You know how to rub it in, don't you, Conway?" needled Tony. "You know if Esteban keeps sending in artwork like that for SATANA, you're going to become the most hated writer in the business."

Gerry nodded. "That's a very distinct possibility."

Roy absent-mindedly chewed on the cap of a black Pen-tel. "Well, we've finally done it," he mused. "It's a shame that John Romita and Stan aren't in right now. You know, Stan was thinking about doing a strip on the Devil's Daughter for years, but until we got into large-sized comics it just didn't seem practical. Then, when we

SATANA

THE DEVIL's DAUGHTER

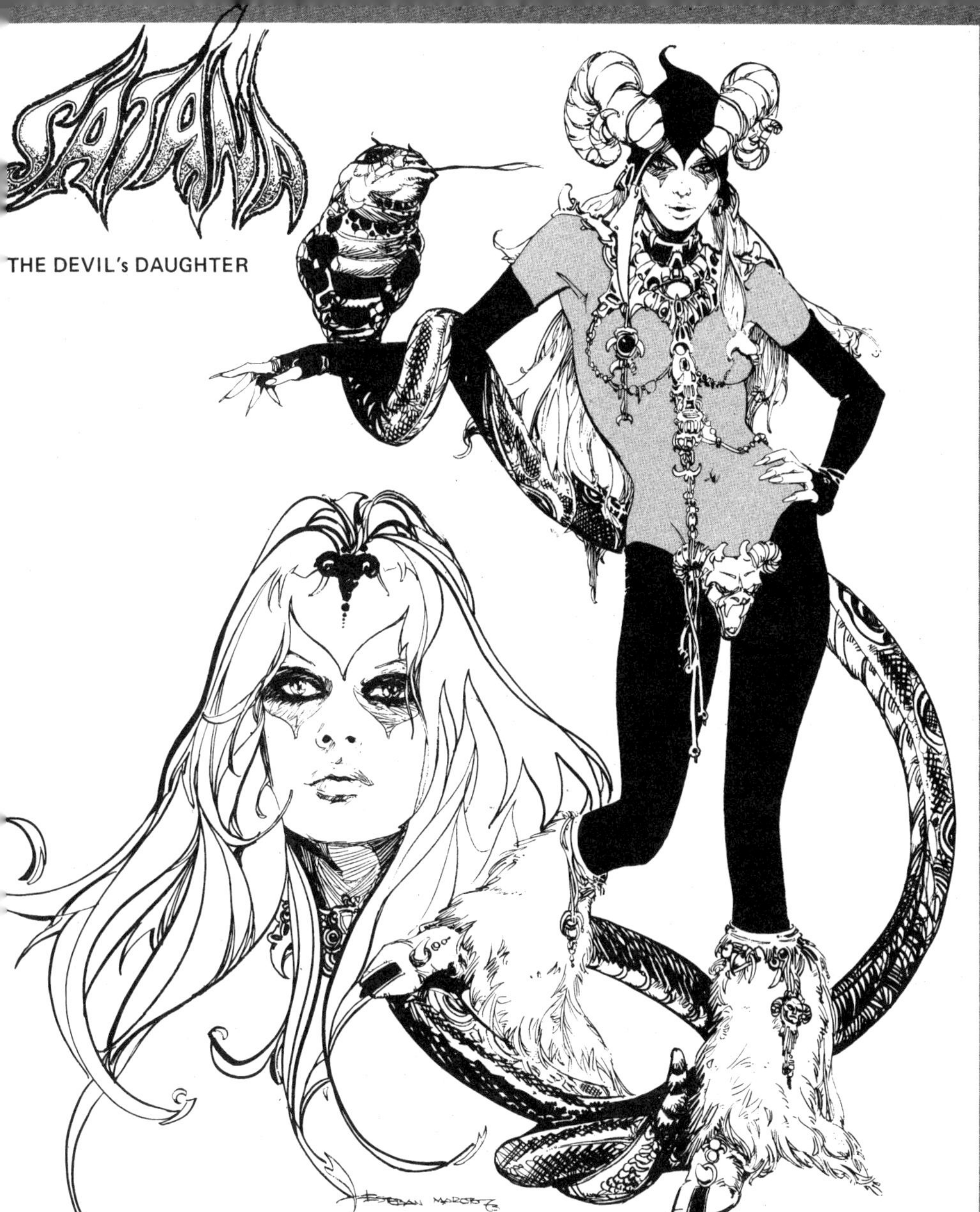
ESTEBAN MAROTO

re first beginning to talk over the possibilities of doing SON OF SATAN series, Stan suggested that we do a ip on the Devil's Daughter also. He told me how he'd ays wanted to do a Devil's Daughter character and inded me out on whether I thought now might be a od time to try it. We started talking about the concept— what she might be like— how she would act— and suddenly she was there in the room with us. Neither of us could picture her or have but the barest inkling of what she was eventually going to be like— but she was there just the same. And we knew that we would have to do her! It was one of those moments when two people link onto a single concept and it becomes so real that you know it just has to be! We knew she'd be a winner and we were right!"

"Esteban did some really far-out things with John Romita's designs," said Gerry.

Roy agreed and then added: "John did some really fine costumes and developed a really great character to begin with. Did you know that John worked up a whole series of character ideas for SATANA? Originally, we were going to have an ad announcing her arrival with three alternate SATANA characters and not telling our readers which she would be. Then we nixed that as too weak an introduction for this character and John took the best features from each character and costume and combined them for Satana. Did any of you ever see John's original roughs?"

We all shook our heads.

"I've got them here someplace. I'll show them to you." Roy searched around in his art drawers 'til he came up with a large envelope used for storing artwork. It was labeled SATANA. "Here we are." Roy slid the contents of the envelope onto his desk. "Here's the rough I was telling you about. You notice the three different characters? The lady with the cape at her face was discarded immediately. Stan thought she looked too much like an ordinary superheroine. But from the other two, John took the locks of hair that give a horned shadow effect from one, the wide forehead from the other, and combined the costumes, resulting in the character that finally appeared in the original ad." Roy pulled out a second page which showed SATANA as she had appeared in her first ad. "We changed her some more once John and I went to work on the first strip. John did a lot of research into the occult and everything he suggested in terms of her costume had a meaning to it. Aside from the hairstyle, the five points to the cape, the cut of the suit, her rhythm of movement— which Maroto carried off beautifully– all were carefully planned out by John. In the final design of the costume we simplified things a great deal. We squared the line across her stomach to add more power to her movements. We wanted her to be capable of dominating a situation physically as well as spiritually. Also, making her a succubus was pretty heavy, and we didn't want to minimize the effect by giving her too complex a costume."

"Who would you say is mostly responsible for her?" Tony asked.

"I don't think any one person can be said to have originated SATANA. Certainly Stan came up with the original concept. As for the actual development of the character, Johnny and I share a goodly portion of that blame with Stan. The succubus idea was mine. But if you want to talk about the responsibility— well, that currently rests with Gerry and Esteban."

All eyes shifted to Gerry, who was sitting in a corner muttering to himself over and over again, "Oh boy, she's all mine...She's All Mine...SHE'S ALL MINE!!!"

"I'd sure like to meet her," mused Tony.

"Wouldn't we all," chuckled Roy.

"Esteban certainly knows how to draw his women," continued Tony.

"Yes," said Roy. "Here are some of Esteban's original thoughts on SATANA before he saw John's version. I asked him for some ideas for her when we originally started getting underway. But Esteban couldn't get to it

until after he finished some previous commitments. So we didn't get his work until after John and I had completed the first strip and it was already in production."

Roy proceeded to show us two of the most exquisite pages of artwork we'd ever seen.

John Verpoorten appeared in the doorway of Roy's office. "Look, you guys— there's work to do. In case you haven't realized it, it's Monday and the weekend's over. So get back to work."

"It's alright, John. The Maroto artwork just came in on SATANA. And we've been going over it."

"Oh, you've got the SATANA job." For a moment John let down his facade of the always-fierce watchdog of the Marvel production schedule. He began to peer curiously at Roy's desk. All-too-quickly, however, he remembered his duties. "Well, everyone, I'll give you til the count of ten to get back to work. McGregor, I want those BLACK PANTHER pages in production today!"

"Easy, John. You know you're just six midgets put together and if you don't watch it I'll take you apart one by one— err...John? Gee, I hope I wasn't out of line with that midgets crack. I...yes, master, I'll get on the book right away!"

"And Roy," John didn't even change his tone when talking to the Editor, "when you're done with the Maroto job, give it to Murray Friedman. He's been worrying about it for weeks." John turned and left.

"Sure John," Roy called after him. "Well folks, you heard John. Now get back to work."

Slowly we filed out of the office. That is, all of us except Gerry who was still sitting in the corner mumbling, "She's mine...She's Mine...SHE'S ALL MINE!!!"

It looked like it wasn't going to be such a bad day after all. FINIS

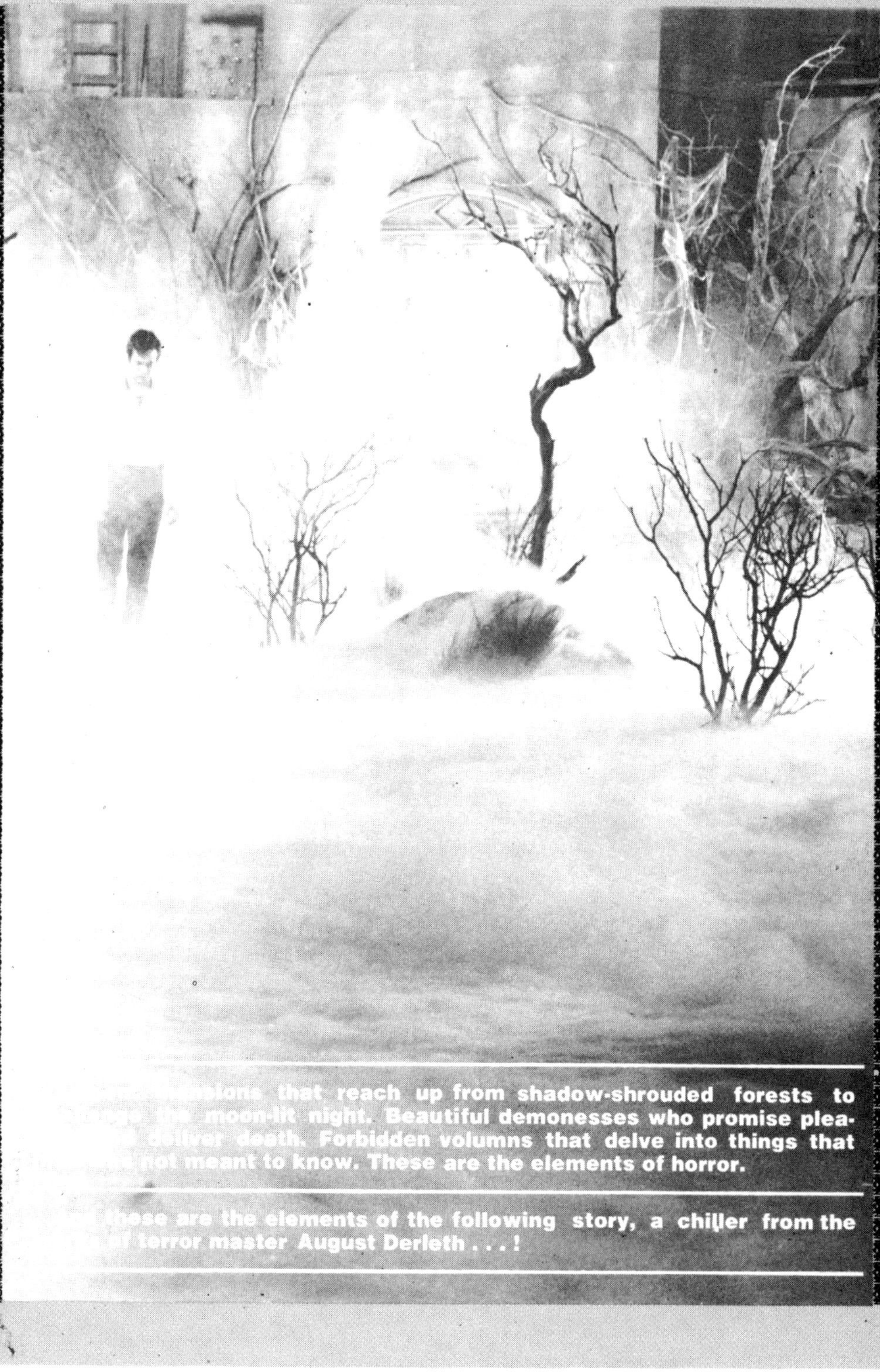

sions that reach up from shadow-shrouded forests to
the moon-lit night. Beautiful demonesses who promise plea-
deliver death. Forbidden volumns that delve into things that
not meant to know. These are the elements of horror.
these are the elements of the following story, a chiller from the
of terror master August Derleth . . . !

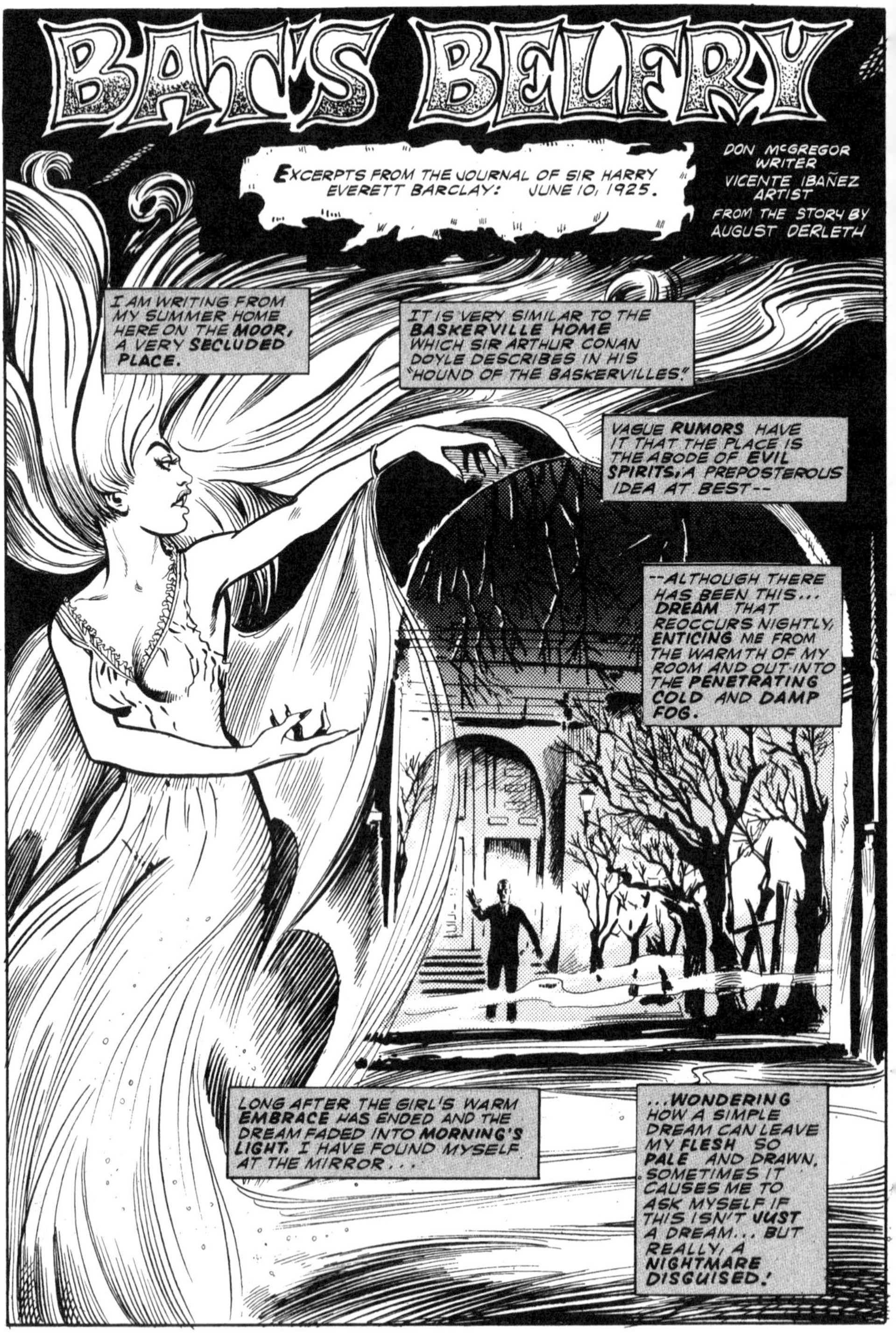

BAT'S BELFRY
DON McGREGOR WRITER
VICENTE IBAÑEZ ARTIST
FROM THE STORY BY AUGUST DERLETH
EXCERPTS FROM THE JOURNAL OF SIR HARRY EVERETT BARCLAY: JUNE 10, 1925.
I AM WRITING FROM MY SUMMER HOME HERE ON THE MOOR, A VERY SECLUDED PLACE.
IT IS VERY SIMILAR TO THE BASKERVILLE HOME WHICH SIR ARTHUR CONAN DOYLE DESCRIBES IN HIS "HOUND OF THE BASKERVILLES."
VAGUE RUMORS HAVE IT THAT THE PLACE IS THE ABODE OF EVIL SPIRITS; A PREPOSTEROUS IDEA AT BEST--
--ALTHOUGH THERE HAS BEEN THIS... DREAM THAT REOCCURS NIGHTLY, ENTICING ME FROM THE WARMTH OF MY ROOM AND OUT INTO THE PENETRATING COLD AND DAMP FOG.
LONG AFTER THE GIRL'S WARM EMBRACE HAS ENDED AND THE DREAM FADED INTO MORNING'S LIGHT, I HAVE FOUND MYSELF AT THE MIRROR...
...WONDERING HOW A SIMPLE DREAM CAN LEAVE MY FLESH SO PALE AND DRAWN. SOMETIMES IT CAUSES ME TO ASK MYSELF IF THIS ISN'T JUST A DREAM... BUT REALLY, A NIGHTMARE DISGUISED!

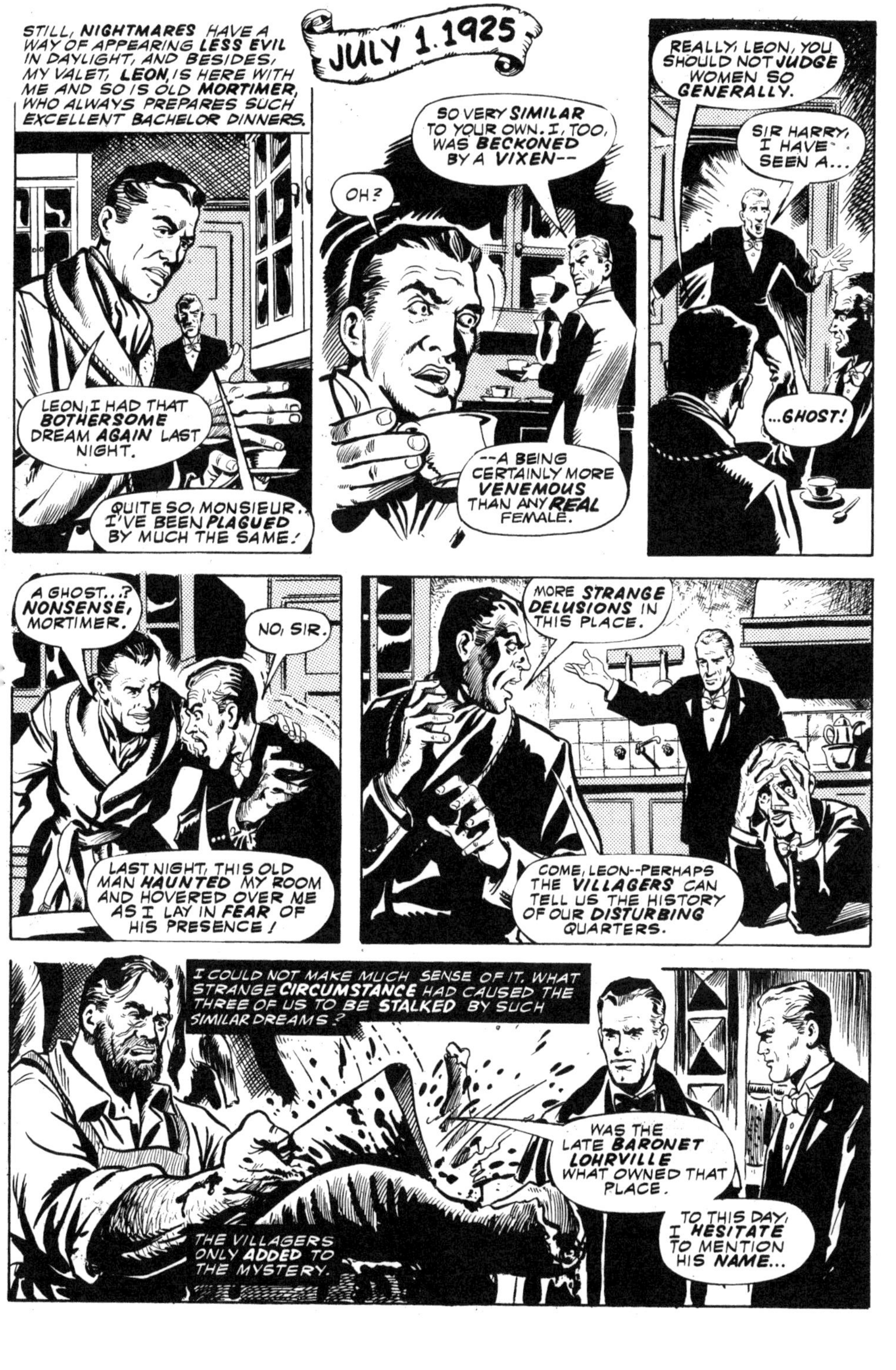
STILL, NIGHTMARES HAVE A WAY OF APPEARING LESS EVIL IN DAYLIGHT, AND BESIDES, MY VALET, LEON, IS HERE WITH ME AND SO IS OLD MORTIMER, WHO ALWAYS PREPARES SUCH EXCELLENT BACHELOR DINNERS.
JULY 1 1925
LEON, I HAD THAT BOTHERSOME DREAM AGAIN LAST NIGHT.
QUITE SO, MONSIEUR. I'VE BEEN PLAGUED BY MUCH THE SAME!
SO VERY SIMILAR TO YOUR OWN. I, TOO, WAS BECKONED BY A VIXEN--
OH?
--A BEING CERTAINLY MORE VENEMOUS THAN ANY REAL FEMALE.
REALLY, LEON, YOU SHOULD NOT JUDGE WOMEN SO GENERALLY.
SIR HARRY, I HAVE SEEN A...
...GHOST!
A GHOST...? NONSENSE, MORTIMER.
NO, SIR.
LAST NIGHT, THIS OLD MAN HAUNTED MY ROOM AND HOVERED OVER ME AS I LAY IN FEAR OF HIS PRESENCE!
MORE STRANGE DELUSIONS IN THIS PLACE.
COME, LEON--PERHAPS THE VILLAGERS CAN TELL US THE HISTORY OF OUR DISTURBING QUARTERS.
I COULD NOT MAKE MUCH SENSE OF IT. WHAT STRANGE CIRCUMSTANCE HAD CAUSED THE THREE OF US TO BE STALKED BY SUCH SIMILAR DREAMS?
THE VILLAGERS ONLY ADDED TO THE MYSTERY.
WAS THE LATE BARONET LOHRVILLE WHAT OWNED THAT PLACE.
TO THIS DAY, I HESITATE TO MENTION HIS NAME...

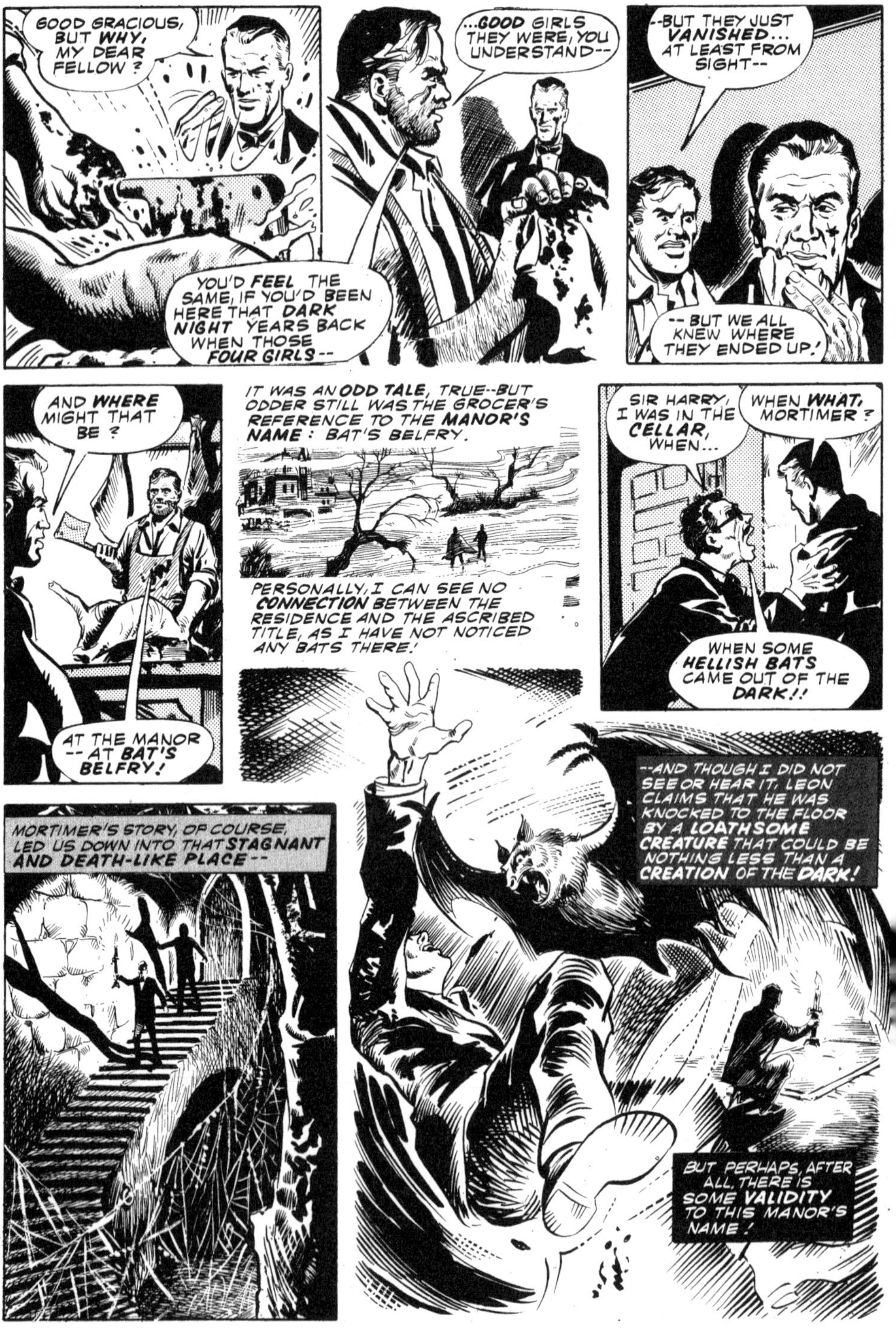
GOOD GRACIOUS, BUT WHY, MY DEAR FELLOW ?
YOU'D FEEL THE SAME, IF YOU'D BEEN HERE THAT DARK NIGHT YEARS BACK WHEN THOSE FOUR GIRLS--
...GOOD GIRLS THEY WERE, YOU UNDERSTAND--
--BUT THEY JUST VANISHED... AT LEAST FROM SIGHT--
-- BUT WE ALL KNEW WHERE THEY ENDED UP!
AND WHERE MIGHT THAT BE ?
AT THE MANOR -- AT BAT'S BELFRY!
IT WAS AN ODD TALE, TRUE--BUT ODDER STILL WAS THE GROCER'S REFERENCE TO THE MANOR'S NAME : BAT'S BELFRY.
PERSONALLY, I CAN SEE NO CONNECTION BETWEEN THE RESIDENCE AND THE ASCRIBED TITLE, AS I HAVE NOT NOTICED ANY BATS THERE!
SIR HARRY, I WAS IN THE CELLAR, WHEN...
WHEN WHAT, MORTIMER ?
WHEN SOME HELLISH BATS CAME OUT OF THE DARK!!
MORTIMER'S STORY, OF COURSE, LED US DOWN INTO THAT STAGNANT AND DEATH-LIKE PLACE--
--AND THOUGH I DID NOT SEE OR HEAR IT, LEON CLAIMS THAT HE WAS KNOCKED TO THE FLOOR BY A LOATHSOME CREATURE THAT COULD BE NOTHING LESS THAN A CREATION OF THE DARK!
BUT PERHAPS, AFTER ALL, THERE IS SOME VALIDITY TO THIS MANOR'S NAME!

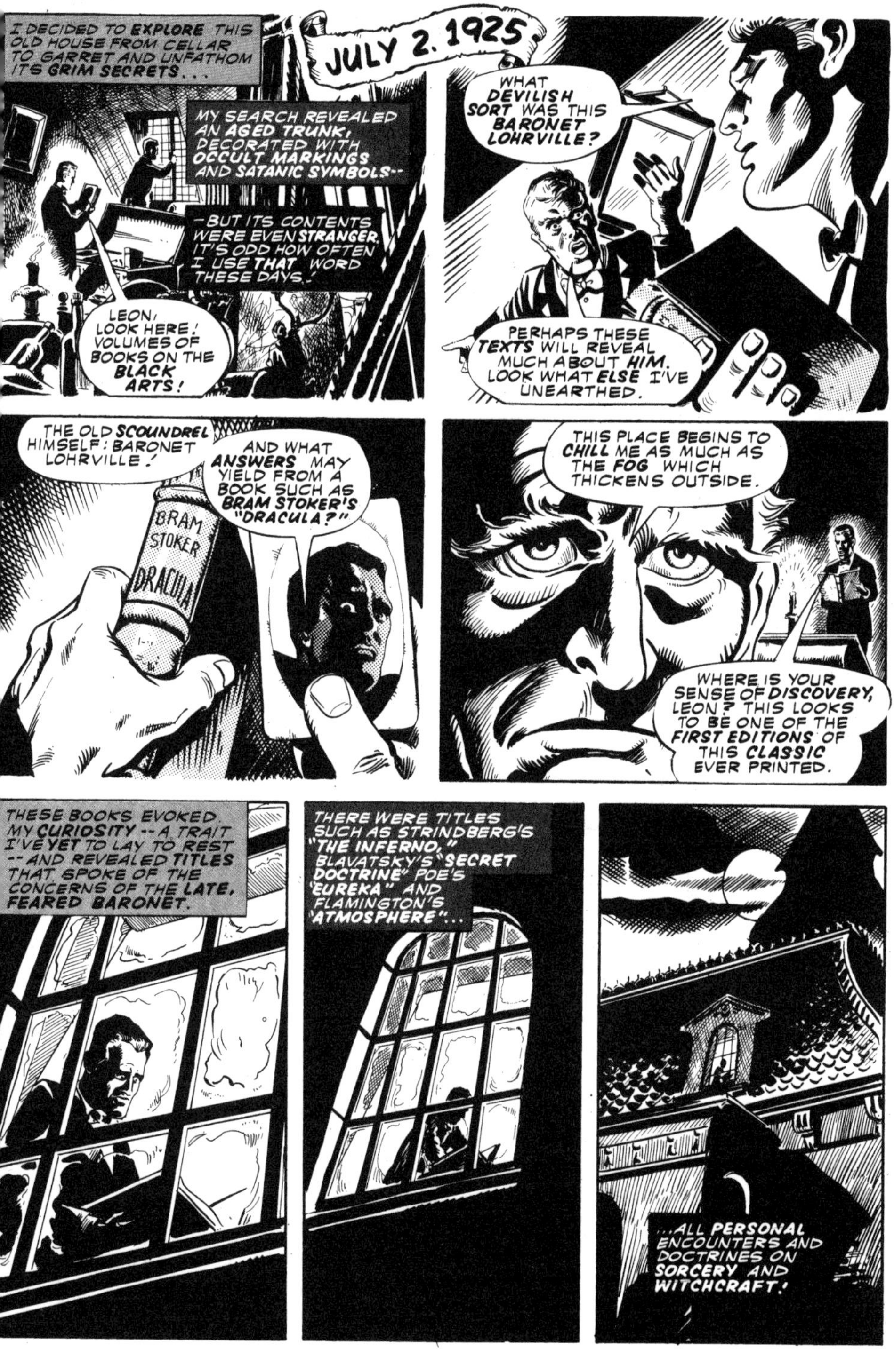
JULY 2, 1925
I DECIDED TO EXPLORE THIS OLD HOUSE FROM CELLAR TO GARRET AND UNFATHOM ITS GRIM SECRETS...
MY SEARCH REVEALED AN AGED TRUNK, DECORATED WITH OCCULT MARKINGS AND SATANIC SYMBOLS--
--BUT ITS CONTENTS WERE EVEN STRANGER. IT'S ODD HOW OFTEN I USE THAT WORD THESE DAYS!
LEON, LOOK HERE! VOLUMES OF BOOKS ON THE BLACK ARTS!
WHAT DEVILISH SORT WAS THIS BARONET LOHRVILLE?
PERHAPS THESE TEXTS WILL REVEAL MUCH ABOUT HIM. LOOK WHAT ELSE I'VE UNEARTHED.
THE OLD SCOUNDREL HIMSELF: BARONET LOHRVILLE!
AND WHAT ANSWERS MAY YIELD FROM A BOOK SUCH AS BRAM STOKER'S "DRACULA?"
BRAM STOKER DRACULA
THIS PLACE BEGINS TO CHILL ME AS MUCH AS THE FOG WHICH THICKENS OUTSIDE.
WHERE IS YOUR SENSE OF DISCOVERY, LEON? THIS LOOKS TO BE ONE OF THE FIRST EDITIONS OF THIS CLASSIC EVER PRINTED.
THESE BOOKS EVOKED MY CURIOSITY -- A TRAIT I'VE YET TO LAY TO REST -- AND REVEALED TITLES THAT SPOKE OF THE CONCERNS OF THE LATE, FEARED BARONET.
THERE WERE TITLES SUCH AS STRINDBERG'S "THE INFERNO," BLAVATSKY'S "SECRET DOCTRINE" POE'S "EUREKA" AND FLAMINGTON'S "ATMOSPHERE"...
...ALL PERSONAL ENCOUNTERS AND DOCTRINES ON SORCERY AND WITCHCRAFT!

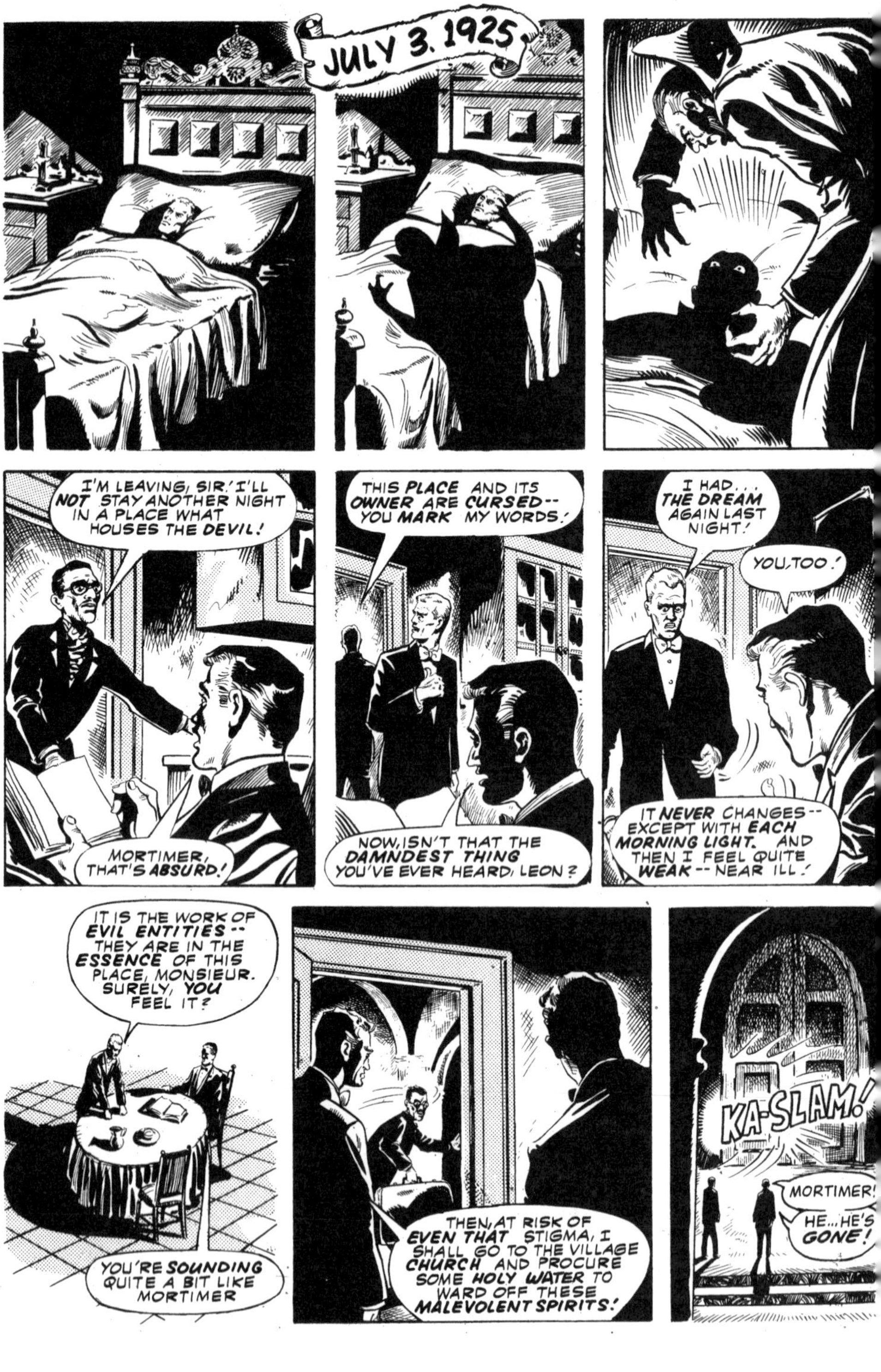
JULY 3, 1925
I'M LEAVING, SIR! I'LL NOT STAY ANOTHER NIGHT IN A PLACE WHAT HOUSES THE DEVIL!
MORTIMER, THAT'S ABSURD!
THIS PLACE AND ITS OWNER ARE CURSED-- YOU MARK MY WORDS!
NOW, ISN'T THAT THE DAMNDEST THING YOU'VE EVER HEARD, LEON?
I HAD... THE DREAM AGAIN LAST NIGHT!
YOU, TOO!
IT NEVER CHANGES-- EXCEPT WITH EACH MORNING LIGHT. AND THEN I FEEL QUITE WEAK-- NEAR ILL!
IT IS THE WORK OF EVIL ENTITIES-- THEY ARE IN THE ESSENCE OF THIS PLACE, MONSIEUR. SURELY, YOU FEEL IT?
YOU'RE SOUNDING QUITE A BIT LIKE MORTIMER
THEN, AT RISK OF EVEN THAT STIGMA, I SHALL GO TO THE VILLAGE CHURCH AND PROCURE SOME HOLY WATER TO WARD OFF THESE MALEVOLENT SPIRITS!
KA-SLAM!
MORTIMER!
HE... HE'S GONE!

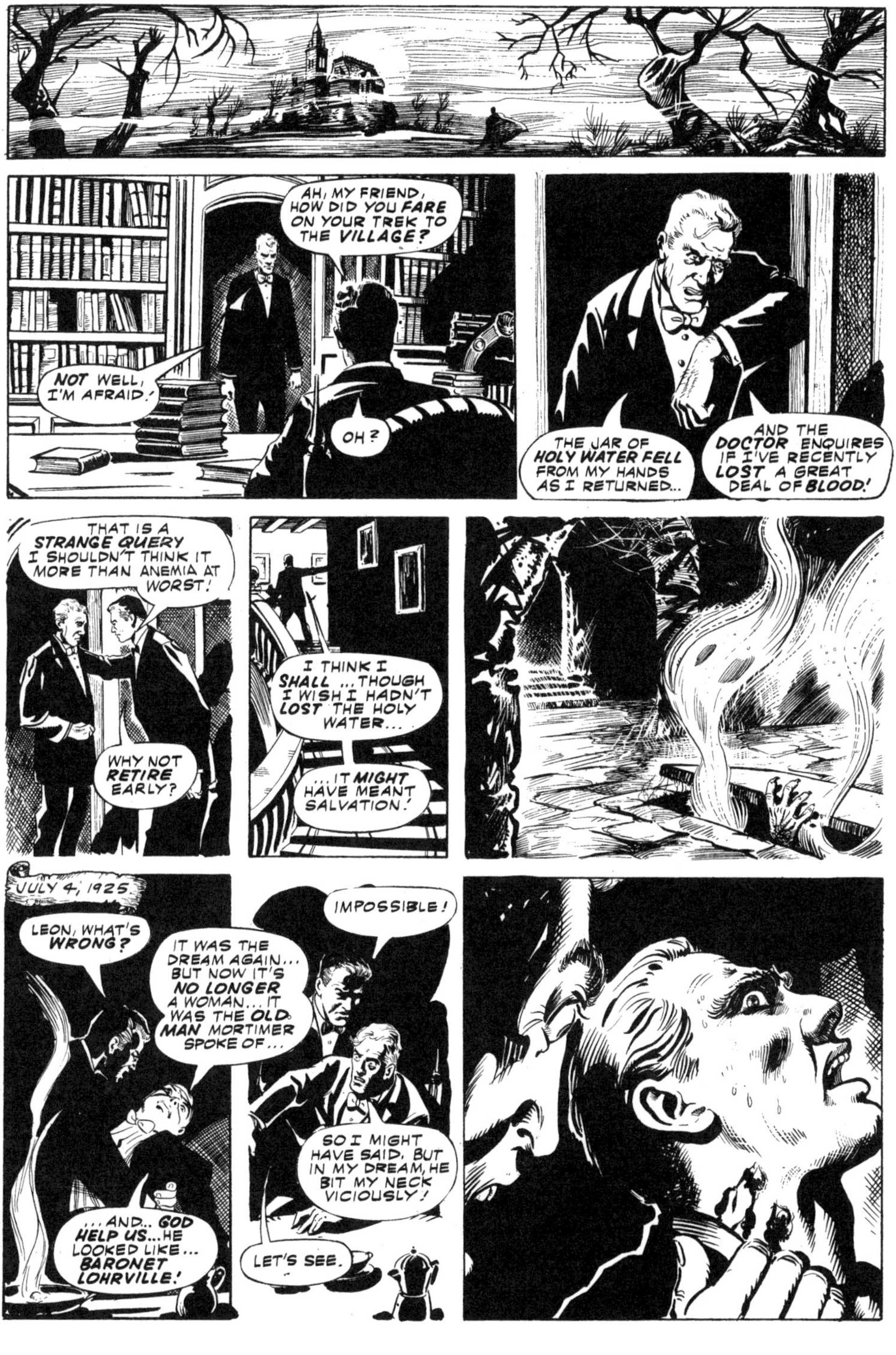
AH, MY FRIEND, HOW DID YOU FARE ON YOUR TREK TO THE VILLAGE?
NOT WELL, I'M AFRAID!
OH?
THE JAR OF HOLY WATER FELL FROM MY HANDS AS I RETURNED...
AND THE DOCTOR ENQUIRES IF I'VE RECENTLY LOST A GREAT DEAL OF BLOOD!
THAT IS A STRANGE QUERY I SHOULDN'T THINK IT MORE THAN ANEMIA AT WORST!
WHY NOT RETIRE EARLY?
I THINK I SHALL ...THOUGH I WISH I HADN'T LOST THE HOLY WATER...
...IT MIGHT HAVE MEANT SALVATION!
JULY 4, 1925
LEON, WHAT'S WRONG?
IT WAS THE DREAM AGAIN... BUT NOW IT'S NO LONGER A WOMAN... IT WAS THE OLD MAN MORTIMER SPOKE OF...
...AND.. GOD HELP US...HE LOOKED LIKE... BARONET LOHRVILLE!
IMPOSSIBLE!
SO I MIGHT HAVE SAID. BUT IN MY DREAM, HE BIT MY NECK VICIOUSLY!
LET'S SEE.

TIME HAS TAKEN ON AN ALTOGETHER NEW MEANING THESE PAST DAYS, SUCH IS THE REASON FOR SUCH A LONG LAPSE IN THESE ENTRIES...

OFTEN I'D LOSE LONG PASSAGES OF TIME... UNAWARE IN MY LETHARGIC STATE THAT THEY'D EVEN PASSED!

JULY 15, 1925

BUT TODAY'S EVENTS HAVE SHARPENED MY WITS. LEON MANAGED TO GET A SMALL QUANTITY OF HOLY WATER INTO THE HOUSE AND SPILLED SOME UPON THAT GREAT SLAB IN THE CELLAR...

LEON, WHAT IN GOD'S NAME IS GOING ON?

THE VERY ENTRANCE TO HELL IS IN THAT CELLER! FAR TOO MUCH TO BE BELIEVED!

LEON, WAIT--

I WAIT NO LONGER, MONSIEUR. YOU SHOULD LEAVE THIS ACCURSED PLACE AT ONCE!

LE DIABLE-- LE DIABLE!

LEON'S WORDS DRIFTED BACK TO ME, MUFFLED BY THE ATMOSPHERE!

--TABLET-- BOOK OF THOTH! --LAMAIS! MON DIEU!

I THOUGHT ON THOSE FRAGMENTED WORDS AS I TURNED BACK TO THE HOUSE. "LE DIABLE" AND "MON DIEU" MEANT "THE DEVIL" AND "MY GOD".

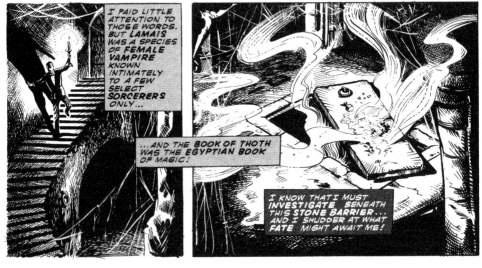

I PAID LITTLE ATTENTION TO THOSE WORDS. BUT LAMAIS WAS A SPECIES OF FEMALE VAMPIRE KNOWN INTIMATELY TO A FEW SELECT SORCERERS ONLY...

...AND THE BOOK OF THOTH WAS THE EGYPTIAN BOOK OF MAGIC!

I KNOW THAT I MUST INVESTIGATE BENEATH THIS STONE BARRIER... AND I SHUDDER AT WHAT FATE MIGHT AWAIT ME!

178

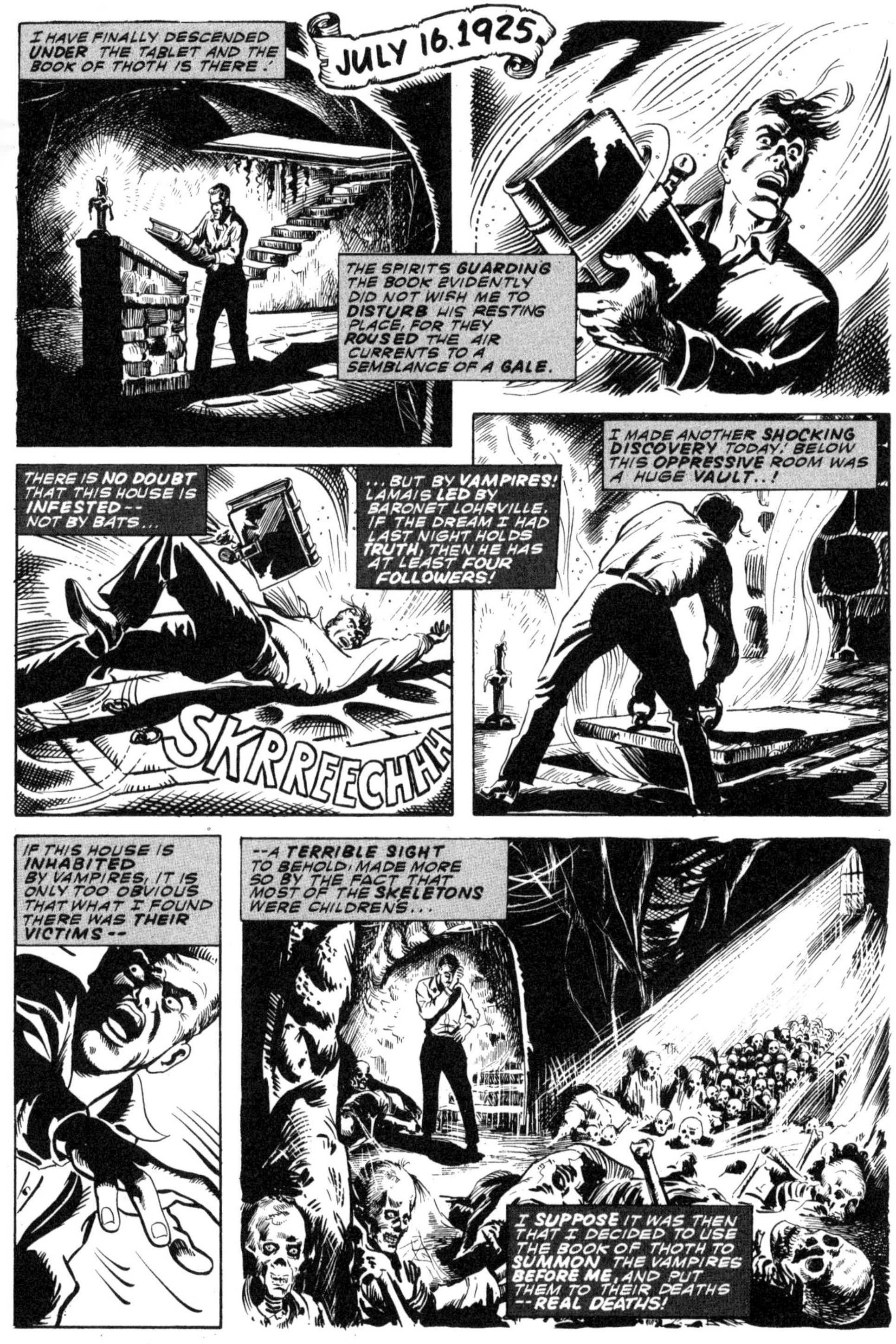
JULY 16, 1925
I HAVE FINALLY DESCENDED UNDER THE TABLET AND THE BOOK OF THOTH IS THERE.'
THE SPIRITS GUARDING THE BOOK EVIDENTLY DID NOT WISH ME TO DISTURB HIS RESTING PLACE, FOR THEY ROUSED THE AIR CURRENTS TO A SEMBLANCE OF A GALE.
THERE IS NO DOUBT THAT THIS HOUSE IS INFESTED-- NOT BY BATS...
...BUT BY VAMPIRES! LAMAIS LED BY BARONET LOHRVILLE. IF THE DREAM I HAD LAST NIGHT HOLDS TRUTH, THEN HE HAS AT LEAST FOUR FOLLOWERS!
SKRREECHHH
I MADE ANOTHER SHOCKING DISCOVERY TODAY! BELOW THIS OPPRESSIVE ROOM WAS A HUGE VAULT..!
IF THIS HOUSE IS INHABITED BY VAMPIRES, IT IS ONLY TOO OBVIOUS THAT WHAT I FOUND THERE WAS THEIR VICTIMS--
--A TERRIBLE SIGHT TO BEHOLD, MADE MORE SO BY THE FACT THAT MOST OF THE SKELETONS WERE CHILDREN'S...
I SUPPOSE IT WAS THEN THAT I DECIDED TO USE THE BOOK OF THOTH TO SUMMON THE VAMPIRES BEFORE ME, AND PUT THEM TO THEIR DEATHS --REAL DEATHS!

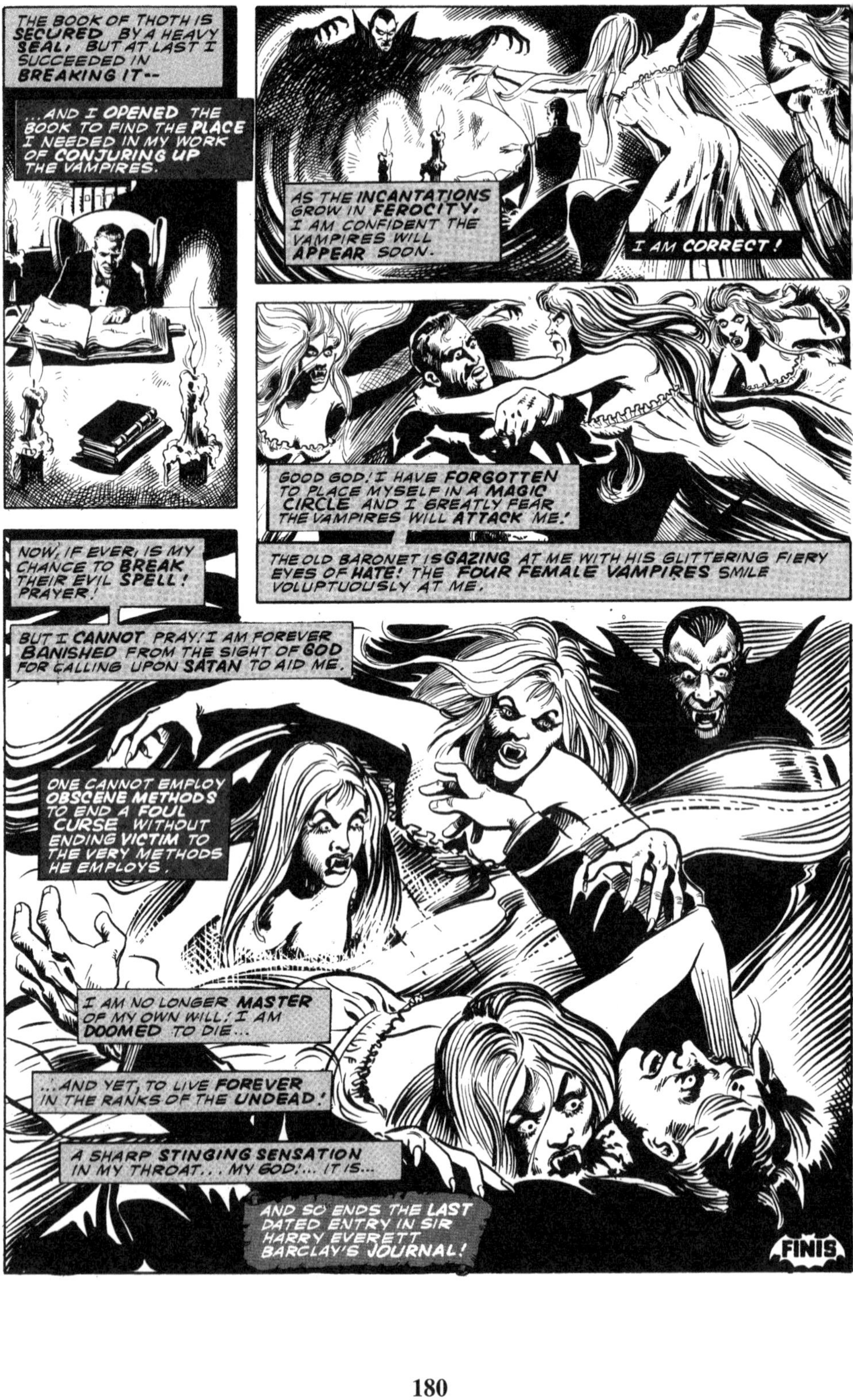
THE BOOK OF THOTH IS SECURED BY A HEAVY SEAL, BUT AT LAST I SUCCEEDED IN BREAKING IT--
...AND I OPENED THE BOOK TO FIND THE PLACE I NEEDED IN MY WORK OF CONJURING UP THE VAMPIRES.
AS THE INCANTATIONS GROW IN FEROCITY, I AM CONFIDENT THE VAMPIRES WILL APPEAR SOON.
I AM CORRECT!
GOOD GOD! I HAVE FORGOTTEN TO PLACE MYSELF IN A MAGIC CIRCLE AND I GREATLY FEAR THE VAMPIRES WILL ATTACK ME!
THE OLD BARONET IS GAZING AT ME WITH HIS GLITTERING FIERY EYES OF HATE! THE FOUR FEMALE VAMPIRES SMILE VOLUPTUOUSLY AT ME.
NOW, IF EVER, IS MY CHANCE TO BREAK THEIR EVIL SPELL! PRAYER!
BUT I CANNOT PRAY! I AM FOREVER BANISHED FROM THE SIGHT OF GOD FOR CALLING UPON SATAN TO AID ME.
ONE CANNOT EMPLOY OBSCENE METHODS TO END A FOUL CURSE WITHOUT ENDING VICTIM TO THE VERY METHODS HE EMPLOYS.
I AM NO LONGER MASTER OF MY OWN WILL; I AM DOOMED TO DIE...
...AND YET, TO LIVE FOREVER IN THE RANKS OF THE UNDEAD!
A SHARP STINGING SENSATION IN MY THROAT... MY GOD!... IT IS...
AND SO ENDS THE LAST DATED ENTRY IN SIR HARRY EVERETT BARCLAY'S JOURNAL!
FINIS

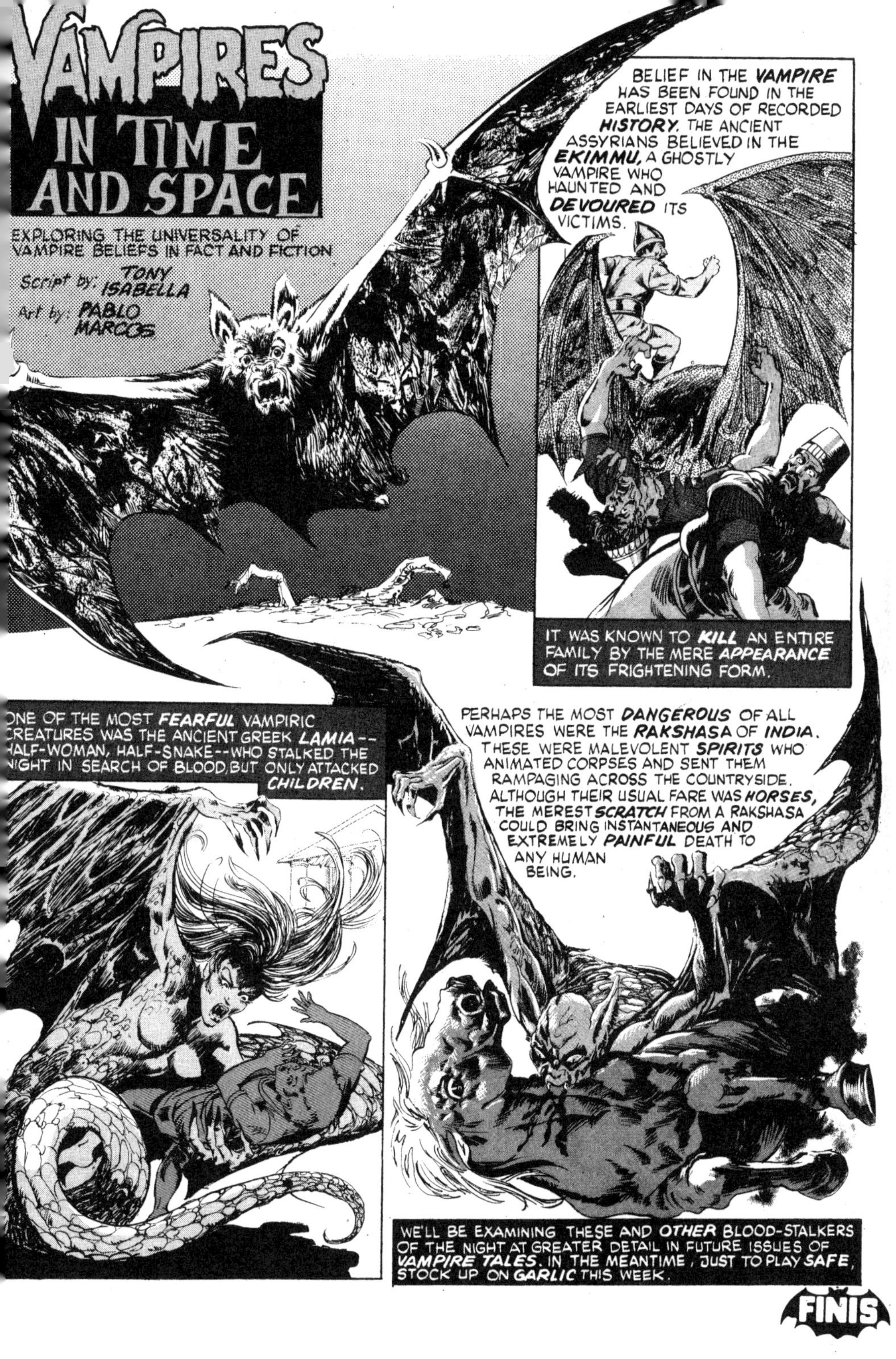
VAMPIRES IN TIME AND SPACE
EXPLORING THE UNIVERSALITY OF VAMPIRE BELIEFS IN FACT AND FICTION
Script by: TONY ISABELLA
Art by: PABLO MARCOS
BELIEF IN THE VAMPIRE HAS BEEN FOUND IN THE EARLIEST DAYS OF RECORDED HISTORY. THE ANCIENT ASSYRIANS BELIEVED IN THE EKIMMU, A GHOSTLY VAMPIRE WHO HAUNTED AND DEVOURED ITS VICTIMS.
IT WAS KNOWN TO KILL AN ENTIRE FAMILY BY THE MERE APPEARANCE OF ITS FRIGHTENING FORM.
ONE OF THE MOST FEARFUL VAMPIRIC CREATURES WAS THE ANCIENT GREEK LAMIA--HALF-WOMAN, HALF-SNAKE--WHO STALKED THE NIGHT IN SEARCH OF BLOOD, BUT ONLY ATTACKED CHILDREN.
PERHAPS THE MOST DANGEROUS OF ALL VAMPIRES WERE THE RAKSHASA OF INDIA. THESE WERE MALEVOLENT SPIRITS WHO ANIMATED CORPSES AND SENT THEM RAMPAGING ACROSS THE COUNTRYSIDE. ALTHOUGH THEIR USUAL FARE WAS HORSES, THE MEREST SCRATCH FROM A RAKSHASA COULD BRING INSTANTANEOUS AND EXTREMELY PAINFUL DEATH TO ANY HUMAN BEING.
WE'LL BE EXAMINING THESE AND OTHER BLOOD-STALKERS OF THE NIGHT AT GREATER DETAIL IN FUTURE ISSUES OF VAMPIRE TALES. IN THE MEANTIME, JUST TO PLAY SAFE, STOCK UP ON GARLIC THIS WEEK.
FINIS

Michael Morbius was *dying.* A blood-cell deficiency was slowly but surely killing him. And so, to counteract this disease within his body, the Nobel Prize-winning scientist added an experimental enzyme to his bloodstream.

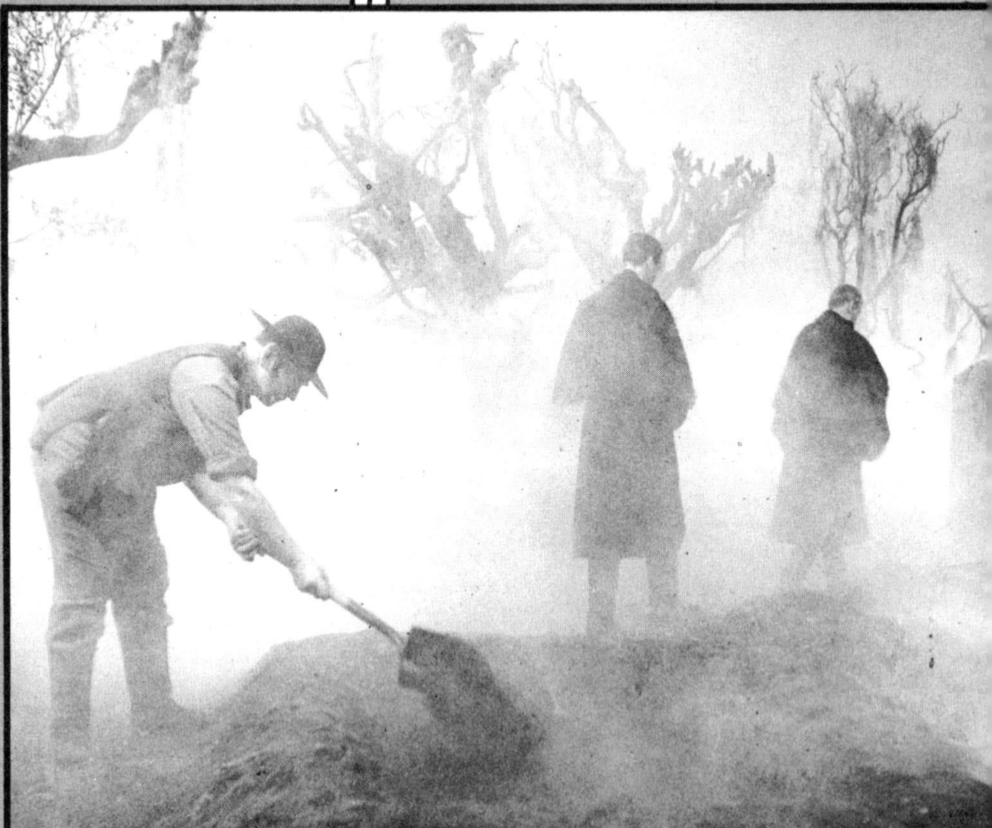

It saved his life—but made him a *vampire,* a stalker of the night. Michael Morbius is *still* dying. But this time, the disease comes from within his *soul!*

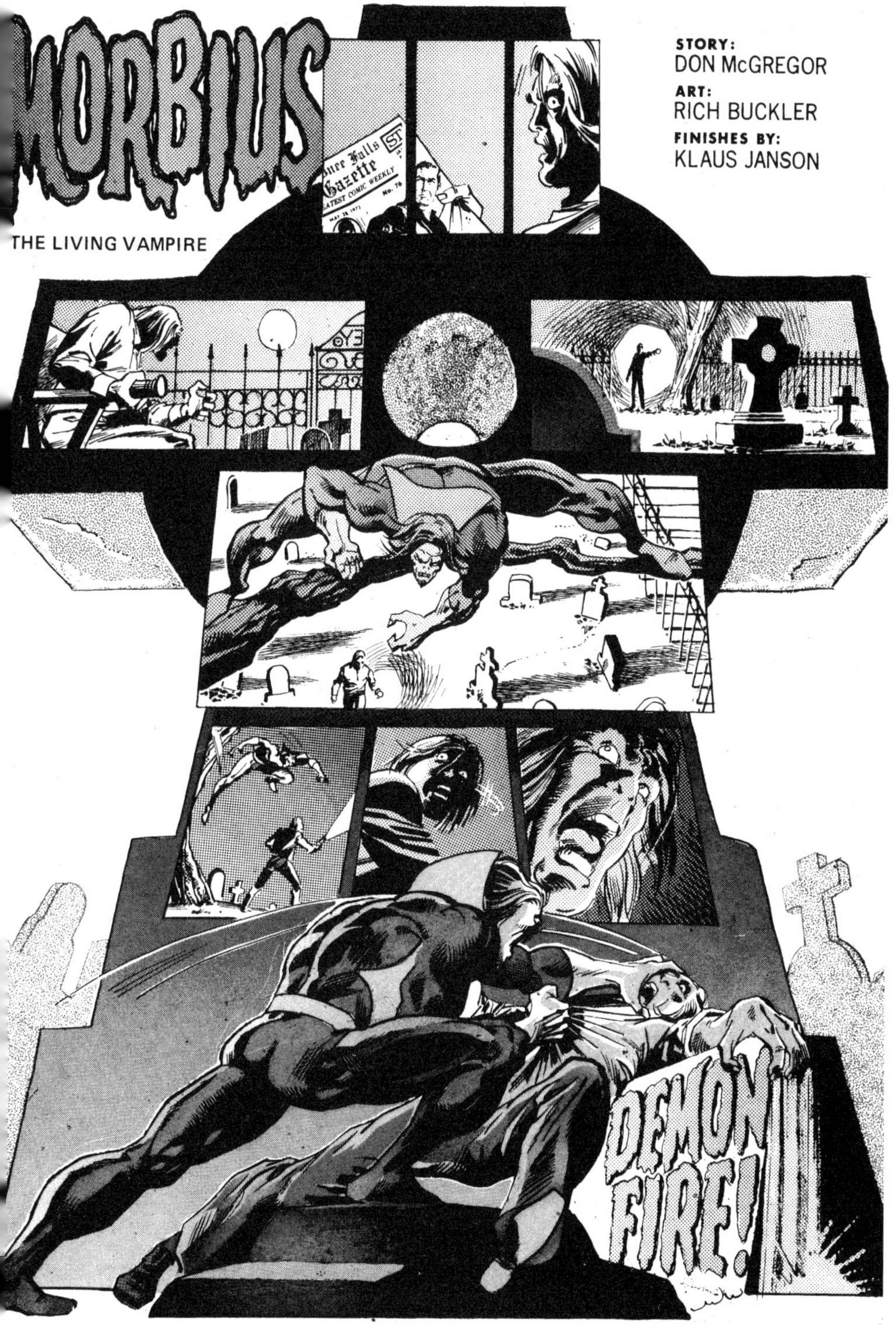
MORBIUS
THE LIVING VAMPIRE
STORY:
DON McGREGOR
ART:
RICH BUCKLER
FINISHES BY:
KLAUS JANSON
Gazette
DEMON FIRE!

WITH FIERCE INTENSITY YOU **PUNCTURE** THE CARE-TAKER'S FLESH, **MICHAEL MORBIUS**...

--AND AS HIS BLOOD LEAVES A **CRIMSON STIGMA** UPON YOUR CORPSE-WHITE FACE, YOU ARE GLAD YOU DO NOT KNOW YOUR VICTIM'S NAME!

SUCH KNOWLEDGE WOULD GIVE YOUR VICTIM AN **IDENTITY**-- AND THE GUILT OF YOUR **MA-CABRE DEEDS** WOULD BE **MAGNIFIED**!

NOW HE LIES **DEAD** AT YOUR FEET, AND THE **CO-AGULATING BLOOD CRUSTS** ABOUT YOUR LIPS.

THE NAUSE-ATING TASTE AND TEXTURE OF **BLOOD** REMAINS ON YOUR TONGUE... AND YOUR INSIDES **HEAVE** WITH THE THOUGHT OF IT!

YOU'VE GOT TO **FEEL** ABOUT THINGS, MICHAEL MORBIUS...

ISN'T THAT WHAT YOU'VE TOLD **YOURSELF** SO MANY TIMES THIS NIGHT? AS IF YOU'LL **FORGET** WHAT THOSE WORDS MEAN!

YOU WON'T LET THIS **SCIENTIFIC VAMPIRISM** STEAL THAT KNOWLEDGE

--THAT ONE MUST LET **PEOPLE** AN **EVENTS** CUT UND THE LAYER OF FLESH--OR ELSE YOU BECOME ANOTHER KIND OF **LIVING DEAD**--

--A KIND OF **PSYCHOLOGICAL DEATH** TOO COMMON ABOUT THE STREETS OF THIS LAND!

YOU GAZE AT THE CARE-TAKER'S **FLASHLIGHT** AND YOU WONDER IF ITS GLARE RE-VEALS HOW DEEPLY THESE DESTRUCT-IONS **HAUNT** YOU.

YOU TURN, MORBIUS, AND **DISCARD** THAT LIGHT. IT DOES NOT HOLD ANY ANSWERS TO THESE **GRIM THOUGHTS**!!

BUT THERE **ARE** ANSWERS **HERE**, AND THAT IS WHY YOU WALK PURPOSEFULLY TOWARD THE **SEPULCHER**.

REMEMBER? YOU CAME TO **RAVENWOOD CEMETERY** NOT TO KILL--

--BUT TO SAVE **AMANDA SAINT**!

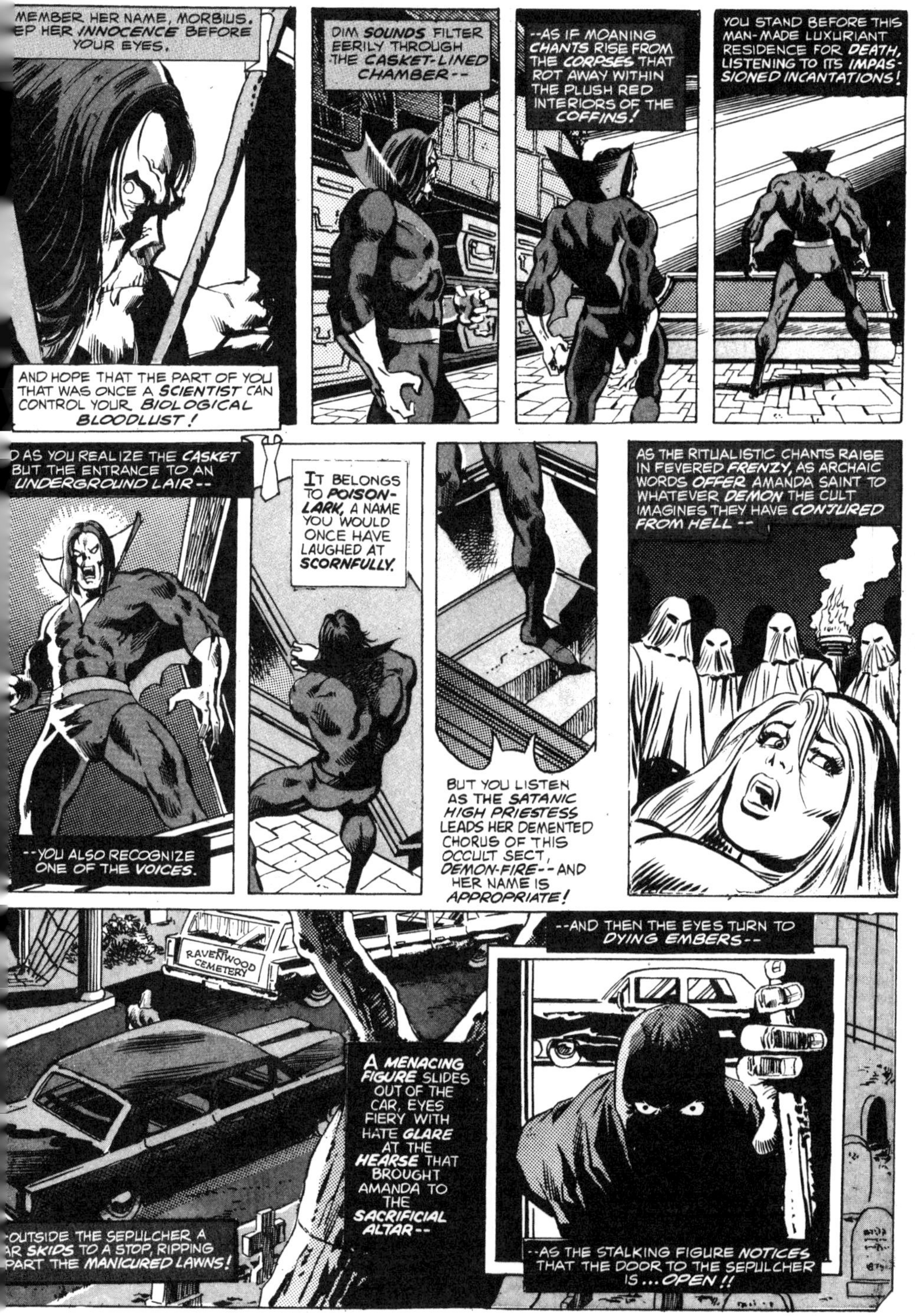
MEMBER HER NAME, MORBIUS. EP HER INNOCENCE BEFORE YOUR EYES.
AND HOPE THAT THE PART OF YOU THAT WAS ONCE A SCIENTIST CAN CONTROL YOUR BIOLOGICAL BLOODLUST!
DIM SOUNDS FILTER EERILY THROUGH THE CASKET-LINED CHAMBER--
--AS IF MOANING CHANTS RISE FROM THE CORPSES THAT ROT AWAY WITHIN THE PLUSH RED INTERIORS OF THE COFFINS!
YOU STAND BEFORE THIS MAN-MADE LUXURIANT RESIDENCE FOR DEATH, LISTENING TO ITS IMPASSIONED INCANTATIONS!
D AS YOU REALIZE THE CASKET BUT THE ENTRANCE TO AN UNDERGROUND LAIR--
--YOU ALSO RECOGNIZE ONE OF THE VOICES.
IT BELONGS TO POISON-LARK, A NAME YOU WOULD ONCE HAVE LAUGHED AT SCORNFULLY.
BUT YOU LISTEN AS THE SATANIC HIGH PRIESTESS LEADS HER DEMENTED CHORUS OF THIS OCCULT SECT, DEMON-FIRE--AND HER NAME IS APPROPRIATE!
AS THE RITUALISTIC CHANTS RAISE IN FEVERED FRENZY, AS ARCHAIC WORDS OFFER AMANDA SAINT TO WHATEVER DEMON THE CULT IMAGINES THEY HAVE CONJURED FROM HELL--
RAVENWOOD CEMETERY
-OUTSIDE THE SEPULCHER A AR SKIDS TO A STOP, RIPPING PART THE MANICURED LAWNS!
A MENACING FIGURE SLIDES OUT OF THE CAR, EYES FIERY WITH HATE GLARE AT THE HEARSE THAT BROUGHT AMANDA TO THE SACRIFICIAL ALTAR--
--AND THEN THE EYES TURN TO DYING EMBERS--
--AS THE STALKING FIGURE NOTICES THAT THE DOOR TO THE SEPULCHER IS...OPEN!!

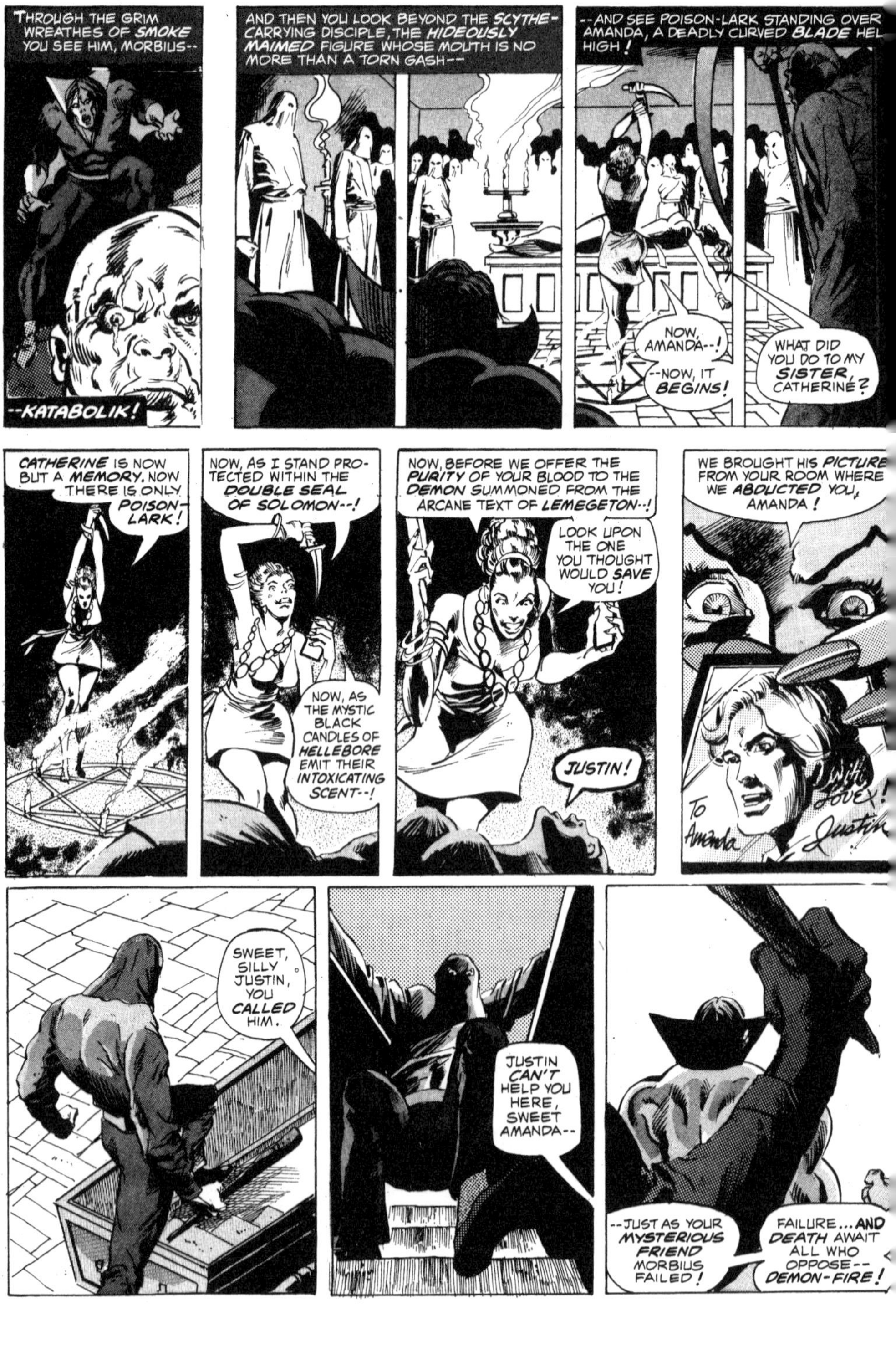
THROUGH THE GRIM WREATHES OF SMOKE YOU SEE HIM, MORBIUS--
--KATABOLIK!
AND THEN YOU LOOK BEYOND THE SCYTHE-CARRYING DISCIPLE, THE HIDEOUSLY MAIMED FIGURE WHOSE MOUTH IS NO MORE THAN A TORN GASH--
--AND SEE POISON-LARK STANDING OVER AMANDA, A DEADLY CURVED BLADE HEL HIGH!
NOW, AMANDA--!
--NOW, IT BEGINS!
WHAT DID YOU DO TO MY SISTER, CATHERINE?
CATHERINE IS NOW BUT A MEMORY. NOW THERE IS ONLY POISON-LARK!
NOW, AS I STAND PROTECTED WITHIN THE DOUBLE SEAL OF SOLOMON--!
NOW, AS THE MYSTIC BLACK CANDLES OF HELLEBORE EMIT THEIR INTOXICATING SCENT--!
NOW, BEFORE WE OFFER THE PURITY OF YOUR BLOOD TO THE DEMON SUMMONED FROM THE ARCANE TEXT OF LEMEGETON--!
LOOK UPON THE ONE YOU THOUGHT WOULD SAVE YOU!
JUSTIN!
WE BROUGHT HIS PICTURE FROM YOUR ROOM WHERE WE ABDUCTED YOU, AMANDA!
To Amanda
With Love! Justin
SWEET, SILLY JUSTIN, YOU CALLED HIM.
JUSTIN CAN'T HELP YOU HERE, SWEET AMANDA--
--JUST AS YOUR MYSTERIOUS FRIEND MORBIUS FAILED!
FAILURE... AND DEATH AWAIT ALL WHO OPPOSE--DEMON-FIRE!

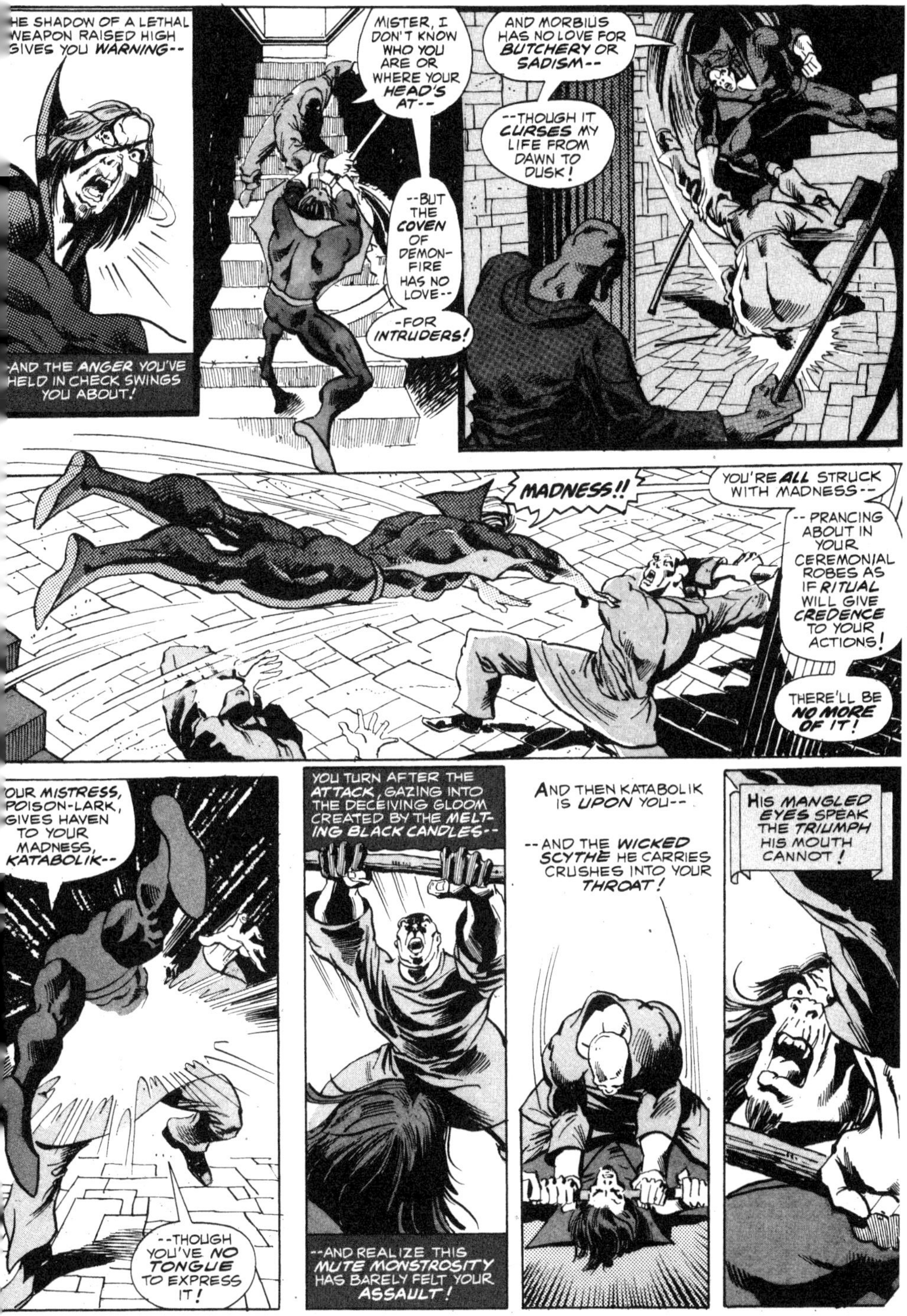

HE SHADOW OF A LETHAL WEAPON RAISED HIGH GIVES YOU WARNING--
-AND THE ANGER YOU'VE HELD IN CHECK SWINGS YOU ABOUT!
MISTER, I DON'T KNOW WHO YOU ARE OR WHERE YOUR HEAD'S AT--
--BUT THE COVEN OF DEMON-FIRE HAS NO LOVE--
-FOR INTRUDERS!
AND MORBIUS HAS NO LOVE FOR BUTCHERY OR SADISM--
--THOUGH IT CURSES MY LIFE FROM DAWN TO DUSK!
MADNESS!!
YOU'RE ALL STRUCK WITH MADNESS--
--PRANCING ABOUT IN YOUR CEREMONIAL ROBES AS IF RITUAL WILL GIVE CREDENCE TO YOUR ACTIONS!
THERE'LL BE NO MORE OF IT!
OUR MISTRESS, POISON-LARK, GIVES HAVEN TO YOUR MADNESS, KATABOLIK--
--THOUGH YOU'VE NO TONGUE TO EXPRESS IT!
YOU TURN AFTER THE ATTACK, GAZING INTO THE DECEIVING GLOOM CREATED BY THE MELTING BLACK CANDLES--
--AND REALIZE THIS MUTE MONSTROSITY HAS BARELY FELT YOUR ASSAULT!
AND THEN KATABOLIK IS UPON YOU--
--AND THE WICKED SCYTHE HE CARRIES CRUSHES INTO YOUR THROAT!
HIS MANGLED EYES SPEAK THE TRIUMPH HIS MOUTH CANNOT!

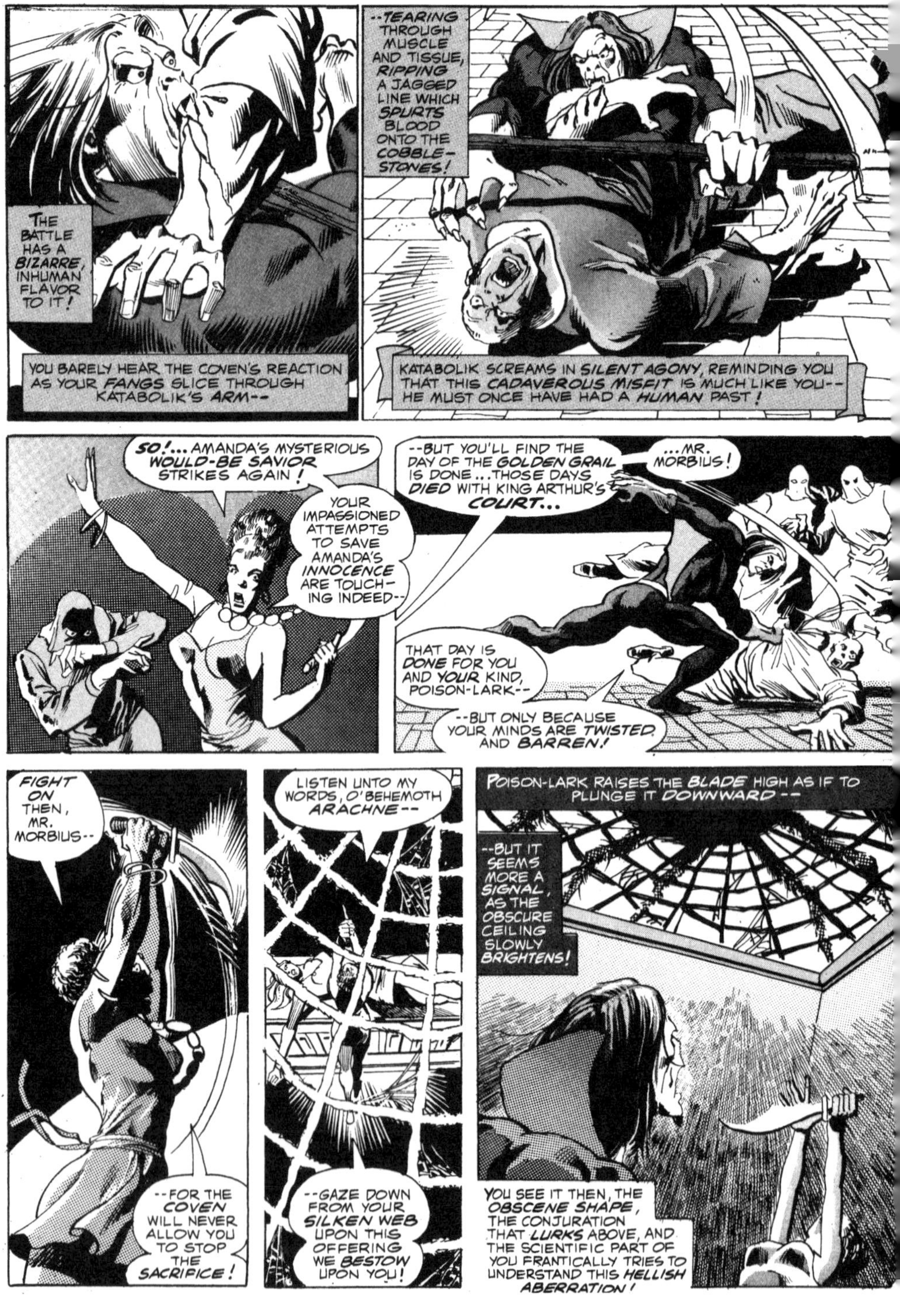
THE BATTLE HAS A BIZARRE, INHUMAN FLAVOR TO IT!
YOU BARELY HEAR THE COVEN'S REACTION AS YOUR FANGS SLICE THROUGH KATABOLIK'S ARM--
--TEARING THROUGH MUSCLE AND TISSUE, RIPPING A JAGGED LINE WHICH SPURTS BLOOD ONTO THE COBBLE-STONES!
KATABOLIK SCREAMS IN SILENT AGONY, REMINDING YOU THAT THIS CADAVEROUS MISFIT IS MUCH LIKE YOU-- HE MUST ONCE HAVE HAD A HUMAN PAST!
SO!... AMANDA'S MYSTERIOUS WOULD-BE SAVIOR STRIKES AGAIN!
YOUR IMPASSIONED ATTEMPTS TO SAVE AMANDA'S INNOCENCE ARE TOUCHING INDEED--
--BUT YOU'LL FIND THE DAY OF THE GOLDEN GRAIL IS DONE... THOSE DAYS DIED WITH KING ARTHUR'S COURT...
...MR. MORBIUS!
THAT DAY IS DONE FOR YOU AND YOUR KIND, POISON-LARK--
--BUT ONLY BECAUSE YOUR MINDS ARE TWISTED AND BARREN!
FIGHT ON THEN, MR. MORBIUS--
--FOR THE COVEN WILL NEVER ALLOW YOU TO STOP THE SACRIFICE!
LISTEN UNTO MY WORDS, O' BEHEMOTH ARACHNE--
--GAZE DOWN FROM YOUR SILKEN WEB UPON THIS OFFERING WE BESTOW UPON YOU!
POISON-LARK RAISES THE BLADE HIGH AS IF TO PLUNGE IT DOWNWARD--
--BUT IT SEEMS MORE A SIGNAL, AS THE OBSCURE CEILING SLOWLY BRIGHTENS!
YOU SEE IT THEN, THE OBSCENE SHAPE, THE CONJURATION THAT LURKS ABOVE, AND THE SCIENTIFIC PART OF YOU FRANTICALLY TRIES TO UNDERSTAND THIS HELLISH ABERRATION!

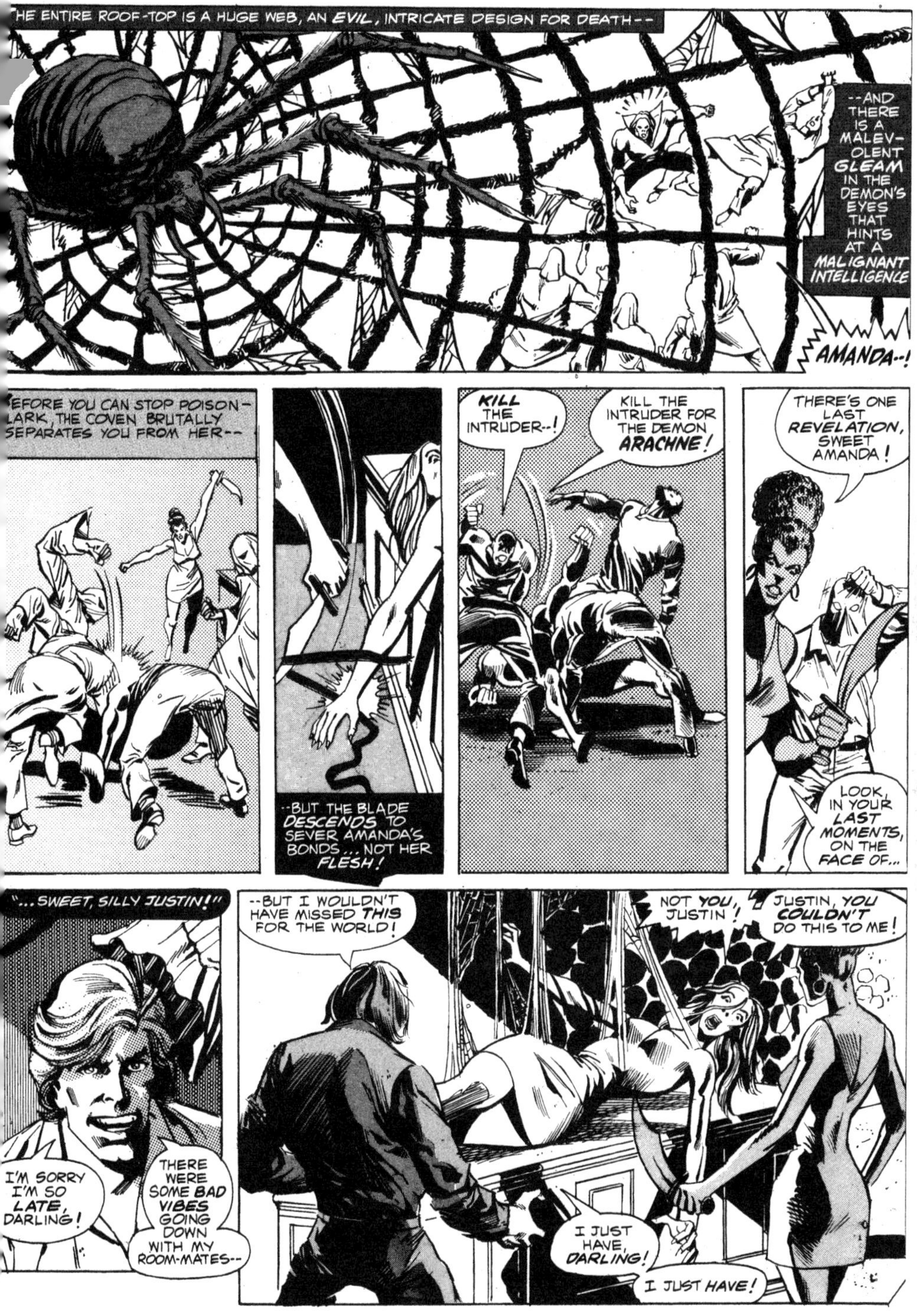

THE ENTIRE ROOF-TOP IS A HUGE WEB, AN EVIL, INTRICATE DESIGN FOR DEATH--
--AND THERE IS A MALEVOLENT GLEAM IN THE DEMON'S EYES THAT HINTS AT A MALIGNANT INTELLIGENCE
AMANDA--!
BEFORE YOU CAN STOP POISON-LARK, THE COVEN BRUTALLY SEPARATES YOU FROM HER--
--BUT THE BLADE DESCENDS TO SEVER AMANDA'S BONDS... NOT HER FLESH!
KILL THE INTRUDER--!
KILL THE INTRUDER FOR THE DEMON ARACHNE!
THERE'S ONE LAST REVELATION, SWEET AMANDA!
LOOK, IN YOUR LAST MOMENTS, ON THE FACE OF...
"...SWEET, SILLY JUSTIN!"
I'M SORRY I'M SO LATE, DARLING!
THERE WERE SOME BAD VIBES GOING DOWN WITH MY ROOM-MATES--
--BUT I WOULDN'T HAVE MISSED THIS FOR THE WORLD!
NOT YOU, JUSTIN!
JUSTIN, YOU COULDN'T DO THIS TO ME!
I JUST HAVE, DARLING!
I JUST HAVE!

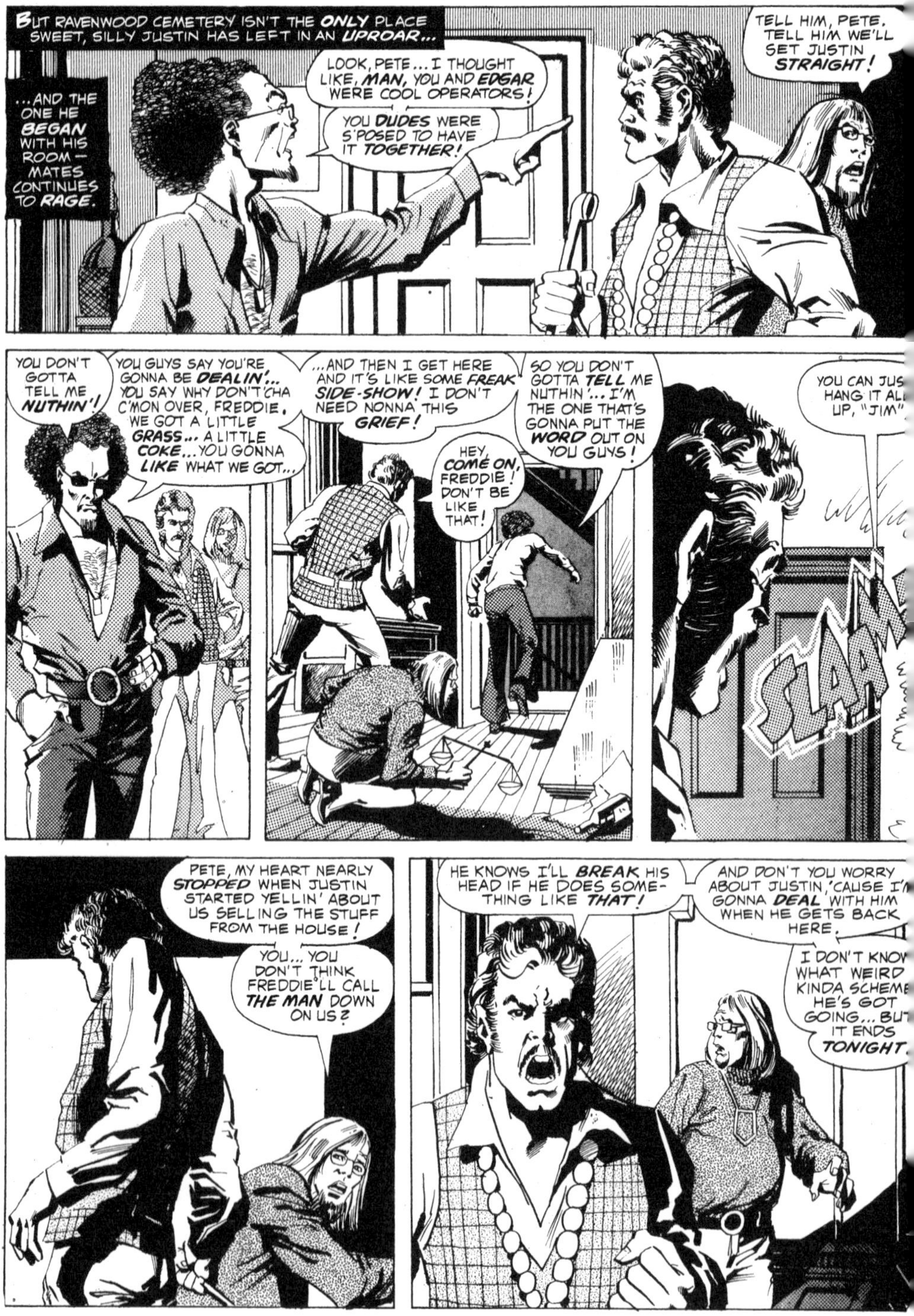
BUT RAVENWOOD CEMETERY ISN'T THE ONLY PLACE SWEET, SILLY JUSTIN HAS LEFT IN AN UPROAR...
...AND THE ONE HE BEGAN WITH HIS ROOM-MATES CONTINUES TO RAGE.
LOOK, PETE... I THOUGHT LIKE, MAN, YOU AND EDGAR WERE COOL OPERATORS!
YOU DUDES WERE S'POSED TO HAVE IT TOGETHER!
TELL HIM, PETE. TELL HIM WE'LL SET JUSTIN STRAIGHT!
YOU DON'T GOTTA TELL ME NUTHIN'!
YOU GUYS SAY YOU'RE GONNA BE DEALIN'... YOU SAY WHY DON'T'CHA C'MON OVER, FREDDIE. WE GOT A LITTLE GRASS... A LITTLE COKE... YOU GONNA LIKE WHAT WE GOT...
...AND THEN I GET HERE AND IT'S LIKE SOME FREAK SIDE-SHOW! I DON'T NEED NONNA THIS GRIEF!
SO YOU DON'T GOTTA TELL ME NUTHIN'... I'M THE ONE THAT'S GONNA PUT THE WORD OUT ON YOU GUYS!
HEY, COME ON, FREDDIE! DON'T BE LIKE THAT!
SLAM
PETE, MY HEART NEARLY STOPPED WHEN JUSTIN STARTED YELLIN' ABOUT US SELLING THE STUFF FROM THE HOUSE!
YOU... YOU DON'T THINK FREDDIE'LL CALL THE MAN DOWN ON US?
HE KNOWS I'LL BREAK HIS HEAD IF HE DOES SOME-THING LIKE THAT!
AND DON'T YOU WORRY ABOUT JUSTIN, 'CAUSE I'M GONNA DEAL WITH HIM WHEN HE GETS BACK HERE.
I DON'T KNOW WHAT WEIRD KINDA SCHEME HE'S GOT GOING... BUT IT ENDS TONIGHT.

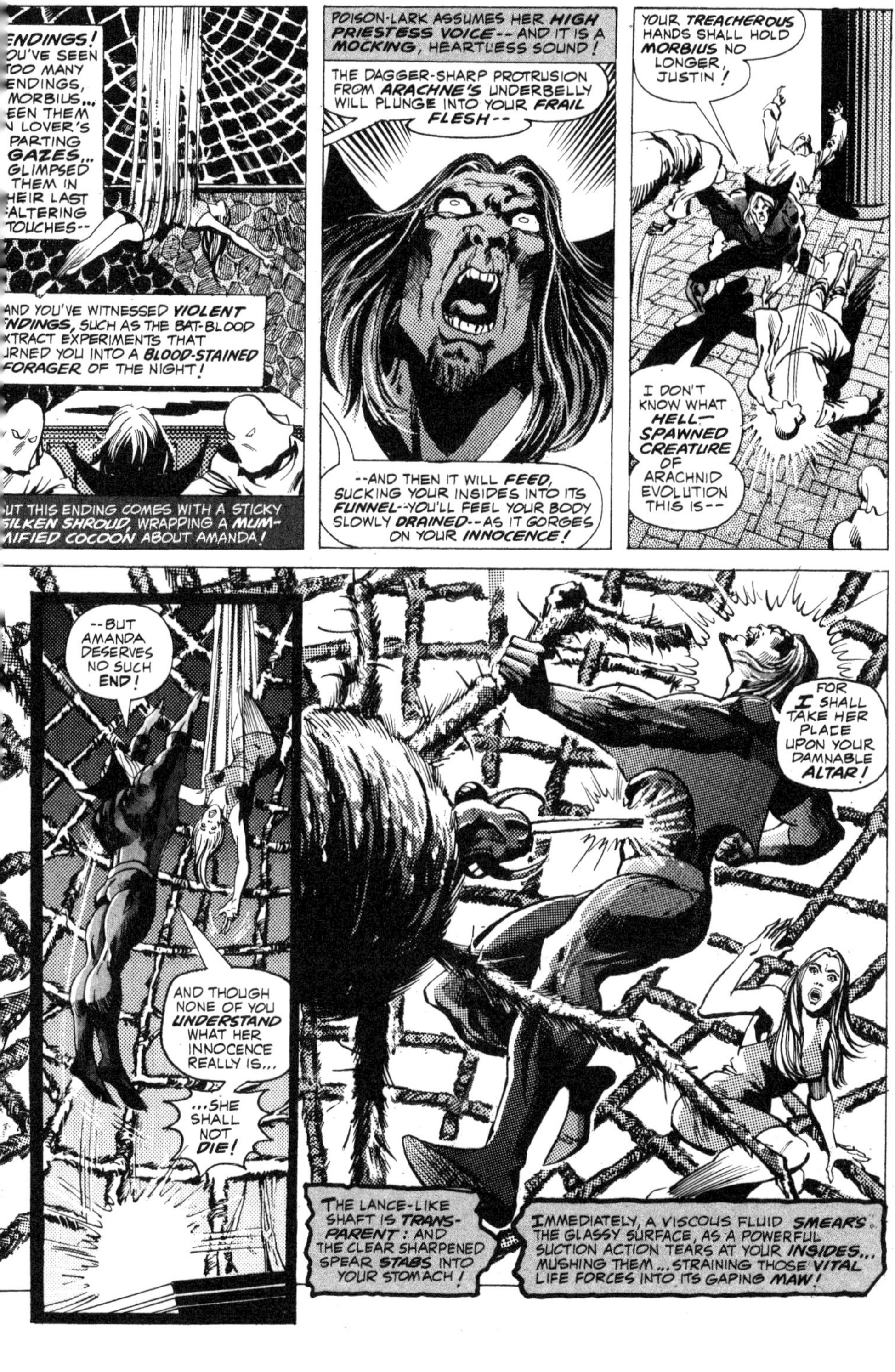
ENDINGS! YOU'VE SEEN TOO MANY ENDINGS, MORBIUS... SEEN THEM IN LOVER'S PARTING GAZES... GLIMPSED THEM IN THEIR LAST FALTERING TOUCHES--
AND YOU'VE WITNESSED VIOLENT ENDINGS, SUCH AS THE BAT-BLOOD EXTRACT EXPERIMENTS THAT TURNED YOU INTO A BLOOD-STAINED FORAGER OF THE NIGHT!
BUT THIS ENDING COMES WITH A STICKY SILKEN SHROUD, WRAPPING A MUMMIFIED COCOON ABOUT AMANDA!
POISON-LARK ASSUMES HER HIGH PRIESTESS VOICE-- AND IT IS A MOCKING, HEARTLESS SOUND!
THE DAGGER-SHARP PROTRUSION FROM ARACHNE'S UNDERBELLY WILL PLUNGE INTO YOUR FRAIL FLESH--
--AND THEN IT WILL FEED, SUCKING YOUR INSIDES INTO ITS FUNNEL--YOU'LL FEEL YOUR BODY SLOWLY DRAINED--AS IT GORGES ON YOUR INNOCENCE!
YOUR TREACHEROUS HANDS SHALL HOLD MORBIUS NO LONGER, JUSTIN!
I DON'T KNOW WHAT HELL-SPAWNED CREATURE OF ARACHNID EVOLUTION THIS IS--
--BUT AMANDA DESERVES NO SUCH END!
AND THOUGH NONE OF YOU UNDERSTAND WHAT HER INNOCENCE REALLY IS...
...SHE SHALL NOT DIE!
FOR I SHALL TAKE HER PLACE UPON YOUR DAMNABLE ALTAR!
THE LANCE-LIKE SHAFT IS TRANSPARENT: AND THE CLEAR SHARPENED SPEAR STABS INTO YOUR STOMACH!
IMMEDIATELY, A VISCOUS FLUID SMEARS THE GLASSY SURFACE, AS A POWERFUL SUCTION ACTION TEARS AT YOUR INSIDES... MUSHING THEM ... STRAINING THOSE VITAL LIFE FORCES INTO ITS GAPING MAW!

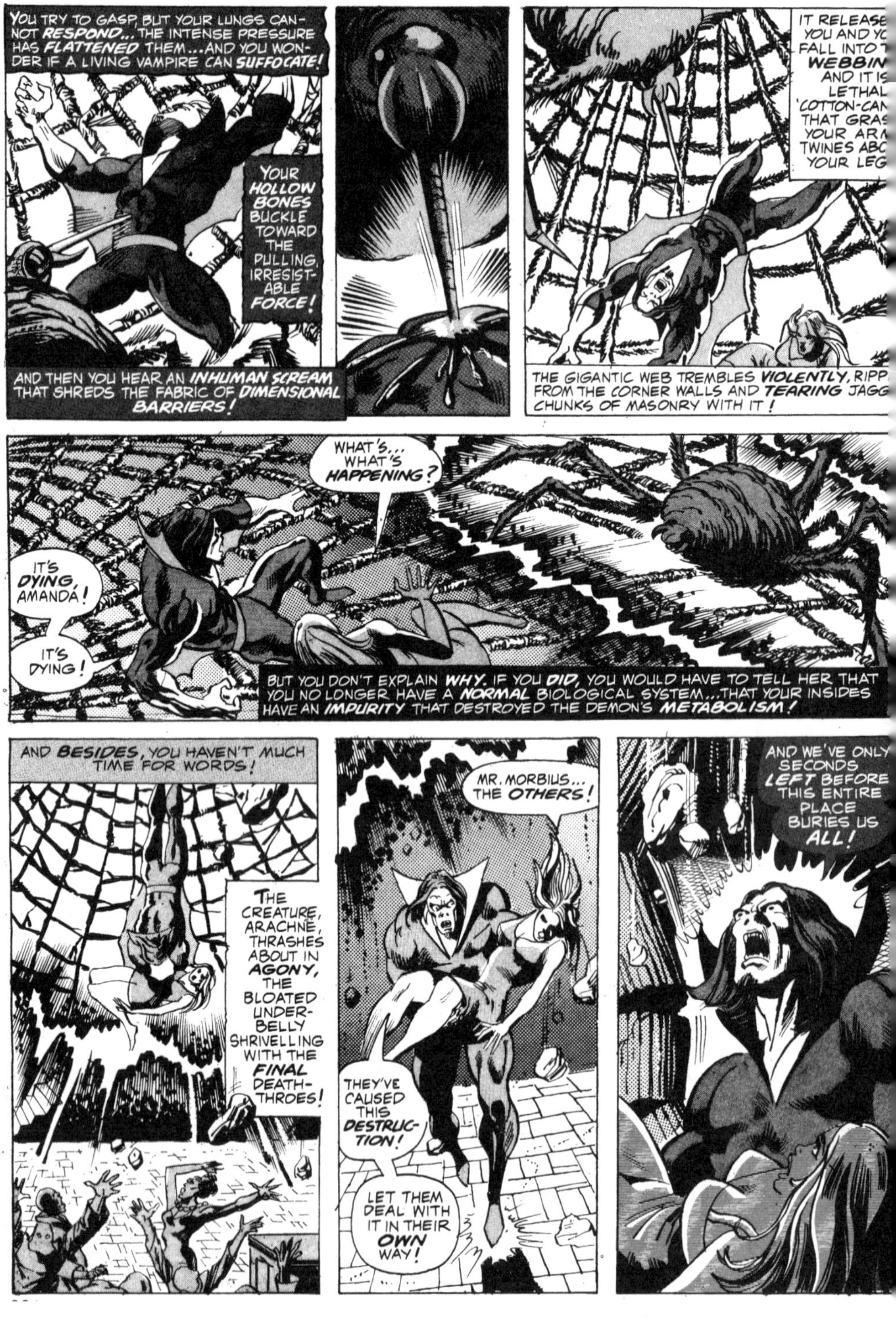
YOU TRY TO GASP, BUT YOUR LUNGS CAN-NOT RESPOND... THE INTENSE PRESSURE HAS FLATTENED THEM ...AND YOU WON-DER IF A LIVING VAMPIRE CAN SUFFOCATE!
YOUR HOLLOW BONES BUCKLE TOWARD THE PULLING, IRRESIST-ABLE FORCE!
AND THEN YOU HEAR AN INHUMAN SCREAM THAT SHREDS THE FABRIC OF DIMENSIONAL BARRIERS!
IT RELEASE YOU AND YO FALL INTO T WEBBIN AND IT IS LETHAL 'COTTON-CAN THAT GRAS YOUR ARM TWINES ABO YOUR LEG
THE GIGANTIC WEB TREMBLES VIOLENTLY, RIPP FROM THE CORNER WALLS AND TEARING JAGG CHUNKS OF MASONRY WITH IT!
WHAT'S... WHAT'S HAPPENING?
IT'S DYING, AMANDA!
IT'S DYING!
BUT YOU DON'T EXPLAIN WHY. IF YOU DID, YOU WOULD HAVE TO TELL HER THAT YOU NO LONGER HAVE A NORMAL BIOLOGICAL SYSTEM...THAT YOUR INSIDES HAVE AN IMPURITY THAT DESTROYED THE DEMON'S METABOLISM!
AND BESIDES, YOU HAVEN'T MUCH TIME FOR WORDS!
THE CREATURE, ARACHNE, THRASHES ABOUT IN AGONY, THE BLOATED UNDER-BELLY SHRIVELLING WITH THE FINAL DEATH-THROES!
MR. MORBIUS... THE OTHERS!
THEY'VE CAUSED THIS DESTRUC-TION!
LET THEM DEAL WITH IT IN THEIR OWN WAY!
AND WE'VE ONLY SECONDS LEFT BEFORE THIS ENTIRE PLACE BURIES US ALL!

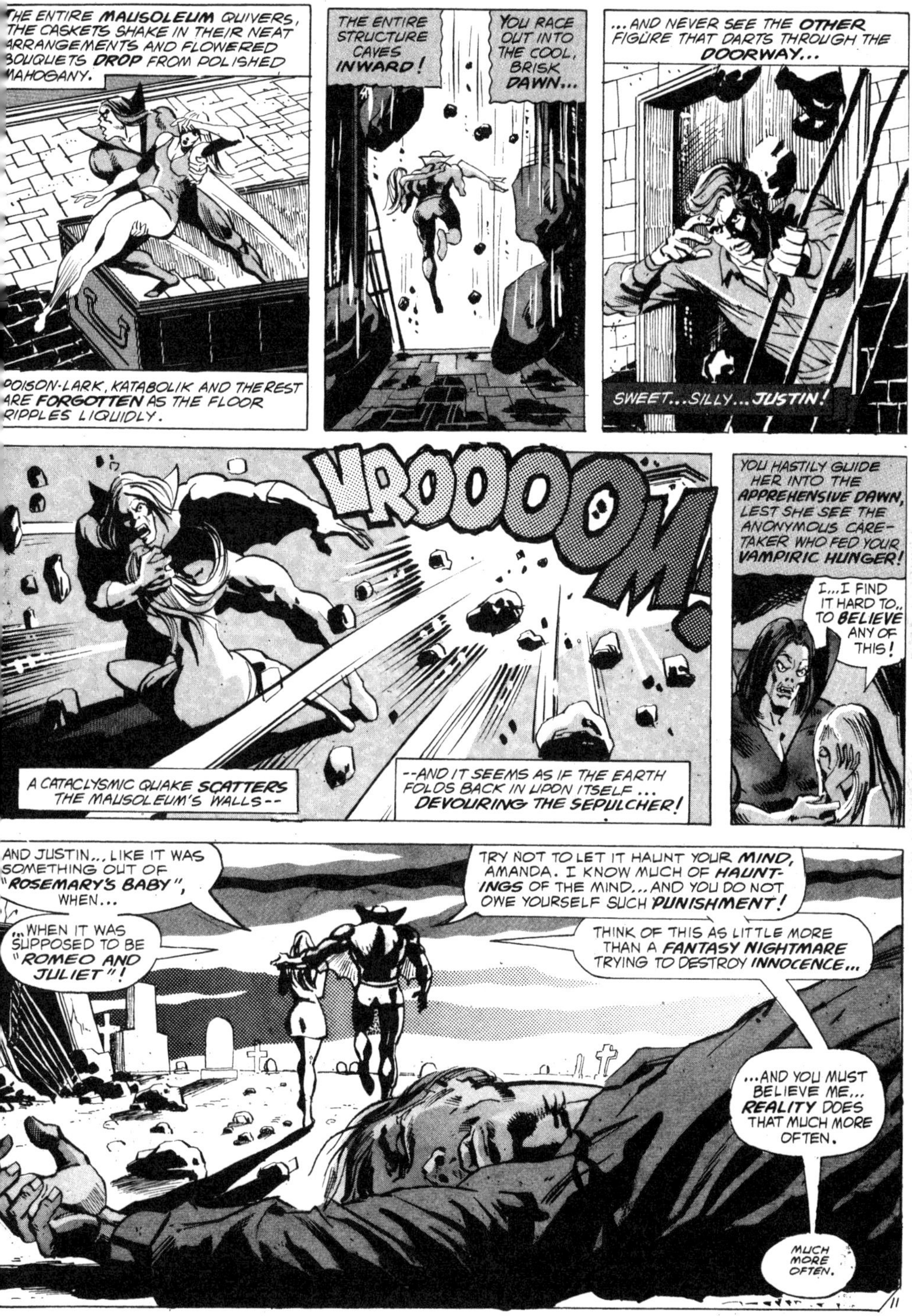
THE ENTIRE MAUSOLEUM QUIVERS, THE CASKETS SHAKE IN THEIR NEAT ARRANGEMENTS AND FLOWERED BOUQUETS DROP FROM POLISHED MAHOGANY.
POISON-LARK, KATABOLIK AND THE REST ARE FORGOTTEN AS THE FLOOR RIPPLES LIQUIDLY.
THE ENTIRE STRUCTURE CAVES INWARD!
YOU RACE OUT INTO THE COOL, BRISK DAWN...
...AND NEVER SEE THE OTHER FIGURE THAT DARTS THROUGH THE DOORWAY...
SWEET...SILLY...JUSTIN!
VROOOOOM!
A CATACLYSMIC QUAKE SCATTERS THE MAUSOLEUM'S WALLS--
--AND IT SEEMS AS IF THE EARTH FOLDS BACK IN UPON ITSELF... DEVOURING THE SEPULCHER!
YOU HASTILY GUIDE HER INTO THE APPREHENSIVE DAWN, LEST SHE SEE THE ANONYMOUS CARE-TAKER WHO FED YOUR VAMPIRIC HUNGER!
I...I FIND IT HARD TO.. TO BELIEVE ANY OF THIS!
AND JUSTIN... LIKE IT WAS SOMETHING OUT OF "ROSEMARY'S BABY", WHEN...
...WHEN IT WAS SUPPOSED TO BE "ROMEO AND JULIET"!
TRY NOT TO LET IT HAUNT YOUR MIND, AMANDA. I KNOW MUCH OF HAUNT-INGS OF THE MIND... AND YOU DO NOT OWE YOURSELF SUCH PUNISHMENT!
THINK OF THIS AS LITTLE MORE THAN A FANTASY NIGHTMARE TRYING TO DESTROY INNOCENCE...
...AND YOU MUST BELIEVE ME... REALITY DOES THAT MUCH MORE OFTEN.
MUCH MORE OFTEN.
11

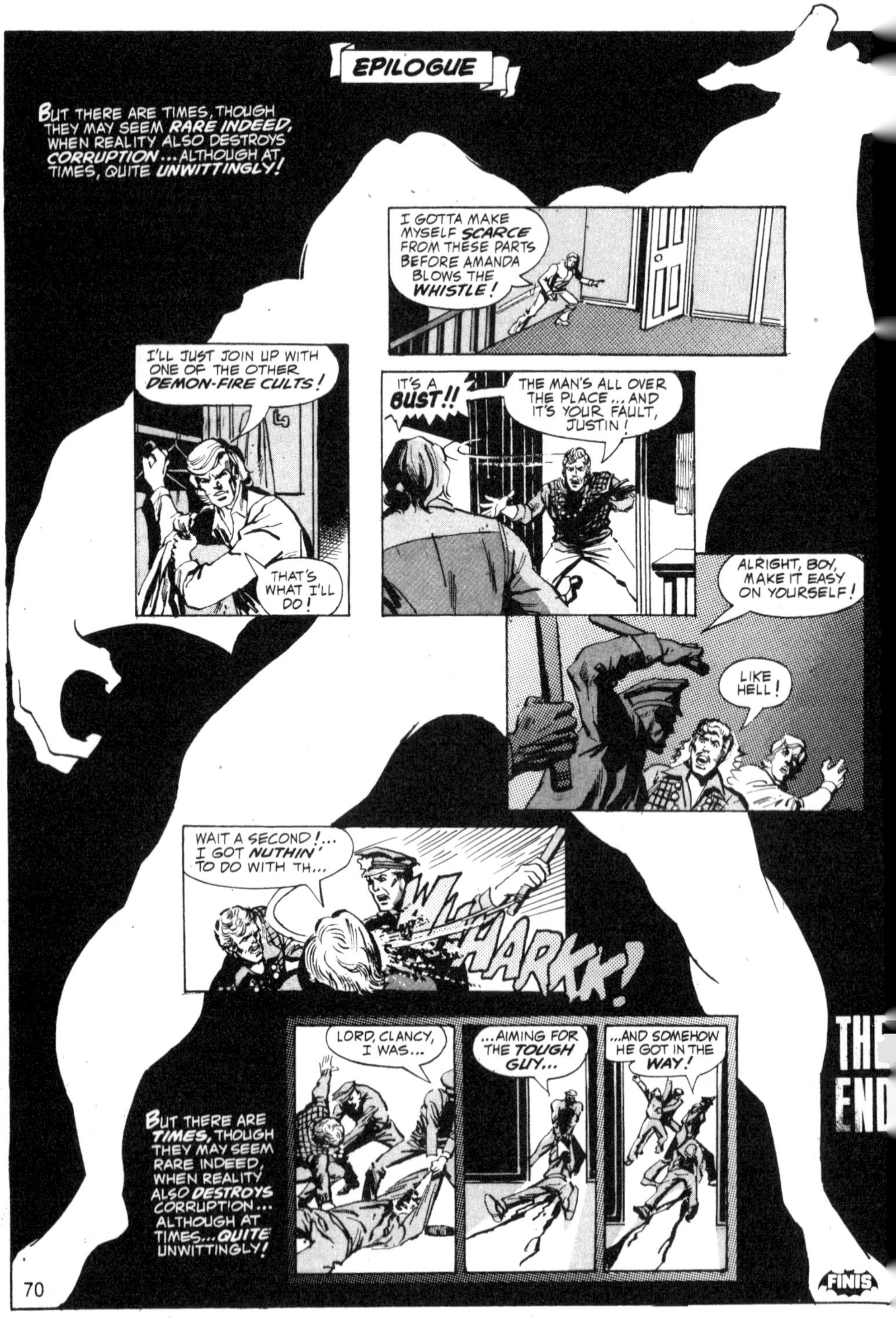
EPILOGUE
BUT THERE ARE TIMES, THOUGH THEY MAY SEEM RARE INDEED, WHEN REALITY ALSO DESTROYS CORRUPTION... ALTHOUGH AT TIMES, QUITE UNWITTINGLY!
I GOTTA MAKE MYSELF SCARCE FROM THESE PARTS BEFORE AMANDA BLOWS THE WHISTLE!
I'LL JUST JOIN UP WITH ONE OF THE OTHER DEMON-FIRE CULTS!
THAT'S WHAT I'LL DO!
IT'S A BUST!!
THE MAN'S ALL OVER THE PLACE... AND IT'S YOUR FAULT, JUSTIN!
ALRIGHT, BOY, MAKE IT EASY ON YOURSELF!
LIKE HELL!
WAIT A SECOND!... I GOT NUTHIN' TO DO WITH TH...
WHHARKK!
LORD, CLANCY, I WAS...
...AIMING FOR THE TOUGH GUY...
...AND SOMEHOW HE GOT IN THE WAY!
BUT THERE ARE TIMES, THOUGH THEY MAY SEEM RARE INDEED, WHEN REALITY ALSO DESTROYS CORRUPTION... ALTHOUGH AT TIMES... QUITE UNWITTINGLY!
THE END
FINIS
70

COMING NEXT ISSUE:
THE COMING OF THE SNOW VAMPIRES

A CHILLING ADAPTION OF AUGUST DERLETH'S *"THE DRIFTING SNOW"* by TONY ISABELLA and ESTEBAN MAROTO

PLUS:

SATANA
THE DEVIL'S DAUGHTER *and*

MORBIUS
THE LIVING VAMPIRE

-- PLUS OTHER PHOTOS, FANTASY *and* FEATURES, ALL IN THE *FOURTH* FAR-OUT ISSUE OF

VAMPIRE TALES

ON SALE NOVEMBER 6TH WHEREVER MAGAZINES ARE DISPLAYED!

SUPPORT YOUR LOCAL SHORT AUTO-BIOGRAPHER

by DONALD F. MCGREGOR

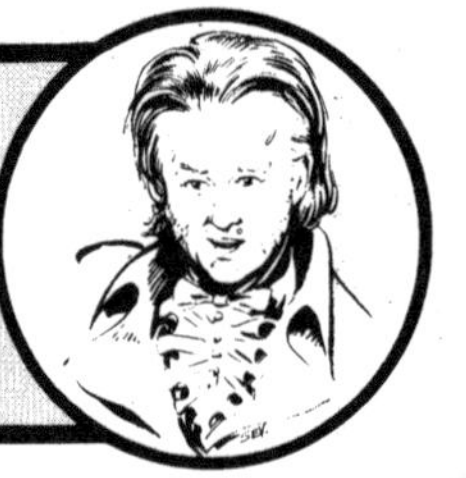

The hardest damn thing to write in the world is a short autobiography. The risks are manifold. First, if it is possible to sum up your entire lifetime in a few short paragraphs, you appear a pretty shallow individual indeed. Shallow— like "not deep," as they say in the vernacular. Second, there is the tendency to turn the whole thing into one of those ego trips which lets everyone in on the fact of how insecure you really are. Insecure— like "having no cool" as Cosby and Culp use to phrase it on I SPY. Or third, there is the "I started out as a child" route which is like piling children's blocks on top of each other: beautiful for the child, boring as Hell for anybody else. Boring— as in "Dullsville," as Edd Byrnes once quipped on 77 SUNSET STRIP. Fourth, the very short nature of the short autobiography means you are bound to slight someone by omitting them or run the risk of alienating all those you do mention which is the reason why, at this moment, I am wondering how in Hell I got talked into this. Peter Cushing; spare my soul!

So I seek a fifth way to do this. Maybe just by doing a bit on those formative years (with apologies to Wonder Bread Commercials) when my father gave the ultimatum in our first floor apartment behind the plumber's shop that no son of his was going to read comic books. Well, Dad, even John Paul Jones had a difficult time with ultimatums. If I had decided to go that route, I could never leave out mention of the magic aura of the "B" Western, that total suspension of reality on Saturday mornings where classical music provided a stirring backdrop for a world where everything was definable rights and wrongs and friendship was more than just an elusive word sought by lost, lone-wolf children. I could have done this thing that way, but that sounded so much like the third classification I mentioned that I decided not to. You can understand that.

I could have explored the High School years where teachers constantly told my Mom that I "had a good head if I would apply it; but you know yourself, he's always somewhere else." (Yeah, I know Neil Diamond sang those lines in a song but can I help it if that's what they said?) The "somewhere else" at the time, if I recall right, was probably a fantasy world of Sunset Strip, Stan Lee extravaganzas and James Bond— a figmentive character that never deserted you while the outside world fostered physical and spiritual beatings upon you. I could also have explored that time and the numerous characters I created to entertain or bore my friends (depending on who you ask). But that had tones of martyrdom, so I looked elsewhere.

"Women" was my next thought. That's what I'll wri about! Everybody digs women! Well, almost everybod And there isn't any subject I'd rather write about. B that has pitfalls, too, unfortunately. If you talk about a individual woman, well that's quite a bit like taking t ego trip route or else playing "show and tell" out kindergarden. Still, I must mention my wife, Sandy, a she definately ended a lot of those lonely night mon logues I used to master. Yep, there she was, dark-eye seductive, straight out of the pages of lurid detecti fiction. She fed my Galahad delusions and conjured u all sorts of dragons for me to slay. Nice girl. Same as m two-year-old daughter, Lauren, who's already convincir me I'm gonna lose the proverbial generation gap.

Well, if that's a dangerous route, perhaps mentioni how one gets involved in writing for illustrated magazin will do. Then, I only have to revert back in time abo three years when I badgered, cajoled, harrassed ar begged my friend Alex Simmons to illustrate ou own magazine DETECTIVES INC. You have find someone to believe in what you want to d Alex believed, especially after I badgered, cajole etc. DETECTIVES INC. became reality.

Or I could relate the hazards of trying to make mov scenes come real that ended up in five terror-fraught (I' been "Marvel" indoctrinated) nights in a cemetery! Bu ain't gonna do that neither, friend!!

Or I could do the "I'd like to thank" scenario, sayir such things as: "I'd like to thank Jim Warren for givi me the chance to first use the comic strip medium wi some of my own designs;" (He once told me he was love with Dorothy Provine's legs before Sinatra ever sa them!) Or: "to Billy Graham in rememberance of frien ship and wild times with burglar alarms, assort thugees and the strips we never finished;" or, even: " Archie Goodwin for his encouragement and acceptan to try new ideas and the same goes for Marv Wolfma born the son of Rudolph the dancing bear, and Cow Bunga, the pretzel bender" (as readers of DRACUL LIVES #4 should know). I could have done that, but th could get so maudlin and who needs maudlin in horr magazines?!

Recently, someone used a phrase that's curren fading out of popularity, and said, "Don, you're coppi out!" Well, that someone was right. So I don't think I write this thing. I'll just cop out. Maybe next year I'll c it. Maybe by then I'll have more of an idea who I a Maybe . . . . .but somehow I doubt it.

FINIS

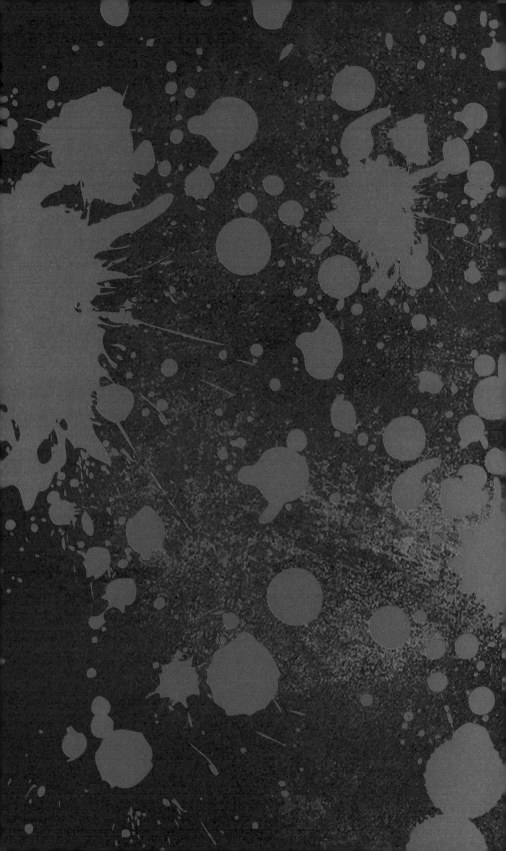

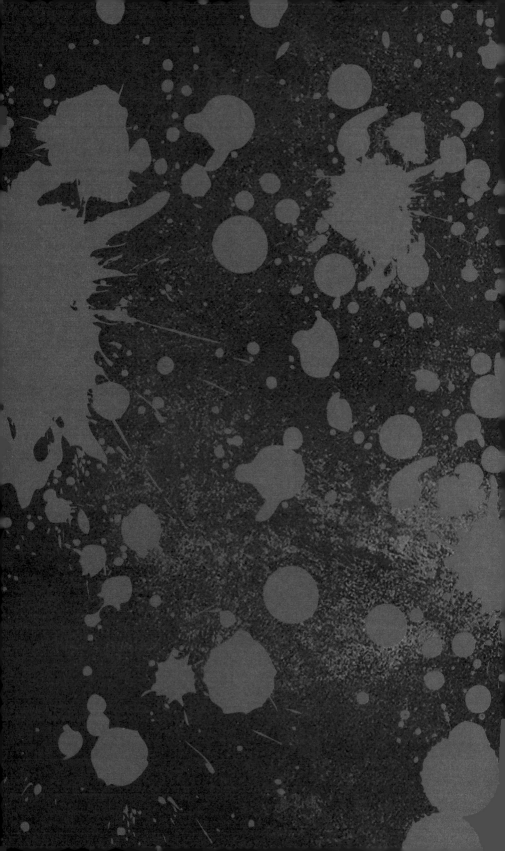